MW00698362

Culturally Adaptive Counseling Skills

To my siblings, Janet, John and Joanie: Thank you for leading the way and for being teachers in my life's journey.

—M. E. G.

For Skye, Lark, and Tai who inspire me always.

—C. J. Y

I wish to dedicate this book to all of those who made a positive difference in the lives of those in need.

—J. E. T.

This book is dedicated to my teachers, mzees, and colleagues in the discipline of African psychology. The struggle for the mental liberation of our people continues, and perhaps this work will enable professionals to serve our people in more culturally appropriate and sensitive ways.

—T. A. P.

Culturally Adaptive Counseling Skills

Demonstrations of Evidence-Based Practices

EDITORS

Miguel E. Gallardo
Pepperdine University

Christine J. Yeh
University of San Francisco

Joseph E. Trimble
Western Washington University

Thomas A. Parham
University of California, Irvine

Los Angeles | London | New Delhi
Singapore | Washington DC

Los Angeles | London | New Delhi
Singapore | Washington DC

FOR INFORMATION:

SAGE Publications, Inc.
2455 Teller Road
Thousand Oaks, California 91320
E-mail: order@sagepub.com

SAGE Publications Ltd.
1 Oliver's Yard
55 City Road
London EC1Y 1SP
United Kingdom

SAGE Publications India Pvt. Ltd.
B 1/I 1 Mohan Cooperative Industrial Area
Mathura Road, New Delhi 110 044
India

SAGE Publications Asia-Pacific Pte. Ltd.
33 Pekin Street #02-01
Far East Square
Singapore 048763

Acquisitions Editor: Kassie Graves
Editorial Assistant: Courtney Munz
Production Editor: Karen Wiley
Copy Editor: Diana Breti
Permissions Editor: Adele Hutchison
Typesetter: C&M Digitals (P) Ltd.
Proofreader: Sarah Duffy
Indexer: Sheila Bodell
Cover Designer: Anupama Krishnan
Marketing Manager: Katie Winters

Copyright © 2012 by SAGE Publications, Inc.

All rights reserved. No part of this book
may be reproduced or utilized in any form
or by any means, electronic or mechanical,
including photocopying, recording, or by
any information storage and retrieval system,
without permission in writing from the
publisher.

Printed in the United States of America

Library of Congress Cataloging-in-Publication Data

Culturally adaptive counseling skills : demonstrations
of evidence-based practices / edited by Miguel E.
Gallardo, Christine J. Yeh, Joseph E. Trimble.

p. cm.
Includes bibliographical references and index.

ISBN 978-1-4129-8721-9 (pbk.)

1. Cross-cultural counseling—United States.
2. Minorities—Counseling of—United States.
I. Gallardo, Miguel E. II. Yeh, Christine J. (Christine
Jean) III. Trimble, Joseph E.

BF636.7.C76C852 2012
361'.06—dc22   2011008510

This book is printed on acid-free paper.

11 12 13 14 15 10 9 8 7 6 5 4 3 2 1

Contents

Acknowledgments_____

Miguel E. Gallardo: I want to acknowledge Dr. Thomas Parham for his tireless work in advocating for, educating, and empowering ethnocultural communities. It is his previous work that laid the foundation for this book. Thank you for always gently pushing, while never wavering.

I also want to acknowledge the National Latina/o Psychological Association for being the womb that nurtures, supports, and guides Latina/o psychologists nationally. I hope this book represents a small segment of the expansive work that represents who we are and what we do.

Christine J. Yeh: I wish to thank my coauthors for giving me the privilege of this incredible journey together. I thank my parents, George and Lillian Yeh for all their sacrifice and support. I also thank the Samoan Community Development Center and the Asian American Psychological Association for supporting me professionally and personally.

Joseph E. Trimble: I wish to acknowledge the thoughtful consideration and generous assistance provided us by our acquisition editor at Sage, Kassie Graves; the invaluable constructive comments and advice provided us by the many anonymous reviewers of our prospectus and chapters; our copy editors; our mentors and advisors who carefully guided us on our paths toward maturity, character, wisdom, and truthfulness; and the enlightenment provided us by our ancestors and the creator. Thank you, also, to my lovely spouse, Molly Ellen, for her love, steadfast encouragement, unfading support, and careful scrutiny of my writing and to our lovely daughters, Gen, Lee, and Casey, for their compassionate encouragement and love.

Thomas A. Parham: In all things, I give honor to the Creator and ancestors. I thank my wife Davida and daughters Tonya and Kenya for their unwavering support and encouragement. I also wish to thank Dorothy Clegern, who helped to produce final drafts of several chapters. Finally, I thank my coauthors, both for the honor and privilege of collaborating with you and for trusting that this was a project that merited a broader audience than a single journal (even TCP) could provide and a broader vision than that journal could appreciate.

We would also like to acknowledge the following reviewers for their helpful suggestions: Norma Day-Vines, Virginia Tech; Kimberly Desmond, Indiana University of Pennsylvania; and Jose Torres, University of Wisconsin-Milwaukee.

Foreword _____

Upon reading this book, *Culturally Adaptive Counseling Skills: Demonstrations of Evidence-Based Practices,* edited by four of this country's leading multicultural psychologists, Drs. Gallardo, Yeh, Parham, and Trimble, and with contributions from other outstanding psychologists, the first thought that came to mind was that during the last 25 years, the specialization of multicultural counseling psychology has come a long way in establishing itself as a legitimate field of study. This is especially evident in the increased quantity, quality, and utility of research and publication works that essentially serve as the core of the specialization. With this thought in mind, I decided to take advantage of having been invited to write this Foreword to identify and address three overriding concerns or issues that I believe gave and continue to give impetus to increasing the quantity and, more important, improving the quality of such works.

The first concern addressed the preeminent, and now widely accepted, need to take culture into consideration across all aspects of counseling psychology: research, training, and practice. The second concern addressed the need to ensure that the inclusion of culture in the work of counseling psychologists is not a random event; it is theory driven and research supported. Finally, the third concern focused on the lack of frameworks/models that could be used to direct and guide counseling psychologists on how to appropriately and effectively include and use culture in the context of their work. From the onset, I would like to say that I believe that this book exemplifies the state of the art with respect to the manner by which these three enduring concerns should be addressed by multicultural counseling psychologists.

This first concern essentially gave impetus to the development of the multicultural counseling movement, by recognizing the failure of counseling psychology to acknowledge, accept, and address the pivotal role that culture plays in the life of an individual as a whole and, more specifically, in all aspects associated with the counseling process. The basis for this concern was rooted in the emerging belief that the psychological needs of individuals, especially those from ethnic, racial, and cultural minority groups (i.e., African Americans, Asian Americans, American Indians, and Latinas/os), could not be effectively met unless their culture and the socioecological context in which they exist were given specific and serious consideration. At the time, the failure to address culture was even more disconcerting given the fact that the ethnic, racial, and cultural makeup of the United States was, and for that matter is, rapidly changing. Recent census reports project that the ethnic, racial, and cultural groups, taken as an aggregate, will comprise a very significant segment of the U.S. population by the year 2050, if not sooner (U.S. Census Bureau, 2004). Given the increase in the size of these groups to date, it is safe to say that at present the majority of counselors/therapists find themselves working with an ever-growing number of individuals from diverse ethnic, racial, and cultural backgrounds.

Recognizing and accepting the pivotal role that culture plays in the sociocultural development and makeup of the individual, counseling psychologists, of whom a significant number were racial/ethnic minority persons, began an initial wave of research and publication endeavors that would eventually serve as the foundation for what is now recognized and accepted as the multicultural counseling specialization within the broader field of counseling psychology. The successful outcome of such endeavors is aptly exemplified in the dramatic increase in research and publication that has occurred in the last 25 years.

Providing a sense of the focus of early endeavors, Ponterotto and Casas (1991) reported the results of a six-year (1983–1988) content analysis of articles published in four major counseling journals. This analysis identified 183 conceptual and empirical articles that focused on racial/ethnic minority populations. The analysis found that the myriad topics addressed in the articles could be placed into five broad categories: client variables, counselor variables, counseling process variables, assessment, and professional issues and development. Demonstrating a growing professional need to develop a more in-depth and comprehensive understanding of the sociocultural characteristics of the racial/ethnic minority client, the largest number of articles fell under the category of client variables. It should be noted that these categories, with the exception of professional issues and development, were similar to those that were identified as applicable for use in a comparable review that included a more extensive selection of counseling-related journals and that covered the five-year period between 1980 and 1984 (Ponterotto, 1988). I would dare to predict that if a similar content analysis were conducted today, the validity and utility of these categories would be supported. In fact, in reviewing the chapters that comprise this book, it quickly becomes apparent that these categories serve to organize the content contained therein.

In addition to journal articles, the last 25 years witnessed a very impressive increase in the publication of chapters and books (e.g., handbooks) that focus directly on the cultural and socioecological factors that must be considered when working with persons from diverse racial and ethnic backgrounds (see Ponterotto, Casas, Suzuki, & Alexander, 2010). With the increase in publications, another concern soon surfaced. This concern was composed of criticism directed at the quality (e.g., the methodological soundness) and utility of the research and publications. Wanting to find empirical evidence that might substantiate or refute the bases of the criticisms, Ponterotto and Casas (1991) conducted the content analysis noted above and concluded that a good number of the criticisms were valid (e.g., disregard for within-group or intra-cultural differences, the use of easily available college student participants, reliance on culturally encapsulated instruments). More recent evidence in support of these criticisms is available (see Prieto, McNeill, Walls, & Gomez, 2001). It bears noting that in recent years, the overall quality and utility of the articles has greatly improved. More specifically, today's publications, as evident in this book, demonstrate an increased academic sophistication and methodological ability for addressing and dealing with the complex and central role that culture and socioecological factors play in the lives of all human beings.

The second concern, the need to ensure that the inclusion of culture in the work of counseling psychologists is not an arbitrary and random event but one that is theory driven and research supported, was initially put forth by multicultural specialists who expressed a deep concern for the lack of theoretically substantiated frameworks to guide and give meaning to their multicultural work (Casas, Vasquez, & Ruiz de Esparza, 2002; Sue, Ivey, & Pedersen, 1996). Lacking such frameworks, these psychologists felt that they were forced to rely on theories and frameworks that solely reflected a Eurocentric perspective and, for all intents and purposes, were found to fall short of meeting the counseling needs of a good number of persons from culturally different groups. Short of developing "new" theories and frameworks, initial efforts were made to adapt the existing theories for use with diverse cultural groups by inserting cultural content, assumed to be of relevance to all and/or to specific cultural groups, throughout the entire Eurocentric-based counseling process. Most frequently, the rhyme or reason for such inclusion was not adequately explained.

Recognizing the fact that without a driving comprehensive theory (i.e., a metatheory), such random and poorly understood inclusion of culture into existing theories and frameworks fell short and would continue to fall short of meeting the counseling needs of diverse cultural groups, a few dedicated counseling psychologists took it upon themselves to develop such a metatheory or paradigm (Sue et al., 1996). While first hesitant to undertake such a development, these psychologists eventually concluded that the multicultural counseling field had matured to the point where the development of such a theory would be beneficial not only for theory building but also for research, training, and practice. Such a theory would be applicable across cultures. That is to say, the guiding principles of the theory would have universal applicability, while the content that gives life to the principles would be culture specific. The metatheory that resulted from their efforts is aptly named "A Theory of Multicultural Counseling and Therapy." In a nutshell, the proposed metatheory sought to provide an organizational framework that would enable psychologists to outline the theoretical, philosophical, ethical, political, and professional underpinnings of the many counseling/helping approaches. Furthermore, such a theory would be culture centered (Pedersen & Ivey, 1993). That is to say, the role of culture in a person's life would be perceived as central and not marginal, fundamental and not merely exotic (Sue et al., 1996).

The implications of accepting and using this metatheory across research, practice, and training were critically examined by leading multicultural counseling psychologists. These psychologists concluded that the theory was conceptually sound and had the potential to stimulate further theory development. More important, these psychologists shared the consensus that being composed of definable and substantive constructs, the theory could easily be used to guide and structure the work of multicultural psychologists. The use of this theory is very easily identified throughout this edited book.

Closely tied to the concern regarding the lack of theory was the third concern, regarding the lack of frameworks that could serve as blueprints on why, when, and how culture might be incorporated into any multicultural-focused work. Early on, Casas and Vasquez (1989) proposed such a framework. While a step in the right direction, their framework was rather broad in its presentation and basically failed to provide the specificity and "hands on" direction that, given the state of development of the multicultural field at that time, was still needed. A more specific and detailed framework/model that actually serves as the basic guiding structure for presenting the content of this book was proposed by Parham (2002). This model is titled the Skills Identification Model. While originally developed to identify specific cultural knowledge and skills that are essential to accurately understand and effectively work with African American communities, it is also applicable, as clearly exemplified in this book, for use with Asian, Latina/o, Native American, and Middle Eastern communities. The use of this skills-focused model has been widely accepted by multicultural psychologists. Its use, within the context of the metatheory described above, greatly helps to give the content of this book unity and direction, while also increasing its pragmatic and applied value.

Yes, the field of multicultural counseling psychology has come a long way in establishing itself as a legitimate, vital, and fruitful field of study. This is due to the efforts of multicultural psychologists who recognized the need to address and overcome concerns and challenges, such as the three that are the focus of this Foreword. The successful outcome of these efforts is exemplified in this book, whose major objective is to clearly demonstrate how to appropriately and effectively address and use culture with all individuals across all counseling endeavors—research, training, and practice. From my reading, I would expect that the structure and content of this book will set the mark for the kinds of publications that are still greatly needed to continue to move the field of multicultural counseling psychology into the future.

J. Manuel Casas, PhD
Professor Emeritus, Counseling,
Clinical & School Psychology
University of California, Santa Barbara

References

Casas, J. M., & Vasquez, M. J. T. (1989). Counseling the Hispanic client: A theoretical and applied perspective. In P. B. Pedersen, J. G. Draguns, W. J. Lonner, & J. E. Trimble (Eds.), *Counseling across cultures* (3rd ed., pp. 153–175). Honolulu: University of Hawaii Press.

Casas, J. M., & Vasquez, M. J. T., & Ruiz de Esparza, C. A. (2002). Counseling the Latino/a: A guiding framework for a diverse population. In P. B. Pedersen, J. G. Draguns, W. J. Lonner, & J. E. Trimble (Eds.), *Counseling across cultures* (5th ed., pp. 133–159). Thousand Oaks, CA: Sage.

Parham, T. A. (2002). Counseling models for African Americans: The what and how of counseling. In T. A. Parham (Ed.), *Counseling persons of African descent: Raising the bar of practitioner competence* (pp. 100–118). Thousand Oaks, CA: Sage.

Pedersen, P. B., & Ivey, A. E. (1993). *Culture-centered counseling and interviewing skills*. Westport, CT: Greenwood/Praeger.

Ponterotto, J. G. (1988). Racial/ethnic minority research in the *Journal of Counseling Psychology*: A content analysis and methodological critique. *Journal of Counseling Psychology, 35,* 410–418.

Ponterotto, J. G., & Casas, J. M. (1991). *Handbook of racial/ethnic minority counseling research*. Springfield, IL: Charles C. Thomas.

Ponterotto, J. G., Casas, J. M., Suzuki, L. A., & Alexander, C. M. (2010). *Handbook of multicultural counseling* (3rd ed.). Thousand Oaks, CA: Sage.

Prieto, L. R., McNeill, B. W., Walls, R. G., & Gomez, S. P. (2001). Chicanas/os and mental health services: An overview of utilization, counselor preference, and assessment issues. *Counseling Psychologist, 29,* 18–54.

Sue, D. W., Ivey, A. E., & Pedersen, P. B. (1996). *A theory of multicultural counseling and therapy.* Pacific Grove, CA: Brooks Cole.

U.S. Census Bureau. (2004). *U.S. interim projections by age, sex, race, and Hispanic origin.* Retrieved January 11, 2011, from http://www.Census.gov/ipc/www/usinterimproj

1

Understanding the Skills Identification Stage Model in Context

Miguel E. Gallardo

Thomas A. Parham

Joseph E. Trimble

Christine J. Yeh

It shouldn't be theories that define the problems of our situation, but rather the problems that demand, and so to speak, select, their own theorization.

Martín-Baró (1994, p. 314)

Introduction and Overview

The Maligned Wolf

The forest was my home. I lived there, and I cared about it. I tried to keep it neat and clean. Then one sunny day, while I was cleaning up some garbage a camper had left behind, I heard footsteps. I leaped behind a tree and saw a little girl coming down the trail carrying a basket. I was suspicious of this little girl right away because she was dressed funny—all in red, and her head covered up as if she did not want people to know who she was. Naturally, I stopped to check her out. I asked who she was, where she was going, where she had come from, and all that. She gave me a song and dance about going

(Continued)

(Continued)

to her grandmother's house with a basket of lunch. She appeared to be a basically honest person, but she was in my forest, and she certainly looked suspicious with that strange getup of hers. So, I decided to teach her just how serious it is to prance through the forest unannounced and dressed funny.

I let her go on her way, but I ran ahead of her to her grandmother's house. When I saw that nice old woman, I explained my problem and she agreed that her granddaughter needed to learn a lesson all right. The old woman agreed to stay out of sight until I called her. Actually, she hid under the bed. When the girl arrived, I invited her into the bedroom where I was in bed, dressed like the grandmother. The girl came in all rosy-cheeked and said something nasty about my big ears. I've been insulted before so I made the best of it by suggesting that my big ears would help me to hear better. Now, what I meant was that I liked her and wanted to pay close attention to what she was saying. But she made another insulting crack about my bulging eyes. Now, you can see how I was beginning to feel about this girl who put on such a nice front but was apparently a very nasty person. Still, I've made it a policy to turn the other cheek, so I told her that my big eyes helped me to see her better.

Her next insult really got to me. I've got this problem with having big teeth, and that little girl made an insulting crack about them. I know that I should have had better control, but I leaped up from that bed and growled that my teeth would help me to eat her better.

Now, let's face it, no wolf could ever eat a little girl; everyone knows that, but that crazy girl started running around the house screaming, me chasing her to calm her down. I'd taken off the grandmother's clothes, but that only seemed to make it worse. All of a sudden the door came crashing open, and a big lumberjack is standing there with his axe. I looked at him, and it became clear that I was in trouble. There was an open window behind me and out I went. I'd like to say that was the end of it. But that grandmother character never did tell my side of the story. Before long the word got around that I was a mean, nasty guy. Everybody started avoiding me. I don't know about that little girl with the funny red outfit, but I didn't live happily ever after (Fern, 1974).

The challenges of preparing for and providing counseling and clinical services that are culturally responsive are areas the helping professions are taking more seriously. In the United States, the ethnic demographics have changed, both nationally and at the state level (U.S. Census Bureau, 2009). Gone are the days when the norm was systemic resistance to engaging in discussions of multiculturalism and diversity. Currently, most professionals, institutions, and agencies seem intellectually committed to the idea of developing greater levels of multicultural responsiveness, yet seem caught in a state of uncertainty about how to best achieve those objectives.

"The Maligned Wolf," the story of Little Red Riding Hood from the Wolf's perspective, provides a template for the underpinnings of the multicultural movement. What the story shapes for us is a much-needed *paradigm shift* or *cultural shift* that appropriately redefines modes of assessing, diagnosing, and intervening with clients (Ancis, 2004; Cardemil & Battle, 2003; D. W. Sue & Sue, 2003). It is clear that viewing therapy through a narrow, culturally encapsulated lens no longer meets the ethical standards as set forth by the counseling professions (American Counseling Association [ACA], 2005; American Psychological Association [APA], 2002, 2003). However, the professions' desire to prioritize clinical responsiveness over cultural responsiveness remains intact (Gallardo, Johnson, Parham, & Carter, 2009). Ultimately, it is still possible for graduate students in most training programs to graduate, complete an internship, and become licensed and not be adequately prepared to meet the needs of underserved and unserved communities. This illustrates the challenges we face in preparing future therapists/counselors to provide services that are culturally and contextually consistent with the lives of those they intend to serve. This also implies that we need to do a better job of assisting graduate training programs to understand the *what* and the *how*.

A continuing concern for us is *who* defines reality for ethnocultural communities as well as *how* it is defined. In essence, we are suggesting that the issue is one of power: The ability to define reality and make others respond to that definition as if it were their own (Nobles, 2010). Consequently, empowerment is a central component to working with ethnocultural communities (Aldarondo, 2007). Prilleltensky, Dokecki, Frieden, and Ota Wang (2007) would argue that "wellness cannot flourish in the absence of justice, and justice is devoid of meaning in the absence of wellness" (p. 19). Therefore, if you are a member of an ethnocultural community, we encourage you not to allow reality to be defined for you by those who do not share or embrace your cultural worldview. Simultaneously, we encourage those readers who may not identify with one of the five ethnocultural communities addressed in this book to avoid defining realities for others based on your own worldview and cultural lens. It is here that well-intentioned therapists can unintentionally violate those they intend to serve responsively.

It has become clear that as we shift our perspective to better understand ethnocultural communities, the need to become culturally responsive at least parallels, and in some cases supersedes, the desire to become clinically competent (D. W. Sue & Sue, 2003). Research addressing the development of cultural competence continues to permeate much of the current psychological and counseling literature (Aldarondo, 2007; Ancis, 2004; Arredondo, 1998; Gallardo et al., 2009; Hays & Iwamasa, 2006; McAuliffe, 2008; S. Sue, 1998; Toporek & Reza, 2001; Vera & Speight, 2003). In response to the growing body of literature in this area, *philosophical mandates* for service providers to develop culturally responsive interventions have emerged. We say "philosophical" simply because the translation from theory to practice has been missing from the literature, which has often personally and professionally challenged training programs and practitioners alike. What is often addressed in these "mandates" for cultural competence is a challenge for all service providers to make this *paradigmatic multicultural shift* when working with ethnocultural communities (APA, 2003). This shift in perspective forces us to reexamine the developmental changes that have occurred in ethical mandates placed on service providers. We are not convinced that our ethical codes should be discarded entirely, but they should be viewed through a cultural lens first and foremost and should integrate culture-specific guidelines for various ethnocultural communities (Gallardo et al., 2009). More specifically, issues such as self-disclosure, multiple relationships, shifting the traditional therapeutic environment, and redefining the traditional therapeutic hour are issues that culturally responsive providers should address with some flexibility, based on the context and culture of their clients, without feeling like they are situating themselves in an unethical predicament. If we struggle in shifting our perspectives, is it because we believe in the universal application of traditional therapeutic techniques? Or, alternatively, does the system that calls for the mandates to make a multicultural shift limit, or present contradictory messages to, service providers and training programs? We argue that in shifting to a more culturally responsive paradigm (rather than making cultural responsiveness secondary or in addition to our clinical responsiveness), we actually broaden our clinical expertise and proficiency. The two should not be separated. In fact, for too long "clinical competence" has existed without the need to also be culturally responsive. Today, with the recent acceptance of the Guidelines on Multicultural Education, Training, Research, Practice, and Organizational Change for Psychologists (APA, 2002), we are challenged to redefine and continuously reevaluate our modes of practice and, at times, the restrictions that are placed on what is considered "ethical" practice.

Evidence-Based Practice in Psychology

A central premise of this book is the current Evidence-Based Practice in Psychology (EBPP) definition, as supported by the American Psychological Association Presidential Taskforce on Evidence-Based Practice (2006). The APA has defined EBPP as "the integration of the best available research with clinical expertise in the context of patient characteristics, culture, and preferences" (p. 273). The EBPP begins with the client/community and asks what already existing research evidence, if any, will assist in achieving the best outcomes. We support this definition of EBPP because it allows for multiple sources of good "evidence" therapeutically, and it begins with a bottom-up perspective. That is, it begins with the client/community and then develops what might work, in what way, and with whom from this perspective. A top-down perspective assumes that what is good for the profession is also good for the communities we serve. There is currently more research being published with this bottom-up perspective in mind, including work with Haitians (Nicolas, Arntz, Hirsch, & Schmiedigen, 2009), cultural adaptations with adolescents (Bernal, Jimenez-Chafey, & Domenech Rodriguez, 2009), and with Chinese Americans (Hwang, 2009). While we are supportive of research to identify what works and with whom (Paul, 1967), we are also aware that an expansion of the "gold standard"—that is, treatments that have been empirically supported—is critical to continuing to advance therapeutic practice with ethnocultural communities. The current EBPP definition allows both the therapist and client to decide what might be the most effective treatment for this person at this moment, based on culture and context. Additionally, the EBPP definition states that "culture is a multifaceted construct, and cultural factors cannot be understood in isolation from social class and personal characteristics that make each patient unique" (APA Presidential Taskforce, 2006, p. 278). The EBPP guidelines state that cultural factors influence not only the nature and expressions of psychopathology, but also clients' understanding of psychological and physical health (La Roche & Christopher, 2009). Griner and Smith (2006) found that interventions that were specifically designed for the cultural groups they were intended to serve were four times as effective as interventions that were implemented with individuals from a variety of cultural groups. Additionally, they found that interventions that were conducted in the client's native language, if other than English, were twice as effective as those conducted in English. For us, it is not an either/or discussion, but a both/and. We ultimately need to know what works best and for whom, but in keeping in sync with our proposed paradigm shift, we also need to employ an expanded perspective in our efforts to push the limits of narrowly defined practice standards. Moreover, Norcross (2002) found that empirically supported treatments fail to include the therapist as a person, the therapeutic relationship, and the client's nondiagnostic characteristics. He further noted that the following therapeutic factors account for variance in therapeutic outcome (the percentages of variance are in parentheses): treatment method (8%), individual therapist (7%), the therapy relationship (10%), patient contributions (25%), interaction (5%), and unexplained variance (45%). Also, a recent study examined the effects of cognitive-behavioral therapy (CBT) and person-centered therapy (PCT) in the treatment of posttraumatic stress disorder (PTSD) (McDonagh et al., 2005). The researchers specifically left out the "specific ingredient" thought to be essential for the treatment of PTSD from a cognitive-behavioral perspective— exposure—when implementing the PCT. They found that while both treatments were well received by patients, significantly fewer dropped out of the PCT than the CBT group, and the benefit to the patients was comparable in both treatment groups. This study further underscores the significance of expanding our perspective of what is good "evidence." This study also highlights the centrality of common factors in the therapeutic context.

Expanding Our Role

There have been several studies that have examined factors common to all healing approaches (Fischer, Jome, & Atkinson, 1998; Frank, 1961; Frank & Frank, 1991). From this body of work, Fischer et al. found support for four "universal healing conditions" that exist in all cultures: (1) The therapeutic relationship serves as a basis for all therapeutic intervention; (2) a shared worldview or conceptual schema or rationale for explaining symptoms provides the common framework within which the healer and client work together; (3) the client has faith or hope in the process of healing; and (4) the therapeutic ritual or intervention is in the form of a procedure that requires the active participation of both the client and the therapist, and the procedure is believed by both to be the means of restoring the client's health. It is our belief that work with ethnocultural communities must focus on the four universal healing conditions, while incorporating any research evidence on the client's culture, context, and presenting concern, within the context of the therapist's clinical expertise and cultural knowledge.

This reexamination of practice with ethnocultural communities also calls for an expansion of our roles as service providers. The importance of shifting from one-on-one counseling to becoming cultural brokers (Stone, 2005), or social advocates (Parham, White, & Ajamu, 1999; D. W. Sue & Sue, 2003; White & Parham, 1990), or creating the good society (Nelson-Jones, 2002), is simply a must. At the foundation of what each of these terms implies is the growing need to further develop our roles as mentors, teachers, advisors, and consultants within the systems in which our clients live and work. Schank, Helbok, Haldeman, and Gallardo (2010) state that clients and community members often see an overlap between the roles of therapist and client as a strength, and so should we as therapists. In fact, clients may seek us out simply because we are a part of the community and seen as someone who understands the client's culture and context. We can no longer assume that helping an individual in the "therapy room" means that the healing process is complete (Vera, Buhin, Montgomery, & Shin, 2005). Failing to examine the social, political, and cultural contexts (La Roche, 2005) in which our clients live indicates that we have placed our desire to be clinically proficient before our desire to be culturally proficient. When we expand our lens into a therapeutic multicultural kaleidoscope, we then bring the systems and social structures that impact our clients in alignment with one another, and only then have we begun the healing process.

Initiating the Process

Outdated modes of thinking about what constitutes "good" practice are now serving as the unofficial "standards of practice." In comparing this tendency to a "low bar" approach, Parham (2002, 2004) has asked the pressing question, "How do we raise the bar of what passes for competence?" More specifically, how can we expand our existing repertoire of clinical skills to include more culturally sound and responsive modes of assessing, diagnosing, and intervening with ethnoculturally diverse clients? We believe that an effective therapist must combine clinical skills and knowledge with a more culturally expanded view of therapy.

Initiating this task has forced us to come to terms with a persistent predicament in the psychotherapy movement concerning cultural sensitivity and responsiveness. Specifically, therapists are more willing to engage in the process of culturally responsive practice, but they may be unsure what specific skills would be useful to facilitate the desired therapeutic outcome. Upon further analysis, we find several culprits that seem to contribute to this state of inertia. One is the body of literature that summarizes demographic trends and population statistics. These writings do acknowledge the recent changes in ethnic demography, but knowing that information provides little help in planning a therapeutic intervention. A second culprit is literature about a cultural group's history, both its past glory and its confrontations with oppression and other negative social forces. This body of literature certainly increases our knowledge, but it still falls short of explaining how to incorporate that knowledge into specific interventions therapeutically. A third problem group is the body of literature that simply describes the limitations of traditional Eurocentric approaches to counseling and therapy in treating culturally diverse clients. This body of literature is very good at describing what doesn't work, but falls short of redirecting the reader to what does work. Each of these elements contributes to the sense of urgency in this book to improve cross-cultural sensitivity and responsiveness.

In distancing ourselves from the three limitations stated above, we have searched for a more crystallized and focused analysis and model that might help us to frame our work in counseling clients who are culturally diverse. The intent of this book is to shift from a top-down to a bottom-up perspective to understand ethnocultural communities. Accordingly, we have resurrected and expanded the Skills Identification Model proposed by Parham (2002). In his model, Parham sought to take the broad concepts of "multicultural counseling and therapy" and break them down into smaller component parts. He reasoned that doing so might enable practitioners and students alike to experience a greater level of confidence in learning and demonstrating specific skills that could be used to conceptualize and intervene. The model was originally designed as a way of deepening our understanding and enhancing our skills in working with African Americans (Parham, 2002). More recently, the model was adapted to working with the Latina/o population (Gallardo, 2004), given the belief in the therapeutic universality of the principles and concepts. This book is a further expansion of the original Skills Identification Model. We have extended the model's utility to include Asian, Latina/o, Native, and Middle Eastern American communities, with implications for other cultural groups as well (see Chapters 2, 5, 8, 11, and 14, this volume). The book contains specific skills therapists can use with all five groups and Case Illustrations as examples of the model's implementation.

Understanding Culture

Any discussion of multicultural skills must, by necessity, begin with both a definition and analysis of culture. The notion of culture is central to our work in this book, and we seek to move beyond simplistic, surface-level manifestations of this concept. Although we have defined our respective cultural communities with "umbrella" terms, we also advocate that readers understand the immense diversity within each cultural community and begin to understand culture as more than race and ethnicity (Lakes, Lopez, & Garro, 2006; Warrier, 2008). In this regard, our profession cannot be so naïve as to assume that the most salient element of culture is the skin color and ethnic/racial background of therapy participants. Culture can include gender, religion and spirituality, sexual orientation, and class. Regardless of what element is most salient, the definition described below can help deepen our understanding of what "culture" means to an individual and/ or community.

To help us to embrace this idea more thoroughly, Ani (1994) has provided us with a definition of culture at the deep structural level. Her work suggests that culture (1) unifies and orders our experience by providing a worldview that orients our experience and interpretation of reality; (2) provides collective group identification built on shared history, symbols, and meanings; and (3) institutionalizes and validates group beliefs, values, behaviors, and attitudes. Nobles (2010) reminds us that culture is a process representing the vast structure of behaviors, ideas, attitudes, values, habits, beliefs, customs, language, rituals, ceremonies, and practices peculiar to a particular group of people that provides them with a "general design for living and patterns for interpreting reality."

As we seek to engage these constructs of culture, Grills (2002); Parham (2002, 2004; Parham, Ajamu, & White, 2011); and King, Dixon, and Nobles (1976) before them provide us with a more formalized structure through which to examine how culture is operationalized across various ethnocultural communities. Individually and collectively, they suggest that there are five domains of information that represent elements of culture at the deep structural level and that these domains are central to developing a better working knowledge of the construct. The five domains are ontology (the nature of reality), axiology (one's value orientation), cosmology (one's relationship to the Divine force in the universe), epistemology (systems of knowledge and discovering truth), and praxis (one's system of human interaction).

Examination of these five domains across the five ethnocultural communities referenced in this book allows us to develop a template that is useful in distinguishing areas of convergence and divergence between the various groups. Table 1.1 illustrates our comparison of cultural manifestations with each specific community.

The Skills Identification Stage Model (SISM)

Having now explored the necessity for more specificity in culturally responsive practice and the notion of culture at the deep structural level, it is now relevant that we turn our attention to the SISM. Parham's (2002)

Table 1.1 Five Domains of Elements Representing Culture

Group / Issue	African American	Latina/o American	Asian American	American Indian/ Alaska Native	Middle Eastern American
Ontology	Reality is a spiritual-material union in which spirit is that energy and life force that permeates everything that exists in the universe; an inner connectedness between all things that exist in the universe.	An integration of personal and familial lived experiences, religious/spiritual insight and history (i.e., an understanding that life is a combination of one's will and efforts and divine intervention), ancestral knowledge and connection, and an understanding that Western forms of health and healthcare can be limitations to one's growth and well-being.	Reality is grounded in a belief in harmony with nature, interconnectedness with family and close relations, the spiritual world, ancestral knowledge, holistic perspectives of health, and faith in external forces (natural world, religious intervention, etc).	To be is to be spirit. To become is to evolve toward one's destiny. All that is has spirit, is interconnected, is conscious, and possesses energy. Everything is to everything else.	Intense reliance on destiny and fate (fatalistic). Reality is based on an integration of personal and familial lived experiences. Espouse a holistic perspective of health and faith in external forces (natural world, religious interventions). Life is a combination of God's interventions and individuals' and families' free will.
Axiology	Collective survival, holistic self, emotional vitality and expressiveness, oral history and language, harmony within the universe, experiencing time in the present with an orientation to the past, contribution to one's community as a measure of worth.	Collectivistic; one's worth is based on one's contribution to the group's well-being and advancement; present and past oriented; group/cultural survival and ownership—*donde hay gana, hay mana; ponle ganas; cuando uno quiere la flor, necesita soportar las espinas*—language preservation and acquisition; connection to cultural traditions; representation	Strong cultural emphasis on family and group needs. Children are socialized to pursue familial goals and avoid shame of embarrassment to the family name. Within a collectivistic value orientation, there is recognition of traditional hierarchies, which are often associated with gender	To give to family and community defines humanity's task in this world. Choice is inviolate, never to be forced. Our past connects us to the spirit world and to our ancestral roots. We learn who we are by learning how we are to contribute to our world—our unique gift and destiny.	Negotiated individualism within the collective. Family is the heart of the community, which is composed of close friends and extended kinship systems. Emphasis is on interdependence and being for others, responsibility for caring for those within the kinship system and those less fortunate. Greatly values education, accepts modern science but with humility and

(Continued)

9

Table 1.1 (Continued)

Group / Issue	African American	Latina/o American	Asian American	American Indian/ Alaska Native	Middle Eastern American
		of motherhood is connected to spirituality and seen as protector, love, and as a source of strength for all.	and age. Cultural focus on hard work and fitting in.		against the backdrop of creationism. Respects knowledge of elders and distrusts those in power. Great deal of respect for parents, elders, and those more educated. Subscribe to a code of honor, shame, personal accountability, and humility.
Cosmology	Spiritual connection to the divine force within the universe; divinity is represented within each person; omnipotence of God.	Spiritual/religious connection as integration of family and culture; divinity falls on a spectrum of ancestral hierarchy that dictates a reverence for those who have preceded us and to our Creator; connection to, conservation, and protection of Mother Earth. Reverence for women and the strength seen therein (e.g., Virgin de la Guadalupe).	High respect for aspects of nature, the spiritual world, and universe. Spiritual and religious beliefs are bound to interdependent connections and community building. Aspects of nature and the spiritual world have significant cultural meanings.	The material and immaterial are parallel aspects to the universe. The eye of the universe is the immaterial energy that imbues all that is. We know this energy as the ineffable, transcendent, and the many aspects of the divine.	Spirituality is defined by the strength of the relationship to an omnipotent God who is invisible, yet near. Divinity is represented within each individual, and all are connected to the divine. The universe in its totality is a creation of an omnipotent God.
Epistemology	Belief in the value of direct experience.	Oral history (i.e., ancestral and cultural history), direct lived experiences; Western science can be limited and may not been seen as the universal truth of insight and	Ancestral and cultural history. Acknowledgment of the hard work and suffering of past generations. Value in the holistic experience	We are born with a history. We are not blank screens. Therefore, we learn of our role and our destiny through the nurturing of family and community.	A combination of values transmitted through the family and the community as well as individual experience. Science is valued, and divine

Group / Issue	African American	Latina/o American	Asian American	American Indian/ Alaska Native	Middle Eastern American
		understanding. The more one is connected to culture and the more solidified one is in one's identity development, the more one understands the limitations to universally accepted truths and discovers and defines one's own reality.	integration of mind, body, spirit, matter, nature, and the universe. Many Asian ethnic groups place a high value on Western science while also recognizing its limitations.	Learning from experience in the world allows our spiritual knowledge to emerge.	knowledge is transmitted through the Prophet. One can reach God through knowledge of the universe. Learning is valued at all levels and for all ages. Inherently skeptical and distrusts systems of power or authority. Means of acquiring knowledge is domain specific: emotions are understood by the heart, and the brain is the seat of reason, yet one needs both for wisdom.
Praxis	Ethical/moral laws and principles (i.e., MAAT) that guide human conduct.	Religious/spiritual guidance as standard for one's thoughts as behaviors; family guidance and shared wisdom; shared lived experiences influence the integration and acceptance into one's behavioral repertoire and provide a source of validation for the way one lives one's life.	Interpersonal and familial obligations that are culturally bound dictate and influence human conduct. Ethical and moral principles strive to maintain social and relational harmony.	Hunters, gatherers, and warriors live in communities of extended family systems. Action is highly valued in terms of how it supports the tribe. Such action includes ceremonies and sacred rituals that sustain the community and enable the people to prosper and mature through culturally specific life stages.	Religious doctrine of Judeo-Christian-Islamic heritage. Obligations are to God, family, and kinship systems. Say no evil, do no evil, think no evil.

Skills Identification Model includes the *what* and *how* of providing culturally responsive interventions to clients. The model proposes that all service providers need to ask two questions: (1) What is important for me to achieve therapeutically with my clients? and (2) How can I achieve these goals using specific culturally appropriate techniques? The SISM assumes that the "cultural competence" notion is comprehensive yet elusive, and thus dissects the therapy process into manageable parts by identifying six tenets that we believe all therapists address during the therapeutic encounter: (1) connecting with clients, (2) conducting a culturally relevant assessment, (3) facilitating awareness, (4) setting goals, (5) taking action and instigating change, and (6) feedback and accountability. The model is a framework that should only be used as a guide to inform therapists about the possibilities that exist when working with ethnoculturally diverse clients. The SISM is not comprehensive, nor is it linear. It is a reflection of the tenets we believe most therapeutic relationships entail, regardless of one's theoretical orientation. For a more indepth understanding of the model, readers are referred to Parham (2002). The purpose of this book is to provide an expanded version of the model to reflect its usability with other ethnocultural populations. Therefore, only a brief description of each issue is provided as a starting point and to frame the discussion for readers.

Connecting With Clients

Townsend and McWhirter (2005) conducted a literature review over a span of 19 years and found that connectedness continues to remain at the forefront of psychologically healthy relationships and personal functioning. The authors go on to state that connectedness is of significant importance when taking into account the economic, political, cultural, ethnic, and social forces that impact people's lives. Their findings also provide support for the common factors literature addressed above, in which the therapeutic alliance serves as the base of all therapeutic relationships. Regardless of the theoretical orientation of the provider, clinical instincts, or diagnostic formulations, the process of remediating clients' concerns cannot happen without the establishment of a therapeutic connection. In essence, our connection with clients becomes the most important therapeutic intervention we can implement in the course of therapy (Lambert & Barley, 2001). This connectedness provides a foundation of trust, commitment, and collaboration between therapist and client. It is the key element by which the therapeutic work impacts and strengthens clients' lives. In order to understand what it means to connect with clients in a cultural context and with cultural consciousness, we must extend our definition of *connecting* beyond the physical realm (e.g., handshakes, visiting one's office) to also include joining at the intellectual, affectual, and spiritual levels (Parham, 2002). Connections on these levels challenge therapists to move beyond the safety of the emotional and professional boundaries that have been enforced through graduate school training programs and professional ethics codes.

Conducting a Culturally Relevant Assessment

In the context of traditional training programs, there has been an emphasis on the use of assessment tools to determine qualitative and quantitative information on a specific person or characteristic. Assessment practices and psychological tests are currently under examination for their use with ethnoculturally diverse populations (Suzuki, Kugler, & Aguiar, 2005). Often, assessment can be conducted using specific screening tools or by simple observations (Parham, 2002). The challenges of establishing the reliability and validity of clinical interview instruments/processes, and of other psychological assessment measures, continue to be a failure in considering cultural and social factors. In addition, research indicates that although some of these instruments may have some clinical usefulness in the counseling setting, the interpretation and results remain culturally inconsistent with ethnocultural groups (Butcher, 1996; Graham, 2006). Culturally responsive assessment avoids pathologizing clients by recognizing their strengths and factors that have contributed to the establishment of sustaining, purposeful, and functional behaviors. The use of culturally appropriate screening tools and assessment measures must be developed from an emic perspective (Butcher, 1996; Cepeda-Benito & Gleaves, 2000; Cheng, Kim, & Abreu, 2004; Velasquez et al., 2002; Whatley, Allen, & Dana, 2003), rather than with an etic foundation (Suzuki et al., 2005). Regardless of the tests used, tests must be interpreted with caution and in a culturally responsive manner and within the client's social, political, and cultural context (Butcher, 1996; Graham, 2006; Suzuki et al., 2005). In addition, we must also acknowledge and culturally assess the unspoken words, the unexpressed emotions in body language, and the unconscious attitudes and beliefs expressed in the behaviors of clients. Ultimately, we encourage therapists to employ these additional strategies when conducting an assessment to acquire information about their clients. In addition to utilizing any culturally interpreted and normed measures, we encourage therapists to consider identifying preexisting strengths, identifying clients' preexisting resources, potentially inviting family into the therapeutic data-gathering process, separating that which is environmental from that which is internal to the client, and investigating the client's cultural background on your own rather than relying solely on the client to educate you about who they are. Although client self-report always supersedes textbook knowledge and information, it is our responsibility as providers to understand and investigate our clients' cultural backgrounds, much like we would when a client presents with a specific diagnosis about which we have limited knowledge. In both the former and latter examples, the information is used as a starting point by which we then understand better what questions we might consider asking, in what way, and at what time during the course of treatment, while understanding the individual who sits before us is unique.

Facilitating Awareness

Insight and awareness have been found to assist clients to feel more in control of their everyday lives (Jinks, 1999), to be helpful factors in successful individual and group therapy (Holmes & Kivlighan, 2000), and to aid in symptom reduction (Kivlighan, Multon, & Patton, 2000). Facilitating awareness reflects the basis of a *psychology of liberation* (Aldarondo, 2007; Comas-Díaz, Lykes, & Alarcon, 1998; Freire, 1970). A psychology of liberation works within the client's own contexts to enhance his or her awareness of surrounding environmental circumstances that contribute to the establishment of behaviors and feelings of oppression, discrimination, and subjugation (Comas-Díaz et al., 1998). It involves recognition of the forces that shape, color, or otherwise exert influence on the physical, psychological, and spiritual aspects of his or her being. Discussion about race and ethnicity in the therapeutic relationship is one example of facilitating awareness in a culturally responsive manner (Cardemil & Battle, 2003). The process of facilitating awareness involves helping our clients to be heard and understood. Facilitating awareness also involves helping clients to understand their language; explore the dynamics of the past, current, and anticipated circumstances; discover how their life experiences color and shape how they engage current situations; and plan for future situations.

Setting Goals

Clients who are optimistic about achieving their valued goals for intrinsic reasons are more likely to actively engage in the therapeutic process, leading to more positive outcomes in therapy (Michalak, Klappheck, & Kosfelder, 2004). Goal setting is one of the most critical aspects of a therapist's work. Goal setting can focus on the outcome clients wish to achieve in therapy and can range from, for example, general goals of feeling less stressed to more specific goals of gaining more independence while continuing to honor and maintain ties to family. Ultimately, transforming therapeutic goals from mere wishes to a realization requires the establishment of a trusting and collaborative relationship between client and therapist. Clients need to feel motivated to achieve their goals and empowered to believe that their goals are achievable. Setting goals in a therapeutic sense is absolutely critical, but the process of crystallizing goals will require elements of realism, specificity (including cultural specificity), and perseverance (Parham, 2002). For some clients, goals can be simply aspirational, in that personal and environmental limitations prevent the realization of the client's stated goals. Incidentally, the client's stated goals and the goals actually achieved are typically the result of a collaborative perspective between what the client and therapist have identified as important to strengthen and empower the client and the client's social, political, and cultural context. Ultimately, "the therapeutic relationship represents the negotiated tasks and goals between counselor and client" (Liu & Pope-Davis, 2005, p. 152). It is also worth noting that the need to balance the focus of goal setting between intrapsychic phenomena and sociocultural and environmental phenomena acknowledges the fact that not all client distress is intrapsychic and that some, or all, of their presenting concerns may be caused by the oppressive, racist, discriminatory, and dehumanizing realities of the environment in which clients interact and live. Consequently, the target of our therapeutic intervention must likewise be sociocultural and environmental.

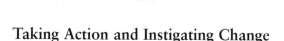

Taking Action and Instigating Change

Taking action and instigating change are the procedural aspects for implementing the goals that have been set by the client and therapist. Taking action and instigating change involve both the conscious commitment to change and the desired actions or behaviors consistent with the intent to change. Of most importance in creating change is the collaborative relationship that has been developed with clients. Furthermore, when attempting to instigate change for the clients, it may be necessary to ask significant others in the client's life to participate in the successful completion of any desired outcomes and changes. This is consistent with our hope that therapists understand the context in which clients live and, in their attempts to extend the couch to the community, include any significant entities and relationships in the therapeutic process. Metaphorically, our clients are never alone in the therapy process, even if they may physically be there on their own. Clients bring with them both past and present relationships and the multitude of ways those relationships have shaped their worldviews, current life situation, and any anticipated future actions they may take. Action and change involve psychological and behavioral dimensions, thereby requiring an interpersonal sense of strength and empowerment, as well as a specific set of skills that clients are comfortable implementing (Parham, 2002). Hays (2009) encourages therapists to ask the following question of their clients: "What is the smallest possible step you could take that would feel like you are making progress?" (p. 358). She encourages clients to consider viewing any change from this perspective because it highlights the importance of breaking goals down into sustainable steps in order to ensure long-term success. We agree.

Feedback and Accountability

Feedback and accountability means providing, and receiving, information reciprocally to both the client and therapist about the change process in therapy. Providing clients with information about their progress and movement in therapy helps them understand areas of particular strength and areas in which further growth may be needed. Feedback is a fundamental aspect in the therapeutic progress because the process itself provides the client and therapist with opportunities to further engage in the change process through periodic review and renewal of commitment (Parham, 2002). In this process, clients are reminded that successful interventions rarely occur as a single moment in time, but rather in a series of steps that continue to change the client's stated goals into tangible transformation in their everyday lives.

Of particular importance is feedback for the therapist. By receiving information about the therapeutic change process, therapists gain a deeper understanding of what the client is experiencing in the moment and what the client has found facilitative or disruptive about his or her therapeutic encounter and change process.

Our task in this book is to provide a framework or model that therapists can use to develop specific skills when working with ethnoculturally diverse clients. We hope that by adapting and integrating these nonexhaustive skill sets into your existing clinical foundation, you will achieve some measure of success during the phases of therapy outlined above.

Understanding the Content in Context

As accompaniments to the specific ethnocultural chapters in this book (Chapters 2, 5, 8, 11, and 14), we have asked our expert colleagues to provide case examples of how the SISM can be implemented. Therefore, Parts I through V include two case examples intended to further crystallize the model in context. What you find as you read through the chapters and case examples are commonalities as well as culturally congruent approaches to working with our ethnocultural communities. Each author and case example author has approached the content and conceptualization in ways that he or she feels resonates with his or her community. We have asked our colleagues to implement the model as they see fit and to critique it, where necessary, as a way to build upon past and current knowledge in this area.

We have also asked Dr. Rebecca Toporek (Chapter 17) to address how the principles put forth in this book can be implemented in the classroom as teaching resource and with students in training. We hope this chapter assists professors to implement the model in training programs. Lastly, we invited Dr. Jeff Harris (Chapter 18) to situate the content of this book within the larger multicultural discussion happening in the field today. It is our intent with this chapter to help readers locate the content of this book within the context of the multicultural literature and mandates. We are not so naïve as to think that this book is the be all and end all, and we understand that we are addressing one component of what it means to be culturally responsive. In fact, we would argue that one needs to have made the paradigm shift, or have the *psychological skill set,* before attempting to implement any behavioral skill set discussed in this book. Chapter 19 outlines future directions and ways we can continue to expand the literature in this area. For the authors of this book, the psychological skill set is primary to any multicultural work one engages in. It is therefore essential that readers, including our Caucasian readers, understand that which is cultural for them before attempting to understand that which is cultural for someone else.

References

Aldarondo, E. (2007). Rekindling the reformist spirit in the mental health professions. In E. Aldarondo (Ed.), *Advancing social justice through clinical practice* (pp. 3–17). Mahwah, NJ: Lawrence Erlbaum.

American Counseling Association. (2005). *ACA code of ethics.* Retrieved May 9, 2011, from http://www.counseling.org/Files/FD.ashx?guid=ab7c1272-71c4-46cf-848c-f98489937dda

American Psychological Association. (2002). Ethical principles of psychologists and code of conduct. *American Psychologist, 57,* 1060–1073.

American Psychological Association. (2003). Guidelines on multicultural education, training, research, practice, and organizational change for psychologists. *American Psychologist, 58,* 377–402.

American Psychological Association Presidential Taskforce on Evidence-Based Practice. (2006). Evidence-based practice in psychology. *American Psychologist, 61,* 271–285.

Ancis, J. R. (Ed.). (2004). *Culturally responsive interventions: Innovative approaches to working with diverse populations.* New York: Brunner-Routledge.

Ani, M. (1994). *Yurugu: An African-centered critique of European cultural thought and behavior.* Trenton, NJ: African World Press.

Arredondo, P. (1998). Integrating multicultural counseling competencies and universal helping conditions in culture-specific contexts. *The Counseling Psychologist, 26,* 592–601.

Bernal, G., Jimenez-Chafey, M., & Domenech Rodriguez, M. M. (2009). Cultural adaptations of treatments: A resource for considering culture in evidence-based practice. *Professional Psychology: Research and Practice, 40*(4), 361–368.

Butcher, J. N. (Ed.). (1996). *International adaptations of the MMPI-2.* Minneapolis: University of Minnesota Press.

Cardemil, E. V., & Battle, C. L. (2003). Guess who's coming to therapy: Getting comfortable with conversations about race and ethnicity in psychotherapy. *Professional Psychology: Research and Practice, 34*(3), 278–286.

Cepeda-Benito, A., & Gleaves, D. H. (2000). Cross-ethnic equivalence of the Hopkins Symptom Checklist-21 in European American, African American, and Latino college students. *Cultural Diversity & Ethnic Minority Psychology, 6*(3), 297–308.

Cheng, R. G., Kim, B. S., & Abreu, J. M. (2004). Asian American multidimensional acculturation scale: Development, factor analysis, reliability, and validity. *Cultural Diversity and Ethnic Minority Psychology, 10*(1), 66–80.

Comas-Díaz, L., Lykes, M. B., & Alarcon, R. (1998). Ethnic conflict and psychology of liberation in Guatemala, Peru, and Puerto Rico. *American Psychologist, 53,* 778–792.

Fern, L. (1974). The maligned wolf. In *Elementary assembly script 5–Topic 3A– Respecting diversity.* Retrieved May 9, 2011, from http://www.sacsc.ca/Resources_ School.htm#AssemblyScripts

Fischer, A. R., Jome, L. M., & Atkinson, D. R. (1998). Reconceptualizing multicultural counseling: Universal healing conditions in a culturally specific context. *Journal of Counseling Psychology, 26,* 525–588.

Frank, J. D. (1961). *Persuasion and healing: A comparative study of psychotherapy.* New York: Schocken Books.

Frank, J. D., & Frank, J. B. (1991). *Persuasion and healing: A comparative study of psychotherapy* (3rd ed.). Baltimore: Johns Hopkins University Press.

Freire, P. (1970). *Pedagogy of the oppressed.* New York: Continuum International.

Gallardo, M. E. (2004, July). *Working culturally and competently with Latinos: Shifting perspectives, facilitating change.* In J. Resnick & J. Carter (Co-Chairs), American Psychological Association pre-convention workshop: Implementation of the Multicultural Guidelines. Workshop conducted at the meeting of the American Psychological Association, Honolulu, HI.

Gallardo, M. E., Johnson, J., Parham, T. A., & Carter, J. A. (2009). Ethics and multiculturalism: Advancing cultural and clinical responsiveness. *Professional Psychology: Research and Practice, 40*(5), 425–435.

Graham, J. R. (2006). *MMPI-2: Assessing personality and psychopathology* (4th ed.). New York: Oxford University Press.

Grills, C. (2002). African-centered psychology: Basic principles. In T. A. Parham (Ed.), *Counseling persons of African descent* (pp. 10–24). Thousand Oaks, CA: Sage.

Griner, D., & Smith, T. B. (2006). Culturally adapted mental health intervention: A meta-analytic review. *Psychotherapy: Theory, Research, Practice, Training, 43*(4), 531–548.

Hays, P. A. (2009). Integrating evidence-based practice, cognitive-behavioral therapy, and multicultural therapy: Ten steps for culturally competent practice. *Professional Psychology: Research and Practice, 40*(4), 354–360.

Hays, P. A., & Iwamasa, G. Y. (2006). *Culturally responsive cognitive-behavioral therapy: Assessment, practice and supervision.* Washington, DC: American Psychological Association.

Holmes, S. E., & Kivlighan, D. M. (2000). Comparison of therapeutic factors in group and individual treatment processes. *Journal of Counseling Psychology, 47*(4), 478–484.

Hwang, W. C. (2009). The formative method for adapting psychotherapy (FMAP): A community-based developmental approach to culturally adapting therapy. *Professional Psychology: Research and Practice, 40*(4), 369–377.

Jinks, G. H. (1999). Intentionality and awareness: A qualitative study of clients' perceptions of change during longer term counseling. *Counseling Psychology Quarterly, 12*(1), 57–67.

King, L., Dixon, V., & Nobles, W. W. (1976). *African philosophy: Assumptions and paradigms for research on black people.* Los Angeles: Fanon Center.

Kivlighan, D. M., Multon, K. D., & Patton, M. J. (2000). Insight symptom reduction in time-limited psychoanalytic counseling. *Journal of Counseling Psychology, 47*(1), 50–58.

La Roche, M. J. (2005). The cultural context and the psychotherapeutic process: Toward a culturally sensitive psychotherapy. *Journal of Psychotherapy Integration, 15*(2), 169–185.

La Roche, M. J., & Christopher, M. S. (2009). Changing paradigms from empirically supported treatments to evidence-based practice: A cultural perspective. *Professional Psychology: Research and Practice, 40*(4), 396–402.

Lakes, K., Lopez, S. R., & Garro, L. C. (2006). Cultural competence and psychotherapy: Applying anthropologically informed conceptions of culture. *Psychotherapy: Theory, Research, Practice, Training, 43*(4), 380–396.

Lambert, M. J., & Barley, D. E. (2001). Research summary on the therapeutic relationship and psychotherapy outcome. *Psychotherapy: Theory, Research, Practice, Training, 38*(4), 357–361.

Liu, W. M., & Pope-Davis, D. B. (2005). The working alliance, therapy ruptures and impasses, and counseling competence: Implications for counselor training and education. In R. T. Carter (Ed.), *Handbook of racial-cultural psychology and counseling: Training and practice* (Vol. 2., pp. 148–167). Hoboken, NJ: John Wiley & Sons.

Martín-Baró, I. (1994). *Writings for a liberation psychology.* Cambridge, MA: Harvard University.

McAuliffe, G. (Ed.). (2008). *Culturally alert counseling: A comprehensive introduction.* Thousand Oaks, CA: Sage.

McDonagh, A., Friedman, M., McHugo, G., Ford, J., Sengupta, A., Mueser, K., et al. (2005). Randomized trial of cognitive-behavioral therapy for chronic post-traumatic stress disorder in adult female survivors of childhood sexual abuse. *Journal of Consulting and Clinical Psychology, 73,* 515–524.

Michalak, J., Klappheck, M. A., & Kosfelder, J. (2004). Personal goals of psychotherapy patients: The intensity and the "why" of goal-motivated behavior and their implications for the therapeutic process. *Psychotherapy Research, 14*(2), 193–209.

Nelson-Jones, R. (2002). Diverse goals for multicultural counseling and therapy. *Counseling Psychology Quarterly, 15*(2), 133–143.

Nicolas, G., Arntz, D. L., Hirsch, B., & Schmiedigen, A. (2009). Cultural adaptations of a group treatment for Haitian American adolescents. *Professional Psychology: Research and Practice, 40*(4), 378–384.

Nobles, W. W. (2010, January). *Rebirthing community: From auset to asset.* Presentation delivered at the Mid-Winter Meeting of the Association of Black Psychologists, Los Angeles, CA.

Norcross, J. C. (Ed.). (2002). *Psychotherapy relationships that work: Therapist contributions and responsiveness to patients.* New York: Oxford University Press.

Parham, T. A. (2002). Counseling models for African Americans: The what and how of counseling. In T. A. Parham (Ed.), *Counseling persons of African descent: Raising the bar of practitioner competence* (pp. 100–118). Thousand Oaks, CA: Sage.

Parham, T. A. (2004). Raising the bar on what passes for competence. *The California Psychologist, 37*(6), 20–21.

Parham, T. A., Ajamu, A., & White, J. L. (2011). *The psychology of blacks: Centering our perspective in the African consciousness.* New York: Prentice Hall.

Parham, T. A., White, J. L., & Ajamu, A. (1999). *The psychology of blacks: An African-centered perspective* (3rd ed.). Englewood Cliffs, NJ: Prentice Hall.

Paul, G. (1967). Strategy of outcome research in psychotherapy. *Journal of Consulting Psychology, 31,* 109–118.

Prilleltensky, I., Dokecki, P., Frieden, G., & Ota Wang, V. (2007). Counseling for wellness and justice: Foundations and ethical dilemmas. In E. Aldarondo (Ed.), *Advancing social justice through clinical practice* (pp. 19–42). Mahwah, NJ: Lawrence Erlbaum.

Schank, J. A., Helbok, C. M., Haldeman, D. C., & Gallardo, M. E. (2010). Ethical issues in small communities: Expanding the definition and discussion. *Professional Psychology: Research and Practice, 41*(6), 502–510.

Stone, J. H. (2005). *Culture and disability.* Thousand Oaks, CA: Sage.

Sue, D. W., & Sue, D. (2003). *Counseling the culturally diverse: Theory and practice* (4th ed.). New York: John Wiley & Sons.

Sue, S. (1998). In search of cultural competence in psychotherapy and counseling. *American Psychologist, 53,* 440–448.

Suzuki, L. A., Kugler, J. K., & Aguiar, L. J. (2005). Assessment practices in racial-cultural psychology. In R. T. Carter (Ed)., *Handbook of racial-cultural psychology and counseling: Training and practice* (Vol. 2., pp. 297–315). Hoboken, NJ: John Wiley & Sons.

Toporek, R. L., & Reza, J. V. (2001). Context as a critical dimension of multicultural counseling. *Journal of Multicultural Counseling and Development, 29,* 13–30.

Townsend, K. C., & McWhirter, B. T. (2005). Connectedness: A review of the literature with implications for counseling, assessment, and research. *Journal of Counseling & Development, 83*(2), 191–201.

U.S. Census Bureau. (2009, May 14). *Census Bureau releases state and county data depicting nation's population ahead of 2010 census: Orange, Fla. joins the list of 'major-minority' counties* [Press Release]. Retrieved May 9, 2011, from http://www.census.gov/newsroom/releases/archives/population/cb09-76.html

Velasquez, R. J., Chavira, D. A., Karle, H. R., Callahan, W. J., Garcia, J. A., & Castellanos, J. (2002). Assessing bilingual and monolingual Latino students with translation of the MMPI-2: Initial data. *Cultural Diversity & Ethnic Minority Psychology, 6*(1), 65–72.

Vera, E. M., Buhin, L., Montgomery, G., & Shin, R. (2005). Enhancing therapeutic interventions with people of color: Integrating outreach, advocacy, and prevention. In R. T. Carter (Ed.), *Handbook of racial-cultural psychology and counseling: Training and practice* (Vol. 2, pp. 477–491). Hoboken, NJ: John Wiley & Sons.

Vera, E., & Speight, S. L. (2003). Multicultural competence, social justice, and counseling psychology: Expanding our roles. *The Counseling Psychologist, 31,* 253–272.

Warrier, S. (2008). "It's in their culture": Fairness and cultural considerations in domestic violence. *Family Court Review, 46*(3), 537–542.

Whatley, P. R., Allen, J., & Dana, R. H. (2003). Racial identity and the MMPI in African American male college students. *Cultural Diversity and Ethnic Minority Psychology, 9*(4), 345–353.

White, J. L., & Parham, T. A. (1990). *The psychology of blacks: An African American perspective* (2nd ed.). Englewood Cliffs, NJ: Prentice Hall.

PART I

African-Centered Applications of the SISM

Delivering Culturally Competent Therapeutic Services to African American Clients

2

The Skills That Distinguish Between Clinical Intention and Successful Outcomes

Thomas A. Parham

A decade ago, the Office of the Surgeon General, under the capable leadership of Dr. David Satcher, issued a report on mental health, and a follow-up report on culture, race, and ethnicity in mental health (U.S. Department of Health & Human Services, 2001). This report was one of the first of its kind issued by the U.S. government that examined issues of mental health and mental illness. Of most importance, these reports painted a sobering portrait of different communities across this nation who wrestled with this psychological duality. Certainly, scholars had been concerned about issues of mental health and illness for decades. Yet the focus never seemed to gain the momentum it needed to place this issue on the "front burner" of our nation's domestic priorities. Clearly, the visibility of a Surgeon General and his office, and the weight of the federal government, helped to bring the issues center stage and even made academia sit up and take note.

Although disparities in mental health care and trends in mental illness and diagnostic profiles were featured prominently in the texts of those monographs, the reports, interestingly enough, also called for the disciplines of counseling, psychology, and psychiatry to address the cultural competence of its clinicians. To say that cultural competence was an issue for the mental health field would be an understatement of significant proportion. In fact, both African-centered (Akbar, 1991; Block, 1980; Grills, 2002; Kambon, 1992; Myers, 1988; Nobles, 1986; Parham, White, & Ajamu, 1999; White, 1972) and multiculturalism scholars (Ponterotto, Casas, Suzuki, & Alexander, 2001; D. W. Sue, Arredondo, & McDavis, 1992; D. W. Sue, Ivey, & Pederson, 1996) generally have been sounding that alarm for the past several decades. Perhaps it was the high rates of premature termination by clients of color reported more than 30 years ago (S. Sue, 1978) that began to catch people's attention. Or maybe it was the recognition by academic and other training institutions of the need to better educate, train, and socialize their students and professionals in how to better serve the mental health needs of clients they purportedly wanted to effectively treat. On the other hand, it could have been a recognition that the cultural incompetence that was so pronounced in the field not only had detrimental effects on clients (misdiagnoses, improper treatment, etc.), but also raised issues of risk and liability for those who did not comply with the new norms for training culturally competent counselors and clinicians that were so well articulated in the counseling and psychology literature (Franklin, 1999; Grills & Ajei, 2002; Ivey, D'Andrea, Bradford-Ivey, & Simek-Morgan, 2002; Parham et al., 1999; D. W. Sue et al., 1992). Whichever factor, or combination thereof, was most responsible for the shift toward a much fuller embrace of the cultural competency movement is unimportant. What is important is the way our helping disciplines have exerted less resistance to this momentum that is sweeping our field.

Now that the disciplines of psychology, psychiatry, counseling, and social work have adopted the language (at least on the surface) of multiculturalism and cultural competence, progress toward a fuller realization of that promise, in my opinion, is being delayed by the lack of specificity about how to engage in treatment interventions with populations that require them. Admittedly, there are a host of culturally generic suggestions about the necessity to enhance awareness, knowledge, and skills (Arrendondo et al., 1996; Ponterotto et al., 2001; D. W. Sue et al., 1992; D. W. Sue et al. 1996); receive continuing education (Parham & Whitten, 2003); and advocate to licensing boards and state accreditation agencies for more accountability in cultural competence among the clinicians they license.

However, what the field has lacked, in spite of the multicultural momentum described above, is a level of cultural specificity that answers the question not of *what* to do (i.e., be multiculturally competent) but *how* to tailor specific interventions to clients of African, Asian, Indian, Latina/o, and Middle Eastern descent. Parham (2002) accepted that challenge in developing a template for working with African American clients. Clearly, much had been written about the nature of providing therapeutic services to persons of African descent over the past three to four decades (Akbar, 1991, 2004; Boyd-Franklin, 1989; Grier & Cobbs, 1968; Jenkins, 1982; Jones, 1972, 1980, 1991; Myers, 1988; Nobles, 1986, 1998, 2008; Parham et al., 1999; Pugh, 1972; A. Thomas & Sillen, 1972; Utsey, Bolden, & Brown, 1995;

Vontress, 1971; White & Parham, 1990; Zhang & Snowden, 1999). That body of work was impressive, indeed, yet seemed to anchor itself in three primary themes: critiquing Eurocentric theories and the assumptions that were inappropriate for use beyond populations for which they were designed (white people); arguing for the uniqueness of an African-centered worldview in treating African Americans; and describing some of the conditions that challenged black people to maintain their mental health and psychological stability in a climate of racial hostility characterized by hardcore racism, discrimination, and oppression. Thus, although many in the discipline were clear about traditional psychology and counseling's limitations, there was little available information on what a clinician, academician, or counselor might use instead if his or her desire was to be more responsive to the cultural needs of clients of African descent. Consequently, Parham developed the model in 2002 to specifically address this void in the black/African psychology literature.

In further operationalizing the tenets of that model, Parham (2000, 2007) developed a videotape for Microtraining Associates and the American Psychological Association in which he illustrated the specific interventions and skills of his model using actual clients who had the benefit of brief therapeutic interventions that were anchored in an African-centered ontological and epistemological system. This is the system or model that we employ here. Thus, the challenge in this section of the book is to first outline the structure of the model and then utilize the case study method to ascertain the functional utility of the model's stages and specific skill recommendations in working with two clients of African descent.

Thus we begin this section on working with African Americans in therapy in a similar way Parham (2002) did, by asking two important questions: What therapeutic outcomes do we want to achieve with African American clients? How do we use specific skills and techniques to facilitate those outcomes? The task here, as Parham reminds us, is to provide a conceptual template by which clinicians can develop specific skills of competence when working with culturally diverse clients. It is hoped that by adapting and integrating these nonexhaustive skill sets into the existing counseling/clinical foundation, clinicians can achieve some measure of success during the phases of therapy outlined below.

African Americans

Although most racial/ethnic demographic forms that we invite clients to fill out imply that African Americans are a monolithic or uniform cultural entity, a more informed perspective reminds us that there is a fair amount of within-group variability in this population. Certainly, many authors have provided some illumination on this issue by challenging members of the profession to explore within-group differences in racial identity, rather than make simple between-group comparisons that yield less relevant findings (Carter, 1995; Cross, 1971, 1980, 1991; Parham, 1989; Parham & Helms, 1981, 1985; C. Thomas, 1971). Beyond discussions of racial and cultural identity, however, Parham, Ajamu, and White (2011) help to profile the more contemporary view of the African American community in their analysis of the black family. They report that there are approximately 8.7 million African American families in the United States according to the 2000 census (the last year in which a full census was taken), but the percentage of married couple families has declined over the past 35 years, from 68% in the 1970s to a mere 48% in the early 2000s (U.S. Census Bureau, 2000). Thus, contrary to societal stereotypes, nearly half of all African American families do enjoy a two-parent lifestyle, a fact that stands in sharp contrast to perceptions commonly portrayed in the larger print and electronic media. Census data also reveal that overall, 66% of African Americans participate in the labor force, with black men participating at a rate of 68% and black women at 64%. Interestingly, some scholars and authors continue to argue that persons of African descent suffer the most persistent forms of racism and discrimination, and there are some data that seem to reinforce that sentiment, especially in the current climate of economic and occupational recession. In 1970, the unemployment rate for blacks was a staggering 10%, compared to just 5% among white workers. In the early 2010s, the national data reveal that black unemployment is still twice that of their white counterparts (17%–18% for African Americans, compared to a national average of 9.7%). Pay equity for persons of African descent continues to be an issue; blacks earn just 61 dollars for every 100 dollars earned by white men and women. Consequently, poverty continues to be an issue that many, but not all, families confront, but the effects are more keenly felt in single-parent households. Issues of academic underachievement; low college eligibility, admission, retention, and graduation rates; violence in communities across the country; disparities in health care access and affordability and impacts of specific medical conditions and diseases; challenges with the law enforcement system and differential police practices; and struggles with personal and reference group identity are also on the list of challenges the black community individually and collectively must confront. And yet, these are the precise conditions that frame African American clients' entry into the mental health system, where they seek relief from anxiety, depression, bipolar disorder, and a host of other ailments and conditions that require therapeutic and sometimes pharmacological intervention. Their defense against many of these challenges is a cultural ethic or mindset that enhances their ability to survive and even thrive amid circumstances that are sobering, to say the least. Clearly, understanding culture in context, and not just which box a client checks on a demographic form, is essential.

Thus, therapeutic work with African Americans does not begin with an initiation of particular skills, but rather with a profound recognition by the treating clinician of some fundamental constructs that relate to the client himself or herself. Although the universe of client characteristics is fairly broad, there are particular elements of a client's essence or character that demand attention. These include, as Grills (2002, 2004); Franklin and Boyd-Franklin (2000); Parham (2002, 2005, 2006); Parham et al. (2011); and others have observed, the notions of spirit/spirituality, the transformative possibilities of the human spirit (Akbar, 1994, 2004; Nobles, 1986), self-healing power (Fu-Kiau, 1991), cultural congruence and self-knowledge (Akbar, 1992; Myers, 1988; Nobles, 2008), and the construct of "mental health" itself.

Spirituality

Spirit and spirituality are fundamental to the African conception of the self. These concepts represent the essence of a person. Spirituality is an animating principle that gives life to each person and reflects the essence and substance of all matter. Spirituality exists before, after, and beyond material existence. Spirit is the basis of all existence, both what is seen and not seen. Spirit is the energy and life force in each person, which like a divine spark gives humans (and all living things) their beingness (Nobles, 1998).

Beyond defining spirituality, it is important to ask what spirituality does for African Americans and, by extension, for all of humankind. First, spirituality is connected to authentic personhood by providing a connection to the divine force in the universe. Second, spirituality provides and affirms a sense of power by acknowledging each person's ability to transform and transcend situational circumstances in ways that are beneficial and yield positive outcomes. Third, spirituality provides a sense of purpose by aligning one's consciousness and one's destiny, consistent with the principle of Ori-Ire, which come from the Yoruba tradition with a similar translation (Parham, 2002).

Transformative Possibilities of the Human Spirit

Spirit is not a static concept; it is dynamic. Thus, because each person is fundamentally spirit at his or her core, he or she is capable of change and transformation. This is a key element for clinicians to remember because too often the life circumstances that prompt a person to attend therapy and counseling are assumed to be characteristic of the client himself or herself. This assumption invites clinicians to label clients in ways that are consistent with their demographic profile or presenting problem, implying that clients are less capable of change.

It is important to remember that clients come from circumstance, but they are not their circumstance. Clients come from poverty, but their spirits can be rich; clients may have a particular challenge in life like alcohol or drug use, but they can overcome that affliction. Clients may have fallen short of a goal or standard or may have transgressed against some social norm that brought

them into contact with an authority figure or institution eager to hold them accountable for their failings. However, clinicians must remember that one's belief in the transformative nature of the human spirit is paramount in understanding a client's ability to rise above circumstance to achieve a higher level of functioning.

Self-Healing Power

In the African tradition, there is a belief that each person is endowed with a self-healing power that can contribute to his or her personal uplifting. This power extends beyond a mere reservoir of energy in each person. When their spirit or energy becomes contaminated, or their energy becomes unbalanced due to some incident, human beings will naturally seek to realign their life force in ways that restore their energy to a state of balance and harmony. Fu-Kiau (1991) helps us to better understand this concept by comparing our energy reserve to a battery in a car. When life events, disappointments, setbacks, or circumstances that challenge our sensibilities decrease our energy, there remains a capacity to restore that energy level to its usual or even maximum level. This process is akin to jumpstarting an automobile when the battery has run low. Therapy, if it is practiced in ways that support and affirm one's humanity and spirituality, helps to recharge that spiritual battery so that the client experiences a greater level of empowerment.

Cultural Congruence and Self-Knowledge

Another fundamental principle of an African-centered psychological perspective is that self-knowledge is the key to mental health (Akbar, 1994; Grills, 2002; Kambon, 1992; Myers, 1988; Nobles, 1998; Parham, 2002; Parham et al., 1999). The more an individual is aligned with his or her natural cultural disposition, the higher the likelihood of living a life that is free of mental debilitations. Conversely, the greater the incongruence between how a person lives and his or her cultural dispositions, the higher the probability that he or she will be vulnerable to mild, moderate, or severe mental debilitations.

The Concept of Mental Health

Embracing the concept of mental health from a traditional Eurocentric frame of reference is a difficult exercise. Not only does the notion of culture and "worldview differences" potentially render such a definition useless, at best, it will be an inaccurate representation of ways African Americans relate to reality. In some respects, traditional definitions are anchored in an "absence of pathology" concept: One infers mental health from an absence of mental illness, particularly as represented by measures that are pathology oriented (e.g., scores on an MMPI assessment instrument). Or mental health is determined by a Mental Status Examination, in which elements like physical appearance, motor activity, speech activity and patterns, mood and affect, alertness and attention, content and organization of thoughts, abstract thinking, perceptions, and memory are examined during a clinical interview.

In other corners of the psychological community, you may find a more hearty and positive definition in which mental health refers to an individual's emotional and psychological well-being, and one's psychological assets are used to help one function effectively and meet the demands of life's daily activities. In this regard, a continuum of high to low functioning can be used to characterize one's adaptation to these daily challenges.

In an African-centered context, Parham (2009) reminds us that mental health, at its core, relates to a more harmonious integration with the universe. This perspective can be seen in the definition of mental health as people functioning in accord with the nature, aim, and purpose of their creation (Farrakhan, 1996). In other models, African-centered clinicians embrace terms like *ordered* and *disordered* behavior (and, by extension, mental health) as that which sustains or inhibits life and fosters and perpetuates the survival or destruction of the human organism in all of its aspects (i.e., physical, mental, emotional). Similarly, Fu-Kiau (1991) argues that to be healthy, one must be in harmony with oneself, one's environment, and the universe. Azibo (1989) proposes that mental health is the achievement of functioning in the psychological and behavioral spheres of life that embraces and is in harmony with the natural order and human nature. Finally, Parham (2002) asserts that mental health is analogous to living in accordance with one's natural essence by achieving an awareness of who one is as a divine and spiritual being, sustaining one's ability to grow, acquiring knowledge and wisdom, exercising free will, and being morally and socially responsible in all human interactions.

Treating African Americans

In articulating this aspect of the book, it is important to stay as consistent with Parham's (2002) original version of the African-centered therapeutic model. Thus, we thank Sage for allowing an extensive reprint of that information. Recall that in the original text, Parham argues that irrespective of which theoretical orientation a clinician elects to use, he or she will need to establish a relationship with his or her client that can facilitate some resolution of the client's presenting problem. As clinicians engage in the therapeutic process, we argue that two of the most important questions in therapy are *what* and *how* (Parham, 2002). The former establishes what a clinician wishes to accomplish in the therapeutic encounter, and the latter provides specific strategies that clinicians can utilize in achieving those outcomes.

In reviewing those strategies and techniques here, it is hoped that the reader might acquire a broader repertoire of skills that will increase the probability of achieving successful outcomes with African American clients. Table 2.1 lists those skills, as first presented by Parham (2002).

Table 2.1   African American Skills Identification Stage Model (AA-SISM)

Connecting With Clients	Creating ambiance within the therapeutic space
	Offering some food or drink
	Using ritual (handshakes, music, poetry, libations)
	Exhibiting congruent realness (self-disclosure)
	Shifting context and setting
	Being with a client (active listening)
Assessment	Understanding and identifying cultural strengths
	Understanding clients
	Distress from a culturally centered frame of reference
	Using culturally normed assessment instruments
	Helping clients and therapist anticipate setbacks
Facilitating Awareness	Rephrasing as a way of helping clients creatively synthesize opposites
	Reflecting
	Use of metaphor
	Analyzing obstacles to growth (defenses)
	Summarizing
	Exploring impact of social forces on client's life
	Assigning readings
	Helping clients understand their language and values
Setting Goals	Becoming a subjective companion
	Reframing the environment while teaching improvisation, transcendence, and transformation
	Helping clients have a cultural corrective experience
	Restoration of balance and harmony
Instigating Change	Empowering clients through self-knowledge
	Teaching clients to problem solve
	Becoming a social advocate on behalf of clients
Feedback/ Accountability	Reviewing what is working in moving toward a goal
	Examining congruence between goals and outcomes
	Examining spiritual energy and sense of harmony
	Reminding clients about the notion of being and becoming (concept of perfectibility)

Connecting With Clients

First, connecting with clients is an essential element in counseling or any therapeutic work because it is this phase of therapy that determines, in part, whether a client will be returning for follow-up visits with the therapist. Emphasis is placed here on this skill because so many clients fail to return to treatment after the first session (Block, 1980; S. Sue, 1978). Several skills can be used to connect with clients so that they can both align their goals with those of their treating clinician and better appreciate the benefits of staying committed to therapy.

Use of Ritual. Ritual is the conscious and deliberate application of words, thoughts, and/or behaviors that bring special meaning to a situation. Rituals can range from basic to elaborate and can be as simple as a handshake or as meaningful as using prayer, pouring libations (water), or embracing each other. Ritual helps to center a client's consciousness on the task at hand. When used in the therapeutic context, ritual has the potential to facilitate a process of joining or connecting for the therapist and client by helping each to develop a sense of collective consciousness that becomes embedded with the spiritual energy created in the moment.

Music. Music is the language of the soul. The sounds that emanate from rhythm and musical notes stimulate feelings as each person seeks to align his or her awareness with the rhythm of the tune or song being played. Rhythms and beats, in turn, provoke a spiritual awakening that helps to create an ambiance for counseling or therapeutic work. Music also becomes central to therapy because the rhythms help to illustrate the need for sustaining movement and momentum in the face of personal struggle and adversity. Much like the natural order and rhythm of life, music helps to stylize space and time for each individual, especially when he or she is talking about a particular problem or concern.

Poetry and Prose. Poetry is a language that stylizes words. Poetry and prose tend to stylize words in ways that use language as a symbolic representation of a particular subject or circumstance. Poetry and prose then serve as a stimulus that instigates exploration of cognitive, affective, behavioral, and spiritual domains of the personality.

Exhibiting Congruent Realness. The notion of "keeping it real" is an important value that is reflected in many African American communities. Essentially, this phrase speaks to the notion that people need to be real, genuine, and authentic in their conversations and interactions with each other. In a similar way, exhibiting congruent wellness through the use of such techniques as self-disclosure, while being vulnerable to questions from the client, enables the therapist to solidify those connections with their clients.

Being real invites the therapist to assume a posture of vulnerability as he or she elects to display a more human side that is less visible amid the ambience of title, degrees, and certifications.

Creating Ambience. Ambience sets the mood or atmosphere in a therapy session, not just the personal contact but also the aesthetics of the room. The furnishings, pictures, figurines, and so on used by the clinician assist the client in locating or adapting to a personal comfort zone. Attention to this dimension recognizes that clients are part of a larger social context from which they cannot be separated. Ambience can be created through office location, artwork on walls, cultural artifacts, or any other items that help the client to engage his or her senses in a search for personal comfort.

Shifting Context and Setting. This skill requires changing the location of the therapeutic work. Traditional therapy is usually conducted in a clinician's office or group room. Arguably, this practice helps to ensure the privacy and confidentiality of the therapeutic session while also creating a comfortable space for a clinician to work in. In the African context, healing and therapy are not necessarily restricted to a specific time and place.

As such, there are a number of activities that occur outside the therapeutic space of an office that can help a therapist to connect with his or her client. Because many of the activities that contribute to healing exist in a larger social context, therapists should consider relocating therapy to settings that allow the therapist to access those healing venues and activities.

Assessment

Several techniques contribute to a therapist's ability to accurately assess what is going on with a client in his or her life, generally as well as in that moment specifically. The following skills are offered as a way of assisting clinicians to make accurate and reliable assessments.

Understanding Cultural Strengths. Working with African American populations requires an assessment of not just what is wrong with clients, but also what is healthy and facilitative in their life. Examining this aspect of their life is particularly difficult when using traditional Eurocentric instruments because most are very pathology oriented and typically assess deficits. In contrast, it is important when working with African American folk to understand the notion of strength. *Strengths* are those skills or attributes that enable an individual or group to meet its needs. Strengths enable individuals to successfully confront and meet the challenges and demands placed upon them by the larger social context. Thus, rather than examine ways in which particular challenges are plaguing the lives of clients you see, first examine ways in which particular skills or attributes have enabled your clients to persevere in the face of adversity.

Understanding Client Distress From a Culturally Specific Frame of Reference. In traditional Eurocentric context, client distress is assumed to be an intra-psychic phenomenon. Although some African American clients do experience distress intra-psychically, much of the stress they encounter is the result of social, cultural, and environmental factors that affect their psyche. Consequently, those assessing African American clients must understand that there is a harmony, balance, and rhythm to life and that distress occurs when clients find that their cognitive, affective, behavioral, and spiritual energies are out of alignment with each other.

Using Appropriate Clinical Instruments. It is very difficult to accurately gauge or measure a particular construct if the instrument or device the therapist is using is one that is not known by and standardized on persons of African descent. Therefore, it is imperative for a therapist to use clinical instruments that, at the very least, have been modified by using more African-centered norms and standards and, at best, have been developed with an African-centered framework in mind.

Facilitating Awareness

Several techniques and skills contribute to a therapist's ability to help clients explore themselves at a deeper level and gain further insights.

Assessing Spiritual Energy. Because African-centered therapists and healers understand and appreciate the importance of spirit, clients need to be helped to access and appreciate their spiritual energy as well. Facilitating awareness requires that therapists be in touch with a client's spiritual energy and that he or she be able to access that energy across positive and negative domains, as well as different levels of intensity. Because spirit is fundamentally energy and life force, therapists are required to understand where a client's energy level is and how he or she can access his or her spiritual energy in times of personal distress. In African tradition, we believe that human beings are endowed with a reservoir of spiritual energy. Consequently, that energy will need to be tapped into in order to ascertain both where clients are in their spiritual space and how that spiritual energy can be used to overcome whatever obstacle they may be confronted with.

Helping Clients Understand Their Pain. Clients often believe that emotional pain and distress are caused by situational phenomena with which they are confronted. It is likely, however, that the particular situations have meaning and importance for clients beyond the circumstances themselves. Therefore, those dimensions of a problem must be thoroughly explored in order for clients to understand their pain. In essence, clients must be assisted with the process of not simply acknowledging their emotions, but also digging deep into the cognitive processes that give meaning to life events.

Analyzing Defenses. Defenses are those qualities and attributes that help to protect the integrity of the individual psyche from assault, harm, or disorder. Because human beings have several needs, which include a need to grow, self-preserve, and regenerate, anything that threatens the stability of that personality integration will likely be attacked by the individual. It is important for therapists and clinicians to examine ways in which individuals impede their growth possibilities by using specific defenses to ward off apparent threats to their psyche.

Helping Clients to "Know Thyself." One of the best things a therapist can do is help a client acquire more self-knowledge. Self-knowledge enables clients to discover aspects of themselves they may have been unaware of. Therapists are encouraged to assist clients in distinguishing between what they do for a living, what material goods they have acquired in their lifetime, and who they are at the core of their being. Too often in our society, individuals are taught that they are what they do, or they are what they acquire.

Rephrasing. In the African tradition, there is an expression: "Life at its best is a creative synthesis of opposites in fruitful harmony" (Parham et al., 1999). In essence, this pearl of wisdom speaks to the necessity of helping clients balance their conversations about distress and turmoil in their life with an awareness of the most positive aspects of that experience that have helped them to arrive at a particular place. When therapists utilize the technique of synthesizing opposites, it helps to not only focus on the emotional distress clients have experienced, but also to understand the positive aspects of that circumstance that allowed them to feel so deeply about their current distress and the positive lessons that can be learned from their circumstance and used in future endeavors.

Understanding Functional Behaviors. In the African tradition, it is believed that all behavior is functional and that specific thoughts, feelings, and actions are intended to meet particular needs that emerge for the individual. Understanding functional behavior requires a therapist to focus less on why a client might engage in a specific action and more on what a client might derive from behaving and responding in a particular way.

Using Metaphors. A metaphor is a direct comparison between seemingly unrelated subjects. This figurative language is an important part of therapy because metaphor helps to identify deeper meanings and situations and can be used to facilitate a broader level of discussion and exploration of a particular issue.

Setting Goals

Goals chart the course for healing. They help the client review strategies that bring some relief of the distress they are experiencing. Specific skills or techniques that are associated with helping a client to set goals include the following.

Becoming a Subjective Companion. Traditional therapy teaches that counselors and clinicians must learn to be objective outsiders. In an African-centered worldview, therapists become subjective companions who articulate very clear, understandable, and deliberate messages to their client that reflect some level of adherence to culturally based assumptions and values. It is not uncommon for a therapist or healer to provide specific advice or counsel to the client, rather than simply listening and reflecting back to that client the essence of the conversation they have heard.

Culturally Corrective Experiences. Much like the human body ingests, digests, and expels substances, the psychological process needs to engage clients in ways that help them to have what we term *culturally corrective experiences.* Many clients are exposed to intellectual, emotional, behavioral, and spiritual experiences that serve as negative rather than positive influences. This "psychic garbage" must be examined, sifted through, and expelled from a client's way of thinking, feeling, and experiencing and this process must become one of the goals of therapy.

Aligning Conscientiousness With Destiny. Within the African tradition, there is a concept called *Ori-Ire,* which means "One whose conscientiousness is aligned with his destiny." When working with African American clients, it is important for therapists to understand that one's thought process must be in tune and in harmony with one's passion in life. This is an important goal of therapy as well; therapists help a client explore those things that provoke a sense of urgency and rise to a level of particular salience in their life.

Restoring Balance and Harmony. Another goal in therapy should be the restoration of balance and harmony in an individual's life. Situations in life can often cause an individual to become unbalanced in his or her energy flow. As such, the restoration of balance is an important technique in helping an individual to not simply synthesize opposites, but to focus more creatively on balancing the energies in his or her life to ensure that he or she does not focus on one domain (positive versus negative) exclusively.

Reframing. Another goal that is important for a therapist to use with a client is the technique of reframing, in which therapists assist their clients to change the structure and quality of a known experience into something that, although unfamiliar, is likely to be of benefit. Reframing is analogous to looking at the proverbial half-empty glass and finding it half-full. It is analogous to taking a negative situation or circumstance and finding some benefit that a person can derive from it, by simply looking at it through a different set of lenses.

Respecting a Client's Need for Distance. On some occasions, clients will come into treatment with a presentation of information that creates a distance between themselves and the actual event. Rather than focus on confronting clients about their need for distance, African-centered therapists understand that healing can occur in the third person, much like it can in the first person. Therefore, there is a respect for distance and understanding that distance creates an emotionally safe place for a client to be in the moment, particularly if he or she is struggling with a particularly distressing issue or event.

Taking Action and Instigating Change

The following skills can assist clients with confronting their circumstances.

Becoming a Social Advocate. Often, the etiology of clients' distress is not intra-psychic, but rather social, cultural, and environmental. If therapists are successful in helping clients to facilitate some healing, they should be careful about sending them out into an environment where they are still vulnerable to the same social pathology that instigated their desire to seek treatment in the first place. As such, working with African American clients requires that therapists consider becoming social advocates. This role requires that therapists often work on behalf of their clients to access social services, institutions, agencies, and other entities in order to help the clients transform their distress into something more positive.

Planning Your Work and Working Your Plan. Therapists who work with African American clients will do well to consider developing a specific plan that an individual can utilize to accomplish his or her goals. Such plans should include details about restating the problem, the strategy being proposed, the specific skills necessary to meet this demand, and a timetable for engaging in the specific action.

Empowering the Client. The self-healing power in individuals is only partially realized if clients restrict their powers to self-revelation. Therapists who work with African American clients should be encouraged to support their clients by helping them to believe that engaging in some type of movement and/or momentum in the face of life's adversities can lead to some level of meaningful change and mastery over their particular life circumstance.

Teaching Clients to Problem Solve. Problem solving is a skill that can be taught to clients. Because situational circumstances often seem overwhelming for the clients that therapists treat, therapists will need to help break down problems into individual, manageable parts. Although clients may not control 100% of the variables that impact an issue, it is entirely possible and probable that they do control some small portion of them. Therefore, therapists should encourage clients to focus on those aspects of a situation or problem that appear to be under their direct control or influence.

Feedback and Accountability

There are several skills that can be used by therapists to provide feedback to clients on how they are utilizing particular suggestions or insights gained during the therapeutic process. Feedback is needed to provide necessary check-in and also to hold clients accountable for being active participants in the therapy process.

Examining Spiritual Energy and Sense of Harmony and Balance. Because there is a rhythm and order to life, therapists will need to check back in with their clients in order to examine how their spirit is doing and whether they have been able to achieve a sense of harmony and balance in their life with the therapeutic strategies they have employed thus far.

Examining Congruence Between Goals and Outcomes. Examining congruence enables a therapist to reflect on a timeline for implementation that considers the level of progress made between stated goals and achieved outcomes. Once determined, clients can sustain some movement toward a desired outcome, never losing sight of what the particular problem was and the specific goal they are trying to achieve.

Remembering Being and Becoming. African-centered therapists understand that clients will sometimes get frustrated at the lack of progress, believing that whatever debilitation they came into therapy with will be gone after an instant or after a short time. It is important to help clients understand that because each personality is endowed with the character of "perfectibility," they must recognize the nature of "being and becoming." The notion of being and becoming relates to the idea that there is a transformative process of the human spirit that each individual can access. Thus, therapists can assist clients to understand that although they are a particular way at a particular moment in time, they have the capability to become more self-empowered, more self-actualized, and more successful in whatever outcomes they are seeking to achieve.

Summary

In considering the use of this model, it is important, if not essential, that practitioners remember several features. Indeed, there can be a gap of profound proportion between clinical intent and a successful therapeutic outcome with any client, but particularly African Americans. This chapter and summary of Parham's (2002) original skill development model is designed to provide readers with specific tools to increase therapeutic and cultural competence. So, what have we learned? First, the model is designed to separate therapy into manageable parts or phases, but it should not be taken to mean that they are anything other than elements of a congruent whole. Second, the techniques described are not selected at random. Rather, they were each recommended based on their ability to contribute to the therapeutic goals the clinician may be seeking. Thus, as you consider adopting any of these techniques, consideration should be given to what outcomes you are trying to achieve. Third, and equally important, the development of the cultural competence described earlier in this chapter will not occur in a single training session or from reading a single description like the one just provided. Rather, like the model presented here, competence will emerge in phases. In this regard, readers are reminded of the work Parham has done in suggesting that competencies develop sequentially, moving from a state of incompetence to states of pre-competence, competence, and ultimately proficiency. Thus, in one phase of therapeutic treatment, a therapist may lack specific competence or even be incompetent. However, in other phases of the model, he or she may be pre-competent or even proficient. Practitioners will have to assess where they believe they are currently regarding the use of particular phases of this model, while also setting goals for developing in ways that demonstrate proficiency across all phases of therapeutic interaction with clients of African descent. Only then will clients begin to receive the services they are rightly entitled to, and clinicians will develop a more realistic cultural comfort zone in addressing the mental health needs of the clients they treat.

References

Akbar, N. (1991). Mental disorders among African Americans. In R. L. Jones (Ed.), *Black psychology* (3rd ed., pp. 339–352). Berkeley, CA: Cobb & Henry.

Akbar, N. (1992). *Chains and images of psychological slavery.* Tallahassee, FL: Mind Productions and Associates.

Akbar, N. (1994). *Light from ancient Africa.* Tallahassee, FL: Mind Productions and Associates.

Akbar, N. (2004). *The Akbar papers in African psychology.* Tallahassee, FL: Mind Productions and Associates.

Arredondo, P., Toporek, R., Brown, S., Jones, J., Locke, D., Sanchez, J., et al. (1996). Operationalizing the multicultural counseling competencies. *Journal of Multicultural Counseling and Development, 24*(1), 42–78.

Azibo, D. A. (1989). *Advances in black/African personality theory.* Unpublished Manuscript.

Block, C. (1980). Black Americans and the cross-cultural counseling experience. In A. J. Marsella & P. B. Pederson (Eds.), *Cross-cultural counseling and psycho-therapy.* New York: Pergamon.

Boyd-Franklin, N. (1989). *Black families in therapy.* New York: Guilford Press.

Carter, R. T. (1995). *The influence of race and racial identity in psychotherapy.* New York: John Wiley & Sons.

Cross, W. E. (1971). The negro to black conversion experience. *Black World, 209,* 13–27.

Cross, W. E. (1980). Models of psychological nigrescence: A literature review. In R. L. Jones (Ed.), *Black psychology* (2nd ed., pp. 81–98). New York: Harper & Row.

Cross, W. E. (1991). *Shades of black: Diversity in African American identity.* Philadelphia: Temple University Press.

Farrakhan, L. (1996, August). *Mental health in the African American community.* Address delivered at the annual convention of the Association of Black Psychologists, Chicago, IL.

Franklin, A. J. (1999). Invisibility syndrome and racial identity development in psy-chotherapy and counseling with African American men. *Counseling Psychologists, 27*(6), 761–793.

Franklin, A. J., & Boyd-Franklin, N. (2000). The invisibility syndrome: A clinical model on the effects of racism on African American males. *Journal of Orthopsychiatry, 70*(1), 33–41.

Fu-Kiau, K. K. (1991). *Self healing power and therapy: Old teachings from Africa.* New York: Vantage Press.

Grier, W. H., & Cobbs, P. M. (1968). *Black rage.* New York: Basic Books.

Grills, C. (2002). African-centered psychology: Basic principles. In T. A. Parham (Ed.), *Counseling persons of African descent: Raising the bar of practitioner competence* (pp. 10–24). Thousand Oaks, CA: Sage.

Grills, C. (2004). African psychology. In R. L. Jones (Ed.), *Black psychology* (4th ed.). Hampton, VA: Cobb & Henry.

Grills, C., & Ajei, M. (2002). African-centered conceptualizations of self and con-sciousness: The Akan model. In T. A. Parham (Ed.), *Counseling persons of African descent: Raising the bar of practitioner competence* (pp. 75–99). Thousand Oaks, CA: Sage.

Ivey, A., D'Andrea, M., Bradford-Ivey, M., & Simek-Morgan, L. (2002). *Theories of counseling and psychotherapy: A multicultural perspective* (5th ed.). Boston: Allyn & Bacon.

Jenkins, A. H. (1982). *The psychology of the Afro-American: A humanistic approach.* New York: Pergamon Press.

Jones, R. L. (1972). *Black psychology.* New York: Harper & Row.

Jones, R. L. (1980). *Black psychology* (2nd ed.). New York: Harper & Row.

Jones, R. L. (1991). *Black psychology* (3rd ed.). Hampton, VA: Cobb & Henry.

Kambon, K. K. (1992). *The African personality in America: An African-centered framework.* Tallahassee, FL: Nubian Nation.

Myers, L. J. (1988). *Understanding the Afrocentric worldview: Introduction to an optimal psychology.* Dubuque, IA: Kendall Hunt.

Nobles, W. W. (1986). *African psychology*. Oakland, CA: Institute for Black Family Life and Culture.

Nobles, W. W. (1998). To be African or not to be: The question of identity or authenticity—some preliminary thoughts. In R. L. Jones (Ed.), *African American identity development* (pp. 183–206). Hampton, VA: Cobb & Henry.

Nobles, W. W. (2008, August). *Ukufa kwa bantu and spirit illness: Shattered consciousness or fractured identity*. Presentation delivered at the annual convention of the Association of Black Psychologists, Oakland, CA.

Parham, T. A. (1989). Cycles of psychological nigrescence. *The Counseling Psychologists, 17*(2), 187–226.

Parham, T. A. (2000). *Innovative approaches to counseling African American clients* [DVD]. North Amhurst, MA: Microtraining and Associates.

Parham, T. A. (Ed.). (2002). *Counseling persons of African descent: Raising the bar of practitioner competence*. Thousand Oaks, CA: Sage.

Parham, T. A. (2005). *Clinical issues in African-centered psychology: Lessons in competence, proficiency, and certification*. Presentation at the annual convention of the Association of Black Psychologists, Miami, FL.

Parham, T. A. (2006, February). *Rediscovering the roots of counseling psychology: Transforming intellectual commitment into social justice and community action*. Invited address at the Winter Roundtable Conference, Teachers College, Columbia University.

Parham, T. A. (2007). *Working with African American clients in therapy* [DVD]. Washington, DC: American Psychological Association.

Parham, T. A. (2009). Foundations for an African American psychology: Extending roots to an ancient kemetic past. In H. Neville, B. Tynes, & S. Utsey (Eds.), *Handbook of African American psychology* (pp. 269–281). Thousand Oaks, CA: Sage.

Parham, T. A., Ajamu, A., & White, J. L. (2011). *The psychology of blacks: Centering our perspective in the African consciousness*. Upper Saddle River, NJ: Prentice Hall.

Parham, T. A., & Helms, J. E. (1981). Influence of black students' racial identity attitudes on preferences for counselor race. *Journal of Counseling Psychology, 28*(3), 250–256.

Parham, T. A., & Helms, J. E. (1985). Relation of racial identity to self-actualization and affective states in black students. *Journal of Counseling Psychology, 32*(3), 431–440.

Parham, T. A., White, J. L., & Ajamu, A. (1999). *The psychology of blacks: An African-centered perspective*. Englewood Cliffs, NJ: Prentice Hall.

Parham, T. A., & Whitten, L. (2003). Teaching multicultural competencies in continuing education for psychologists: A last stance. In D. Pope-Davis & H. Coleman (Eds.), *Handbook of multicultural competencies*. Thousand Oaks, CA: Sage.

Ponterotto, J. G., Casas, J. M., Suzuki, L. A., & Alexander, C. M. (Eds.). (2001). *Handbook of multicultural counseling*. Thousand Oaks, CA: Sage.

Pugh, R. (1972). *The psychology of the black experience*. Monterey, CA: Brooks/Cole.

Sue, D. W., Arredondo, P., & McDavis, R. J. (1992). Multicultural counseling competencies and standards: A call to the profession. *Journal of Counseling and Development, 70*, 477–484.

Sue, D. W., Ivey, A. E., & Pedersen, P. B. (1996). *A theory of multicultural counseling and therapy.* Pacific Grove, CA: Brooks/Cole.

Sue, S. (1978, May). *Ethnic minority research: Trends and directions.* Paper presented at the National Conference on Minority Group Alcohol, Drug Abuse, and Mental Health. Denver, CO.

Thomas, A., & Sillen, S. (1972). *Racism in psychiatry.* Secaucus, NJ: Citadel Press.

Thomas, C. (1971). *Boys no more.* Beverly Hills, CA: Glenco Press.

U.S. Census Bureau. (2000). *Current population survey and demographics.* Washington, DC: Author.

U.S. Department of Health & Human Services. (2001). *Mental health: Culture, race and ethnicity (a supplement to the Report of the Surgeon General).* Rockville, MD: Office of the Surgeon General.

Utsey, S. O., Bolden, M. A., & Brown, A. L. (1995). Visions of revolution from the spirit of Frantz Fanon: The psychology of liberation for counseling African Americans confronting societal racism and oppression. In J. G. Ponterotto, J. M. Casas, L. A. Suzuki, & C. M. Alexander (Eds.), *Handbook of multicultural counseling* (pp. 311–336). Thousand Oaks, CA: Sage.

Vontress, C. (1971). Racial differences: Impediments to rapport. *Journal of Counseling Psychology, 18,* 7–12.

White, J. L. (1972). Toward a black psychology. In R. L. Jones (Ed.), *Black psychology.* New York: Harper & Row.

White, J. L., & Parham, T. A. (1990). *The psychology of blacks: An African American perspective* (2nd ed.). Englewood Cliffs, NJ: Prentice Hall.

Zhang, A. Y., & Snowden, L. R. (1999). Ethnic characteristics of mental disorders in five U.S. communities. *Cultural Diversity and Ethnic Minority Psychology, 5,* 134–146.

Case Illustration: Reflections on the Culturally Adaptive Model of Counseling for Persons of African Descent

3

An African-Centered Perspective

Cheryl Tawede Grills

The objective of the Skills Identification Stage Model (SISM) is to provide a framework for clinicians to develop specific skill competencies when working with culturally diverse clients. Parham (Chapter 2) appropriately counsels that "therapeutic work with African Americans does not begin with an initiation of particular skills, but rather with a profound recognition by the treating clinician of some fundamental constructs that relate to the client." This evolved skill set is expected to lead to cultural proficiency and will require more than a mere "technique" fix. If the field is truly going to raise the bar, therapeutic work with African American clients must also include serious reflection about what has become complicit adherence to culturally prescribed Western treatment paradigms.[1] A narrow

---

[1]The use of the term *African American* is rather limiting but is herein used with reference to not only people of African descent born in the United States but to diasporan African descendants, some of whom may be from the Caribbean, South and Central America, Europe, and Continental Africa.

band of intervention modalities is imposed upon helpers, ungrounded in the cultural ethos or social realities associated with mental health among African Americans.

Although the field may be intellectually committed to the legitimacy of cultural proficiency, uncertainty remains about our readiness to question its internal logic regarding what constitutes praxis. Particularly striking is the nearly complete absence of environmental or community change strategies in deference to an emphasis on interventions targeting individual change. The SISM would do well to incorporate principles from Social Ecological Theory to expand the framework of intervention (Centers for Disease Control and Prevention, 2009). The Social Ecological Model draws attention to the complex interplay between individual, relationship, community, and societal factors such that multiple issues are considered in the conceptualization of presenting problems, prompting multiple levels of intervention. This approach is particularly important for historically oppressed groups whose communities were/are as much impacted by sociopolitical and economic pressures as the individuals therein.

We do not have to rely solely on an individual change model because other options abound. The efficacy of approaches focused on changing the social and physical environment to reduce threats and challenges to mental health, namely, stress, youth violence, and substance abuse, are sorely neglected in psychology discourse and praxis. Community psychology, positive psychology, and resiliency theory recognize what African traditional thought has known and practiced for centuries. By building sense of community, social capital, and community safety nets, community and individual well-being can be achieved and sustained (Bell, Bhana, McKay, & Petersen, 2005; Grills, 2009; Prilleltensky & Prilleltensky, 2006). I posit that implementing a community change perspective/approach enables us to think more deeply about processes that invigorate a community, particularly for its members steeped in alienation. Using a community change lens, we can think more deeply about transformative processes that move a community whose members experience alienation from reluctant participation to meaningful engagement. In this context, critical targets of intervention include creating environments, policies, and a variety of community building services that promote mental health.

Appropriately, the SISM attempts to unpack the broad concept of cultural competence by partitioning the therapy process into six manageable areas: (1) connecting with clients, (2) conducting culturally relevant assessment, (3) facilitating awareness, (4) setting goals, (5) taking action and instigating change, and (6) feedback and accountability. To increase cultural proficiency with African Americans, I would add a seventh: connecting with community. Interventions must become more community-centric to contribute to or enhance individual change efforts. This shift in framework is discussed below and followed by brief commentary specific to other components of the SISM.

_____ **Connecting With Community**

*A man outside his clan [community] is like a grasshopper which
has lost its wings.*

Bantu-Kongo proverb

"Communality, relationality, and fundamental interconnection underlie the
African mode of seeing and being in the world" (Ogbonnaya, 1994a, p. 4).
Even in one's individuality, there is *never* a true separation from a communal
connection, regardless of the artificial separation created in a therapeutic
space. Weak-to-strong ties to a communal social world are central to mental
health. Additionally, community wellness is critical to personal wellness.
Interventions with African Americans that ignore these basic principles have
already diminished their cultural proficiency and relevance.

Culturally proficient treatment for African Americans requires an appreciation of the fact that the African social order was, and continues to be,
communal (Diop, 1978; Gyekye, 1995; Ogbonnaya, 1994a,1994b). "I am
because we are; I exist because the community exists" (African proverb). The
foundation for health, well-being, and resolution of challenges to mental
health is a strong community. In this African-centered worldview, community is a space where one can suffer neither social nor cultural alienation
(Onwubiko, 1991). It is the place wherein people are encouraged, through
ritual, structures, and practices, to act and behave in ways that increase common good (Katz, 1982). When common good is protected, individuals are
protected. In other words, raising the bar requires us to bring greater balance
to psychology's biopsychosocial model, a model that overemphasizes the
biological and individual behavior/psyche while compromising the social and
communal dynamism of human behavior. The issue that the SISM must contend with, then, is not whether we shall have community, but how we will
relate to one another in community and how this connection is legitimized
(Ogbonnaya, 1994a).

The era of exaggerated, unbridled individualism in Western theory and
praxis has not served African American clients well. Its Hobbesian view of
community as a network of relations between separate individuals who are
first and foremost themselves and only secondly placed within association
with one another does not keep the individual and community in balance
(Ogbonnaya, 1994a, 1994b). These models of mental health reduce us to
concepts of communities with limited resources for which people must
compete. Healing, therefore, remains a scarce, nonexpanding resource
(Katz, 1982; Ott & Pinard, 2007). We must address the hidden crisis in
mental health and education: the gap between mental health needs and
existing supports. For example, only one in five children with mental health
problems receives specialty mental health services (Burns et al., 1995).
Thus, for every young person who receives treatment, four to five go

without (Malti & Noam, 2009). In truth, mental health specialists are able to meet the needs of only 10% of all children with mental health issues. This results in focusing on children with the most severe symptoms while neglecting preventive and early intervention services for less severe, yet still troubling, cases (Tolan & Dodge, 2005).

Bobby Wright (1974) cautioned African American psychologists about the scourge of *mentacide* (to willingly think and act from another's location and/or interpretation of reality at the expense of one's own survival). For an ethnocultural group whose heritage is communal, is it not mentacide to deemphasize the significance of community in deference to individual dimensions of human beingness? Is it not mentacide to act as though there is balance between the need for one-on-one psychotherapy and the availability of mental health services and practitioners to meet that need? Community *is* the custodian of the individual. The person is known and identified in, by, and through her community (Onwubiko, 1991). Connection to community and sense of community contribute to and protect mental health (Dorsey & Forehand, 2003; Dworkin, Larson, & Hansen, 2003; Kawachi, Kennedy, & Glass, 1999). Treatment modalities, if culturally proficient for African Americans, should reflect appropriate attention to community in theory and praxis.

The SISM poses two organizing questions: "What do I want to achieve therapeutically with my clients?" and "How can I achieve these goals using specific techniques?" For African American clients, answers should include the idea of connecting with community (i.e., connecting the client to community and/or you as service provider connecting to the client's community as part of the intervention strategy). This is essential given that keys to mental health from an African-centered perspective include positive relationships with self *and* others, communal self-knowledge, and understanding how connection to others is intricately related to self-preservation and fulfillment in life. In fact, the World Health Organization's (WHO; 2007) definition of mental health is closely aligned with this African-centered perspective ("a state of well-being in which every individual realizes his or her own abilities and potential, can cope with the normal stresses of life, can work productively and fruitfully, and is able to make a contribution to her or his community" [para. 1]). The WHO casts mental health as a set of positive attributes in a person *and* community. Any semblance of mental health, then, must ultimately occur within the context of community.

African Americans are members of multiple intersecting social networks that collectively guide and provide meaning to behavior. To maintain, recover, and sustain health and well-being, interventions must be able to align with clients' constant and continuous interaction with self, others, environmental contexts, and spiritual forces. In its present iteration, the SISM does not offer enough traction to fully engage more than the person side of the biopsychosocial equation, nor does it promote cultural proficiency and microskills at the community level of intervention. Extension of the model's six components could assist practitioners to expand their frame so that interventions more broadly reflect a relational, connective orientation to life that is more characteristic of African American culture. In other words, we need a framework that allows development of more "client in community" strategies and "community change" strategies.

In the expanded framework, interventions can pay greater attention to engaging and impacting a client's community because community plays an enormous role in mental health and resilience. Communities that foster mental health and resilience are (1) characterized by availability of social organizations that provide an array of resources to residents, (2) offer consistent expressions of social norms so that community members understand what constitutes desirable behavior, and (3) provide opportunities for their members (including children and youth) to participate in the life of the community as valued members (Benard, 1991).

The expanded frame also broadens our lens to include consideration of resilience, to balance psychology's tendency to emphasize pathology and deficits. Resilience is the capacity of people to exhibit positive behavior and cope with stress, adversity, or trauma (Luthar & Cicchetti, 2000; Luthar, Cicchetti, & Becker, 2000). Protective factors that support resilience are found in three contexts: personal attributes (e.g., positive self-concept, sense of efficacy); family (e.g., having close bonds with at least one family member or an emotionally stable parent); and community (e.g., receiving support). Again, this calls attention to the need to expand the multicultural framework. This is particularly true for its application to an African cultural framework in which "a person is a person because there are people" (African proverb). The symbiotic person-community relationship is essential to mental health and resolution of psychological problems. To be fully human (and, therefore, mentally healthy), one has to be connected to other human beings.

> A person whose existence and personality are dependent on the community is expected in turn to contribute to the continued existence of the community. . . . The meaning of one's life is therefore measured by one's commitment to social ideals and community existence. (Gbadegesin, 1998a, p. 168)

Interventions, if they are to be culturally aligned for African Americans, must intervene beyond the individual client, couple, or nuclear family system.

From a skills point of view, intervention strategies must include service that focuses on building the health and capacity of the community or neighborhood-level systems for those seeking treatment. The SISM alludes to this but must give more explicit attention to incorporating community structure/social organizations. The clearest sign of a cohesive and supportive community is the presence of *social organizations* that provide healthy human development (Garmezy, 1991). What promotes and sustains treatment gains for the African American client for whom community is the bedrock of mental health? Where are the gathering places where people can be "in" and "do" community? Where does the social, political, economic, and organizational work of the local neighborhood occur, or do such structures even exist? Where are community issues discussed? What mechanisms are in place to do the work of basic family socialization and education? How are community safety nets of support (i.e., related to parenting, human development, promoting resilience, networking, enhancing support systems, disseminating community history, cultivating leadership, etc.) created and sustained? Community centers are one practical way to understand this African cultural praxis of boko (Fu-Kiau, 2007).[2] *Boko* means creating within communities a space or an environment where "everyone is expected to be the keeper and protector of the interests of others" (Gbadegesin, 1998b, p. 132).

Community-centric multicultural strategies encourage praxis that supports communities to

- involve elders to contribute to the sense of community as a whole;
- develop and encourage a desire in clients to give back to the community through service;
- expand therapeutic interventions to include development of (a) cultural awareness and sense of identity through activities like music, art, dancing, rituals, and rites of passage and (b) internalize principles to guide behavior, mentoring, celebrations, and inclusive education in school system curricula because psychological well-being is anchored within the community through a strong cultural foundation and racial self-identity (Grills, 2002; Kambon, 1999; Nobles, 1986; Vontress, 1991); and
- create spaces and mechanisms for mutual support, socialization, and governance.

The following case example reflects a community-centric intervention. The individual clients are not directly the focus of intervention but rather their newly created community that emphasizes a shared mission greater than themselves that accrues benefits for the individual, immediate community and broader society.

---

[2]*Boko* is a Bantu term referring to a defined community space where Mbongi can occur. In the boko common shelter, "Mbongi Assemblies" convene to take care of and/or address the human as well as material good of the community. To take responsibility for the community meant to become responsible for lightening the weight of social and economic problems among the people. To sit in a Mbongi Assembly was to have one's eyes wide open (toward the secrecy of life) and to be able to honestly tell the story of the community. The Mbongi was a way of structurally (1) gathering together the best minds and practices; (2) taking, seizing, or accepting responsibility for solving and resolving the community problems; (3) capturing, critiquing, and clarifying those "things which concern us dearly"; (4) exposing the "truth" of our reality as reflected and represented by our spiritual, intellectual, social, and artistic memory and creations; and (5) uncovering, correcting, and utilizing the core meaning and purpose of a people in the service of human development and well-being (Association of Black Psychologists, 2008).

Case Example

A group of clients early in recovery from psychoactive substance addiction were engaged in a project in South Central Los Angeles in response to the Northridge earthquake (1994). All eyes were on the devastation sustained in the San Fernando Valley area of Los Angeles County, the epicenter of the quake. Considerable damage, however, was sustained in other parts of the county, including South Central L.A. Little attention was given to this poor, predominantly African American and Latino community filled with red-tagged homes (homes designated uninhabitable due to structural damage caused by the earthquake). A local community-based organization needed help to document the devastation to South L.A. and the mental health impact on residents, in an attempt to have federal and local dollars directed to the community. Contrary to "standard practice" in mental health and substance abuse treatment, the local community organization assembled a team of 25 men and women in early recovery from addiction to help canvass South L.A. neighborhoods. They had one month to one year of sobriety from a variety of substances, with the average recovery time being less than six months. They were led by a peer with more than 10 years of sobriety. They conducted daily community surveys of red-tagged homes and residents about the damage sustained and their mental health and well-being. In their daily door knocking and documenting of earthquake-related issues, the team went to the very neighborhoods considered risky environments to their recovery. Inspired by the urgent needs of the community, their focus was no longer on their "individual" recovery. Instead, they were connected to familiar spaces, places, and people as part of their early community-centric recovery strategy. *Throughout the four-month community canvassing process, not a single member of the team relapsed.* In fact, in daily debriefing sessions, participants highlighted the importance of being able to give back to the very communities they had abused during their addiction. They noted the healing power of being connected to a community change and protection process for their perceptions of themselves and their sense of community. They heralded the importance of this sense of community found as a member of the Emergency Response Team and the broader community-based organization to their daily sense of well-being and reason for maintaining a commitment to recovery. Ultimately, this community-centric focus stabilized their recovery and aided the community. As a result of their documentation, federal resources were redirected to South L.A. through policy advocacy, supported by valid and reliable data, which they had collected.

What was the therapeutic objective? Abstinence and behavior change with respect to substance abuse and underlying causative factors. This was achieved using a strategy that extended far beyond the bounds of current evidenced-based practice. The community-centric approach created for each individual a community of peers with shared abstinence goals, relational needs, and a way to reconnect to a community where they were now valued and valuable. They were contributors to a positive social change process. The very neighborhoods harmed by their addiction were now beneficiaries of their activism. The community change process provided a deeper sense of purpose for their recovery and reconnected them to their communal core and heritage. The community-centric process impacted commitment to recovery, identity, and self-image, and a different kind of behavioral conditioning to their previously risky spaces and places.

Connecting With Clients

As noted previously, connecting with clients also entails connecting to the community, such that interventions reinforce strong *community safety nets*— the extent to which individuals have access to naturally existing (or created) and supported systems of community care, connection, and opportunities to be "in" community. Bell's Seven Principles to Decrease Risk and Increase Resiliency (Bell et al., 2005) provide a useful framework. Bell argues practitioners' work should

1. Reweave the social fabric/recreate a sense of community;

2. Provide models, tools, skills and techniques to facilitate implementation of the concept or program;

3. Create situations/programs/relationships that foster a sense of connection/attachment/belonging to a larger group or common goal;

4. Provide opportunities to learn social and emotional skills;

5. Provide opportunities to increase self-esteem;

6. Provide an adult protective shield for young people; and

7. Minimize trauma.

To connect with African American clients in a culturally proficient manner, interventions must artfully weave in spirituality, communalism, harmony, sensitivity to emotional cues, oral communication, relationship to time, special role of elders, interest in one's history and culture, sense of humor, resilience, critically addressing race and class oppression, and more (Akbar, 2003; Belgrave & Allison, 2010; Boyd-Franklin, 2003; Grills, 2004, 2009; Hartling, 2008; Lambert & Smith, 2009; Myers, 1998; Nobles, 1998, 2006; Nobles, Goddard, & Gilbert, 2009; Ogbonnaya, 1994b; Parham, 2009).

In the application of the SISM to African American clients, Parham (2002) includes reference to the use of ritual. This is a very important point. Ritual is a salient feature of cultural processes in general and particularly so within African culture. Ritual is knowledge and custom embodied in ceremony, formal procedure, and rites that serve to remind, reorient, and habitualize behavior. It has the capacity to tap into the power of the spoken word (speech), rhythm (movement), the language of symbols (images), and various levels of reality and consciousness. It codifies cultural values, principles, and norms and provides opportunities for instruction, healing, and reconciliation. There are degrees of meaning, praxis, and knowledge in the application of a ritual. For example, in some traditional African medicine techniques, candle lighting and incense burning are ritual techniques. When used, they appeal to sensory modalities, such as the olfactory system, often ignored in Western psychotherapy. They have the capacity to be centering and have impact on the therapist as well as the client. Unfortunately, a textbook reference or an isolated workshop will not reveal the theory or African science behind how burning a candle or certain incense can impact the distribution of energy, cognition, emotion, behavior, or spiritual processes. These are areas Western psychology would do well to fold into its lexicon of constructs, theories, and science if it is to move toward greater global relevance and universalism.

Nonetheless, the Multicultural Model is broad enough to permit the practitioner to address many cultural principles, elements, modes of expression, and engagement central to a therapeutic process with African American clients, including the importance of the following:

- interdependence, collective responsibility, communal orientation, and relational emphasis (i.e., encouraging community and familial support, respect for elders, generosity, cooperativeness/mutual help);
- spirituality and an understanding of the "self as a community within itself" (Ogbonnaya, 1994b, p. 83);
- understanding the *Maafa*, the diasporan African holocaust experience;
- managing racism, relentless racial microaggressions, and defending against social realities in the United States that reflect an "anti-black" ethos;
- connecting with purpose and meaning in life;
- fostering self-determination;
- affirming an African identity as the "real self," coupled with conscientious rejection of internalized racism;
- consciously reclaiming and utilizing cultural heritage and knowledge;
- enlisting oral patterns, vernacular, use of metaphors, and humor;
- working within a flexible understanding of kinship patterns; and
- incorporating spontaneity and fluid thought processes (leaving room for intuition/hunches rather than strict adherence to logic, reasoning, and typical thought processes attended to in cognitive behavioral interventions).

Commendably, the SISM acknowledges the importance of connecting on a spiritual level, but it does not show the clinician *how* to do that. Reading about African spirituality or sporadically attending isolated cultural awareness workshops does not accomplish an appropriate level of depth or proficiency in understanding how to integrate the concept of spirituality into praxis. Consider the analogy of the Freemasons. Within this organization, there are "33 degrees" of knowledge that require years of training and demonstration of worthiness to hold in good faith deeper, more esoteric information. Likewise, in the application of psychology's empirically supported treatments, there are degrees of knowledge and understanding about techniques being applied in intervention strategies.

There is basic knowledge and proficiency in the application of a technique (e.g., Cognitive Behavioral Therapy [CBT] in the treatment of anxiety disorders). Then, there is the deeper understanding of the underlying cognitive neuroscience and what occurs and contributes to client outcomes. Here, I am referring to changes in brain physiology and "wiring." Therapy, or changing one's thinking and behavior, is associated with changes in neural circuitry (Baxter et al., 1992; Gorman, Kent, Sullivan, & Coplan, 2000; Linden, 2006; Paquette et al., 2003; Saxena et al., 2009; Schwartz, 1999; Schwartz, Stoessel, Baxter, Martin, & Phelps, 1996; Straube, Madlen, Dilger, Mentzel, & Miltner, 2006). In addition to psychological and behavioral improvement (reduction in symptoms) made by CBT for phobias and Obsessive-Compulsive Disorder, there is significant difference in brain activation between people with these afflictions and people without them. There is some inconsistency about the areas of the brain that are activated, but studies suggest that having fears or anxieties and treatment of them is associated with certain changes in brain activation levels. In other words, changes made at the mind level, in a psychotherapeutic context, could functionally "rewire" the brain. As Paquette et al. (2003) noted, "change the mind and you change the brain" (p. 401).

As with the Freemasons and CBT, there are also degrees of knowledge in the application of spirituality in treatment. One can merely talk about spirituality and a client's ontological and cosmological philosophy, but then there is a deeper understanding of preterrational consciousness and what is being shifted in the process of spiritually focused change. This deeper knowledge and capacity to engage comes through either a natural gift or intensive training. We have not even begun to explore this in Western psychology, perhaps because it does not lend itself in any discernable way to Western empiricism and is, therefore, likely to be left to physicists to explore in their discussions of the "spooky effect." More attention to what is meant by spirituality and degrees of spiritual connection and practice must be articulated in the field and conveyed to practitioners in a way that enables them to practically work with this dimension of human beingness to the benefit of clients and communities.

The Zen koan "What is the sound of one hand clapping?" is echoed by the physics question "How can a particle be in two places at once?" This line of inquiry and thinking is akin to the African worldview of spirituality. African traditional thought has recognized for some time a position now held by some progressive scientists. Science and spirit (and spirituality) are not so different. They are different disciplines trying to understand the same thing. With this in mind, African-centered psychology challenges us to question "what reality is."

Our training instructs us to think reality is what our senses present to us, a perspective Western science has embraced for well over 400 years. Science only gives us *models* of the world, not the world itself, and these models are often time and culture bound (Arntz, Chasse, & Vicente, 2005).

Case Example

A very gifted African American traditional healer (Afia) in the United States provides consultations (divination readings) upon request for those who seek insight into their life circumstances, challenges, and opportunities. Afia uses chants and sometimes divination objects to help her spiritually "see" her clients. Consultations are often done by phone with clients whom she has never seen and about whom she has no background information. These clients are not typically in the same geographic location as Afia, let alone in the same room. In a recent one-hour consultation with a middle-aged African American woman, Afia accurately predicted health issues recently experienced and not yet fully resolved; saw marital relationship tensions and longstanding critical relationship issues warranting further reflection by the client, including an unsuccessful outcome to a project the client was working on, with recommendations on managing reactions to this so the project could be salvaged and made successful; and finally changes in employment and residence on the near horizon. The client also inquired about her children and a few family members and was provided with information about one of her children about which the client was unaware. The client was encouraged to implement several simple techniques (meditations, burning certain incense, shifts in nutrition, and cleansings) to strengthen her spiritual well-being and sensitivities so that her ancestors and spirit guides could more effectively work in and through her. At the conclusion of the consultation, the client was impressed with the insights Afia had into details of her personal life without having ever met her or her family and friends. The client was, nonetheless, skeptical about the predictions of residence and job changes because she had no intention to change either. In fact, she was opposed to any changes of this sort. Finally, she was amused about the information about her son, believing it to be unlikely, knowing her son as she did. The outcome: within two weeks of the consultation, the unsuccessful project outcome came true; within four to six weeks, the opportunity for a significant employment change revealed itself, and an unwanted residence change came to fruition. When she queried her son about the business and personal issues he was pondering in his own life, he was stunned that his mother knew about them and wanted to know the source of her information. Spiritually informed and fortified, the client's management of these major life issues was definitively impacted in a positive way, cognitively and emotionally. Afia never told her what to do. She still had "choice" in her management of each issue and was able to marshal her own spiritual reserves and community resources to navigate what came to pass.

This was a spiritual assessment and intervention strategy. We have yet to develop concepts in Western psychology to understand, let alone practice, this form of healing. I hesitated sharing this example, in part because my colleagues in Western psychology are prone to scoff at such accounts or view them as mere coincidence (or self-fulfilling prophecy). I could recount many more examples of Afia's assessments and interventions with African American *and* Latino clients that would defy chance occurrence or these easy dismissals. I also realize these same colleagues cannot disprove or logically discredit the accuracy of Afia's spiritual insights. Unfortunately, Western empiricism lacks the sophistication to examine processes like the above, which severely limits our ability to incorporate these types of culturally based strategies. Afia did as Parham (2002) suggested. She joined the client at the intellectual, affectual, *and* spiritual levels.

Social science research and psychology need a new paradigm to go where the positivist paradigm and its empirical methods cannot go: the essence of human beingness, the metaphysical world of consubstantiation and human consciousness. This new research paradigm would allow for preterrational process and enable us to examine and model things like the following:

- intuition
- distance communication
- déjà vu experience, remote viewing, near death experience, miraculous healing, prophetic dreams, joint coincidences
- the influence and presence of spiritual entities and ancestors
- foreknowledge and past knowledge gleaned through divination
- creativity
- reframing of "bad luck," "good fortune," and more

Conducting a Culturally Relevant Assessment

We are at a deficit in the field of psychology with respect to assessment with African Americans. "Empirical research and scale development has not kept pace with the theoretical and conceptual literature in African-centered psychology" (Utsey, Belvet, & Fisher, 2009, p. 84). Glaringly, we are missing tools for use with African Americans on a host of variables (e.g., racial stress, ethnic identity, cultural affiliation and spiritual attunement,[3] communalism).

To its credit, the SISM puts forth a broader understanding of human beingness. Parham (Chapter 2) states "mental health, at its core, relates to a more harmonious integration with the universe." This suggests the need for an expanded repertoire of factors to be assessed and assessment tools. For example, a client might be asked to reflect upon a question such as, When did

---

[3]Attunement is to be in sync with preterrational means of access to information. It is information gleaned without reliance upon logic or sentience.

you last feel like you were operating in harmony—even if there were stressors and challenges in your life? That is, when did things seem to flow, operate more smoothly, and feel like you were in sync with something greater than yourself? What were you doing and thinking? Who were you associating with and where did you spend your time?

The SISM does not provide guidance or offer latitude in the clinician's use of herself or himself in the assessment process, and this is where intuition and/ or preterrational knowledge could be used (Grills, 2004). The following case example provides one illustration.

Case Example

In the case of preschool teacher Gina, the use of clinical intuition or preter-rational knowledge is illustrated (Grills, 2004). Gina came in for an African-based spiritual consultation because she was concerned about relationship issues. During her consultation, I intuited that there was something else that required her more immediate attention. Over the course of the session, it eventually became clear there was an impending health issue for her pre-school-age son. I inquired about his health, to which she responded everything was okay. I pursued the line of inquiry further and asked when was the last time he had an eye exam, to which she responded within the last 12 months. I encouraged her to consider taking him back for a new eye exam immediately, which she did. The doctor discovered her child was in the early stages of a serious eye condition, which was diagnosed and treated early enough to abate the condition. The full impact of this case study is felt when one recognizes the client's child was not even present at the session. There were no concrete pieces of evidence to suggest this as an issue to pursue in the consultation.

In an African worldview, human beings are intimately linked beyond time and space and have access to knowledge beyond that available through mere sentient processes and the rudiments of logic. African American young people talk about this all the time in their colloquial expressions and mannerisms. For example, sayings like "I feel you" communicate a connection to one another beyond the physical and emotional senses.

One final assessment issue to note addresses what Parham (2002) refers to in the SISM as the two most important questions in therapy: What? and How? In an African-centered framework, there is often one additional question that lurks in the shadows if not explicitly posed by the client: Why? and, perhaps, Why now? The *why* question is, in fact, very Africentric. It turns attention to the broader realm of the spiritual, the communal, the plurality of selves (Ogbonnaya, 1994b), and the alignment with personal destiny, all of which impact human behavior. Illness has physical, social/communal, psychological, and spiritual causes and cures (Ademuwagun, 1978).

Facilitating Awareness

An African-centered understanding of facilitating awareness is difficult to fully capture within the Eurocentric frame and training. The continued arrogance and disrespect of things spiritual as invalid, unreal, and unconnected to human behavior is pervasive. This worldview tends to limit the extent to which we train emerging clinicians to be more attentive to their preterrational faculties, and it dissuades practitioners from giving any credence to attending to and utilizing spiritual foci as a technique in treatment. With disdain, scholars and media still refer to this line of knowledge acquisition and skill as voodoo, without any substantive knowledge or study of this area of awareness.

For example, in encouraging clients to discover how their life experiences color and shape how they engage situations and plan for the future, tapping into the spiritual realm can be expanded to include the legacy of their families. For African American families so inclined, one could invite the ancestors or a specific family ancestor to join in the space of a therapy session to offer guidance, heightened awareness, and support. As part of the therapeutic encounter, clients could be asked, "What would this ancestor say?" "How would he or she see this issue?" "How can he or she be helpful to you?" On the surface, one might argue this is merely a version of a Gestalt empty chair technique. On one level, it might be. On a deeper level, consistent with an African ontological, cosmological, and epistemological worldview, this is more than mere symbolic enactment of the presence of one's ancestor. The ancestor is believed to actually be present. Western epistemology would argue this presence cannot be verified empirically. This supposition may be true, but we also must admit Western epistemology cannot prove the ancestor is nonexistent either.

Another way to further facilitate awareness with African American clients is through the use of metaphor to promote insight, shared understanding, and perceptual lens shifts. While seemingly subtle, the use of metaphor has been found to be a particularly powerful tool. Barrett and Cooperrider (1990) suggest that one way to help a group liberate itself from an entrenched cognitive mindset is through the use of generative metaphor. Generative metaphor has great potential as an agent for group development change. It has been successfully used to help groups (1) build liberated aspirations and develop hope, (2) decrease interpersonal conflict, (3) broaden strategic consensus around a positive vision for the future, (4) renew collective will to act, and (5) enhance egalitarian language reflecting a new sense of unity and mutuality in the joint creation of a group's future. "Metaphors are filters that screen some details and emphasize others" (Barrett & Cooperrider, 1990, p. 219). In short, they "organize our view of the world" (Black, 1962). They are powerful because of their semantic and cognitive reconstruction capacity. (This reflects a different angle than what is covered in typical CBT.)

Metaphor is, at its simplest, a way of proceeding from the known to the unknown. It is a way of cognition in which the identifying qualities of one thing are transferred in an instantaneous, almost unconscious flash of insight to some other thing that is by remoteness or complexity unknown to us. (Nisbett & Kunda, 1985, p. 4)

Metaphors can capitalize on African Americans' artful use of language and can present a way of seeing difficult issues in a clearer light. They can transfer meaning from one domain to another, enriching and enhancing the ability to see many dimensions and implications of dilemmas. They can also act as a way to organize perceptions and can provide a framework for selecting and naming characteristics of experience by asserting similarity with a different, seemingly unrelated object or experience. For example, "trying to help an oppressed person is like trying to put your arm around somebody with a sunburn" (Florynce Kennedy, cited in Grothe, 2008, p. 51).

The potential for semantic transformation is what makes artists, poets, leaders and scientist alike so attuned to the power of metaphor, and aware of its potential for directing perception-enriching awareness, and transforming the world. Good metaphors provoke new thought, excite us with novel perspectives, vibrate with multivocal meanings, and enable people to see the world with fresh perceptions not possible in any other way. (Barrett & Cooperrider, 1990, p. 219)

Metaphors invite active experimentation in areas of well-entrenched thinking and help people overcome self-defeating, often unconscious defenses and resistance to change. Fresh insights are transferred instantaneously, almost unconsciously, bringing about semantic and perceptual changes. Metaphors can create space for active thought experimentation, testing, and correction so that expansion of cognitive frames can occur. It provides a mechanism for movement.[4]

Taking Action and Instigating Change

Taking action and instigating change are the procedural aspects for implementing the goals that have been set by the client and therapist. Parham (2002) aptly notes that "often, the etiology of client's distress is not intra-psychic, but rather

---

[4]"Metaphor provides a steering function for future actions and perceptions. Social order and social structure are not preordained, but are achieved through members' construction of reality. Social action achieves form through the metaphor in actors' heads (Turner, 1974). As Pepper (1942) pointed out, 'root metaphors' provide the social group with a whole set of categories through which the social group interprets the world. For example, in the 17th century the universe was seen as a machine, which affected not only the activities of physical science, but whole fields of moral philosophy and human psychology. In the 19th century, for example, Marxist theory operated according to an embryonic metaphor. Social orders were seen as proceeding from the 'womb' of preceding others, with transformation periods likened to the 'birth' of a new order. The state of capitalism was seen as carrying the 'seeds' of its own destruction. These metaphors spawn categories and terms that drive people to initiate actions congruent with the metaphors informing their beliefs" (Barrett & Cooperrider, 1990).

social, cultural, and environmental" (p. 9). Therapists and counselors, trained in individual-level behavior change interventions, are encouraged to spend equal time in reflection on this point with their clients. Our training makes us particularly vulnerable to the context minimization error.[5] Action and change involve not only psychological and behavioral dimensions, which emphasize individual-level empowerment, they also involve community and societal change requiring a communal skill set that emphasizes a client and family/community level of implementation. Strategies that promote lasting change and resolution of presenting problems (a.k.a. symptoms) must include the family or community in more substantive and creative ways than currently found in Western practice.

Case Example

In the case of a middle-aged African American female client suffering from depression and marital problems, a marked shift in emotional and behavioral change occurred only when a family-level intervention occurred that mirrored her religious and communal cultural realities. The turning point in therapy was a gathering of the client, her husband, and both sets of their parents. The extended family joined in a circle in the center of the couple's kitchen to "pray" together on the marital problems. The issues faced by the couple were given public voice, and the racial stressors impacting the couple became clearer to both husband and wife. They were given practical and spiritual support that lead to practical steps toward resolution, steps that incorporated an understanding of generations of racial stress that negatively impact African American male/female relationships and families. In that circle, prayer did not include a discussion of or detailing of actual issues between the couple. Rather, it focused on contextualizing their life sociohistorically and calling for spiritual guidance, insight, fortitude, and healing. All of the cognitive behavioral interventions to that point did not lead to the insights and shifts in the change process brought about by that moment of family prayer, contextualization, and insight. One might argue this was merely a heightened sense of social support that emboldened the couple to take the necessary risk to face their challenges and own their personal responsibility. Both the husband's and wife's parents had, however, up to that point offered emotional and practical support, but to no avail. What inspired the quantum leap in the change process? An African-centered intervention would argue the naming of the external stressors, coupled with the spiritual fortitude, simultaneously altered conscious awareness, and increased psychological empowerment proffered the spiritual empowerment/protection needed to amplify change.

---

[5]The context minimization error is the "tendency to ignore the impact of enduring neighborhood and community contexts on human behavior. The error has adverse consequences for understanding psychological processes and efforts at social change" (Shinn & Toohey, 2003, p. 428).

All of the above require that during the assessment process, the change agent must gain some insight into the client's worldview. In other words, what is the client's level of acculturation? I intentionally include African Americans in a discussion of acculturation. How is culture operating in their life? How amenable are they to the inclusion of certain aspects of their cultural heritage in the consciousness raising and change process? To what extent can their culture be used as a tool for change? Are there family or community resources available? To what extent and in what way is internalized racism a factor in this client's presenting problem? How much will the client's religious beliefs collide with African cultural heritage's spiritual beliefs and his or her ability to tap into his or her spirituality? How can his or her religious beliefs be incorporated into instigating action strategies and change?

Feedback and Accountability

In the AA-SISM, accountability is discussed in relationship to the individual client. In an African-centered model, accountability involves the client, family, and community. Current intervention practice and ethical proscriptions typically do not offer us a way to engage accountability beyond the individual level. That does not mean we ignore the relevance of the others. We must apply creative thought and reflection to this apparent conundrum.

Conclusion

I applaud the authors for challenging the assumption that counseling theories and skills are universal and may be applied to various populations. I have argued that for communally oriented people of African descent, healing is culturally informed and influenced and effective treatment can be enhanced if conceptualized as collective. Order (mental health and well-being) can be reestablished when people are integrated into the social fabric of community and family. Intervention strategies that incorporate sociocommunal systems that replicate the client's African-centered values can be more authentic, develop critical social supports, and lead to substantive and sustained change. African Americans are a heterogeneous group, variably influenced by generations of racial oppression, and this requires the counselor to gauge how any given client engages with his or her ethnic identity and culture and his or her collective, communal movement and inclination toward health.

Connecting with African American clients from an African-centered perspective includes and extends beyond what is typically understood in standard Western practice. In an African paradigm of consciousness and reality, healing begins with a clear distinction between the user and the thing used. The user is the soul. The thing used is the human body. Further, it makes a distinction between the manifestations and source of consciousness. The manifestation of consciousness and awareness is cognition, but the source is the soul conferred upon the individual by the divine. What does this mean for connecting with clients? To facilitate empathy, one might expect the counselor to enlist the following in his or her efforts to connect with a client:

- perceptual role taking (the ability to imagine the literal visual perspective of another)
- cognitive role taking (the ability to imagine others' thoughts and motives)
- affective role taking (the ability to infer another's emotional state)

From the African-centered perspective, what is missing, among other things, is spiritual role sharing: the ability to connect with another person at the level of spirit (*sunsum*) and soul (*okra*; Grills, 2002).

Finally, it is hard to imagine that interventions culturally tailored to African Americans will have lasting impact if they occur in the absence of community voice, community context, and community-level interventions. Further, I argue, interventions with African Americans need to cogently interweave cultural values familiar to our experiences of spirituality, communalism, harmony, sensitivity to emotional cues, oral communication, relationship to time, special role of elders, interest in one's history and culture, humor, and resilience, while critically addressing race and class oppression, social justice, and more (Akbar, 2003; Belgrave & Allison, 2010; Boyd-Franklin, 2003; Foster, Phillips, Belgrave, Randolph, & Braithwaite, 1993; Gordon, 2004; Grills, 2004, 2006, 2009; Hartling, 2008; Lambert & Smith, 2009; Myers, 1998; Nobles, 2006; Parham, 2009; Peres, Franco, Santos, & Zanetti, 2008; Potts, 2003; Thompson & Alfred, 2009; Utsey et al., 2009; Wallace & Constantine, 2005; Watts & Serrano-Garcia, 2003). The AA-SISM offers promise as we expand the definition of what it means to be human, so that a broader share of worldviews that comprise the human race are reflected.

References

Ademuwagun, Z. A. (1978). Alafia—the Yoruba concept of health: Implications for health education. *International Journal of Health Education, 21*(2), 89–97.

Akbar, N. (2003). *Akbar papers in African psychology.* Tallahassee, FL: Mind Productions & Associates.

Arntz, W., Chasse, B., & Vicente, M. (2005). *What the bleep do we know!? Discovering the endless possibilities for altering your everyday reality.* Deerfield Beach, FL: Health Communications.

Association of Black Psychologists. (2008). *To be African from the beginning to now: 40 years of meeting the challenges of black mental health. ABPsi 40th Annual International Convention Program Book.* Washington, DC: Author.

Barrett, F. J., & Cooperrider, D. L. (1990). Generative metaphor intervention: A new approach for working with systems divided by conflict and caught in defensive perception. *The Journal of Applied Behavioral Science, 26*(2), 219–239.

Baxter, L. R., Schwartz, J. M., Bergman, K. S., Szuba, M. P., Guze, B. H., Mazziotta, J. C., et al. (1992). Caudate glucose metabolic rate changes with both drug and behavior therapy for obsessive-compulsive disorder. *Archives of General Psychiatry, 49*, 681–689.

Belgrave, F. Z., & Allison, K. W. (2010). *African American psychology: From Africa to America* (2nd ed.). Los Angeles: Sage.

Bell, C. C., Bhana, A., McKay, M. M., & Petersen, I. (2005). A commentary on the triadic theory of influence as a guide for adapting HIV prevention programs for new contexts and populations: The CHAMP-South Africa story. *Social Work in Mental Health, 5*(3/4), 237–261.

Benard, B. (1991). *Fostering resiliency in kids: Protective factors in the family, school, and community.* Portland, OR: Northwest Regional Educational Laboratory.

Black, M. (1962). *Models and metaphors.* Ithaca, NY: Cornell University Press.

Boyd-Franklin, N. (2003). *Black families in therapy: An African American experience* (2nd ed.). New York: Guilford Press.

Burns, B. J., Costello, E. J., Angold, A., Tweed, D., Stangl, D., Farmer, E. M., et al. (1995). Children's mental health service use across service sectors. *Health Affairs, 14*(3), 147–159.

Centers for Disease Control and Prevention. (2009). *Violence prevention—The social-ecological model: A framework for prevention.* Retrieved May 10, 2011, from http://www.cdc.gov/ViolencePrevention/overview/social-ecologicalmodel.html

Diop, C. A. (1978). *The cultural unity of black Africa.* Chicago: Third World Press.

Dorsey, S., & Forehand, R. (2003). The relation of social capital to childhood psychosocial adjustment difficulties: The role of positive parenting and neighborhood dangerousness. *Journal of Psychopathology and Behavioral Assessment, 25*(1), 11–23.

Dworkin, J., Larson, R., & Hansen, D. (2003). Adolescents' accounts of growth experiences in youth activities. *Journal of Youth and Adolescence, 32*(1), 17–26.

Foster, P. M., Phillips, F., Belgrave, F. Z., Randolph, S. M., & Braithwaite, N. (1993). An Africentric model for AIDS education, prevention, and psychological services within the African American community. *Journal of Black Psychology, 19*(2), 123–141.

Fu-Kiau, K. B. (2007). *Simba simbi: Hold up that which holds you up.* Pittsburgh, PA: Dorrance.

Garmezy, N. (1991). Resiliency and vulnerability to adverse developmental outcomes associated with poverty. *American Behavioral Science, 34*, 416–430.

Gbadegesin, S. (1998a). Eniyan: The Yoruba concept of a person. In P. H. Coetzee & A. P. Roux (Eds.), *The African philosophy reader* (pp. 149–168). New York: Routledge.

Gbadegesin, S. (1998b). Yoruba philosophy: Individuality, community, and the moral order. In E. C. Eze (Ed.), *African philosophy: An anthology* (pp. 130–141). Malden, MA: Blackwell.

Gordon, M. (2004). *Media images of women and African American girls' sense of self.* Unpublished doctoral dissertation, University of Michigan.

Gorman, J. M., Kent, J. M., Sullivan, G. M., & Coplan, J. D. (2000). Neuroanatomical hypothesis of panic disorder, revised. *American Journal of Psychiatry 157,* 493–505.

Grills, C. (2002). African-centered psychology. In T. Parham (Ed.), *Counseling persons of African descent* (pp. 10–24). Thousand Oaks, CA: Sage.

Grills, C. (2004). African psychology. In R. Jones (Ed.), *African psychology* (pp. 171–208). Hampton, VA: Cobb & Henry.

Grills, C. (2006). Afterward. In W. Nobles (Ed.), *Seeking the sakhu: Foundational writings for an African psychology* (pp. 363–367). Chicago: Third World Press.

Grills, C. (2009). I am because we are: Locating health, well-being, and intervention in community. *Psych Discourse, 43*(4), 9–17.

Grothe, M. (2008). *I never metaphor I didn't like: A comprehensive compilation of history's greatest analogies, metaphors, and similes.* New York: HarperCollins.

Gyekye, K. (1995). *An essay on African philosophical thought: The Akan conceptual scheme.* Philadelphia: Temple University Press.

Hartling, L. M. (2008). Strengthening resilience in a risky world: It's all about relationships. *Women & Therapy, 31*(2/3/4), 51–70.

Kambon, K. K. K. (1999). *African/black psychology in the American context: An African-centered approach.* Tallahassee, FL: Nubian Nation.

Katz, R. (1982). *Boiling energy: Community healing among the Kalahari Kung.* Cambridge, MA: Harvard University Press.

Kawachi, I., Kennedy, B. P., & Glass, R. (1999). Social capital and self-rated health: A contextual analysis. *American Journal of Public Health, 89*(8), 1187–1193.

Lambert, M. C., & Smith, W. K. (2009). Handbook of African American psychology. In H. A. Neville, B. M. Tynes., & S. O. Utsey (Eds.), *Behavioral and emotional strengths in people of African heritage: Theory, research, methodology, and intervention* (pp. 385–402). Thousand Oaks: Sage.

Linden, D. E. J. (2006). How psychotherapy changes the brain—The contribution of functional neuroimaging. *Molecular Psychiatry, 11,* 528–538.

Luthar, S. S., & Cicchetti, D. (2000). The construct of resilience: A critical evaluation and guidelines for future work. *Child Development, 71*(3), 543–562.

Luthar, S. S., Cicchetti, D., & Becker, B. (2000). Research on resilience: Response to commentaries. *Child Development, 71*(3), 573–575.

Malti, T., & Noam, G. G. (2009). *Where youth development meets mental health and education: The RALLY approach.* San Francisco: Jossey-Bass.

Myers, L. J. (1998). *Understanding an Afrocentric worldview: Introduction to an optimal psychology.* Dubuque, IA: Kendall/Hunt.

Nisbett, R. E., & Kunda, Z. (1985). Perception of social distributions. *Journal of Personality and Social Psychology, 48*(2), 297–311.

Nobles, W. W. (1986). *African psychology: Toward its reclamation, reascension, and revitalization.* Oakland, CA: Black Family Press.

Nobles, W. (1998). To be African or not to be: The question of identity or authenticity—some preliminary thoughts. In R. Jones (Ed.), *African American identity development* (pp. 185–207). Hampton, VA: Cobb & Henry.

Nobles, W. (2006). *Seeking the sakhu: Foundational writings for an African psychology.* Chicago: Third World Press.

Nobles, W., Goddard, L., & Gilbert, D. (2009). Culture, ecology, women, and African-centered HIV prevention. *Journal of Black Psychology, 35*(2), 228–246.

Ogbonnaya, A. O. (1994a). *On communitarian divinity: An African interpretation of the trinity.* New York: Paragon House.

Ogbonnaya, A. O. (1994b). Person as a community: An African understanding of the person as an intrapsychic community. *Journal of Black Psychology, 20,* 75–87.

Onwubiko, O. A. (1991). *African thought, religion and culture.* Enugu, Nigeria: Snapp Press.

Ott, J., & Pinard, R. (Ott and Associates). (2007). *Concept paper for CIMH on county departments of mental health.* Professional Report.

Paquette, V., Levesque, J., Mensour, B., Leroux, J., Beaudoin, G., Bourgouin, P., et al. (2003). "Change the mind and you change the brain": Effects of cognitive-behavioral therapy on the neural correlates of spider phobia. *NeuroImage, 18,* 401–409.

Parham, T. A. (2002). Counseling African Americans: The current state of affairs. In T. A. Parham (Ed.), *Counseling people of African descent: Raising the bar of practitioner competence* (pp. 1–9). Thousand Oaks, CA: Sage.

Parham, T. A. (2009). Handbook of African American psychology. In H. A. Neville, B. M. Tynes., & S. O. Utsey (Eds.), *Foundations for an African American psychology: Extending roots to an ancient kemetic past* (pp. 3–18). Thousand Oaks, CA: Sage.

Pepper, S. (1942). *World hypotheses.* Berkeley and Los Angeles: University of California Press.

Peres, D. S., Franco, L. J., Santos, M. A., & Zanetti, M. L. (2008). Social representations of low-income diabetic women according to the health-disease process. *Revista Latino-Americana de Enfermagem, 16*(3), 389–395.

Potts, R. G. (2003). Emancipatory education versus school-based prevention in African American communities. *American Journal of Community Psychology, 31*(1–2), 173–183.

Prilleltensky, I., & Prilleltensky, O. (2006). *Promoting well-being: Linking personal, organizational, and community change.* Hoboken, NJ: John Wiley & Sons.

Saxena, S., Gorbis, E., O'Neill, J. Mandelkern, M. A., Maidment, K. M., Chang, S., et al. (2009). Rapid effects of brief intensive cognitive-behavioral therapy on brain glucose metabolism in obsessive-compulsive disorder. *Molecular Psychiatry, 14,* 197–205.

Schwartz, J. M. (1999). A role for volition and attention in the generation of new brain circuitry: Toward a neurobiology of mental force. *Journal of Consciousness Studies, 6*(8–9), 115–142.

Schwartz, J. M., Stoessel, P. W., Baxter, L. R., Martin, K. M., & Phelps, M. E. (1996). Systemic changes in cerebral glucose metabolic rate after successful behavior modification treatment of obsessive compulsive disorder. *Archives of General Psychiatry, 53,* 109–113.

Shinn, M., & Toohey, S. M. (2003). Community context of human welfare. *Annual Review of Psychology, 54,* 427–459.

Straube, T., Madlen, G., Dilger, S., Mentzel, H., & Miltner, W. H. R. (2006). Effects of cognitive-behavioral therapy on brain activation in specific phobia. *NeuroImage, 29,* 125–135.

Thompson, C. E., & Alfred, D. M. (2009). Handbook of African American psychology. In H. A. Neville, B. M. Tynes., & S. O. Utsey (Eds.), *Black liberation psychology and practice* (pp. 48–49). Thousand Oaks, CA: Sage.

Tolan, P. H., & Dodge, K. A. (2005). Children's mental health as a primary care and concern: A system for comprehensive support and service. *American Psychologist, 60*(6), 601–614.

Turner, B. (1974). *Weber and Islam: A critical study.* London: Routledge & Kegan Paul.

Utsey, S. O., Belvet, B., & Fisher, N. (2009). Assessing African-centered (Africentric) psychological constructs: A review of existing instrumentation. In H. A. Neville, B. M. Tynes., & S. O. Utsey (Eds.), *Handbook of African American psychology* (pp. 75–90). Thousand Oaks, CA: Sage.

Vontress, C. E. (1991). Traditional healing in Africa: Implications for cross-cultural counseling. *Journal of Counselling and Development, 70*(1), 242–249.

Wallace, B. C., & Constantine, M. G. (2005). Africentric cultural values, psychological help-seeking attitudes, and self-concealment in African American college students. *Journal of Black Psychology, 31,* 369–385.

Watts, R. J., & Serrano-Garcia, I. (2003). Special section: The psychology of liberation: Responses to oppression. *American Journal of Community Psychology, 31*(1–2), 73–78.

World Health Organization. (2007). *What is mental health?* Retrieved May 10, 2011, from http://www.who.int/features/qa/62/en/index.html

Wright, B. (1974). The psychopathic racial personality. *Black Books Bulletin, 2*(2), 24–32.

4

Case Illustration: Exploring an African American Case With the AA-SISM

Anderson J. Franklin

The purpose of presenting this case is to demonstrate the utility of Parham's (2002) African American Skills Identification Stage Model (AA-SISM) in the conceptualization and practice of counseling a client of African descent. It will illustrate another path toward counselor cultural competence and how knowledge and skills in this area are essential to effective counseling and serving more appropriately the needs of clients. To accomplish this objective, I will briefly summarize my thoughts about cultural competence, summarize a case, and then discuss utilizing Parham's model as a conceptual and intervention framework and make concluding observations.

Cultural Competence

Understanding cultural competence, of course, is beset with the complexity of defining "culture." Nevertheless, cultural competence, for me, is having awareness and a working knowledge of the development and socialization that is the source of people's beliefs, values, and spirituality and informs the way they think about, respond to, and interpret what is meaningful to them. Moreover, when I think of cultural competence it is integrated with counselor competence, for it is only another element of many skills required in effective counseling. As with counseling in general, the goal of our theory, research, and practice is to develop competence in thinking about client's issues and then know how to work with them. Parham's (2002) AA-SISM is another contribution to that goal and highlights critical skills necessary to achieve it. We must have cultural competence as an essential contextual framework for understanding our clients because we need theory to aid conceptualization of our social interactions, research to validate our hypotheses about them, and practice to prove their utility in transforming the client.

Case Example

The Case of Kojo, a client of mine, will be used to consider some of the approaches and interventions I could have used during counseling, if Parham's AA-SISM had been more intentionally employed. To accomplish this goal, it is important to first understand my approach to counseling as a means to understand the divergence and convergence of original thinking with a hypothetical interface with Parham's model. As I undertake this endeavor, it is important to understand that in individual counseling, my fundamental approach is an integrative psychotherapy orientation, primarily guided by a systems framework, with both psychodynamic and behavioral approaches informing conceptualization and practice. Moreover, central to my thinking is the interface of sociocultural contexts (such as gender, race, racism, and classism) with development of behavior and outlook of clients.

Kojo is a 35-year-old black male, oldest of two sons of a single mother who raised them in New York City. In Yoruba, Kojo means "unconquerable," a conscious choice made by him when he adopted this name years ago. He came into counseling expressing stress about his early career decisions, marital relationship, and sense of life direction. His job was secure as a tenured teacher in the public school system. Kojo presented with several adjustment disorders with underlying depression. He was sophisticated about racial contexts and, through his observations, comments, and self-evaluations in counseling, provided multilayered sociopolitical interpretations for conditions of the black community in society. Kojo was married with two children, an older daughter and younger son. He did not like his teaching job and saw ministry as his true calling but an unfulfilled career aspiration. He was conflicted, however, about his ability to make it a primary source of income, much less success. His work as an inner-city public school teacher was necessary for job security in support of his family, but it was also aligned with his social justice values of helping black people. Kojo was very concerned, vocal, and active in advocacy for equity in the education of black schoolchildren in the community.

Approaching the Case of Kojo

Counseling Kojo involved assessing and evaluating his presenting problems and understanding the psychosocial context of his life history, career choices, and aspirations. Equally important in the assessment process was the Mental Status Examination. As a result, the issues were conceptualized, goals were set, and counseling strategies were determined and applied in work with

Kojo. Consistent with my approach, Kojo's stress about early career decisions, his marital relationship, sense of direction, and symptoms of depression were viewed from a multisystem perspective (Boyd-Franklin, 2003). This perspective included, for example, not only considering the structure and function of the many contexts in his life that he spends time in (e.g., work, home) but also how Kojo connected his sense of self-efficacy to his job, family, and community.

Critical Questions in the Counseling Process

Parham (2002) raises two questions for counselors to ask when providing services: (1) What is important for me to achieve therapeutically with my clients? and (2) How can I achieve these goals using specific culturally appropriate techniques? These are two questions counselors certainly need to be mindful of when working with clients, along with properly understanding the presenting problems and determining their capacity to address those problems. The questions highlight content mastery and self-integrity in professional competence. We as counselors are bound by ethical standards of practice that rely upon honesty in recognizing when we don't understand, much less know how to address, issues presented by clients. In those instances, making a referral is perhaps the more appropriate counselor intervention. I raise this in response to the larger goals of this book, which is counseling in multicultural contexts with ethnically diverse populations. Too often, we practice counseling with a professional arrogance by not acknowledging when we truly do not understand the client's issues, much less the cultural context from which they evolved. Without such acknowledgment, we are less likely to admit shortcomings or seek professional development training in multicultural competence. Expertise can be a slippery slope of flexible boundaries that get ignored and sometimes crossed when the number and complexity of clients' needs are greater than we recognize or have the capacity to meet. Therefore, Parham's fundamental questions for counselors treating clients who are culturally different gain credence as essential first steps in providing culturally competent counseling.

Connecting With Clients Is Essential

It was important for me to listen to what Kojo presented as concerns, how he presented them, and the manner in which he achieved a comfort level with counseling sessions. Toward this end, I consider initial greeting as an important first step in therapeutic listening. It creates context and sets tone. For example, Kojo was dressed in a suit with shirt and tie. We had a firm handshake upon greeting. I was in business casual attire. He had a trench coat, which I offered to hang on an unobtrusive hook behind the door, as I noted his searching for where to put it.

This gesture was as natural for me as deliberate, for in my judgment, Kojo appeared fastidious, preferring to not throw his coat on a chair as he surveyed the room, something other clients do without inhibition. In the parlance of the elder generation, he was "clean" or well dressed. He said "thank you" to my gesture, with what I interpret as gratefulness for not rumpling his coat. He sat down carefully, organizing his suit jacket and pants to get comfortable. These observations were part of my assessment tool bag, to learn something about his "deportment values." I observed his mannerisms without comment but interpreted them as important to his presentation of self. (I was associating his behaviors with those black men, brothers, who stay "clean," in other words, for whom dressing stylishly is part of their persona.) I asked whether he had any difficulty finding the office. He jokingly commented that getting there was no problem but getting out of his neighborhood was. I knew the neighborhood, particularly its double-parked cars and folk all over the street. I said I knew "getting out of Bed-Sty [slang for a Brooklyn neighborhood] can be a hassle, particularly coming down Fulton Street." (This was deliberate self-disclosure on my part.) He said, "So you know what I'm talking about." The connecting process reached another level.

Within this short span of interpersonal transactions, there was awareness of and respect for the way he carried himself as well as acknowledgment of his neighborhood that subsequently unfolded as an important area of counselor-client bonding and social context for him in counseling. I consider knowing how to connect and join with African American clients to be important skills in cultural competence. Parham (2002) deconstructs "connecting" with African American clients by identifying such skills as recognizing symbolism of prose in jargon (e.g., "Bed-Sty"), exhibiting congruent realness or "keeping it real" (e.g., nonverbally recognizing his coat was of value to his persona, casual chatting about getting to the appointment). Consistent with Parham's model, I was creating ambience, while recognizing in unspoken ways his embrace of a cultural strength (e.g., carrying yourself well-dressed; you represent the "race," a cultural mantra of many generations of black mothers and fathers).

Sanchez-Hucles (2000) notes the importance of first sessions to bond with African American clients, to reduce their leaving counseling prematurely. This is a particular risk when the session triggers their protective mechanisms, especially if the counselor's interactions are perceived as racial slights, cultural ignorance, or unintentional racism (Boyd-Franklin, 2003; Ridley, 1995). This is important in work with black men, who shy away from counseling and are guarded when they do come. Franklin (2004) notes that stereotypes about black men frequently predetermine, and moderate, their social interactions with others. Stereotypes make black men highly sensitive to slights that make them feel their genuine personhood is overshadowed by untrue preconceptions of them. Counselors, including those of the same ethnicity, are not immune from holding stereotyped beliefs and attitudes about people. They can and have manifested in counseling sessions.

Consequently, while working with Kojo I was mindful of these complexities during our initial sessions. I was also interested in how Kojo presented his cultural, racial, and gender orientation in that first session because it provide insight into how congruent Kojo's perspectives were with my working cultural knowledge of the black community and experiences of men of African descent in racial contexts, and how they were different. This fundamental assessment of perspectives and value orientations was typical of my array of counselor tools and approach to the counseling process. Helping Kojo to disclose his degree of stress about early career decisions, marital relationship, and sense of life direction over time evolved into a working therapeutic frame.

Conceptualizing the Approach With Deep Cultural Knowledge

Although I typically incorporate a cultural perspective and value orientation in the assessment process with clients, thinking more about the deep structure of culture (Ani, 1994) provided in Parham's model can be added to my steps in the counseling process. In particular, there are two concepts that could have been helpful in understanding the client's view of the world, if used by me as a consistent part of my assessment tools: (1) Ori-Ire and (2) cosmology.

Parham (2002) represents Ori-Ire as a level of spirituality that "provides an assumed sense of purpose, by instigating alignment between one's consciousness and one's destiny" (p. 116). This is connected to Ani's (1994) deep cultural knowledge perspective. They both represent a phenomenological as well as multidimensional construct akin to religion. This experiential aspect of the human experience is also an underrepresented and undervalued dimension of analysis engaged in counselor practice. I very much incorporate religion and spirituality in assessment and practice; however, it is sometimes too informed by conventional theology and practice of organized religion. Ori-Ire as a concept expands spirituality, and therefore religion, asking us as counselors to broaden and deepen our notions of conventional spirituality not just beyond organized religious beliefs and practices, but also into a greater realm of the human experience brought by destiny. It asks us to consider "destiny" in the lives of our clients, that which is generated by the person, his or her unique aura, in relationship to a somewhat existentialist understanding of what it means to "be in the world." It also urges us as counselors to affirm a belief in "the transformative possibilities of the human spirit" (Chapter 2, this volume).

Given earlier statements by Kojo that ministry was an unheeded "calling," suggesting a deep intrinsic spiritual sense of his career destiny, Ori-Ire therefore becomes salient to his counselor as a significant area for exploration and understanding. Furthermore, because Ori-Ire refers to how one is aligned with one's destiny and brings proper passion and commitment to fulfilling it, exploring this possibility with Kojo might be helpful to sort out his doubts.

Some adherents to this belief say we are, by nature, drawn to our destiny if not fully aware of it. This may explain Kojo's nagging sense of lack of fulfillment and restlessness. Perhaps embedded in his wistful unfulfilled career pondering ("one's consciousness") is an unconscious alignment with his destiny that, with properly focused counseling, will be exposed and lead to the appropriate intervention and resolution.

Clinical Application and Intervention With the AA-SISM

Thinking beyond conventional assumptions about career conflicts internalized by Kojo, including concomitant behaviors such as his depressive symptoms, how would this deeper understanding have provided different practice? Or, "how can I achieve these goals using specific culturally appropriate techniques?" Conventional career counseling practice often looks at the alignment of particular careers with clients' interests or personality attributes, with little consideration of social equity (Blustein, 2008). I in part followed convention in this respect, sorting out Kojo's interests and bookmarking identified personality attributes. What is asked of us in expanding our skills as counselors is how do we accomplish our goals with cultural competence? For me, it is expanding an existing repertoire of cultural insights and skills toward that gold standard of multicultural competence. The concept of Ori-Ire and thinking about the elements of deep culture (Ani, 1994) inform and strengthen competence for me with new knowledge and awareness. The AA-SISM organizes practice toward the gold standard of multicultural competence. Therefore, in using this model, the question for me becomes what was done and could have been done differently, or at least illuminated, in counseling Kojo. This will be briefly discussed by considering the elements of the AA-SISM.

Connecting With Clients

Connecting with clients is critical in the counseling process. This is an important reminder for even the experienced counselor. Throughout our professional literature, there is discussion of the significance of joining and bonding early in counseling sessions. It is no less important with African American clients. Knowing some of the expectations and meanings behind African Americans' greeting behaviors is helpful for counselors who want to be culturally competent. This includes not only the physical act of greeting but also the set of expectations they launch. Adult and older African American clients, for example, may be expecting proper deportment on the part of the counselor as a professional. This means behavior commensurate with our accomplishments, thus earning credibility and respect for the title "doctor." Kojo certainly had this expectation, as shown by his highlighting the status of the persons who made the referral and their confidence in my experience, which he underlined with, "You came highly recommended."

Informality in greetings and subsequent first-name basis with a professional is not expected in traditional African American culture. Throughout the first sessions, it was apparent that calling me "doctor" was central to my client's values of respect for me and set a condition for our counseling process. Like Kojo, however, going forward in counseling sessions, African American clients not only expect a professional stance but also want to feel you are interactive, engaging, and genuine, not hiding behind a mask of professionalism, indiscernible and distant. It is not only youth who expect you to "keep it real."

Conducting Culturally Relevant Assessment

Following a protocol in assessing and evaluating the client's concerns and mental health status is important. Integrating cultural sensitivity into assessment has long been a concern of mine. This includes how psychometric properties of standardized tests contain cultural bias, which is too often overlooked in our haste to have reliability and prediction, much less validity. Even the intake methods employed by counselors as we gather and interpret family, developmental, and work history is not free from cultural bias. Let me be clear: It is important to have useful and accurate metrics as well as a protocol for collecting and utilizing information gathered on our clients. Sometimes, however, we overlook important areas in the lives of our clients because of overreliance on conventions in assessment.

Therefore, as an effort to counterbalance the diagnostic classifications of pathology, I routinely assesses the personal strengths and dreams of clients. This helps to provide perspective on the client's patterns of resilience, motivation, and capacity to overcome adversity while in pursuit of dreams. It was an integral part of evaluating Kojo's representation of why ministry was an unfulfilled ambition. In that regard, the cultural theoretical framework of invisibility (Franklin & Boyd-Franklin, 2000) representing the psychological consequences of racist public stereotypes of black males became an important sociocultural lens in my assessment process. Moreover, awareness and knowledge of the racial context, for example, was essential when challenging Kojo's claims that it was racism rather than, at times, his lack of personal responsibility that was behind his inability to fulfill the goal to be a minister.

Facilitating Awareness

This was a sensitive area to handle, for too often black male experiences, like those of Kojo, are immersed in the quicksand of misconceptions, stereotypes, disillusionment, and confusion. Disentangling oneself from this contemplative quagmire is difficult and can readily lead to inaccurate attributions. However, for the counselor to successfully facilitate awareness in these nuanced areas of racial attributions requires knowledge of African American history and cultural adaptations such as Posttraumatic Slave Syndrome (Leary, 2005) or the Invisibility Syndrome (Franklin, 1999, 2004). Even with this knowledge, helping a client to gain awareness of his or her role in immobility, for example, independent of racism, can be difficult. I facilitated Kojo's awareness by using history and interpreting cultural adaptations to racism during the counseling process, as a way to educate and promote self-integrity in him. This is my *psychoeducational module* in the counseling process. A psychohistorical interpretation for Kojo's behavior helped him put into perspective his indignation as well as his lack of real commitment to pursue his dreams of ministry. Therefore, facilitating client awareness is very much associated with the counselor's cultural knowledge.

Setting Goals

Achieving awareness, however, nicely dovetails with another skill of the counselor: setting goals. Awareness, like insight, does not necessarily lead to action. In fact, it has the potential to bog a person down by the enormity of challenges to overcome and possibilities discovered in making steps toward resolution. We are now talking about self-agency and self-efficacy. Setting goals becomes necessary to focus the process as well as to generate pathways to their attainment. Cultural awareness on my part was important in setting goals with Kojo. Although through counseling he had gained a more sophisticated awareness of his dilemma, as well as his part in it, he was at a loss to get out of it. Goal setting had to be realistic but also culturally compatible. It was easy to say, "Pursue admission to a school of theology," but that ignored some cultural realities. Two that come to mind are (1) Kojo's sense of his competence to take the GRE and gain admission, which was tied to his school history of average achievement as a black child in New York City Public Schools, as well as his perception of how poorly black people do on tests, that is, what Claude Steele and Joshua Aronson (1995) consider the risks of "stereotype threat"; and (2) his knowledge that many ministers in the black community did not have to attend theology school to have a church or become successful. For me, sometimes setting goals with a client gets focused more upon conventional paths to success, ignoring, for example, in Kojo's case, that paths to success in the black community have often not been by traditional educational routes.

The AA-SISM becomes an aid to increase awareness that there are both obvious and not-so-obvious paths in counseling clients, too. Moreover, many not-so-obvious elements remain unseen by us professionally because we are victims of our training and are not sufficiently competent in understanding our clients' other "cultural" perspectives brought into the counseling process.

Taking Action and Instigating Change

It becomes apparent that there is more to achieving goals than just setting them. Failure is the death knell to client motivation. There is an even greater risk when forms of empowerment and advocacy assumed by the counselor are perceived, or proved, to be ineffectual. Counselors' advocacy and steps toward clients' empowerment can be a slippery slope. For example, I counseled Kojo to go to theology school, given my values and personal bias toward higher education and advanced degrees. However, as noted in this self-development model for counselors, situational circumstances for the client can be overwhelming and prohibitive. It can come from within or from perceived legitimate external constraints. Moving clients to take control of their lives and instigate change can be frustrating. Even as an experienced counselor working with people of African descent, it remains important when formulating strategies of action to be mindful of the diversity of interpretations and responses by people to decades of structural inequities that prevent African Americans from benefiting from presumed societal opportunities. There are clients as paralyzed by existing inequitable barriers as they are by their own inability to believe in what Parham refers to as "the transformative possibilities of the human spirit." Therefore, the counselor taking action and instigating change must be mindful of client readiness as well as cultural context.

Feedback and Accountability

In light of my client's reluctance to pursue obvious steps toward his unfulfilled goal, framing feedback and accountability became important to breaking the logjam of immobilization. To do this also required cultural competence. As counselors, we need to know what to say, when to say it, and how to say it to assist our clients. These facets of communication are also immersed in a cultural context. In my professional relationship with Kojo, it was apparent that he had great respect for me, which meant he would hear my feedback as a directive to follow without question because I was the "doctor." It robbed him of his own self-agency in solving his dilemma. I was the professional, so therefore I must know what I am talking about. These are experiences counselors can have with all clients, but they can also have a cultural overlay to them if one is not perceptive of how they manifest in the counseling process. In this circumstance, feedback and accountability were embedded in cultural values of respect for the wisdom of professionals and elders. Empowering self-agency, without compromising those esteemed values about professionals and elders held by Kojo, required restructuring his orientation to professional and elder advice and self-agency while acknowledging his deferential stance to both. This, therefore, enabled Kojo to generate his own possibilities to resolve his problems through our collaborative counseling process and see it as not insulting or disrespectful of me, but appropriate in a new paradigm of collaborative decision making.

Conclusion

Even for the counselor as experienced in practicing cultural competence as I am, knowing the deep structure of culture and the AA-SISM is useful. They are steps toward achieving cultural competence. Articulating the gold standard of cultural competence remains elusive, but every effort toward this objective brings us closer to that goal. These guiding principles help counselors to be mindful of what to consider when counseling in a culturally competent way. It is not a recipe book, nor an inflexible template to lockstep follow to achieve cultural competence. Rather, as the author notes, it is a guide. Even the best cooks see recipe books as a guide to cooking rather than the only method to make a cooked meal. Therefore, our aim should be to utilize these guidelines to facilitate our own generative processes toward better understanding and practicing effective counseling, which incorporates the gold standard of cultural competence.

References

Ani, M. (1994). *Yurugu: An African-centered critique of European cultural thought and behavior.* Trenton, NJ: African World Press.

Blustein, D. L. (2008). The role of work in psychological health and well-being: A conceptual, historical, and public policy perspective. *American Psychologist, 63,* 228–240.

Boyd-Franklin, N. (2003). *Black families in therapy: Understanding the African American experience* (2nd ed.). New York: Guilford Press.

Franklin, A. J. (1999). Invisibility syndrome and racial identity development in psychotherapy and counseling African American men. *The Counseling Psychologist, 27,* 761–793.

Franklin, A. J. (2004). *From brotherhood to manhood: How black men rescue their relationships and dreams from the invisibility syndrome.* New York: John Wiley & Sons.

Franklin, A. J., & Boyd-Franklin, N. (2000). Invisibility syndrome: A clinical model towards understanding the effects of racism upon African American males. *American Journal of Orthopsychiatry, 70,* 33–41.

Leary, J. D. (2005). *Post-traumatic slave syndrome: America's legacy of enduring injury and healing.* Milwaukie, OR: Uptone Press.

Parham, T. A. (2002). Counseling models for African Americans: The what and how of counseling. In T. A. Parham (Ed.), *Counseling persons of African descent: Raising the bar of practitioner competence* (pp. 100–118). Thousand Oaks, CA: Sage.

Ridley, C. R. (1995). *Overcoming unintentional racism in counseling and therapy: A practitioner's guide to intentional intervention.* Thousand Oaks, CA: Sage.

Sanchez-Hucles, J. (2000). *The first session with African Americans: A step-by-step guide.* San Francisco: Jossey-Bass.

Steele, C. M., & Aronson, J. (1995). Stereotype threat and the intellectual test performance of African Americans. *Journal of Personality and Social Psychology, 69,* 797–811.

PART II

Socioculturally Specific Therapeutic Skills for Latinas/os

Expanding Our Evidence-Based Practice Perspectives

Therapists as Cultural Architects and Systemic Advocates

Latina/o Skills Identification Stage Model

Miguel E. Gallardo

An individual has not started living until he can rise above the narrow confines of his individualistic concerns to the broader concerns of all humanity.

Martin Luther King, Jr.

Introduction and Demographics

The cultural landscape in this country has already changed, as indicated by 2008 census data that reported for the first time, Latinas/os, Blacks, Asians, and other non-white residents accounted for half the populations of the nation's largest cities (U.S. Census Bureau, n.d.-b). As the Latina/o population continues to grow in the United States, we can no longer assume that to know one means we understand all. According to the most recent census figures, there are approximately 50.5 million Latinas/os, representing 16.3% of the total U.S. population, thus comprising the largest racial/ethnic group in the United States and accounting for 56% of all growth in the U.S. (U.S. Census Bureau, 2010).

The Latina/o population consists of heterogeneous groups in terms of ethnicity, physical appearance, cultural practices, traditions, and Spanish language dialects (Comas-Díaz, 2001; Santiago-Rivera, Arredondo, & Gallardo-Cooper, 2002). Latinas/os are a diverse group of multigenerational immigrants from different Spanish-speaking countries as well as long-term residents. We are also very diverse in terms of national origin, level of acculturation, length of residency in the United States, socioeconomic status (SES), and other demographic variables. In many Latin American countries, there are at least three major groups: (1) the indigenous groups that may still speak their native languages and have beliefs and traditions from their native cultures; (2) a large mestizo group, which is a mixture between the indigenous and the Spanish blood and culture; and (3) the "pure" descendants of the Spanish colonizers (Falicov, 1998). In addition to these three groups, one can often find a smaller number of descendants from other countries in Western and Eastern Europe and an even smaller number of immigrants from the Middle and Far East. The diversity within Latina/o cultures is vast, but although the culture continues to evolve and diversify within, most Latinas/os continue to have some fundamental core values that transcend all groups. More important, although it is critical to examine the psychology of Latina/o subgroups in order to understand both similarities and differences, for the purposes of this chapter, an introduction and overview to the Latina/o population will be examined utilizing some of the cultural characteristics that are common to the various Latina/o subgroups. Additionally, self-identification and terminology are rooted in geographic and regional locations throughout the United States and will be discussed within this context.

Terminology

The frequently used term "Hispanic" was imposed by the U.S. Census Bureau as a pan-ethnic or umbrella term that emphasizes white European colonial heritage while excluding the indigenous, slave, mestizo, and non-European and non-Spanish-speaking heritages (Delgado-Romero, Galvan, Hunter, & Torres, 2008). This is a term that has been used to describe Mexican, Cuban, Central, South, and Puerto Rican Americans, and it has been rejected by some as a designation imposed from the outside (Albert, 1996). The gender-appropriate Latina/o is often, and more frequently, used within and outside the social sciences as a "culturally inclusive" (although there is still much debate about this term as well) umbrella term that emphasizes roots in Latin American countries of origin. The term Latina/o is considered to include, as an example, Brazilians, who were conquered by the Portuguese and are therefore not Hispanic (Delgado-Romero et al., 2008). As was stated, preferences for terminology associated with self-identification can also be regional. For example, the term Chicana/o, used in the Western region of the United States, was coined as a means of self-identification for U.S.-born Americans of Mexican descent, and it is associated with the sociopolitical and civil rights movements of the late 1960s, thus connoting an important political awareness reflective of resistance, defiance, and ethnic pride (Gallardo, 2006). Similarly, other Latinas/os may simply identify as Cuban, Puerto Rican, Colombian, and so on. La Raza is another term that Latinas/os have identified with and traditionally used as a reference to "the people." For the purposes of this chapter, the umbrella term Latina/o will be used to encompass the breadth and depth of this group in the United States.

Latina/o Cultural and Environmental Considerations

The cultural characteristics/assumptions below are not intended to be exhaustive, but more an outline by which therapists can begin to understand and conceptualize Latina/o culture and specific lived experiences. The chapter's primary focus is on helping practitioners develop culturally responsive interventions, rather than discussing cultural characteristics that can be found in most other areas of the literature.

It has been highlighted in the literature on resiliency and protective factors with Latinas/os that cultural values remain a consistent source of protective factors in the development of resiliency (German, Gonzalez, & Dumka, 2009; Holleran & Waller, 2003; Parra-Cardona, Bulock, Imig, Villarruel, & Gold, 2006). Various groups of Latinas/os differ in cultural characteristics as well as immigration status and history, socioeconomic level, and racial/ethnic makeup, and as McNeill et al. (2001) have noted, it can be problematic to assume that all Latinas/os share similar psychological issues and responses. For example, the fusion and cross-influence of Native American and European cultures results in a culture that is unique to Mexicans and descendants of Mexican people, as does the amalgamation of the Spanish and African in Afro-Cuban culture, which influences beliefs and worldviews. Latina/o cultures are further influenced by residency in the United States, immigrant or generational status, pressures to acculturate or assimilate to the dominant culture, and level of ethnic identification. In addition, in any discussion of cultural or ethnic characteristics, it is important to acknowledge that we can only speak in terms of generalities and that many within-group differences related to ethnic identity and behavior vary across levels of generation, socioeconomic status, and acculturation (McNeill et al., 2001). With these qualifications in mind, it is important for clinicians to be aware of some primary Latina/o cultural attributes, especially in regard to family structure and interpersonal relationships.

Connectedness as Identity

Many Latina/o families and individuals are best described as demonstrating the values of allocentrism or collectivism, emphasizing the needs and objectives of the in-group, as opposed to individualistic needs and values (Marín & Marín, 1991), characteristics central to other Latina/o groups but different from Anglo-American culture (Albert, 1996). Other commonalities include the concept of familismo or family interdependence, which involves extended family members sharing such parenting tasks as nurturing and disciplining children, financial responsibilities, and problem solving (Falicov, 1998). This interdependence extends to family obligations of emotional and financial support, mutual generosity, and intimacy or personal involvement with others, as the needs of the family are always prioritized over the needs of the individual. Pride in the dignity of the family is a fundamental value (Delgado-Romero et al., 2008; Gallardo & Paoliello, 2008; Organista, 2006; M. E. Ruiz, 2007). For example, Parra-Cardona et al. (2006) conducted qualitative interviews with migrant farm workers of Mexican origin and found that despite inconsistent living arrangements and financial instability, these individuals found comfort in estando todos juntos (being all together) and working to provide for their families. The authors noted that the role of family and community for these farm workers served as a buffer to many of the environmental barriers of racism and discrimination they experienced. Holleran and Waller (2003) also conducted ethnographic interviews with Chicanos and found that for adolescents and young adults, the cultural value of familismo served as a protective factor from discriminatory environments, gang activity, and high-risk behaviors. Recent research on familismo links this cultural characteristic to more positive well-being (Rodriguez, Mira, Paez, & Myers, 2007), as a buffer against psychological distress, and to enhancement of emotional well-being during many phases in life (Fuligni & Pedersen, 2002; Gil, Wagner, & Vega, 2000; M. E. Ruiz, 2007).

The investigation by Parra-Cardona et al. (2006) also noted the importance of personalismo for these Mexican farm workers. Many Latina/o relationships are guided by the concept of personalismo, or the tendency to prefer personal, although not necessarily informal, contacts over impersonal or institutional ones. Falicov (1998) states that personalismo signifies the development of meaningful interpersonal relationships in a variety of contexts. Additionally, respeto (respect) governs all family relationships as well as interpersonal relationships outside of the family and dictates appropriate deferential behavior toward others on the basis of age, socioeconomic position, gender, and authority status. Confianza is the trust needed to develop interpersonal and professional relationships. Jenkins and Cofresi (1998) found that confianza was an important variable in the development of interpersonal social networks for Latinas and that a loss of confianza in these relationships led to the development of mental and emotional concerns for these women. It is clear that for many Latina/o individuals and families, family, trust, and meaningful interpersonal relationships serve as protective factors.

Religion and Spirituality

Additionally, the role of spiritual and religious beliefs within Latina/o culture, and in one's connectedness to the larger world and in the development of one's worldview, needs to be considered because these beliefs can be a particular source of healthy development and a protective factor for many Latinas/os (Comas-Díaz, 2006; McNeill & Cervantes, 2008). Spirituality and religion can be the guiding force that sustains healthy development and also provide clarification to unanswered questions and life dilemmas. Catholicism is prevalent among Latina/o groups and can provide spiritual guidance, especially in promoting the values of enduring human suffering and practicing self-denial. According to Espinosa, Elizondo, and Miranda (2003), 70% of Latinas/os are Catholic; 23% are Protestant or "other Christian"; 37% identify as "born-again" or evangelical; 1% identify with a world religion such as Buddhism, Islam, or Judaism; and .37% identify as atheist or agnostic. Many Latinas/os also practice other indigenous forms of spiritual rituals and cultural practices (Altarriba, 1998; Gielen, Fish, & Draguns, 2004; McNeill & Cervantes, 2008). The influence of the Catholic Church may also be seen in parents' preferences for children's attendance at parochial schools or a Catholic college. Churches in a barrio (neighborhood) may also serve a variety of public and community functions that build community and resiliency. Holleran and Waller (2003) found that religiosidad acted as a protective factor for the Chicanas/os with whom they conducted ethnographic interviews. In their study, Mexican-Catholic traditions were supported by the community and family and served as protection from high-risk activities in the barrio.

For many Latinas/os, folk beliefs may coexist with both mainstream religious and medical practices. An example of this is the belief in curanderismo (folk healing), which is rooted in Mexican culture and which can be classified as a popular syncretism of indigenous and Catholic beliefs. Curanderas/os (folk healers) are consulted for many problems involving both medical and psychological components, which may require the use of herbal treatments as well as prayer to Catholic saints. The curandera/o is believed to have supernatural powers that are a "gift from God" as she or he attempts to restore balance or harmony, perhaps even involving the family or community in treatment. Professional curanderas/os may diagnose and treat physical ailments (e.g., diabetes), social/interpersonal problems (e.g., marital conflicts), or psychological disturbances (e.g., depression). Susto (fright or spirit loss), mal de ojo (evil eye caused by envy), and empacho (indigestion) are common ailments treated through curanderismo (Ortiz, Davis, & McNeill, 2008; Trotter & Chavira, 1997). Similar spiritual traditions such as Santería and Espiritismo, which exist within Cuban and Puerto Rican communities respectively, provide guidance and support for many, especially those without access to conventional psychological and medical services (see McNeill & Cervantes, 2008).

Additionally, the interpretation of Latinas/os' spiritual and religious beliefs and practices from a dominant cultural perspective has often resulted in equating a religious/spiritual Latina/o worldview with having no control over one's life or being fatalistic. As with any stereotype, this interpretation may be a reality for some Latinas/os. However, for most, the idea of maintaining a sense of control in their own life is widespread and often serves as a buffer to the more social and environmental aspects of their life over which they have little to no control. Valuing spirituality and religion in one's life should not be mistaken for a loss of control over one's life. Although some Latinas/os believe that their control begins and ends with the Divine power, some may believe simultaneously in the Divine gift of free will. The statement Si Dios quiere ("If God wants it . . . it will happen") has become a statement that many outside Latina/o culture have associated with Latinas/os having no personal control. It is important that we begin to move beyond this narrowly defined explanation to a more accurate description, which includes a more expansive way of defining a Latina/o spiritual/religious worldview. The ways in which Latinas/os live their life are more consistent with "knowing thyself," which translates into knowing one's capabilities as well as limitations, which can serve as protective factors in the development of resiliency. Ultimately, what this enforces for Latinas/os is a sense of trust that no matter what occurs, life will unfold the way it needs to. The Spanish dicho (saying), No hay mal que por bien no venga ("There is nothing bad from which good does not occur") defines the lived realities for many Latinas/os.

Immigration

As you reflect on your own assumptions, biases, and belief systems, Deaux (2006) suggests that you reflect on three critical questions: (1) What does the immigrant bring? (2) What does the immigrant encounter? and (3) What does the immigrant do? If, upon reflection, your initial responses to these three questions reflect negativity or misguided or narrowly defined concepts, without recognizing the strengths and sources of resilience and overall contributions of Latina/o immigrants, then it is essential that you continue to seek further education and experiences and reflect critically on how your limitations negatively impact your current views and your ability to culturally respond therapeutically, and may lead to the perpetuation of social policies that collectively impact those who have the least power and no voice in society.

Latina/o immigrants are also incredibly diverse. In fact, Alegria, Shrout et al. (2007) found differences between Latina/o subgroups and the prevalence of psychiatric disorders among Latinas/os in the United States Some of the findings from this study indicated that time of immigration to the United States, whether before the age of six or after, accounted for differences in psychiatric disorders between various Latina/o sub-ethnic groups. For example, Mexican immigrants who arrive in the United States. after age six demonstrated a lower risk of depressive disorders than those Mexican individuals who arrived prior to age six or who were born in the United States. Additionally, in comparison to Mexican individuals who immigrated prior to age six or who were born in the United States, Cubans who immigrated prior to age six or who were born in the United States differed in their levels of perceived discrimination, believed they lived in safer neighborhoods, and endured less family conflict, which contributed to decreased prevalence of depressive disorders. The findings of this study help us begin to separate unique differences between Latina/o immigrants in the United States, rather than label all immigration experiences the same.

Voluntary versus involuntary immigration status (Ogbu & Simons, 1998) is an important distinction for practitioners to understand, given the sociopolitical and sociocultural impact this has on adjustment, acceptance, and adaptation to U.S. culture. Voluntary immigrants are those individuals who voluntarily engage in intercultural contact. This group consists of some immigrant groups, sojourners, and various ethnocultural groups. Involuntary immigrants are those individuals who have been forced by necessity into involuntary interactions as a result of war, genocide, poverty, and political instability, to name a few. This would include refugees, asylum seekers, indigenous peoples (Ward, 2008), and Cuban immigrants who fled to the United States during the Castro regime. Similarly, the rights and privileges of Puerto Ricans who live in Puerto Rico, who many argue have voluntary status to and from the United States given Puerto Rico's status as a U.S. territory, are limited due to political and economic ambiguity and U.S. influence. Alegria, Mulvaney-Day et al. (2007) found that foreign-born nativity is protective for some Latina/o groups (i.e., Mexicans) but not for others (i.e., Puerto Ricans). Differentiating immigration history, reasons for immigration, and issues such as mobility (one's ability to freely travel back and forth from country of origin), permanence (temporarily here in the United States vs. permanent resident), and voluntariness are critical. These distinctions become important as we shift to a U.S. cultural context and the impact the individual's/family's journey has on their cultural and social status here in the United States.

A discussion of immigration would be incomplete without discussing social status and social policy. Social stratification in the United States has direct implications on immigrant status and any resultant psychological challenges and barriers immigrants might experience. How we situate Latina/o communities in U.S. society based on power and wealth impacts Latina/o immigrants in a multitude of ways. As we consider culturally responding to the needs of these communities, it is important that we consider an ecological framework (Bronfenbrenner, 1977, 1979). Falicov (2007) identifies immigrants who arrived after 1965 as *economic immigrants* whose transnational context needs to be understood within an ecological framework consisting of expanded meanings of family, community, and culture, while considering the cultural and sociopolitical contexts. In taking into account an ecological perspective, we begin to expand our understanding of how to best respond to and respect immigrants from diverse backgrounds. In adapting Bronfenbrenner's ecological model, we can conceptualize the immigrant experience on three different levels: the micro, meso, and macro. According to Deaux (2006), at the micro level are the individual immigrant's "attitudes, values, expectations, identities, motivations and memories" (p. 5). The meso level includes "intergroup attitudes and behaviors, stereotypes, and social networks" (p. 5). The macro level includes immigration policy and law. In comparing U.S. immigration policies to Canada's, Deaux found that one notable difference between the United States and Canada is the adoption of the "mosaic" metaphor by Canadians to describe immigration, as a opposed to the "melting pot" metaphor widely adopted in the United States. The social context can influence the risk for psychiatric disorders. Living in unsafe neighborhoods, ethnic discrimination, and perceptions of low social status all play an important role in the increased risk for psychological challenges among many Latinas/os. Additionally, outcomes of macro-level social policy influences include the fears of the children of immigrants, who worry that their parents will be deported.

The immigration process is ongoing for most families. Symptoms such as depression, anxiety, psychosomatic illnesses, and behavior problems can appear at any time for family members, including at the time of departure, during the migration process, at the time of a life-cycle event (death, divorce), or during reunions with separated family members (Falicov, 1998), and when women may be raped and sexually assaulted. Additionally, the pre-migration trauma and the impact this has on the development of psychological challenges, particularly for involuntary immigrants, is important to understand (Bemak & Chi-Yung Chung, 2008). Suarez-Orozco, Todorova, and Louie (2002) found that children who were separated from their parents during the immigration process were more likely to report depressive symptoms than children who were not. The process of serial migration, or the "step-wise" manner (Hondagneu-Sotelo, 1992) in which families migrate, can have detrimental effects on both the children and parents. It is not uncommon for one parent to immigrate first, leaving the other parent and children behind, or for both parents to immigrate first, leaving children with grandparents or extended family. Consequently, children may leave their country of origin together with parents or leave separately, depending on the circumstances of the family and country of origin. This process could take months to years before all family members are reunited. A consequence of this process is that family relationships can become strained, some siblings may be more acculturated to U.S. society than others, and conflict may arise if there are intergenerational differences between parents and children. Gender roles may also shift, resulting in conflict between the parents (Hondagneu-Sotelo, 1992). All these factors are important considerations when working therapeutically with immigrant communities. Nothing is more important than our ability to see the immigrant as a human being first and foremost and not as the culmination of our individual and societal fears and unwillingness to see the connections we all share (Gallardo, 2010). Deaux (2006) states that "the trend over the past forty years in the United States has been toward diminished support for immigration" (p. 43). She gives two salient reasons for negative attitudes toward immigration: perceived economic threats and beliefs in a status hierarchy. It is the development of negative attitudes, driven by fear, that has led to increased stereotypes and discrimination faced by many Latina/o immigrant groups, resulting in increased psychological challenges for these communities as a whole as they attempt to adapt to U.S. culture as a means of survival.

Acculturation

Issues of acculturation continue to both challenge Latina/o mental health and provide a source of protection against discrimination. Although an examination of the research on the effects of acculturation yields many complexities, a number of studies and reviews of the literature indicate that more acculturated Latinas/os have more substance abuse problems, poorer dietary practices, less healthy psychological profiles, and worse birth outcomes than less acculturated Latinas/os (Cuéllar, Sils, & Bracamontes 2004; Lara, Gamboa, Kahramanian, Morales, & Hayes-Bautista 2005; Leigh & Huff, 2006). According to Leigh and Huff, immigrants from Mexico have lower prevalence rates of alcohol abuse, major depression, and phobias than U.S.-born Mexican Americans. Additionally, Escobar (2000) found that in general, Mexican immigrants have fewer mental health problems than U.S.-born Mexican Americans. Balls Organista, Organista, and Kurasaki (2003) also found that Mexican Americans' acculturation to the United States is rife with a broader array of mental health concerns. They posit that much of this is due to entering a working poor labor force and environmental segregation, resulting in a deterioration of extended support within nuclear and extended families. These studies raise important questions about the social and environmental context for many Latinas/os in the United States and indicate that many Latina/o immigrants exhibit strengths that provide resilience and protection from factors before entering the United States. Although these data suggest that more acculturated Latinas/os appear to have poorer health outcomes, Lara et al. also found that more acculturated Latinas/os are more likely to report having information on preventative health measures than less acculturated Latinas/os, but are less likely to implement that knowledge as preventative behaviors in their personal lives. Understood within context, these more acculturated Latinas/os may continue to feel misunderstood and discriminated against and display cultural reservation in connecting with a system that, upon contact, may further oppress them and lack the necessary support Latinas/os need. In essence, it appears that becoming more acculturated may have disadvantages (Flaskerud, 2007). Vega et al. (1998) found that Mexican immigrants had much better mental health profiles than those individuals of Mexican descent born in the United States. Place of birth also had a greater impact than other demographic information, such as age, gender, and socioeconomic status. The findings of Heilemann, Lee, and Kury (2002) suggest that Mexican American women who suffered from depression and who were more acculturated were also less resilient. Another trend in the research on acculturation is that "biculturalism" or an intermediate level of acculturation among Latinas/os, may be less detrimental to their mental health (Cuéllar et al., 2004). Does being bicultural imply better adjustment and better health? There are still debates and dialogues about this in the literature and field, but it does appear that the more one retains a level of cultural connectedness to one's ethnic and cultural heritage, the more one is affirmed and protected against any challenges one may face. Because most of the studies on acculturation have been conducted primarily with populations of Mexican origin, it is important that these results not be overgeneralized or extended to other Latina/o subgroups, unless there is information to support such findings.

Identity and Language

As we continue to understand the nuances and intricacies of working with a diverse heterogeneous Latina/o cultural group, it is important that we increase our conceptual understanding of ethnic identity. Components of ethnic identity include self-identification, phenotypical features, cultural heritage, recognition of prejudice and discrimination, and intra-ethnic attitudes and interactions (Vera & Quintana, 2004). Ethnic socialization or enculturation is the process by which children learn they have ethnic group membership, behaviors, and preferences (Knight, Bernal, Cota, Garza, & Ocampo, 1993), and it interacts with the processes of acculturation and assimilation to influence ethnic identity development. Padilla (2006) reviewed the literature on biculturalism and found that parents transmit culture in different ways, depending on their history of immigration. Padilla noted that individuals' awareness of who they are culturally, that is, their cognitive understanding of their connection to to culture, was salient for first- and second-generation immigrant children and less salient for third-generation and bicultural children. Umana-Taylor and Fine (2004) found that Mexican adolescents' ethnic identity formation was influenced by the family's ethnic socialization experiences, the ethnic composition of their school, and the family's generational status. Although a solid body of research on the processes of ethnic identity development exists for Latina/o children and adolescents, less is known about these processes across the lifespan (Pizarro & Vera, 2001; Vera & Quintana, 2004). However, Spencer-Rodgers and Collins's (2006) study on risk and resilience with Latinas/os found that although the experiences of belonging to a disadvantaged, culturally devalued community might negatively impact self-concept and create feelings of low self-worth, these experiences also increased racial centrality, or the salience of belonging to an ethnic group. In essence, these authors found that threats to negative self-concept are buffered by the individual increasing his or her connectedness to ethnic group membership, thereby increasing the sense of personal worth. Their study supports social identity theory's "self-esteem hypothesis" (Tajfel & Turner, 1986) and is a rejection of the residual colonized mentality many within the community may be attempting to counter. In essence, ethnic identity is a way for Latinas/os to decolonize our minds and empower and solidify our place in U.S. context and culture.

Although there are numerous generic models of ethnic identity development proposed (e.g., Atkinson, Morten, & Sue, 1998; Phinney, 1993), as well as Latina/o-specific models (e.g., Bernal & Knight, 1993; Casas & Pytluk, 1995), A. S. Ruiz's (1990) model of Latina/o ethnic identity in young adults was designed to assist in the therapy and counseling process. Ruiz makes four assumptions about Latina/o culture: (1) marginality correlates with poor adjustment, (2) marginalization and assimilation create challenges for the individual, (3) ethnic pride correlates with good mental health, and (4) a sense of pride in the acculturation process affords more flexibility of choice for the individual. His model outlines five stages: casual, cognitive, consequence, working through, and successful resolution. Ruiz's model, like the more generic models, makes assumptions ranging from the idea that individuals receive negative messages about their association with ethnic-specific communities, thereby resulting in a rejection of culture, to dissonance between attempting to assimilate and continuing to feel compelled to identify ethnically, resulting in successful ethnic identification and resolution or integration. Subsequently, V. Torres (1999) developed and validated the Bicultural Orientation Model for Latina/o college students, outlining four Latina/o orientations: (1) bicultural orientation, (2) Latina/o orientation, (3) Anglo orientation, and (4) marginal orientation. His model describes a range from individuals who feel comfortable in both U.S. culture and Latina/o culture to individuals who feel alienated from both cultures. Torres defines four conditions that impact Latina/o ethnic identification/orientation: the environment in which the individual grew up, family influences and generational status in the United States, self-perception of status in the United States, and dissonance between the environment in which the individual grew up and the current environment in which the individual lives.

Additionally, Abraido-Lanza, Guier, and Colon (1998) studied thriving, or an individual's ability to grow beyond the minimum development needed for normal growth, and found that thriving was associated with increased personal resources that included psychological well-being, self-esteem, and self-efficacy, all variables related to positive ethnic identity development (Phinney, 1990). As with acculturation, our understanding of ethnic identity is further complicated by country of origin because an immigrant from Mexico may encounter different messages than a Cuban, Peruvian, or Colombian immigrant. In addition, second-, third-, and fourth-generation Latinas/os will have very different ethnic identity developmental processes than those who have more recently immigrated. These models and factors are important for consideration in a therapeutic context because they provide us with concepts and experiences to consider, as well as some cultural characteristics that can determine the treatment and course of therapy. For example, it is problematic when a Spanish-speaking client, who prefers to speak Spanish, seeks treatments but is unable to locate a Spanish-speaking therapist. In addition, a client who may have a bicultural orientation as conceptualized by V. Torres (1999) may have a good foundation in the English language, yet may prefer to utilize Spanish when in treatment, particularly when discussing emotionally charged experiences and situations. Thus, a lack of culturally responsive bilingual and bicultural therapists is a barrier to many Latinas/os receiving the care they need (Altarriba & Santiago-Rivera, 1994; Santiago-Rivera, 1995; Santiago-Rivera & Altarriba, 2002). As a result, there is increasing attention being paid to the incorporation of linguistic competencies in training and in treatment. It is important that readers are mindful that simply being a bilingual therapist does not equate to being culturally responsive as a therapist. Greater attention needs to be paid to evaluating linguistic competencies, as much as we attend to the evaluation of cultural competencies. Linguistic competencies must be evaluated as a "skill" when intervening with Latinas/os in therapy. When providing therapeutic services to Latinas/os, it is critical that therapists assess the language proficiency of the client as well as their own linguistic and cultural competencies. Too often, agencies hire "bilingual" therapists to provide services to monolingual Spanish-speaking communities, without the needed linguistic and cultural competencies to ethically do the job. It is important that therapists meet not only a cultural mandate, but an ethical one as well (Cervantes, 2009).

Gender

The role of men and women in Latina/o culture is also shifting. As will be highlighted in the case illustrations that follow, gender and gender roles can have an impact on individual development in the context of culture and family. Gender role conflict is defined as "a psychological state in which socialized gender roles have negative consequences for the person or others" (O'Neil, 2008, p. 362). More specifically, for Latinas/os, gender role conflict helps us understand how traditional masculine ideals can have potentially negative consequences for both men and women. One of the best predictors for the development of depressive symptoms in Latino men is a lack of intercultural competence, that is, the ability to manage group-specific skills that facilitate cultural transitions (L. Torres & Rollock, 2007). Valentine and Mosley (2000) found that Mexican Americans' gender role attitudes toward sex role stereotypes tend to shift toward the dominant culture over time, rather than retain any culturally sanctioned roles they may assume. Machismo, a form of masculine ideology, is often a misunderstood cultural value of Latinas/os. Until more recently, the masculinity literature on Latino men primarily sustained a monolithic negative perspective (Quintero & Estrada, 1998). As a result, the socially sanctioned systems in the United States have redefined the term and reduced it to a one-sided negative stereotype. The positive elements of machismo, or cabellerismo, have been neglected in Western interpretation.

Studies have shown that Caucasian Americans are second only to Latinas/os in valuing traditional masculinity. In fact, Abreu, Goodyear, Campos, and Newcomb (2000) found higher rates of endorsement for traditional male gender roles in European American men than in Latino men. A noteworthy difference between the masculine construct valued by Caucasian Americans and the Latino machismo is the social acceptance of these concepts when applied to Caucasians rather than Latinas/os (Mirande, 1997). For example, when masculine traits such as toughness, competition, and assertiveness are associated with Caucasian males, the terms are more culturally and socially accepted than when applied to Latino males (Gallardo & Curry, 2008). J. B. Torres, Solberg, and Carlstrom (2002) found that the majority of the Mexican American men in their study supported a more expanded, multidimensional perspective on the machismo construct, while only 10% endorsed a more stereotypic view of the construct. Fragoso and Kashubeck (2000) found that the Mexican American men in their study who endorsed higher levels of machismo with restricted emotionality also endorsed higher levels of stress and depression. The literature in this area clearly directs us to rethink any outdated perspective about Latino men and masculinity we may hold. No place is this more important than when attempting to provide therapeutic services to Latinas/os. For Latino men, machismo is multidimensional, consisting of both positive (cabellerismo) and negative (macho) elements (Arciniega, Anderson, Tovar-Blank, & Tracey, 2008; Neff, 2001). The positive dimensions include honor, respect, bravery, dignity, and family responsibility (Arciniega et al., 2008). These virtues are of tremendous importance and a source of great strength for the Latina/o community. Viewing machismo from the more dialectical perspective of both positive and negative aspects allows for more flexibility and utility within a therapeutic or counseling setting (Gallardo & Curry, 2008). Most important, it highlights the importance of changing the stereotype of machismo to be more consistent with the variations in Latino male identity (J. B. Torres, et al. 2002). An expansion of the definition of machismo and a deeper appreciation for gender role adherence in Latino men provides insights into what is needed to be successful in counseling, outreach, education, and community interventions. More notably, Un buen gallo en cualquier gallinero canta (A good man will be a good man in whatever context he finds himself).

As the Latina/o community grows and becomes more culturally situated in the United States, shifts in gender roles are also taking place. Much like the progress mainstream society has begun to make with regard to women's rights and equality, many of these same transitions are occurring in Latina/o culture. It is impossible to talk about Latino masculinity and male identity development without talking about Latina women. Privately, women in the culture have always been the dominant force in domestic life and family life, but more than ever today, Latinas are providing for their families outside the home, in addition to continuing to provide a warm home environment. While the roles of Latina women have evolved in more public ways, the shift in men's roles has been slow to follow, in much the same way as in mainstream culture. In many ways, Latina women are more prepared to exist in a male-dominated world while also subscribing to the tenets of marianismo. Although men's roles are shifting, we still struggle to co-exist in our comfortable male-dominated world and the publicly changing female world. Marianismo is the female counter to machismo; women are taught to be women and mothers who honor the model of the Virgin Mary and are "virtuous, humble, yet spiritually stronger than men" (Santiago-Rivera et al., 2002, p. 49). Similarly, like Latino men, women are subscribing less to the gender role socialization process due to educational attainment, acculturation, and involvement in relationships that endorse a more equal partnership (Santiago-Rivera et al., 2002). This is important to note because we can no longer assume that Latino men or Latina women endorse any preconceived stereotypical notion we may have about who they are. Ultimately, both men and women are finding their place and expanding their roles, in a U.S. context that has historically narrowly defined their roles within the culture.

Sociopolitical Context

We cannot assume that our Latina/o clients can afford, access, or are aware of treatment options (Delgado-Romero et al., 2008; McAuliffe, Grothaus, Pare, & Wininger, 2008). Consequently, the existence of various barriers related to the underutilization of mental health services by Latinas/os leads us to a discussion of the sociopolitical context.

There are a number of reasons for the underutilization of mental health services by Latinas/os. Sevilla Martir et al. (2007; as cited in Willerton, Dankoski, & Sevilla Martir, 2008) found the following barriers to the utilization of health care by Latinas/os: (1) cost of services, (2) lack of health insurance, (3) language, (4) fear of the system, (5) transportation, and (6) lack of knowledge. Although their study was conducted in the Midwest, their findings transcend other geographic locations throughout the country, particularly for a less acculturated and lower-socioeconomic-status Latina/o population. Additionally, while we have made much progress in providing mental health services for Latinas/os, issues of availability, accessibility, acceptability, and accountability still remain (Willerton et al., 2008). Similarly, it is impossible to discuss Latinas/os and challenges to mental health care without a discussion of perceptions of discrimination in the United States. In the United States, race, like immigrant status, is not simply the color of one's skin, but is a process used to designate Latinas/os into socially ranked or stratified locations in society. Although this socially constructed concept of race does not provide a valid system of classification biologically, phenotypic expression continues to influence status and privilege in societies throughout the world (Harrell & Gallardo, 2008).

Ogbu (1994) defines racial stratification as the "hierarchical organization of socially defined 'races' or groups symbolized by skin color" (p. 268). Skin color has direct implications for the status afforded to certain groups in society, as defined by members of the dominant group. Ogbu states, "In a system of racial stratification people are prohibited from changing their group membership" (p. 269). The racial stratification process, as outlined by Ogbu, directly influences and limits distribution of and access to resources and social mobility. As a result, a disproportionate segment of Latinas/os live in barrios or neighborhoods with substandard housing, ineffective education systems, and unequal access to good healthcare. Consequently, as a reflection of this sociopolitical cultural context, Latinas/os' ways of coping, interpreting, and making sense of the world develop as a means of survival, or protection, and as a way to counter any forms of stigmatization, subjugation, and marginalization imposed upon us. Members of disenfranchised groups establish cultural and familial adaptations for the survival of the group's people and traditions, as a way to combat any social forces that may negatively impact social, familial, and cultural values and ways of living. In addition, they face a healthcare system that, when accessible, is dominated by poor-quality services and discriminatory or racist practices (U.S. Public Health Service, Office of the Surgeon General, 2001). These challenges are compounded by the stigma that experiencing mental health problems is unacceptable to many Latinas/os (Alegria et al., 2002). For example, it is not uncommon for Latinas/os to seek care from a primary care physician (Diaz-Martinez & Escobar, 2002), as a more acceptable means of addressing any mental health concern they may have. For many Latinas/os, there are differing cultural viewpoints of health and illness, help-seeking behaviors, and communication. These challenges, among others, continue to relegate the Latina/o community to limited access to services, combined with a sociopolitical system that, when health services are accessed, makes the community feel further marginalized and disenfranchised. Ultimately, sociopolitical forces and racial stratification impact the formation of worldviews, as well as trust in the mental healthcare system, which can present obstacles to the development of positive health outcomes. As a result, our service delivery models must include a strength-based, social justice approach as we attempt to address the mental health needs of Latinas/os. Additionally, therapists need to intervene systemically. Expanding the role of the therapist to include a systemic orientation is essential when providing services to Latinas/os.

Latina/o Skills Identification Stage Model

The Latina/o Skills Identification Stage Model (L-SISM) is intended to shape therapists' focus and responsiveness to some core issues that are facilitative in the therapeutic process, but not exhaustive. In addition, the model is not linear, although it is outlined as such. Therapy, when done within the context of Latina/o culture, will include the tenets of the L-SISM throughout the course of therapy and not at specific times in a specific, structured manner.

If we are to understand Latinas/os from a more culturally heterogeneous perspective, it is critical that we shift our attention to examine individuals in a local context, rather than a global one. When we examine the local, social world, we begin to see more clearly the multiple intersections that shape the multiple identities, worldviews, behaviors, and values of each Latina/o individual. Additionally, as was identified in our introductory chapter, but is worth noting again, it is imperative that we look beyond our simplistic definitions of ethnicity and race (Lakes, Lopez, & Garro, 2006; Warrier, 2008) as a basis upon which we explain our interventions.

Culture is dynamic and changing; as a community's interactions with the larger society change, so does its culture and our understanding of culture. Examining culture as stable minimizes the sociopolitical and historical processes that shape how traditions or cultural practices are central to a culture (Warrier, 2008). With this in mind, it is important that the reader understand that the information provided throughout the remainder of this chapter contains one aspect of a multidimensional approach to providing culturally responsive therapeutic services to Latinas/os. Using this multidimensional and systemic perspective, therapists will have a more holistic understanding of their client/family. Culturally responsive practice with the

Table 5.1   Latina/o Skills Identification Stage Model

Connecting With Clients	Allow the initial process to be informal and personal, using small talk, if needed. Implement *personalismo* and *platica* as priorities over any other task at hand.
	Address members of the family with formal greetings depending on age, status, etc. and also by their specific ethnic self-designation (don't assume that they are "Hispanic" when "Latino" or Mexican American, or Dominican may be preferred; ask how they identify).
	Allow for nontraditional therapeutic hour/process, if needed.
	Create culturally congruent therapeutic space (i.e., help develop a sense of "home" for clients).
	Use self-disclosure as a therapeutic intervention and as a way to build a respectful relationship.
	Assess cultural strengths and existing resources.
	Shift environmental context, if necessary (i.e., meet client outside office space).
	Use of rituals (*dichos,* music, poetry, prayer, bibliotherapy, *cuentos*).
	Educate client about counseling process.
	Identify what role your client wants you to take (e.g., limited, seek assistance only, gain deeper insight).
	Gift giving (i.e., provide client with a sense of hope that therapeutic work might make a difference in their lives). It is not a guarantee, but a demonstration of faith in the healing process.

Assessment	Assess generation status/ethnic identification/education history and acculturation history (information from these areas will help guide what the therapy process will look like).
	Trauma assessment: identify what, if any, traumas exist, either present or past.
	Ecosystemic understanding and influences (i.e., understand the context in which the client lives and the influences of any environmental factors).
	Language usage: provide treatment in language of preference and adapt language to meet client's educational level and acculturation levels (avoid using psychobabble when not necessary and when incompatible with client's educational and linguistic competencies).
	Assess Spiritual/religious beliefs and the role they play in the client's life, if any.
	Family and community relationships: involve in therapy when appropriate.
	Use culturally appropriate clinical instruments/measures.
	Beliefs about healthcare: understand the client's cultural explanatory model.
	Understand client distress from a Latina/o-centered frame of reference (i.e., compare clients to a standard that matches their own developmental, cultural, and life histories).
Facilitating Awareness	Use cultural strengths and existing resources to help client gain awareness.
	Assess social and political forces: depathologize client and presenting concerns and separate what is connected to the individual from the environment.
	Increase insight into cultural coping methods.
	Use reflecting and reframing and validate, validate, validate before questioning, challenging, or confronting.
	Help clients understand their own language and values for explaining symptoms and where they come from.
	Help clients understand their struggle (social context).
	Use *dichos*, cultural and community-specific stories.
	Possibly connect clients to resources, people, or services in community where further understanding can be developed.
	Analyze any obstacle that may be preventing growth.
	Assign readings, when necessary and when appropriate.
Setting Goals	Understand and assess therapist's own process variables in therapy with Latinas/os (e.g., belief systems about Latinas/os, how one feels about empowering Latina/o clients, beliefs about the possibility of change for Latinas/os).
	Incorporate level of education, SES, etc. (feasibility of goal attainment).
	Use a collaborative approach with client/family/community, when necessary and appropriate.

(Continued)

Table 5.1 (Continued)

	Address immediate and concrete concerns first.
	Develop a clear, specific, focused treatment plan designed in collaboration with client/community.
	Expand role to community activist, consultant, advisor, case manager, etc. when needed and appropriate.
	Include family and community in achieving goals, when appropriate.
Instigating Change	Understand the research and culturally adapt any existing model, treatment, or intervention developed to address client's concerns, when needed and when appropriate.
	Get out and get connected; immerse and extend cultural learning experiences as a way to develop cultural empathy for your clients.
	Be a role model for clients.
	Empower the client (self-knowledge) and help client develop a stronger sense of connectedness to individuals in community and community context.
	Teach clients to problem solve.
	Become a social advocate on behalf of the client (cultural broker).
	Use collaborative/active approaches in which you and client are participating in the process of change.
	Involve family and community, when appropriate.
Feedback/ Accountability	Assessing one's credibility: many Latina/o clients may see the therapist's overlapping roles in the community as a strength and as someone they can trust.
	Understand and measure "success" in a Latina/o-specific context, not majority, universal standard of success.
	Examine congruence between goals and outcomes achieved.
	Assess therapist's role in creating change (i.e., understand what is helpful or not).
	Involve family and community if needed.
	Seek feedback from client, but know that feedback may not be direct, or may be limited, due to your professional role as a therapist/doctor/professional.

Latina/o community calls for an expansion of our roles as therapists (Comas-Díaz, 2006; Falicov, 2007; Robbins, Schwartz, & Szapocznik, 2004; Santiago-Rivera et al., 2002).

Discussion on providing services to Latinas/os is never an either/or, but always a both/and. We cannot rely solely on broad general assumptions about or characteristics of various cultural groups, so we must also remain diligent in building a foundation of knowledge about each cultural group outside our own.

As was mentioned in our introductory chapter, we view this approach and recommendations to working with Latinas/os as consistent with the recent movement toward Evidence-Based Practices in Psychology (EBPP). EBPP also attends to factors related to clients' developmental and life stages (American Psychological Association Presidential Taskforce on Evidence-Based Practice, 2006). Additional client characteristics to consider include gender, gender identity, culture, ethnicity, race, age, family context, religious/spiritual beliefs, and sexual orientation, along with the impact of these variables on the treatment process, relationship, and outcome. Finally, tenets of this Latina/o-centered framework are largely grounded within a Cultural Explanatory Model (CEM), a term used by medical anthropologist Arthur Kleinman (Kleinman, Eisenberg, & Good, 1978). CEM refers to socioculturally based belief systems that individuals hold. Health professionals who adhere to a biomedical model would base their work on empirical, observable, measurable, objective, individualistic, absolute, and rational tenets. Lay individuals' CEMs are vague, are dynamic, have emotional meaning, and are embedded in a person's sociocultural context (i.e., cultural beliefs, socioeconomic factors, and community social networks; Rajaram & Rashidi, 1998). CEMs help us understand the multitude of ways individuals conceptualize an illness, its causes, signs and symptoms, modes of prevention and diagnosis, treatment, prognosis, and expectations of their role as a patient and the role of the treatment provider. Therefore, the goal of therapeutic encounters may vary across cultures and individuals, and CEMs certainly should be considered when working with Latinas/os.

Connecting With Clients

If we begin with the Western premise that for therapy to be successful the client must arrive at an unfamiliar place at a specified time to receive unfamiliar services, it becomes evident why the therapeutic foundation may need to be revisited. In addition, most clients are expected to discuss concerns quickly, with openness and self-expression, and ultimately create the needed change by working hard enough to accomplish their goals. Although this therapeutic framework may be perfectly acceptable for some Latinas/os, for many, depending on generation and acculturation status, seeking services from this particular perspective can be intimidating. The process of reformulating a culturally consistent framework in working with Latinas/os does not equate to discarding one's existing model of therapy or therapeutic foundation but, more appropriately, broadening one's approach to include the tenets of cultural responsiveness within this framework. In doing so, it is clear that therapists must challenge themselves to redefine the therapeutic hour, self-disclose personal and professional information when therapeutically appropriate, and, of most significance, change the environmental context in which the therapeutic relationship is established and maintained.

The transcending variable throughout the process of therapy with Latinas/os is education. With most clients there is some educational aspect, but with Latina/o clients an assessment of generation status and acculturation level will provide insight into the need to educate and "socialize" Latina/o clients into the therapeutic journey.

Personalismo

As was stated previously, personalismo (see earlier discussion for research support on the use of personalismo) can be critical when attempting to build a therapeutic relationship with Latinas/os. One avenue for developing a personal relationship is to redefine the therapeutic hour, which conveys to the Latina/o client the importance of establishing genuine and authentic relationships with others over formalities. In addition, it makes the notion of personalismo a therapeutic intervention, rather than just a concept or value that one understands theoretically. Slowing the initial process down to convey a more present-oriented mindset—rather than a future-oriented perspective of needing to identify, treat, and solve any problems—communicates the therapist's willingness to place the relationship before the problem. In doing so, therapists acknowledge the importance of building a therapeutic relationship and joining the client in his or her culturally specific context and level of comfort, rather than simply trying to seek out a problem and solve it. As indicated above, with most Latinas/os, the way in which the therapist approaches the establishment of a therapeutic relationship depends on the generation and educational level and acculturation status of the client. Conducting an assessment of these factors provides information on what a culturally relevant approach will look like for the individual, rather than for an entire culture.

Self-Disclosure

Another important intervention in connecting with Latina/o clients, and in maintaining the therapeutic relationship, is self-disclosure on the part of the therapist. Although historically not seen as a therapeutic intervention, self-disclosure can serve the purpose of connecting and building rapport (Gallardo, 2006). The use of self-disclosure needs to occur for the client's benefit only and not as a way for therapists to use the relationship for their own growth and development. In cases where it is therapeutically appropriate to self-disclose, it may be important for therapists to express information about their family history and relationships, marital status, and ethnic identity. Manoleas, Organista, Negron-Velasquez, and McCormick (2000) found that one of the primary characteristics of Latina/o clinicians working with Latina/o clients was implementing "a flexible 'sense of boundaries' and view[ing] clients and their families holistically" (p. 388). In addition, they also found that Latina/o clinicians were more likely to self-disclose to their Latina/o clients, versus with non-Latina/o clients. Self-disclosure is communicated verbally and also through environmental stimuli and atmosphere. For example, the pictures and decoration, or lack thereof, therapists have in their offices communicates personal information about who you are and how the client might perceive you in therapy. It is important that therapists assess their own levels of comfort in self-disclosing information prior to beginning therapeutic work. It is also important that therapists remain centered and genuine when working with Latinas/os. Therefore, self-awareness is critical when developing a level of comfort in self-disclosing and in building the therapeutic relationship.

Environmental Context

As has been stated throughout this book, shifting the environmental context, or creating the good society (Nelson-Jones, 2002) in which therapy occurs, is another important way to make therapy accessible, less amorphous, and more acceptable for Latina/o clients. In reaching out to Latina/o clients, it may be important to truly meet the client where he or she is. Meeting the clients where they are does not mean meeting the clients in their readiness to address problems or access uncomfortable feelings. Although that is important, meeting the client means meeting him or her in his or her environment, when feasible and appropriate. An intervention such as this can include visiting a client's home to begin the therapeutic process or connecting with a local community center or local business where individuals and families can drop in to talk with you. As was noted by Schank, Holbeck, Haldeman, and Gallardo (2010), clients may specifically seek those providers who are a part of the community because they are seen as someone who understands clients' needs. Most important, clients and community members see this overlap between deliverer of services and connection to community as a strength, and so should we as therapists. Manoleas et al. (2000) also reported that Latina/o clinicians were more likely to follow up after a missed appointment by calling their Latina/o clients and/or by talking with neighbors, family, and compadres about the client's status, when appropriate. Although some of these "interventions" may seem "unethical," it is critical that students and therapists alike understand the implications of professional ethical guidelines and requirements but not restrict their capacity to respond in ways that might be culturally attuned to the needs of their Latina/o client. As with all interventions, issues of safety and appropriateness need to be assessed by all therapists. However, to assume that these interventions are not viable options is to limit or narrowly define the successful creation of therapeutic relationships and interventions with Latina/o clients.

Cultural Costumbres

The use of rituals, which can include music, cuentos (Costantino & Malgady, 2000; Costantino, Malgady, & Rogler, 1986), or other Latina/o spiritual or religious ceremonial activities, is also an important consideration when connecting with the client. By asking the client how you can make the therapeutic encounter culturally congruent and more defined for him or her, you are also inviting the client to build a relationship centered on his or her values, beliefs, and customs. Therapists may find themselves in situations where they need clients to educate and guide them through this process, and by acknowledging your own limitations, you are also humanizing the process of therapy between you and the client. This can be essential in establishing a therapeutic foundation.

What's In a Name?

Finally, addressing clients by their preferred ethnic self-identification, personal names, geographic identification (e.g., Nuyorican: New York–born Puerto Rican), titles, or by place in the family are all important. Therapists should consider directing their questioning in a way that elicits information about the roles and responsibilities of family members or individuals, if necessary. In doing so, therapists acknowledge the established family structure and relationships. Whether you are seeing one individual or the entire family, for Latinas/os, the observance of the family is central in conveying respect and honor. The family bond can be so strong for many Latinas/os that even when there is distance or conflict in the family, the desire to protect and maintain family dignity remains present. It is not safe to assume that because your Latina/o client is seeking assistance with family issues, he or she does not want to remain connected to, or protective of, family.

Assessment

The Latina/o Dimension of Personal Identity (Arredondo & Santiago-Rivera, as cited in Santiago-Rivera et al., 2002), the Multidimensional Ecosystemic Comparative Approach (MECA; Falicov, 1998), and cultural family genograms (Hardy & Laszloffy, 1995; McGoldrick, 1998) can all be useful frameworks to use when conducting a cultural assessment with Latina/o clients. These models provide an opportunity for the culturally responsive therapist to broaden his or her perspective, understanding, and assessment of Latinas/os. Moreover, these cultural assessment tools provide greater clarity regarding clients' strengths and allow for the implementation of existing resources, which can guide treatment planning, goal setting, and intervention strategies from a strength-based foundation, rather than a pathological one. Additionally, McAuliffe, Grothaus, Wininger, and Corriveau (2006) found that culturally oriented questioning can also be a useful assessment with culturally diverse populations. Culturally oriented questioning includes assessing the importance of culture for the client, understanding experiences of oppression, and understanding cultural values that shape the individual's life. The Latina/o client's life story, or personal narrative, is often the best source of information. The cultural characteristics of a particular Latina/o subculture can be a useful beginning point in treatment, but it must be supplemented and validated through the use of culturally oriented questioning, to avoid any unintentional violations on the part of the therapist. It is critical that the therapist's "therapeutic bar" or measure of what is "normal" behavior connect to the identity, generational status, and context of each Latina/o client. Manoleas and Garcia (2003) provide three clinical algorithms as tools for psychotherapy with Latina/o clients: engagement, assessment-formulation, and intervention, which all encompass decision-making processes that integrate clinical, cultural, and environmental factors. In each of the three algorithms, Manoleas and Garcia provide the clinician with a decision-making sequence whereby the clinician engages in methodical decision making to inform the process of engaging, assessing, and finding the best treatment and intervention plan for the client. Their decision-making model can be used as a foundation and implemented throughout the L-SISM.

As was mentioned above, when assessing a Latina/o client, it is important to develop a cultural narrative with the client, perhaps utilizing a cultural genogram, and to demonstrate cultural responsiveness when diagnosing and using tests. More specifically, it is important to understand the ethnic identification of Latina/o individuals and families. A client who states he or she is Mexican American may yield very little information to the therapist if he or she does not strongly identify with that culture or have a strongly integrated Latina/o worldview. Identifying the roles gender, sexual orientation, religion/spirituality, or class play in the individual/family's social context is important when working with Latinas/os. It is safe to assume that your Latina/o client will identify within multiple life spaces and identities (e.g., third-generation Latina lesbian who is from a upper-middle-class background and living in New York vs. first-generation Latino heterosexual male who is from the working poor social class, and living in California). The multiple dimensions of geography, generation status, social class, sexual orientation, and context all play critical roles in understanding what may work with each of these individuals therapeutically. Hays's (2008) ADDRESSING model (Age and generational influences, Developmental disabilities and Disabilities acquired later in life, Religion and spiritual orientation, Ethnic and racial identity, Socioeconomic status, Sexual orientation, Indigenous heritage, National origin, and Gender) is another framework that includes a broader approach to understanding the multiple identities of each client. We suggest using this model as an outline when assessing any client.

Culturally Congruent Diagnosis

When shifting perspectives, it is also crucial for therapists to understand diagnostic categories as social constructions (McAuliffe & Associates, 2008). The use of diagnostic measures, particularly the Diagnostic and Statistical Manual of Mental Disorders (DSM-IV-TR; American Psychiatric Association, 2000), is a reflection of a specific cultural context that may or may not reflect the cultural reality for many Latinas/os. McAuliffe et al. (2008) recommend engaging in a three-step process to culturally responsive diagnosis: "(1) assessing client cultural identity and salience before diagnosing; (2) considering local descriptions of mental distress; and (3) working through the DSM in an Axis IV-III-I-II order" (p. 592). Assessing levels of connectedness to a Latina/o worldview, or identity orientation, can be useful because it may not be necessary to modify the therapeutic encounter if your Latina/o client strongly identifies with U.S. culture more than Latina/o culture.

There are varying ways of understanding mental distress and health concerns in various Latina/o cultural groups. For example, terms such as mal puesto (hexing), mal de ojo (evil eye), and ataques de nervios (feelings of panic or anxiety) are important Latina/o-specific terms to consider that may be more salient in one Latina/o subgroup over another (Harris, Velásquez, White, & Renteria, 2004; Ortiz et al., 2008). Finally, utilizing the *DSM-IV-TR* in an Axis IV-III-I-II hierarchy of consideration enables the therapist to assess any environmental and psychosocial issues (Axis IV) first, such as housing problems, relationship concerns, acculturation issues, discrimination, and so on. The Latina/o-responsive therapist can then move to assess any medical concerns (Axis III). This sequence can be important because the overlap between the physical and mental may have become more intertwined and connected. An assessment of other conditions that can be the focus of clinical insights (Axis I) should follow. It is important to consider culture in all aspects of treatment. "Disorders" that may be viewed as "abnormal" from a mainstream perspective may be acceptable cultural expressions for many Latina/o clients. For example, a Latina/o client may state that he or she "talks to the spirits" (McAuliffe & Associates, 2008). Although some therapists may consider such behavior a manifestation of personality concerns, this manifestation might be culturally congruent for the client and his or her community. As a result, assessment of personality disorders (Axis II) should be the last step for Latina/o clients. Because culture is as influential in determining personality as any other variable, it is critical that therapists use culture as a foundation to understand personality functioning and not as a last resort. Additionally, although we believe that culture is important to consider, we also understand that culture should not supplant therapists' existing clinical knowledge by assuming that culture can explain all behavior as "appropriate."

Finally, there are times when it becomes necessary to use traditional clinical assessments to assess and culturally diagnosis Latina/o clients and families. When these circumstances arise, it is vital that culturally appropriate instruments are used (Costantino, Flanagan, & Malgady, 2001; Graham, 2006; Suzuki, Kugler, & Aguiar, 2005; Velasquez et al., 2002) and interpreted accordingly, to take into account the social and cultural realities of Latina/o clients. In essence, it becomes essential that culture provide the framework for interpretation and analysis. McAuliffe and colleagues' (2006) three-step guide can also be useful here. In practice, the three-step process can help us learn, early on, the salience of culture for the individual (Step 1), learn what miedo (fear) may mean within the client's local context (Step 2), while considering the psychosocial and environmental factors (Step 3) that may have contributed to the client's connection to culture, or lack thereof, and the causes of miedo. Although miedo, literally translated, means fear, it can also imply panic attacks, nervousness, and general anxiety. An examination of the ecological-systemic factors helps the therapist account for any generational and identity concerns, housing problems, health issues, and family relational concerns that impact the development of coping strategies, miedo in this example, or distress for the client. Ultimately, the therapist can use this information and insight to facilitate awareness for the client.

Facilitating Awareness/Sociopolitical Context

Once a therapist has moved beyond simply connecting with clients and culturally assessing and understanding presenting concerns from a cultural frame of reference, it then becomes important to transfer and join your clinical understanding of the client's presentation to that of the client and his or her context. The therapist's understanding of the sociopolitical context (discussed earlier) is critical to help facilitate awareness for the client, without invalidating his or her experiences or attempting to change any existing beliefs prematurely. It is important to help Latina/o clients make sense of their environments and understand the ways in which their problems may be byproducts of social injustices and political forces around them. This helps clients shift perspectives and reframe any socially constructed definitions they may hold regarding their presenting concerns and potential solutions.

Bronfenbrenner (1977, 1979, 1986) outlined a model that has been adapted for use with Latina/o communities. Bronfenbrenner's use of the micro, meso, exo, and macro systems provides clinicians with a framework from which the social context of Latina/o clients can be understood. Robbins et al. (2004) describe a structural ecosystems approach in working with Latinas/os that emphasizes the importance of understanding the intersection of systems that Latinas/os influence and are influenced by. This model was adapted from earlier work by Szapocznik (Szapocznik, Scoppetta, & King, 1978; Szapocznik et al., 1997).

Ethnic Psychology

Ethnic psychology, another facilitative model, highlights the importance of adapting "mainstream" psychotherapy to Latina/o clients, while remaining culturally and clinically ethical. Comas-Díaz (2006) uses the term *Latino ethnic psychology* to describe the application of cultural traditions and practices to healing and liberation. Latina/o ethnic psychology attempts to restore connectedness, foster liberation, and facilitate ethnic identity reformulation. It also aims to achieve sabiduría, a spiritual and existential type of wisdom.

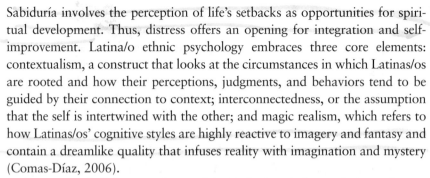

Sabiduría involves the perception of life's setbacks as opportunities for spiritual development. Thus, distress offers an opening for integration and self-improvement. Latina/o ethnic psychology embraces three core elements: contextualism, a construct that looks at the circumstances in which Latinas/os are rooted and how their perceptions, judgments, and behaviors tend to be guided by their connection to context; interconnectedness, or the assumption that the self is intertwined with the other; and magic realism, which refers to how Latinas/os' cognitive styles are highly reactive to imagery and fantasy and contain a dreamlike quality that infuses reality with imagination and mystery (Comas-Díaz, 2006).

Cuentos and dichos can be used in Latina/o ethnic psychology. Cuento therapy (Costantino & Malgady, 2000; Costantino et al., 1986) involves the use of folktales with ethnoculturally relevant stimuli in a social learning approach. Dichos (Aviera, 1996, 2002; Zuniga, 1992), or proverbs in the Spanish language, can be used by Latinas/os to capture the perception that life's challenges are opportunities for personal development and growth. For example, La gota de agua labra la piedra (A drop of water can carve a rock) can be used to illustrate how thoughts can gradually affect one's view of life and produce and maintain depression (Múnoz & Mendelson, 2005). Dichos teach the art of living by overcoming losses and celebrating one's blessings (Comas-Díaz, 2006). A therapist does not need to be fluent in Spanish to learn and incorporate dichos in therapy. However, as with all interventions, it is simply not enough to "know" the information; it is essential that therapists assess their linguistic competency to implement such interventions therapeutically.

Liberation Psychology

The Psychology of Liberation theory (Comas-Díaz, Lykes, & Alarcon, 1998; Martin-Baro, 1994) is another cultural frame that contextualizes for therapists what it means to "free" one from the forces that contaminate the lives of many Latinas/os. The need to expand the roles of "therapists" becomes fundamental in truly helping Latina/o clients heal. If we simply heal our clients in the "room," without intervening in the environments that created the distress to begin with, how much have we really accomplished? Therefore, in order to begin to depathologize our clients from socially created labels, helping them reflect and reframe their concerns in context and helping them understand obstacles that they have potentially created for themselves in learning to cope are imperative.

Postmodern Perspectives

The postmodern social deconstructionalist approaches of Solution-Focused Therapy (de Shazer, 1985; de Shazer & Berg, 1992) and Narrative Therapy (White, 1991, 1995) enable an externalization of problems from a strength-based perspective that focuses on the client's existing strengths and exceptions. McAuliffe and Associates (2008) also highlight the importance of implementing a narrative approach to counseling culturally diverse individuals by re-authoring personal life stories, externalizing problems, and socially deconstructing labels that may have been imposed on the client as a result of distress. Semmler and Williams (2000) state that when implementing a narrative approach to understanding life stories, culture is inextricably connected to the client and cannot be seen as separate. In essence, attempts at separating culture from client are culturally irresponsible. Culture permeates the life stories clients disclose. Whether they are discussing religion, sexual orientation, or the intersections of both, culture is the guiding force that therapists can utilize to assess areas of strength and areas needing growth. Assigning readings for the client, being in the moment with the client, engaging in culturally oriented questioning, using dichos, and assessing the client's spiritual energy are ways of helping Latina/o clients gain insight.

Setting Goals

When setting goals with Latina/o clients, it is important to engage in a collaborative process that includes the client, the family, and community members, when appropriate. Goal setting can play a major role in maintaining an ongoing relationship with Latina/o clients. Inappropriate goal setting that is not congruent with the client's needs and cultural context can lead to early and more frequent drop-out rates and poor follow-through in therapy. In addition, assessing the client's identity status, level of education, socioeconomic status, and available resources is central to goal setting. Identity status, level of education, SES, and available resources become important in goal setting simply because goals may need to be modified and tailored to assist the client in achieving any aspired outcomes in therapy. This may seem like more of the same, but essentially this transforms the therapeutic relationship into a symbiotic one in which the therapist and client become active participants in the achievement of therapeutic goals. This further elaborates the need for clinicians to become cultural brokers (Stone, 2005) and social advocates (Sue & Sue, 2003) for their clients by joining with the client in a collaborative process. This sets in motion another shift in the traditional therapeutic role, from therapist to teacher, advocate, social architect, and problem solver. Moreover, therapists will need to manage the maintenance of goals set and implemented throughout the process of therapy.

Taking Action and Instigating Change

In order to truly create the needed change for Latina/o clients, it is important that therapists connect with the Latina/o community holistically. This translates into therapists seeking out educational and cultural experiences. Latina/o-centered therapists should consider redefining what progress means in therapy from a Latina/o-centered frame of reference; how culture may change the way progress unfolds in treatment; and how to achieve change within the individual's local, cultural context and standards, and not by a generic standard typically used to measure effectiveness therapeutically. For some Latina/o clients, the "generic standard" may apply, depending on generational level or identity status, but therapists should not make the assumption that it does. Extending the couch to the community is important for this reason. As therapists begin to build more collaborative and consistent relationships with Latinas/os through immersion in the culture and extensive efforts to learn about cultural differences and similarities, they begin to genuinely and authentically understand what change and progress means in a culturally consistent and affirmative way for Latinas/os. More important, by engaging in extensive efforts to learn about Latina/o clients and culture, therapists automatically modify their role as "therapist." Their role must transform, at times, into the role of cultural engineers advocating on behalf of clients as clients attempt to problem solve and access existing internal strengths. Role modeling on the part of the therapist also demonstrates to Latina/o clients how to advocate and negotiate social and institutional barriers. In role modeling, therapists expand their roles from "traditional" provider to cultural architect, assisting clients to draw a personal blueprint of the needed changes in their lives, while building a cultural environment that is consistent with who they are, where they come from, and where they would like to go.

Additionally, the inclusion of family and important members of the community can play a significant role in initiating and achieving goals in therapy. The inclusion of trusted community members (e.g., indigenous healers, community leaders, church leaders) and family creates a systemic intervention that is culturally consistent with the client. Including the most important and significant people in the lives of Latinas/os can be helpful in developing ways to support clients beyond the therapy room. These processes, together, facilitate the empowerment of clients by helping them assume control over their lives, understand their Latina/o-ness in relation to the world around them, and gain self-knowledge. Extending the couch to the community implies seeking personal and professional experiences while also connecting with the client's community network through the client and his or her personal life story.

Feedback and Accountability

Another important tenet in the process of conducting therapy with Latina/o clients is obtaining feedback and ensuring that therapist and client are accountable for their commitment to treatment. There are four goals in understanding accountability on the part of the therapist: (1) to understand the helpfulness of therapy by seeking ongoing clarification; (2) to facilitate the creation of change for the client, by the client; (3) to assess one's own process variables in therapy with Latinas/os; and (4) to understand Latinas/os and the Latina/o community enough to assess what a "successful" outcome means within a cultural context.

   It is important for therapists to understand the role their clients want them to play in therapy. It is not safe to assume any particular role in therapy; rather, one should seek out clarification in this process. For many Latinas/os, engaging in therapy may mean seeking ongoing treatment when deeper insights into life circumstances are desired or seeking time-limited treatment for assistance with navigating one aspect or challenge in their life. Either of these roles may mean that therapists will need to take an active collaborative role with their clients and provide advice, consultation, and ongoing feed-back, when necessary and appropriate. Whatever the therapist's role may be in therapy, therapists should always ensure that they have first taken respon-sibility to understand the culture enough to facilitate awareness for the client and to accurately assess a measure of success within the specific cultural context of the client. It is also important for therapists to understand that soliciting feedback from Latina/o clients may look different. Out of respect for the therapist, Latinas/os may not want to directly state what is working or what is not working. Therefore, it is important for the therapist to look beyond face value at times, to ensure that therapy is making a difference. Hopefully, therapists develop a greater sense of comfort in involving family and community in clients' stated outcome goals in therapy, where appropri-ate. This is a great way to solicit feedback in a way that may be more accept-able for Latina/o clients and their families.

Conclusion

The L-SISM is a foundation for conceptual consideration. Although the L-SISM highlights specific skills that can be used where appropriate, the process by which therapists choose to understand, extend their efforts to learn about Latina/o culture, and resist the urge to limit their capacity to understand and intervene in therapy is more critical to culturally attending to the needs of Latinas/os in therapy. Culturally responsive "skills" in ther-apy may not simply be the implementation of techniques, but more the process by which one engages in the therapeutic encounter. It is here that the "skill" of knowing what you know, knowing what you do not know, and knowing that there is information that you do not even know you do not know, is foundational to being culturally responsive. The case examples in the following chapters illustrate evidence-based practices within an L-SISM framework. Consistent with the EBPP definition, the authors have outlined any available research in the context of their clients' presenting problems, included their own clinical expertise and experience in their work, and have placed culture as primary to their work with these cases.

References

Abraido-Lanza, F. F., Guier, C., & Colon, R. M. (1998). Psychological thriving among Latinas with chronic illness. *Journal of Social Issues, 54*(2), 405–424.

Abreu, J. M., Goodyear, R. K., Campos, A., & Newcomb, M. D. (2000). Ethnic belonging and traditional masculinity ideology among African Americans, European Americans, and Latinas/os. *Psychology of Men & Masculinity, 1*(2), 75–86.

Albert, R. D. (1996). A framework and model for understanding Latin American and Latino/Hispanic cultural patterns. In. D. Landis & R. S. Bhagat (Eds.), *Handbook of intercultural training* (2nd ed., pp. 327–348). Thousand Oaks, CA: Sage.

Alegria, M., Canino, G., Rios, R., Vera, M., Calderon, J., Rusch, D., et al. (2002). Inequalities in the use of specialty mental health services among Latinas/os, African Americans, and non-Latino whites. *Psychiatric Services, 53,* 1547–1555.

Alegria, M., Mulvaney-Day, N., Torres, M., Polo, A., Cao, Z., & Canino, G. (2007). Prevalence of psychiatric disorders across Latino subgroups in the United States. *American Journal of Public Health, 97,* 68–75.

Alegria, M., Shrout, P. E., Woo, M., Guarnaccia, P., Sribney, W., Vila, D., et al. (2007). Understanding differences in past-year psychiatric disorders for Latinas/os living in the U.S. *Social Science and Medicine, 65,* 214–230.

Altarriba, J. (1998). Counseling the Hispanic client: Cuban Americans, Mexican Americans, and Puerto Ricans. *Journal of Counseling and Development, 76*(4), 389–399.

Altarriba, J., & Santiago-Rivera, A. L. (1994). Current perspectives on using linguistic and cultural factors in counseling the Hispanic client. *Professional Practice: Research and Practice, 25,* 388–397.

American Psychiatric Association. (2000). *Diagnostic and statistical manual of mental disorders* (4th ed., Text rev.). Washington, DC: Author.

American Psychological Association Presidential Taskforce on Evidence-Based Practice. (2006). Evidence-based practice in psychology. *American Psychologist, 61,* 271–285.

Arciniega, G. M., Anderson, T. C., Tovar-Blank, Z. G., & Tracey, J. G. (2008). Toward a fuller conception of machismo: Development of a traditional machismo caballerismo scale. *Journal of Counseling Psychology, 55*(1), 19–33.

Atkinson, D. R., Morten, G., & Sue, D. W. (1998). *Counseling American minorities: A cross-cultural perspective* (5th ed.). Boston: McGraw-Hill.

Aviera, A. (1996). "Dichos" therapy group: A therapeutic use of Spanish language proverbs with hospitalized Spanish-speaking psychiatric patients. *Cultural Diversity and Mental Health, 2*(2), 73–87.

Aviera, A. (2002). Culturally sensitive and creative therapy with Latino clients. *California Psychologist, 35*(4), 18.

Balls Organista, P., Organista, K. C., & Kurasaki, K. (2003). The relationship between acculturation and ethnic minority mental health. In K. M. Chun, P. Balls Organista, & G. Marin (Eds.), *Acculturation: Advances in theory, measurement, and applied research* (pp. 139–161). Washington, DC: American Psychological Association.

Bemak, F., & Chi-Yung Chung, R. (2008). Counseling refugees and migrants. In P. R. Pederson, J. G. Draguns, W. J. Lonner, & J. E. Trimble (Eds.), *Counseling across cultures* (6th ed., pp. 307–324). Thousand Oaks, CA: Sage.

Bernal, M. E., & Knight, G. P. (1993). *Ethnic identity: Formation and transmission among Hispanics and other minorities.* Albany: State University of New York Press.

Bronfenbrenner, U. (1977). Toward an experimental ecology of human development. *American Psychologist, 32,* 513–531.

Bronfenbrenner, U. (1979). *The ecology of human development.* Cambridge, MA: Harvard University Press.

Bronfenbrenner, U. (1986). Ecology of the family as a context for human development: Research perspectives. *Developmental Psychology, 22,* 723–742.

Casas, M. J., & Pytluk, S. D. (1995). Hispanic identity development: Implications for research and practice. In J. G. Ponterotto, M. J. Casas, L. A. Suzuki, & C. M. Alexander (Eds.), *Handbook of multicultural counseling* (pp. 155–180). Thousand Oaks, CA: Sage.

Cervantes, J. M. (2009). Ethical reminders in the evaluation of undocumented, immigrant Spanish-speaking families. *The California Psychologist, 42*(3), 10–13.

Comas-Díaz, L. (2001). Hispanics, Latinas/os, or Americanos: The evolution of identity. *Cultural Diversity and Ethnic Minority Psychology, 7*(2), 115–120.

Comas-Díaz, L. (2006). Latino healing: The integration of ethnic psychology into psychotherapy. *Psychotherapy: Theory, Research, Practice, Training, 43*(4), 436–453.

Comas-Díaz, L., Lykes, M. B., & Alarcon, R. (1998). Ethnic conflict and psychology of liberation in Guatemala, Peru, and Puerto Rico. *American Psychologist, 53,* 778–792.

Costantino, G., Flanagan, R., & Malgady, R. G. (2001). Narrative assessment: TAT, CAT, and TEMAS. In L. A. Suzuki, J. G. Ponterroto, & P. Meller (Eds.), *Handbook of multicultural assessment: Clinical, psychological, and educational applications* (2nd ed., pp. 217–236). San Francisco: Jossey-Bass.

Costantino, G., & Malgady, R. G. (2000). Multicultural and cross-cultural utility of the TEMAS (Tell-Me-A-Story) test. In R. H. Dana (Ed.), *Handbook of cross-cultural and multicultural personality assessment* (pp. 481–513). Mahwah, NJ: Lawrence Erlbaum.

Costantino, G., Malgady, R. G., & Rogler, L. H. (1986). Cuento therapy: A culturally sensitive modality for Puerto Rican children. *Journal of Consulting and Clinical Psychology, 54,* 639–645.

Cuéllar, I., Sils, R. I., & Bracamontes, E. (2004). Acculturation: A psychological construct of continuing relevance for Chicana/o psychology. In R. J. Velásquez, L. M. Arrellano, & B. W. McNeill (Eds.), *The handbook of Chicana/o psychology and mental health* (pp. 23–42). Mahwah, NJ: Lawrence Erlbaum.

de Shazer, S. (1985). *Keys to solutions in brief therapy.* New York: W. W. Norton.

de Shazer, S., & Berg, I. K. (1992). Doing therapy: A post-structural re-vision. *Journal of Marital and Family Therapy, 18*(1), 71–81.

Deaux, K. (2006). *To be an immigrant.* New York: Russell Sage Foundation.

Delgado-Romero, E. A., Galvan, N., Hunter, M. R., & Torres, V. (2008). Latino/Latina Americans. In G. McAuliffe (Ed.), *Culturally alert counseling: A comprehensive introduction* (pp. 323–352). Thousand Oaks, CA: Sage.

Diaz-Martinez, A. M., & Escobar, J. I. (2002). Assessing and treating depressed Latino patients in primary care. *New Jersey Medicine, 99,* 37–39.

Escobar, J. (2000). Immigration and mental health: Mexican Americans in the United States. *Harvard Review of Psychiatry, 8*(2), 64–72.

Espinosa, G., Elizondo, V., & Miranda, J. (2003, January). *Hispanic churches in American public life: A summary of findings* (Interim Report 2). Notre Dame, IN: University of Notre Dame, Institute for Latino Studies.

Falicov, C. J. (1998). *Latino families in therapy: A guide to multicultural practice.* New York: Guilford Press.

Falicov, C. J. (2007). Working with transnational immigrants: Expanding meanings of family, community, and culture. *Family Process, 46*(2), 157–171.

Flaskerud, J. H. (2007). Cultural competence column: Acculturation. *Issues in Mental Health Nursing, 28,* 543–546.

Fragoso, J. M., & Kashubeck, S. (2000). Machismo, gender role conflict, and mental health in Mexican American men. *Psychology of Men & Masculinity, 1*(2), 87–97.

Fuligni, A. J., & Pedersen, S. (2002). Family obligation and the transition to young adulthood. *Developmental Psychology,* 856–868.

Gallardo, M. E. (2006). Self-disclosure. In Y. Jackson (Ed.), *Encyclopedia of multicultural psychology* (pp. 418–420). Thousand Oaks, CA: Sage.

Gallardo, M. E. (2010). Latina/o immigration: Humanizing communities and unifying voices. *The National Psychologist, 19*(4).

Gallardo, M. E., & Curry, S. (2008). Machismo. In F. Leong (Ed.), *Encyclopedia of counseling* (Vol. 3, pp. 1207–1208). Thousand Oaks, CA: Sage.

Gallardo, M. E., & Paoliello, Y. (2008). Familismo. In F. Leong (Ed.), *Encyclopedia of counseling* (Vol. 3, pp. 1149–1150). Thousand Oaks, CA: Sage.

German, M., Gonzales, N. A., & Dumka, L. (2009). Familism values as a protective factor for Mexican-origin adolescents exposed to deviant peers. *Journal of Early Adolescence, 29*(1), 16–42.

Gielen, U. P., Fish, J. M., & Draguns, J. G. (Eds.). (2004). *Handbook of culture, therapy, and healing.* Mahwah, NJ: Lawrence Erlbaum.

Gil, A. G., Wagner, E. F., & Vega, W. A. (2000). Acculturation, familism, and alcohol use among Latino adolescent males: Longitudinal relations. *Journal of Community Psychology, 28*(4), 443–458.

Graham, J. R. (2006). *MMPI-2 assessing personality and psychopathology* (4th ed.). New York: Oxford University Press.

Hardy, K. V., & Laszloffy, T. A. (1995). The cultural genogram: Key in training culturally competent family therapists. *Journal of Marriage and Family Therapy, 21,* 227–237.

Harrell, S., & Gallardo, M. E. (2008). Sociopolitical and community dynamics in the development of a multicultural worldview. In J. K. Asamen, M. L. Ellis, & G. Berry (Eds.), *The SAGE handbook of child development, multiculturalism, and media* (pp. 113-127). Thousand Oaks, CA: Sage.

Harris, M. L., Velasquez, R. J., White, J., & Renteria, T. (2004). Folk healing and curanderismo within the contemporary Chicana/o community: Current status. In R. J. Velasquez, L. M. Arellano, & B. W. McNeill (Eds.), *The handbook of Chicana/o psychology and mental health* (pp. 111–125). Mahwah, NJ: Lawrence Erlbaum.

Hays, P. A. (2008). *Addressing cultural complexities in practice: Assessment, diagnosis, & therapy* (2nd ed.). Washington, DC: American Psychological Association.

Heilemann, M. V., Lee, K. A., & Kury, F. S. (2002). Strengths and vulnerabilities of women of Mexican descent in relation to depressive symptoms. *Nursing Research, 51*(3), 175–182.

Holleran, L. K., & Waller, M. A. (2003). Sources of resilience among Chicano/a youth: Forging identities in the Borderlands. *Child and Adolescent Social Work Journal, 20*(5), 335–350.

Hondagneu-Sotelo, P. (1992). Overcoming patriarchal constraints: The reconstruction of gender relationships among Mexican immigrant women and men. *Gender and Society, 6*, 393–415.

Jenkins, J. H., & Cofresi, N. (1998). The sociosomatic course of depression and trauma: A cultural analysis of suffering and resilience in the life of a Puerto Rican woman. *Psychosomatic Medicine, 60*, 439–447.

Kleinman, A., Eisenberg, L., & Good, B. (1978). Culture, illness, and care: Clinical lessons from anthropologic and cross-cultural research. *Annals of Internal Medicine, 88*, 251–258.

Knight, G., Bernal, M., Cota, M., Garza, C., & Ocampo, K. (1993). Family socialization and Mexican American identity and behavior. In M. Bernal & G. Knight (Eds.), *Ethnic identity: Formation and transmission among Hispanics and other minorities* (pp. 105–130). Albany: State University of New York Press.

Lakes, K., Lopez, S. R., & Garro, L. C. (2006). Cultural competence and psychotherapy: Applying anthropologically informed conceptions of culture. *Psychotherapy: Theory, Research, Practice, Training, 43*(4), 380–396.

Lara, M., Gamboa, C., Kahramanian, M. I., Morales, L. S., & Hayes-Bautista, D. E. (2005). Acculturation and Latino health in the United States: A review of the literature and the sociopolitical context. *Annual Review of Public Health, 26*, 367–397.

Leigh, W. A., & Huff, D. (2006). *Women of color health data book: Adolescents to seniors*. Washington, DC: National Institutes of Health, Office of Research on Women's Health.

Manoleas, P., & Garcia, B. (2003). Clinical algorithms as a tool for psychotherapy with Latino clients. *American Journal of Orthopsychiatry, 73*(2), 154–166.

Manoleas, P., Organista, K., Negron-Velasquez, G., & McCormick, K. (2000). Characteristics of Latino mental health clinicians: A preliminary examination. *Community Mental Health Journal, 36*(4), 383–394.

Marín, G., & Marín, B. V. (1991). *Research with Hispanic populations*. London: Sage.

Martin-Baro, I. (1994). *Writings for a liberation psychology*. Cambridge, MA: Harvard University Press.

McAuliffe, G. J., & Associates (Eds.). (2008). *Culturally alert counseling: A comprehensive introduction*. Thousand Oaks, CA: Sage.

McAuliffe, G., Grothaus, T., Pare, D., & Wininger, A. (2008). The practice of culturally alert counseling. In G. McAuliffe & Associates (Eds.), *Culturally alert counseling: A comprehensive introduction* (pp. 570–631). Thousand Oaks, CA: Sage.

McAuliffe, G. J., Grothaus, T., Wininger, A., & Corriveau, S. (2006). *Content analysis of the multicultural counseling intervention literature*. Unpublished manuscript, Old Dominion University, Norfolk, VA.

McGoldrick, M. (1998). Introduction: Re-visioning family therapy through a cultural lens. In M. McGoldrick (Ed.), *Revisioning family therapy: Race, culture, and gender in clinical practice* (pp. 3–19). New York: Guilford Press.

McNeill, B. W., & Cervantes, J. (2008). *Latina/o healing practices: Mestizo and indigenous perspectives*. New York: Routledge.

McNeill, B. W., Prieto, L., Niemann, Y. F., Pizarro, M., Vera, E. M., & Gómez, S. (2001). Current directions in Chicana/o psychology. *The Counseling Psychologist, 29,* 5–17.

Mirande, A. (1997). *Hombres y machos: Masculinity and Latino culture.* Boulder, CO: Westview Press.

Múnoz, R. F., & Mendelson, T. (2005). Toward evidence-based interventions for diverse populations: The San Francisco General Hospital prevention and treatment manuals. *Journal of Clinical and Counseling Psychology, 73,* 790–799.

Neff, J. A. (2001). Confirmatory factor analyses of a measure of "machismo" among Anglo, African American, and Mexican American male drinkers. *Hispanic Journal of Behavioral Sciences, 23*(2), 171–188.

Nelson-Jones, R. (2002). Diverse goals for multicultural counseling and therapy. *Counseling Psychology Quarterly, 15*(2), 133–143.

Ogbu, J. U. (1994). Racial stratification and education in the United States: Why inequality exists. *Teachers College Record, 98*(2), 264–298.

Ogbu, J. U., & Simons, H. D. (1998). Voluntary and involuntary minorities: A cultural-ecological theory of school performance with some implications for education. *Anthropology & Education Quarterly, 29*(2), 155–188.

O'Neil, J. M. (2008). Summarizing twenty-five years of research on men's gender role conflict using the Gender Role Conflict Scale: New research paradigms and clinical implications. *The Counseling Psychologist, 36*(3), 358–445.

Organista, K. (2006). Cognitive-behavioral therapy with Latinos and Latinas. In P. A. Hays & G. Y. Iwamasa (Eds.), *Culturally responsive cognitive-behavioral therapy* (pp. 73–96). Washington, DC: American Psychological Association.

Ortiz, F. A., Davis, K. G., & McNeill, B. W. (2008). Curanderismo: Religious and spiritual worldviews and indigenous healing traditions. In B. W. McNeill & J. M. Cervantes (Eds.), *Latina/o healing traditions: Mestizo and indigenous perspectives* (pp. 271–302). New York: Routledge.

Padilla, A. (2006). Bicultural social development. *Hispanic Journal of Behavioral Sciences, 28,* 467–497.

Parra-Cardona, J. R., Bulock, L. A., Imig, D. R., Villarruel, F. A., & Gold, S. J. (2006). Trabajando duro todos los dias: Learning from the life experiences of Mexican-origin migrant families. *Family Relations, 55,* 361–375.

Phinney, J. (1990). Ethnic identity in adolescents and adults: Review of research. *Psychological Bulletin, 108,* 499–514.

Phinney, J. (1993). A three-stage model of ethnic identity development in adolescence. In M. Bernal & G. Knight (Eds.), *Ethnic identity: Formation and transmission among Hispanics and other minorities* (pp. 61–80). Albany: State University of New York Press.

Pizarro, M., & Vera, E. L. (2001). Chicana/o ethnic identity research: Lessons for researchers and counselors. *The Counseling Psychologist, 29,* 91–117.

Quintero, G. A., & Estrada, A. L. (1998). Cultural models of masculinity and drug use: "Machismo," heroin and street survival on the U.S.-Mexican border. *Contemporary Drug Problems, 25,* 147–168.

Rajaram, S. S., & Rashidi, A. (1998). Minority women and breast cancer screening: The role of cultural explanatory models. *Preventive Medicine, 27,* 757–764.

Robbins, M. S., Schwartz, S., & Szapocznik, J. (2004). Structural ecosystems theory with Hispanic adolescents exhibiting disruptive behavior disorders. In J. R. Ancis (Ed.), *Culturally responsive interventions: Innovative approaches to working with diverse populations* (pp. 71–99). New York: Brunner-Routledge.

Rodriguez, N., Mira, C. B., Paez, N. D., & Myers, H. F. (2007). Exploring the complexities of familism and acculturation: Central constructs for people of Mexican origin. *American Journal of Community Psychology, 39,* 61–77.

Ruiz, A. S. (1990). Ethnic identity: Crisis and resolution. *Journal of Multicultural Counseling and Development, 18,* 29–40.

Ruiz, M. E. (2007). Familismo and filial piety among Latino and Asian elders: Reevaluating family and social support. *Hispanic Health Care International, 5*(2), 81–89.

Santiago-Rivera, A. L. (1995). Developing a culturally sensitive treatment modality for bilingual Spanish-speaking clients: Incorporating language and culture in counseling. *Journal of Counseling and Development, 74,* 12–17.

Santiago-Rivera, A. L., & Altarriba, J. (2002). The role of the language in therapy with the Spanish-English bilingual client. *Professional Psychology: Research and Practice, 33*(1), 30–38.

Santiago-Rivera, A. L., Arredondo, P., & Gallardo-Cooper, M. (2002). *Counseling Latinas/os and la familia: A practical guide.* Thousand Oaks, CA: Sage.

Schank, J. A., Holbeck, C. M., Haldeman, D. C., & Gallardo, M. E. (2010). Ethical issues in small communities: Expanding the definition and discussion. *Professional Psychology: Research and Practice 41*(6), 501–510.

Semmler, P. L., & Williams, C. B. (2000). Narrative therapy: A storied context of multicultural counseling. *Journal of Multicultural Counseling and Development, 28,* 51–62.

Spencer-Rodgers, J., & Collins, N. L. (2006). Risk and resilience: Dual effects of perceptions of group disadvantage among Latinas/os. *Journal of Experimental Social Psychology, 42,* 729–737.

Stone, J. H. (2005). *Culture and disability.* Thousand Oaks, CA: Sage.

Suarez-Orozco, C., Todorova, I. L. G., & Louie, J. (2002). Making up for lost time: The experience of separation and reunification among immigrant families. *Family Process, 41*(4), 625–643.

Sue, D. W., & Sue, D. (2003). *Counseling the culturally diverse: Theory and practice* (4th ed.). New York: John Wiley & Sons.

Suzuki, L. A., Kugler, J. K., & Aguiar, L. J. (2005). Assessment practices in racial-cultural psychology. In R. T. Carter (Ed.), *Handbook of racial-cultural psychology and counseling: Training and practice* (Vol. 2, pp. 297–315). Hoboken, NJ: John Wiley & Sons.

Szapocznik, J., Kurtines, W., Santisteban, D. A., Pantin, H., Scoppetta, M., Mancilla, Y., et al. (1997). The evolution of structural ecosystems theory for working with Latino families. In J. G. Garcia & M. C. Zea (Eds.), *Psychological interventions and research with Latino populations* (pp. 156–180). Boston: Allyn & Bacon.

Szapocznik, J., Scoppetta, M., & King, O. E. (1978). Theory and practice in matching treatment to the special characteristics and problems of Cuban immigrants. *Journal of Community Psychology, 6,* 112–122.

Tajfel, H., & Turner, J. (1986). The social identity theory of intergroup behavior. In W. Austin & S. Worchel (Eds.), *The social psychology of intergroup relations* (pp. 7–24). Monterey, CA: Brooks/Cole.

Torres, J. B., Solberg, S. H., & Carlstrom, A. H. (2002). The myth of sameness among Latino men and their machismo. *American Journal of Orthopsychiatry, 72*(2), 163–181.

Torres, L., & Rollock, D. (2007). Acculturation and depression among Hispanics: The moderating effect of intercultural competence. *Cultural Diversity and Ethnic Minority Psychology, 13*(1), 10–17.

Torres, V. (1999). Validation of a bicultural orientation model for Hispanic college students. *Journal of College Student Development, 40*(3), 285–299.

Trotter, R. T., & Chavira, J. A. (1997). *Curanderismo: Mexican-American folk healing* (2nd ed.). Athens: University of Georgia Press.

Umana-Taylor, A. J., & Fine, M. A. (2004). Examining ethnic identity among Mexican-origin adolescents living in the United States. *Hispanic Journal of Behavioral Sciences, 26*, 36–59.

U.S. Census Bureau. (2010). Race and Hispanic or Latino: 2010-United States— States; and Puerto Rico 2010 Census National Summary File of Redistricting Data.

U.S. Census Bureau. (n.d.-b/May 22, 2011). Population estimates. Retrieved May 23, 2011, from http://www.census.gov/popest/estbygeo.html

U.S. Public Health Service, Office of the Surgeon General (2001). *Mental health: Culture, race, and ethnicity: A supplement to* Mental health: A report of the Surgeon General. Rockville, MD: U.S. Public Health Service, Department of Health and Human Services.

Valentine, S., & Mosley, G. (2000). Acculturation and sex-role attitudes among Mexican Americans: A longitudinal analysis. *Hispanic Journal of Behavioral Sciences, 22*, 104–113.

Vega, W. A., Kolody, B., Aguilar-Gaxiola, S., Alderete, E., Catalano, R., & Caraveo Anduaga, J. (1998). Lifetime prevalence of DSM-III-R psychiatric disorders among urban and rural Mexican Americans in California. *Archives of General Psychiatry, 55*, 771–778.

Velasquez, R. J., Chavira, D. A., Karle, H. R., Callahan, W. J., Garcia, J. A., & Castellanos, J. (2002). Assessing bilingual and monolingual Latino students with translation of the MMPI-2: Initial data. *Cultural Diversity & Ethnic Minority Psychology, 6*(1), 65–72.

Vera, E. M., & Quintana, S. M. (2004). Ethnic identity development in Chicana/o youth. In R. J. Velásquez, L. M. Arrellano, & B. W. McNeill (Eds.), *The handbook of Chicana/o psychology and mental health* (pp. 43–60). Mahwah, NJ: Lawrence Erlbaum.

Ward, C. A. (2008). The ABCs of acculturation. In P. R. Pederson, J. G. Draguns, W. J. Lonner, & J. E. Trimble (Eds.), *Counseling across cultures* (6th ed., pp. 291–306). Thousand Oaks, CA: Sage.

Warrier, S. (2008). "It's in their culture": Fairness and cultural considerations in domestic violence. *Family Court Review, 46*(3), 537–542.

White, M. (1991). Deconstruction and therapy. *Dulwich Centre Newsletter, 3*, 21–40.

White, M. (1995). *Re-authoring lives: Interviews and essays*. Adelaide, Australia: Dulwich Centre.

Willerton, E., Dankoski, M. E., & Sevilla Martir, J. F. (2008). Medical family therapy: A model for addressing mental health disparities among Latinas/os. *Families, Systems, and Health, 26*(2), 196–206.

Zuniga, M. E. (1992). Using metaphors in therapy: Dichos and Latino clients. *Social Work, 37*(1), 55–60.

6

Case Illustration: Evidence-Based Practice With Latina/o Adolescents and Families

I. David Acevedo-Polakovich

Cheryl Gering

This chapter uses the Latina/o Skills Identification Stage Model (L-SISM; Chapter 5, this volume) to frame the description of a culturally responsive, empirically supported intervention delivered to a Latina/o family, the Mercaders, who experienced conflict, in part associated with their adolescent son's behavior. Because the intervention was not originally guided by the L-SISM, this chapter examines the L-SISM's ability to accurately capture culturally responsive features of this intervention. The chapter includes seven subsections: The first six describe how each one of the treatment issues identified by the L-SISM (i.e., connecting with clients, assessment, facilitating awareness, setting goals, facilitating change, feedback and accountability) was addressed in the intervention, and the last section offers some final considerations. Some basic background on the Mercaders and their treatment is provided in this introduction.

The Mercader family included a father, a mother, and an adolescent son (Miguel, aged 16). The family owned and operated a Mexican goods store in a mid-sized city in the Midwestern United States. The growing Latina/o community in this city primarily consisted of recently arrived immigrants, of whom a majority came from Mexico. The intervention occurred in a community services center offering a range of bilingual (English and Spanish) health and human services. The family was referred for treatment by Mrs. Mercader's primary care provider, to whom she had confided that her family was experiencing conflict as a result of her adolescent son's behavior. According to Mrs. Mercader, it had become virtually impossible for her and Miguel to communicate without arguing, Miguel ignored her advice and direction, and her frustration with Miguel had led to arguments with her husband.

Because Mr. Mercader's occupation involved frequent overnight absences in order to supply the family store, most of the in-clinic meetings were conducted with Miguel and Mrs. Mercader (individual sessions were held occasionally). However, in order to facilitate engagement with treatment, the interventionist[1] regularly consulted with Mr. Mercader over the telephone and occasionally visited him at the family's store. It is consistent with both the L-SISM and the services research literature that this expansion of professional practices beyond the traditional intervention room can enhance accessibility, utilization, effectiveness, and client satisfaction with treatment (Acevedo-Polakovich, Crider, Kassab, & Gerhart, in press; Hernandez, Nesman, Mowery, Acevedo-Polakovich, & Callejas, 2009). As such, this expansion of practices is directly responsive to the ethical principles and guidelines of the mental health professions (e.g., American Psychological Association, 2002).

The intervention delivered to the Mercader family—Bicultural Effectiveness Training (BET; Szapocznik et al., 1986; Szapocznik, Santiesteban, Kurtines, Perez-Vidal, & Hervis, 1984)—was developed in response to research suggesting that differential acculturation patterns within Latina/o families are associated with increased degrees of family stress and adolescent problem behaviors (Szapocznik et al., 1986). BET's objectives are to encourage a focus on how culture influences family life, to reframe cultural conflict as a common family foe, to develop a balanced understanding of the cultures that influence family functioning, and to develop shared family goals and a shared worldview. These objectives are accomplished by 12 psychoeducational sessions incorporating didactic, experiential (e.g., role play), and discussion components (e.g., awareness group techniques, cognitive classroom tasks), with the emphasis on specific components varying across phases and sessions. The process of BET, and a rationale for its use with the Mercader family, will be further explained in the course of this chapter.

Connecting With Clients

The L-SISM identifies connecting with clients as a central issue in culturally responsive treatment and points to several skills that facilitate this outcome. At the outset of the intervention with the Mercaders, several of these skills were implemented to ensure that the intervention reflected a respect for the parents' roles as strong family leaders, which characterizes many Latina/o

---

[1]The terms *interventionist* and *intervention* are used throughout the chapter in order to be inclusive of the wide variety of professionals and paraprofessionals that Latinas/os might encounter when seeking a psychosocial intervention.

families with adolescents (Roselló & Bernal, 2005). For instance, the initial appointment was conducted with Miguel and his parents rather than with Miguel alone, and the formal *usted* was used when speaking in Spanish with Miguel's parents.

As suggested by the L-SISM, self-disclosure and informal conversation were used during the first session and throughout the intervention, in order to connect with the Mercaders. Noticing Mr. and Mrs. Mercader's Mexican accents, the interventionist, who had lived in central Mexico until emerging adulthood, shared this fact in Spanish and inquired whether they might be Mexican as well. This led to a conversation in Spanish about the interventionist's and the parents' familiarity with each other's hometowns and to self-disclosure of personal immigration narratives (e.g., at what age and under what circumstances each of the adults had immigrated). During the conversation, Mr. and Mrs. Mercader shared their relief at learning that a *paisano* (countryman) who understood their background would be working with their family.

As described by the L-SISM, deciding what language to use in treatment can play an important role in establishing rapport with bilingual Latina/o families (Santiago-Rivera & Altarriba, 2002). Early in the first session, the interventionist facilitated a discussion about each family member's preferred language. Collectively, it was decided that sessions would be conducted primarily in Spanish because Miguel was more fluent in Spanish than his parents were in English. However, Miguel would speak English when he needed to clarify Spanish conversations or felt that he could better express his emotions this way. The Mercaders and the interventionist agreed that everyone shared responsibility for ensuring that Miguel's parents understood any discussions conducted in English.

Illustrating another skill highlighted in the L-SISM, the interventionist followed the discussion about language fluency with a brief description of the counseling process, including information about its usual format, content, purpose, potential length, and the interventionist's typical role. As suggested by the L-SISM, culturally responsive examples and metaphors were used in this discussion (and throughout treatment). One particularly helpful metaphor was the use of the Spanish terms *consejero* (advice giver) and *motivador* (motivator) to describe the role of the interventionist (who is trained as a clinical psychologist). This metaphor was used because the majority of clients seen in this particular setting perceived psychologists as providers who treated the relatively severe symptoms of *locura* (craziness or insanity) through medication or hospitalization. By contrast, providers such as familial or religious authority figures were seen as the best recourse for less severe problems and usually addressed them by giving advice or intervening directly. This mental health belief system is not uncommon among Mexican and Mexican-origin populations (Guarnaccia, Lewis-Fernandez, & Rivera Marano, 2003).

Some benefits of using the *consejero* metaphor were evident in Mr. and Mrs. Mercader's stated relief about seeing a professional in this role. Prior to the use of this metaphor, they had worried that members of the community who learned that the family was seeing a psychologist might believe someone in their family was seriously disturbed, causing embarrassment to the family. Mr. Mercader's comfort with this metaphor was also evident later in treatment when he brought a personal friend to the intervention setting to meet the family's *consejero* and to refer this friend for an appointment.

Although the L-SISM addresses interpersonal skills that are important for developing rapport with clients, client engagement begins prior to actually meeting the clients and is facilitated by characteristics of service settings (Callejas, Hernandez, Nesman, & Mowery, 2009). For example, like Mrs. Mercader, many Latinas/os first share behavioral health problems with trusted primary care providers (Callejas et al., 2009). Because of this, blending health and human services in one setting can facilitate Latina/o client engagement (Acevedo-Polakovich et al., 2010; Callejas et al., 2009; Hernandez et al., 2009). For example, collaboration between service providers enabled the primary care provider to personally introduce the behavioral health interventionist to Mrs. Mercader at the time the referral was made and prior to the intervention. This strategy facilitated engagement by introducing the interventionist in the context of *personalismo*, a characteristic of many Latina/o cultures that emphasizes personal relationships in social behavior (Evans, Coon, & Crogan, 2007). The role of *personalismo* in psychosocial interventions with Latinas/os is further elaborated in Chapter 5 of this volume.

Assessment

Consistent with existing recommendations for U.S. Latina/o assessment practices (e.g., Acevedo-Polakovich et al., 2007), the L-SISM suggests that the culturally responsive assessment of Latinas/os must attend to immigration histories, acculturation, ethnic identity, family relationships, spiritual or religious beliefs, and the ecosystemic understanding of problem behaviors and their causes, and must use appropriate clinical instruments. Several of these factors were important in the case of the Mercader family. In terms of immigration history and acculturation, Miguel's parents were born and raised in a rural village in Mexico's central high plain region and immigrated to the United States as young adults. By contrast, Miguel was born in one of the largest cities in the United States and, until the age of 12, was raised in a predominately Mexican neighborhood within this city.

The differences in immigration history and acculturation among the members of the Mercader family were associated with important cultural and cultural identity differences and ultimately also with the family's presenting concerns. Miguel identified most strongly as a *Chicano,*[2] was most comfortable

---

[2]Term adopted by some Americans of Mexican descent, often connoting the adoption of a political identity that emphasizes Chicanos' historical origins as people native to the Americas and now living in an oppressive political system arising from European occupation (Ramirez, 2005). Also see Chapter 5, this volume.

speaking English, and perceived some of his parents' beliefs about proper young adult behavior as foreign and antiquated. By contrast, Miguel's parents identified as Mexican, preferred speaking Spanish, and interpreted Miguel's lack of formality when addressing familial and other authority figures as *faltas de respeto* (lack of respect) that often caused the family shame and embarrassment. In the course of the intervention (during the second phase of BET, described later in this chapter), it would come to light that some of Miguel's behavior and his parents' concerns arose from differing interpretations of the Latina/o value of *respeto*. His parents viewed *respeto* as interpersonal behavior that conveyed appreciation to others, whereas Miguel viewed *respeto* as guiding actions and interactions that reinforced a personal image of toughness and others' deference to him.

Miguel and his parents viewed each other's interpretations of their shared Mexican heritage (of which the difference in the understanding of *respeto* was but one example) as incorrect, which—at each of the frequent times that behavioral issues could be connected to this "mistaken" interpretation of Mexican identity—seemed to facilitate mutual dismissal of each other's concerns as unfounded and irrelevant (e.g., "Miguel wouldn't be like that if he could just act like a proper Mexican gentleman instead of the thug his friends want him to be."). By dismissing each other's perspective, the Mercaders created an obstacle to arriving at a solution even when problems were discussed within the family. Differential acculturation patterns, such as those observed among the Mercaders, are not uncommon in immigrant Latina/o families whose teenage children are exhibiting problem behaviors (Gonzales, Fabrett, & Knight, 2009).

An important ecosystemic influence on family conflict arose from the mismatch between the Mercaders' traditional beliefs and practices and prevalent mainstream U.S. beliefs and practices about normal adolescent behavior and development. The Mercaders shared the belief that Miguel had reached an age at which he should successfully tackle responsibilities, such as making sure that Mrs. Mercader was safe and economically provided for while Mr. Mercader was out of town. Although these types of expectations for adolescents are not uncommon in U.S. ethnic minority communities (Phinney, 2005), their mismatch with mainstream U.S. adolescent expectations was the source of significant stress for the family. Foremost was the tension existing between the Mercaders and the public school system as a result of Miguel's absences from school in order to oversee the family store during his father's frequent business trips. These school absences had become associated with decreased academic performance and school involvement, which in turn sparked an increasingly conflicted relationship between the Mercaders and school personnel (e.g., school personnel had threatened to contact Child and Family Services if Miguel's absences continued to be enabled by the family).

Although Mrs. Mercader agreed that Miguel should be living up to his "adult responsibilities" by managing the family store while his father was away, she was concerned about the escalating conflict with school personnel and the possibility that they would follow through on their threats. Because of this, she would often instruct Miguel to go to school while his father was absent. Hoping to meet his father's expectations, and confused by his mother's ambivalence about his being absent from school (note that her concern was with the school's threats and not with Miguel's absences), Miguel would often disregard these instructions unless his mother became visibly upset (e.g., crying, screaming). Miguel's disregard increased Mrs. Mercader's frustration, and this in turn created tension in her marital relationship. Because Mr. Mercader experienced both disappointment that Miguel had defied Mrs. Mercader and pride that he had engaged in his adult responsibilities, he frequently gave Miguel contradictory feedback about his behavior (e.g., saying it made him both proud and ashamed), which further prevented a family solution from being reached before Mr. Mercader had to take another work-related trip.

In outlining the implementation of the L-SISM with Latina/o clients, Gallardo highlights the importance of assessing cultural and personal strengths (Chapter 5). Assessing clients' strengths offers important advantages to treatment planning and implementation, and—as discussed below—providing feedback about these strengths can, in its own right, offer some therapeutic benefit to clients (Dishion, Nelson, & Kavanagh, 2003; Tharinger et al., 2008). Moreover, as introduced below, such feedback seems particularly warranted in work with historically marginalized populations in which a singular focus on maladaptive patterns can unintentionally serve to perpetuate the processes of marginalization and alienation.

Throughout the assessment and intervention process, several cultural features of the Mercader family were identified that served as positive change factors. First, the Mercaders' shared sense that Miguel was old enough to take responsibility for his own behavior facilitated his involvement in the intervention, particularly when reframed as taking responsibility for his role in the family. Second, the close relationship between personal identity and family belongingness exhibited by each of the Mercaders facilitated their engagement in the intervention. This was perhaps most clearly articulated by Mr. Mercader who, during his first meeting with the interventionist, stated, "How can I say I am OK when my family is not OK? That cannot be."[3]

Third, consistent with existing data about Latina/o family structures (Falicov, 1998) but counter to gender stereotypes often held in the mainstream United States about Latinas/os (Felix-Ortiz, Abreu, Briano, & Bowen, 2001; Neff, 2001; Torres, Solberg, & Carlstrom, 2002), although Mr. Mercader was referred to as the head of the family, Mrs. Mercader held a significant degree of internal power over family decisions. Because of this, Mrs. Mercader's active interest in the family intervention facilitated her

---

[3]This statement is consistent with *familismo*, a cultural value often encountered among Latina/o families that emphasizes the importance of the family and family harmony in personal constructions of identity and well-being (Cauce & Domenech-Rodriguez, 2002).

son's and husband's engagement in the intervention. Accordingly, intentional efforts were made throughout the intervention to engage the family in a manner that recognized both parents' roles as family leaders. For example, the interventionist respected the family's privacy by giving the family some time for private discussion whenever controversial decisions that impacted the entire family needed to be made. As can be the case in some Latina/o families, these decisions—though usually reflecting Mrs. Mercader's original stand on the issue—were frequently communicated to the interventionist by Mr. Mercader, in his role as head of the family.

Finally, each member of the Mercader family possessed unique personal strengths that facilitated successful assessment and intervention. Despite demanding employment obligations, Mr. Mercader took great care to maintain some level of involvement in the family intervention through frequent phone calls with the interventionist. Miguel's strong sense of personal and familial responsibility facilitated his engagement in treatment and successful completion of treatment tasks. Mrs. Mercader's notable skill as a soft-power leader with strong influence on her son's and husband's behavior provided an additional source of motivation and support for the entire family system during the course of the intervention.

In sum, the assessment information pointed to important family and individual strengths, often rooted in cultural beliefs and practices, but also to an important negative influence of differential acculturation patterns on family functioning and, ultimately, on Miguel's behavior. Specifically, intergenerational differences in cultural identity seemed to prevent mutual understanding and successful family communication. Although Mr. and Mrs. Mercader appeared to be closely aligned with their culture of origin, Miguel embraced the Mexican American culture of the inner-city ethnic neighborhood he grew up in. The available literature has primarily focused on intergenerational cultural differences in families with adolescents who identify with U.S. culture and immigrant parents who identify with a Latina/o culture (Gonzales et al., 2009). The Mercader family presented an interesting variant of this pattern: Although *all* members of the family strongly identified with their Mexican heritage, their differing interpretations of this Mexican heritage negatively influenced family processes.

Facilitating Awareness

As reflected in discussions of the nonlinear nature of the L-SISM, efforts at facilitating awareness are particularly salient when providing assessment feedback but should occur throughout the intervention. For example, later sections of this chapter expand on how Mrs. Mercader was assisted—during the first phase of the intervention—in reaching awareness that her family's situation was not unlike those of other immigrant families. Similarly, later sections explain how the entire family became aware—during the final phase of the intervention—that the insights gained through BET helped them better understand their relationship with school personnel and identify possible approaches to improving this relationship.

In terms of facilitating awareness during assessment feedback, it is worth noting that assessing strengths along with factors contributing to the maintenance of presenting problems facilitated the adoption of a collaborative assessment feedback strategy, with practical and ethical advantages. The interventionist first presented the family's strengths (including the strengths of each member of the family), described the implications these strengths might have for intervention, and facilitated a family discussion about these strengths and their potential relevance. When findings were perceived as accurate by the family, the interventionist asked for examples of times when this strength had been observed by the family. If findings were perceived as inaccurate, the interventionist facilitated a collaborative reinterpretation of data. After each strength had been discussed in this manner, intervenable factors contributing to the presenting problem were presented in a similar sequential fashion.

There is practical value to the collaborative and sequential feedback approach used with the Mercader family; existing research suggests that it facilitates client engagement and has therapeutic value in its own right (Dishion et al., 2003; Tharinger et al., 2008). For example, Mrs. Mercader commented on the way that the assessment findings provided the family with a new language with which to approach family communication. Moreover, by providing clients from a historically marginalized population with information about their personal strengths (often rooted in cultural values), this approach is consistent with ethical mandates to avoid perpetuating the processes of marginalization and alienation (e.g., APA, 2003).

Setting Goals

The L-SISM suggests that working collaboratively with clients in order to establish clear, specific treatment plans that incorporate family and community elements is an integral component of culturally responsive work. In the case of the Mercaders, as intervention alternatives were discussed during the assessment feedback phase, each approach in which the family showed interest was explained in greater detail, including its possible demands and consequences. As presented in the introduction, because of the hypothesized effects of differential acculturation patterns on family functioning, BET was suggested as a preferred comprehensive intervention approach. Other presented alternatives included various forms of family therapy, individual therapy for one or more family members, and no intervention. After some discussion (including, as previously described, some time for family discussion without the interventionist), the Mercader family agreed to try BET. The primary treatment goals agreed to by the family were to reduce conflict between Miguel and his mother and to increase overall family harmony.

After additional discussion, the family also agreed to include a secondary goal of improving relations with school personnel, which the interventionist suggested might also reduce some external sources of stress on the family.

Facilitating Change

The L-SISM highlights the interventionist's role as cultural broker, a role that is forefront in the empirically supported intervention used with the Mercader family. BET is organized in three treatment phases, and the goal of the first phase is to begin establishing a shared family view by introducing core concepts in healthy bicultural family functioning (e.g., biculturalism, cultural conflict, family systems). The Mercader family reported having a positive experience during this phase. In Mrs. Mercader's terms, it "helped us know that we are normal and gave us the words to talk about the things we experience every day." During BET's second phase, the interventionist addresses issues in which cultural differences interact with intergenerational differences, including family composition and relational styles as well as family stress and conflict. As discussed earlier in this chapter, one salient example of the type of process occurring during this second stage involved the Mercader family's identification of differences in their understanding of *respeto* and of the ways these differences often led to miscommunication and family conflict.

The goal of the final BET phase is to encourage a family's maintenance of gains by summarizing the skills learned, views developed, and progress made throughout the first two phases of BET and by helping them apply these skills to arrive at shared goals for future growth. In the Mercaders' case, once the family relationship issues were understood and had improved significantly, one shared goal for future growth was the improvement of the family's relationship with the personnel at Miguel's school. By the third phase of BET, the family spoke of these relationships as cultural differences between their family and the school personnel. In problem solving about how to improve this relationship, the family often used parallels between their improved "family biculturality" and the manner in which they might create a more harmonious relationship with the school by understanding its culture and expectations, making sure that school personnel clearly understood the family's culture and expectations, and finding a workable common ground.

Feedback and Accountability

The nonlinear nature of the intervention elements highlighted in the L-SISM is again emphasized when considering the various moments at which culturally responsive skills were implemented to ensure that the intervention with the Mercader family included feedback and accountability. For instance, the conversation about language use during the first family session served as a first opportunity for informal feedback. Later, as assessment data were gathered, the use of direct questioning—sometimes serving a hypothesis-testing function—also served a feedback purpose (e.g., "Miguel, I hear you and your parents talk a lot about *respeto,* but your parents talk mostly about showing *respeto* to others and you talk mostly about others showing you *respeto.* Could it be that you are using the same word but are not talking about the same thing?"). Finally, the interactive process used to provide the Mercader family with assessment feedback, which encouraged them to share their reactions regarding the accuracy of the interventionist's interpretations, is another example of the incorporation of feedback and accountability throughout the intervention.

Several additional characteristics of feedback and accountability recognized by the L-SISM were relevant to the work with the Mercaders. As highlighted by the L-SISM, the Mercaders had their own definition of success regarding Miguel's behavior and development. Specifically, their goals were for him to behave in a manner that—from their perspective—represented the family well, to help reduce conflict with school personnel, and to achieve this while continuing to meet his adult responsibilities to the family. Although alternative versions of Miguel's successful development were at times introduced by the interventionist (e.g., specific tools and avenues to enable the pursuit of higher education), neither Miguel nor his parents demonstrated interest in further exploring these alternatives. The lack of congruence between the family's goals and the interventionist's hopes for Miguel also highlights the importance of understanding one's own belief systems about Latinas/os and empowering Latina/o clients. Although the interventionist wished (and continues to wish) the Mercaders could envision a future for Miguel that involved higher education, it was by definition unresponsive to continue emphasizing these goals once they were clearly discussed with, and rejected by, the family. Continued emphasis by the interventionist in this direction could have compromised rapport with the family and may be interpreted as a socioeconomic class bias on the part of providers that can often permeate interventions with working class clients (APA Task Force on Socioeconomic Status, 2007). With some difficulty for the interventionist, the Mercaders and he had to agree to disagree.

Conclusions and Recommendations

The work with the Mercaders highlights two important aspects of the L-SISM. One aspect is the nonlinear nature of the treatment issues and specific skills that it incorporates. Although connecting with clients, considering contextual and historical influences on behavior, facilitating awareness, and facilitating change may become salient issues at predictable points in the intervention process, this order of salience neither is invariant across clients nor suggests that other issues become irrelevant when one of them seems particularly salient. A second aspect is that culturally responsive mental health care benefits from assessment and feedback that is reciprocal between clients and interventionists. Stated plainly, just as clients benefit when interventionists provide ongoing feedback on their efforts toward change, interventionists benefit when they receive ongoing feedback from clients, colleagues, and supervisors on the skills, strategies, and techniques they deploy in order to be culturally responsive. This may be particularly important when circumstances dictate interventionists practice near (but not beyond) the borders of their cultural competence (Ancis, 2004).

One particular advantage of the L-SISM is its focus on implementation skills, which some research suggests may account for an equal or greater proportion of intervention effects than the choice of intervention approach (Chatoor & Krupnick, 2001; Sparks, Duncan, & Miller, 2008). As such, when used, as in this case example, to direct the application of interventions with empirically supported effects on the types of problems being presented by clients, it may facilitate maximally effective interventions. Mastery of specific intervention skills (such as those emphasized in the L-SISM) and mastery of specific intervention approaches (e.g., BET) may each constitute necessary, but not sufficient, conditions for successful culturally responsive interventions.

Our experience in writing this case study suggests to us that, with some caveats, the L-SISM has practical utility in capturing many features of a culturally responsive intervention. Nevertheless, research is needed that examines the reliability, stability, and usefulness of the issues and skills that it incorporates, and, perhaps most important, the practical utility of this model in directing culturally responsive interventions and the training of culturally responsive interventionists. We hope that along with the comparative examination of skill and intervention effects on therapy outcome, such research includes the consideration of setting characteristics (i.e., blended community services centers offering bilingual services) as an integral component of effective cultural responsiveness. The L-SISM offers an interesting possibility for the conceptualization of culturally responsive interventions and the training of culturally responsive interventionists, which are increasingly important activities in a diversifying United States where interventionists are ever more likely to encounter families like the Mercaders.

References

Acevedo-Polakovich, I. D., Crider, E., Kassab, V. A., & Gerhart, J. I. (in press). Organizational approaches to reducing Latina/o mental health service disparities. In L. Buki & L. M. Piedra (Eds.), *Building infrastructures for Latino mental health*. New York: Springer.

Acevedo-Polakovich, I. D., Reynaga-Abiko, G., Garriot, P. O., Derefinko, K. J., Wimsatt, M. K., Gudonis, L. C., et al. (2007). Beyond instrument selection: Cultural considerations in the psychological assessment of U.S. Latinas/os. *Professional Psychology: Research and Practice, 38,* 375–384.

American Psychological Association. (2002). Ethical principles of psychologists and code of conduct. *American Psychologist, 57,* 1060–1073.

American Psychological Association. (2003). Guidelines on multicultural education, training, research, practice, and organizational change for psychologists. *American Psychologist, 58,* 377–402.

American Psychological Association Task Force on Socioeconomic Status. (2007). *Report of the APA Task Force on Socioeconomic Status.* Washington, DC: American Psychological Association.

Ancis, J. R. (2004). Culturally responsive practice. In J. R. Ancis (Ed.), *Culturally responsive interventions* (pp. 3–22). New York: Brunner-Routledge.

Callejas, L. M., Hernandez, M., Nesman, T., & Mowery, D. (2009). Creating a front porch in systems of care: Improving access to behavioral health services for diverse children and families. *Evaluation and Program Planning, 33,* 32–35.

Cauce, A. M., & Domenech-Rodriguez, M. (2002). Latino families: Myths and realities. In J. M. Contreras, K. A. Kerns, & A. M. Neal-Barentt (Eds.), *Latino children and families in the United States: Current research and future directions* (pp. 3–26). Westport, CT: Praeger.

Chatoor, I., & Krupnick, J. (2001). The role of non-specific factors in treatment outcome of psychotherapy studies. *European Child & Adolescent Psychiatry, 10*(Supp.1), 19–25.

Dishion, T., Nelson, S., & Kavanagh, K. (2003). The family check-up with high-risk young adolescents: Preventing early-onset substance use by parent monitoring. *Behavior Therapy, 34,* 553–571.

Evans, B., Coon, D., & Crogan, N. (2007). Personalismo and breaking barriers: Accessing Hispanic populations for clinical services and research. *Geriatric Nursing, 28,* 289–296.

Falicov, C. J. (1998). *Latina/o families in therapy: A guide to multicultural practice.* New York: Guilford Press.

Felix-Ortiz, M., Abreu, J. M., Briano, M., & Bowen, D. (2001). A critique of machismo measures in psychological research. In F. Columbus (Ed.), *Advances in psychology research* (Vol. III, pp. 63–90). Huntington, NY: Nova Science.

Gonzales, N. A., Fabrett, F. C., & Knight, G. P. (2009). Acculturation, enculturation, and the psychological adaptation of Latino youth. In F. A. Villarruel, G. Carlo, J. M. Grau, M. Azmitia, N. J. Cabrera, & T. J. Chahin (Eds.), *Handbook of U.S. Latino psychology: Developmental and community perspectives* (pp. 115–134). Thousand Oaks, CA: Sage.

Guarnaccia, P. J., Lewis-Fernandez, R., & Rivera Marano, M. (2003). Toward a Puerto-Rican popular nosology: Nervios and ataquede nervios. *Cultural Medicine and Psychiatry, 27,* 339–366.

Hernandez, M., Nesman, T., Mowery, D., Acevedo-Polakovich, I. D., & Callejas, L. M. (2009). Cultural competence: A review and conceptual model for mental health services. *Psychiatric Services, 60,* 1046–1050.

Neff, J. A. (2001). A confirmatory factor analysis of a measure of "machismo" among Anglo, African American, and Mexican American male drinkers. *Hispanic Journal of Behavioral Sciences, 23*(2), 171–188.

Phinney, J. S. (2005). Ethnic identity exploration in emerging adulthood. In J. J. Arnett & J. L. Tanner (Eds.), *Emerging adults in America: Coming of age in the 21st century* (pp. 117–134). Washington, DC: American Psychological Association.

Ramirez, M. (2005). Mestiza/o and Chicana/o psychology: Theory, research, and application. In R. J. Velásquez, L. M. Arellano, & B. W. McNeill (Eds.), *The handbook of Chicana/o psychology and mental health* (pp. 3–22). Mahwah, NJ: Lawrence Erlbaum.

Roselló, J., & Bernal, G. (2005). New developments in cognitive-behavioral and interpersonal treatments for depressed Puerto Rican adolescents. In E. D. Hibbs & P. S. Jensen (Eds.), *Psychosocial treatments for child and adolescent disorders: Empirically based strategies for clinical practice* (2nd ed., pp. 187–217). Washington, DC: American Psychological Association.

Santiago-Rivera, A. L., & Altarriba, J. (2002). The role of language in therapy with the Spanish-English bilingual client. *Professional Psychology: Research and Practice, 33,* 30–38.

Sparks, J. A., Duncan, B. L., & Miller, S. D. (2008). Common factors in psychotherapy. In J. L. Lebow (Ed.), *Twenty-first century psychotherapies: Contemporary approaches to theory and practice* (pp. 453–497). Hoboken, NJ: John Wiley & Sons.

Szapocznik, J., Rio, A., Perez-Vidal, A., Kurtines, W., Hervis, O., & Santisteban, D. (1986). Bicultural effectiveness training (BET): An experimental test of an intervention modality for families experiencing intergenerational/intercultural conflict. *Hispanic Journal of Behavioral Sciences, 8*(4), 303–330.

Szapocznik, J., Santiesteban, D., Kurtines, W., Perez-Vidal, A., & Hervis, O. (1984). Bicultural effectiveness training: A treatment intervention for enhancing intercultural adjustment in Cuban American families. *Hispanic Journal of Behavioral Sciences, 6,* 317–344.

Tharinger, D. J., Finn, S. E., Hersh, B., Wilkinson, A., Christopher, G. B., & Tran, A. (2008). Assessment feedback with parents and preadolescent children: A collaborative approach. *Professional Psychology: Research and Practice, 39,* 600–609.

Torres, J. B., Solberg, V. S. H., & Carlstrom, A. H. (2002). The myth of sameness among Latino men and their machismo. *American Journal of Orthopsychiatry, 72*(2), 163–181.

Case Illustration: Implementation and Application of Latina/o Cultural Values in Practice

The Case of Julia

Susana Ortiz Salgado

This case illustration addresses culturally responsive therapy grounded in a feminist-interpersonal framework. Congruent with my cultural values and feminist-interpersonal orientation, I make reference to what I bring to the therapeutic relationship and how I use myself as a therapeutic tool. This case further illustrates therapeutic work from an Evidence-Based Practice in Psychology (EBPP) perspective, defined as the integration of the best available research with clinical expertise based on the client's culture and unique individual characteristics (American Psychological Association [APA], 2006). The Latina/o Skills Identification Stage Model (L-SISM; Chapter 5, this volume) operationalizes skills that can be implemented while working with Latina/o clients. Due to the nonlinear nature of my therapeutic style and the L-SISM, this case illustration will strategically demonstrate usage of the L-SISM tenets throughout, versus addressing the outline of the model in the order stated. The L-SISM can be applied throughout the course of therapy. Therefore, in the hope of maintaining the integrity of my therapeutic work and demonstrating how the L-SISM can be applicable, I first describe how I worked with Julia and then highlight the corresponding L-SISM tenet. An early encounter is described in detail because it illustrates how I addressed what could have been a barrier to her continuing therapy. Similarly, the institutional context is briefly described to provide a backdrop for Julia's context and highlight the need for a model like the L-SISM.

Client's Background

Julia is a student in a community college that is recognized for being an Hispanic-serving institution. The majority of the students are of Latina/o descent, and the local community is composed primarily of Latinas/os. Julia, a predominantly Spanish speaker, walked into Psychological Services and in her best English, which is broken but comprehensible, asked to schedule an appointment with a Spanish-speaking psychologist. The receptionist did not make an effort to clarify or ask anyone to interpret, and instead thought she was in crisis and had Julia meet with the crisis counselor, who is a monolingual English speaker. The crisis counselor conducted a risk assessment utilizing simple English, while Julia responded in broken English and nonverbals to convey that she was not a danger to self or others, but was seeking therapeutic services to talk about her life. Julia was deemed safe and was referred to me, as the only Spanish-speaking therapist in the center the following day. This interaction was of chief concern because it inadvertently discriminated against Julia and communicated that in order to access services, she must speak Standard English, therefore demoralizing her and creating a language barrier (Sue & Sue, 2003).

Julia is a 56-year-old heterosexual Mexican woman who emigrated from Mexico seven years prior to seeking therapy. She was simultaneously enrolled in English Language Learner classes and Child Development courses at the community college. Julia is divorced and has two adult children. She is the eldest of 12 siblings, few of whom reside in the United States. She sought therapy because she experienced bouts of sadness, increasing feelings of loneliness, a need to cry, loss of confidence in her skills, and disconnection from herself and her family. She stated that she wanted to recuperate *la Julia que se quedo en la frontera al cruzar a los EE.UU* [the Julia who symbolically stayed at the border right before she crossed to the U.S.]. Services were rendered at a community college counseling center where a brief therapy model of six to eight sessions is followed.

Theoretical Orientation

I would like to offer a brief overview of how a feminist-interpersonal theoretical orientation was used to guide Julia's therapeutic process. Feminist-interpersonal theories are often integrated because of their compatibility and overlap in their emphasis on individuals' relationship to the therapist, to others outside therapy, and with systems (Miville, Romero, & Corpus, 2009). Specifically, the interpersonal theory tenets that are relevant to this case example are (1) people are social beings who develop their personalities and conflicts in relation to others; (2) themes that emerge in childhood will later be reenacted in adult relationships; and (3) interpersonal strategies are developed by people in response to others as a way to maintain self-esteem

(Teyber, 2000). Interpersonal and feminist therapies emphasize transparency and the use of the therapist as a therapeutic "tool." However, feminist therapy further emphasizes an egalitarian relationship and an analysis of power within the multiple systems the client occupies.

Intake: Julia's Story

As suggested by the L-SISM, self-disclosure and transparency were used to build rapport and attempt to repair the unintentional cultural violation committed by our agency. It was my intention to be transparent about how terrible I felt that she was misunderstood and that she was set up to speak with a non-Spanish-speaking therapist. I tried to convey that this was not her fault but rather a culturally insensitive oversight on our part. I acknowledged her persistence and courage for returning and agreeing to meet with me. I explained that it was unacceptable and that all efforts should have been made by our agency to ascertain her needs, and she should have been scheduled to meet with a Spanish-speaking therapist from the beginning. Although the intake meeting was not under my control, I felt a responsibility to her as a Chicana psychologist to correct this mistake and provide her with a corrective, culturally responsive therapeutic experience. Julia was very gracious and clearly demonstrated her value for *personalismo* and *simpatía;* she expressed feeling bad for the crisis counselor because they had to communicate with charades but appreciated her effort to ensure that she was safe.

As I attempt to write about my therapeutic process with Julia, I realize the interconnectedness between the six tenets of the L-SISM in my work with Latinas/os. Attempting to separate these tenets would certainly structure this process, but in doing so, the therapeutic process would lose the natural synergy and reciprocal nature between tenets that transpired in my work with Julia. Therefore, I will integrate and refer to the tenets throughout this case study.

Consistent with my cultural values as a Chicana, and in concert with my theoretical orientation, I wanted to create a safe space that would foster a strong therapeutic relationship that engendered *personalismo, respeto, simpatía,* and *confianza.* After learning about Julia's first contact with our agency, I automatically addressed her in Spanish and referred to her as *usted,* which is a term of respect that denotes authority and reverence in many Latina/o cultures. It was evident that Julia had some formal education in her country of origin because her Spanish proficiency was sophisticated, specific, and selective. I quickly adjusted my Spanish to a level that was more consistent with middle-class Mexican culture, to ensure that she felt understood (Santiago-Rivera, Arredondo, & Gallardo-Cooper, 2002). In addition to assessing language preference, it is important to assess the level or proficiency of Spanish that a client speaks because it can provide insight about educational level and/or social class. Unlike many of my Mexican and Mexican

American clients, Julia used very few colloquialisms and spoke more formal Spanish. Matching her language sparked curiosity in Julia. She asked questions pertaining to my national origin and where my family was from, which led to *charlas* (chats) and self-disclosure on my part. I reciprocated and specifically asked her the name of the *colonia* (in Mexico, the term refers to a neighborhood) where she lived in Mexico City and the name of the town where she was raised. We engaged in a brief conversation about Mexico's landscape and history and talked about the natural beauty that is found where she was raised. For a moment she was full of nostalgia, and shortly thereafter she seemed ready to delve into her story. As we engaged in what appeared to be a casual conversation, we were establishing a relationship. The purpose of eliciting specifics about where she lived in Mexico was to contextualize her within her sociocultural environment while also communicating to her that I was relatively knowledgeable about where she came from. The complexity and translinear application of the L-SISM brings this example to life because it illustrates that while connecting with a client, I was simultaneously assessing and gathering information about her interpersonal style and her social class based on how she engaged with me, while also developing hypotheses regarding her sociocultural worldview to "test" in our future work. Making a genuine effort to connect with Latina/o clients conveys that we value them enough to get to know and understand them.

After our *charla* and a few laughs, I shifted my demeanor to one that was slightly more formal, to convey that we were about to transition into a more serious domain. While remaining personable in my tone, I asked her a general question, "What brings you to therapy today?" She smiled, cried, and responded in a story-like fashion. *Tengo cincuenta y seis maravillosos años* [I have 56 marvelous years]. Julia's story started at the point when she was five years old and consisted of life-changing events (e.g., getting married, getting divorced, becoming a mother, educational trajectory, immigration to the United States) and existential revelations (e.g., realizing "her place" as a woman, not having a childhood, identity issues, faulty beliefs about herself). Her passion for words was matched by her adept ability to express her emotions. Her storytelling was animated, full of facial expressions, hand gestures, intonations in her voice, and expression of a range of emotions (e.g., cried, smiled, laughed, expressed anger and sadness) as she transitioned through the various "chapters" of her life. As suggested by the L-SISM, I used the Latina/o cultural value of *personalismo* as an intervention by allowing the process to unfold organically and by creating space for Julia to tell her story. At times her story was disjointed and nonsequential, yet she captured salient aspects of what she considered relevant to her current concerns and potential therapeutic goals. As stated in the L-SISM, engaging the client in setting goals, instigating change, and helping define "success" based on her cultural worldview was critical. In addition to the content of her story, I paid attention to her process of communication and how she communicated about specific experiences and people (Santiago-Rivera et al., 2002; Sue & Sue, 2003). This gave me a sense of her values, her priorities, and where she focused her interpersonal and intrapersonal energy. The purpose of the initial intake was to mend her relationship with the agency, to connect with her, and to begin the assessment process.

Establishing *Confianza*

Julia is more than 20 years older than me; therefore, it was important to address our age difference and power dynamics early in our work together. I used this opportunity to discuss the role that we would each have in therapy and our power dynamics. The purpose was to develop a collaborative relationship in which parameters were clear and to convey to her that she could directly ask to be taken care of in therapy and that I would "be there" for her. I began by eliciting feedback about what it had been like to talk with someone who was significantly younger. Upon learning that Julia assumed I had all the answers because I was "*la doctora*," I realized I had a clinical and cultural dilemma. I was unsure whether I would violate her cultural assumption by "returning" the power she ascribed to me. I also wanted to "take care of her" because I knew that in some ways this would be therapeutic, given that one of her concerns was that she was not taken care of by others. However, consistent with a feminist framework, I needed to empower and encourage her to have a voice in her healing process. As we openly discussed our differences and some core themes that she wanted to address in therapy, she realized she needed to explore these themes to begin her healing process but was too afraid to do it alone. She asked me to accompany and guide her in her journey as she processed the various losses she had experienced throughout her life. Consistent with the L-SISM, I elicited feedback at various points throughout the course of treatment; however, engaging her early on set a precedent and conveyed that she needed to be involved in every aspect of her healing process in order for therapy to be successful.

As my work with Julia progressed, I simultaneously engaged in tenets put forth by the L-SISM, such as assessment and increasing awareness of her family and cultural dynamics. Assessment begins and continues throughout the therapeutic process. This enables therapists to correct and adjust as needed, allowing for the development of culturally congruent goals and interventions. Without a careful exploration of Julia's history, I could have made many erroneous assumptions about her and her presenting concerns. Because her father owned land and cattle, her family of origin was considered *los ricos del pueblo* (the wealthy ones in the village), but Julia, her mother, and younger siblings did not benefit directly from *his* wealth. Instead, Julia recalled that her father was physically and emotionally abusive toward her and her family. He abused his power by withholding earnings from the family, which forced Julia to sell *tamales*, *tortas*, and *pastelitos* at the *Zócalo* at the age of five, in order to earn money so that her younger siblings could eat and have some autonomy from their father. As I assessed for an accurate sociocultural representation of her worldview, I reflected what she said to me, attempting to increase her awareness about the fact that neither parent allowed her to have a childhood. I expressed sadness for the five-year-old child who was not taken care of, but instead was abused and placed in a position where she had to be the adult. I also increased her awareness regarding her personality development and invited her to co-create an understanding about how her self-sufficiency and tough demeanor have been protective and functional within her multiple ecological contexts (micro: family and self, macro: Mexican culture in her pueblo). Similarly, working from a strength-based approach (Bettendorf & Fischer, 2009), I increased awareness and saliency of the cultural values and strengths she referred to throughout our sessions (e.g., *familismo, respeto,* being a strong woman, ethnic identity), to help anchor her when she felt overwhelmed. She slowly began to shift her perspective and realized that as a child she did not have much power and was "forced" into the role of caretaker and protector, but she is now an adult, with power and a choice about her role in the family.

Goals and Interventions

After clarifying some of her concerns that brought her to therapy, we collaboratively established therapeutic goals and began to implement treatment interventions. Her goals entailed decreasing her depressive symptoms, changing her role in her family of origin, and reclaiming her identity and sense of self in the United States. Her goals and our approach to reaching those goals were interconnected. For example, Julia identified many kinesthetic activities that brought her emotional joy. Therefore, we developed a regimen of activities that promoted both physical and psychological well-being (e.g., swimming, yoga, running). Another treatment intervention consisted of challenging negative internalized messages (e.g., I am not important and neither are my needs). By engaging in self-care activities, she learned to attend to her needs and alter how she responded to herself. This process further validated that her needs were important and that she was worthy of attention and care (Teyber, 2000). The L-SISM identifies collaboration in the development of treatment goals as an important skill for maintaining a connection with Latina/o clients. Similarly, it enables the client to have ownership of the healing process and promotes application of the skills outside the therapy. It is important to note that Julia did not meet the criteria for a Mood Disorder, and based on her presentation, sociocultural history, and context, an approach that only focused on symptom reduction would have been incompatible with her. Julia described depressive symptoms that appeared to be normative responses to a complicated life history that was coming to culmination.

As suggested by the L-SISM, in order to understand Julia's distress and her interpersonal style, an exploration of her identity development within her sociohistorical culture, using an ecological model, was warranted

(Bronfenbrenner, 1977, 1979, 1986). In Julia's case, this meant understanding her development in the context of her personal and familial history, within the context of Mexican culture in the late 1950s and early 1960s. Julia's gender identity is contextualized within her ethnic identity, and it is grounded in her cultural value of *familismo*. However, she received mixed messages about womanhood and her role in the family throughout her life. Specifically, there was a clear contradiction between her family of origin's microsystem and the culture of her *pueblo*. Little girls in her pueblo were supposed to work within confines of their household, not sell food on the street. She was often ostracized by peers and extended family and referred to as a *niña malcriada* (poorly reared girl) and *niña de la calle* (a girl from the streets). Confused by the mixed messages, she embraced being a rebel and rejected the standards of womanhood of that era in her pueblo. While exploring her gender identity and her view of womanhood, she discussed moments that elucidated that although it was functional for her family that she rejected cultural gender roles, there were parameters to gender role bending. She recognized she was allowed to occupy masculine roles but that her values were expected to remain consistent with the ideals of womanhood of her culture and generation.

It was critical that I placed her story in a generational sociocultural context because failure to do so would have marginalized her further (Falicov, 1998; McNeill et al., 2001; Santiago-Rivera et al., 2002). I needed to be mindful of my feminist identity and values and know when to validate her and when to allow her to struggle in finding her own balance and sense of womanhood that was consistent with her sense of self. Respecting her cultural and familial values, I facilitated awareness of the mixed messages she and other women receive about femininity. We discussed *marianismo* as a cultural value (Lopez-Baez, 1999), and I encouraged her to think about the cultural messages underlying her family's reactions to her desire to pursue a professional career. We explored relevant "commandments" of Latina womanhood and contextualized them in her life (e.g., Do not forget a women's place; Do not put your own needs first; Do not wish for more in life than being a housewife; Gil & Vazquez, 1996).

Further assessment of her interpersonal style revealed that as she matured, she was characterized as having *carácter fuerte,* which encompasses being strong willed, possessing strong convictions, having control over one's life, and having the ability to respond to whatever life throws one's way. However, she also conveyed that she did not need anyone and further pushed people away. As suggested by the L-SISM, we co-created a framework that encompassed cultural and personal values (e.g., *familismo, respeto, orgullo* [pride], *personalismo*) identified by Julia, in order for her to understand how her current relational style was no longer congruent with these values. By increasing awareness of how she contributed to this interpersonal dynamic, she felt empowered and hopeful that she could change her relational style and develop reciprocal relationships with others, including her siblings. She concurrently expanded on this framework and applied this model to other relationships and began to identify patterns in her life. The L-SISM identifies specific domains to facilitate awareness that enhances understanding of the client's cultural strengths, conceptualizes the client's concerns within his or her social-political context, facilitates the client's understanding of his or her values, and increases insight into cultural coping mechanisms.

Consistent with feminist therapy, the L-SISM suggests that we understand a client's distress from a culturally centered frame of reference. This allows for an acknowledgment of the systemic influences and an analysis of power dynamics in the client's life. As suggested by L-SISM, I attempted to depathologize her symptoms of sadness, feelings of loss and loneliness, and the loss of sense of self by helping her understand the impact her context, family of origin, and her responses had on her development. An analysis of power in her family revealed that although she felt powerless when her father would physically abuse her, she conversely felt powerful because she was the only one in her family who could protect her siblings, and she knew that her mother and siblings relied on her to provide for them. At this point, I knew we had *confianza;* therefore, I took a risk and I offered a cultural interpretation of how her father defied her values of *familismo* and *caballerismo.* I explained that unlike most men of that time, he did not provide for or protect his family and instead abused his power. She began to recognize that she missed her mother's *caricias* (caresses) and that she had not acknowledged the impact her father had on her development. She began to grieve the loss of a childhood she never had the opportunity to live.

Congruent with recommendations that Gallardo makes (Chapter 5, this volume), I elaborated on Julia's metaphor of identity (i.e., leaving the old Julia at the border) because it encompassed a loss of self and culture. Utilizing her metaphor enabled her to reconnect with the reasons she emigrated to the United States while further contextualizing her loss of power. She came to realize that she felt *tonta* (dumb) in the United States because she was not the highly esteemed professional she had been in Mexico. She realized that by immigrating, she lost her sense of purpose and needed to establish goals that were relevant to her identity and compatible with United States culture. We also addressed how her inability to speak English properly further demoralized her because it made her invisible in our society. Using this and other culturally related metaphors and *dichos* (Zuniga, 1992), she began to "recuperate" herself by contextualizing her feelings, given the many losses she had had throughout her life. She realized that the loss of power was connected to her loss of identity, which triggered feelings related to other unprocessed losses (e.g., no childhood, having parents who did not protect her, not feeling cared for by her family). By discussing past challenges and losses, she identified previous positive coping strategies and began to reconnect with aspects of her identity, such as being a *mujer de carácter fuerte* (woman of strong character) and enjoying the small things in life. She began to recognize aspects of her personality that were *cruzando la frontera* (crossing the border). By dissecting specific relationship issues in her current life, she learned to identify recurring themes and began to implement problem-solving skills and set limits with her siblings. I challenged her to consider that they are adults and that *familismo* and *respeto* extends to every member of the family, including her. We discussed her role in the family as an illusion of power that enabled her to maintain her self-esteem. I facilitated identification of her needs and had her role-play asking for support. It is important to note that she understood that the solidification of changes would happen outside therapy and would likely happen after therapy had terminated. That is why the notion of assisting clients in developing a personal blueprint of the needed changes (Chapter 5, this volume) is well suited to a brief therapy model. It enables therapists to empower clients and cultivate the idea that clients should be active agents of change, not passive recipients. It also dispels the myth that all change needs to happen in the therapy room. Instead, time can be devoted to planting seeds and giving clients the tools needed to problem solve.

Termination and Conclusion

Consistent with the L-SISM, I elicited feedback from Julia about the overall process. She acknowledged that talking about her family initially made her nervous because she loved her family in spite of how they hurt her. However, she stated that after she realized I understood her cultural worldview, values, and emotional connection to her family, she felt that I could accompany her and not judge her for being angry at her family. She stated that she felt validated, rather than selfish, when she saw how sad I was when she talked about not having a childhood and other traumatic events. She continued to support her siblings but also learned to take care of herself in the process. She set limits with them when she felt she was being taken advantage of, and she allowed her brother to try to provide support for her. Based on her cultural worldview, therapy was successful (Chapter 1, this volume). Julia "validated" the therapeutic utility of many of the skills identified by the L-SISM. Specifically, she identified many culturally congruent interventions (e.g., *personalismo*, *simpatia*, *charlar*, *respeto*, knowledge of her cultural worldview) as helpful. She expanded her feedback by stating that she felt secure with me because I was a professional, yet I allowed myself to be human and be touched by emotions. She noted specific times she felt I was accompanying her because she could see the sadness on my face. Her comment elicited an internal emotional response that I addressed by being transparent about the fact that she has overcome many challenging situations and that as another human being, it would be insensitive of me to not have a reaction. I also self-disclosed that I value personal integrity and authenticity and that I allow myself to experience emotions in therapy because it helps me understand the emotion in the room while appreciating the person sitting across from me. As we concluded our work, I conveyed that I learned a lot through our work together and enjoyed working with her.

References

American Psychological Association. (2006). Evidence-based practice in psychology. *American Psychologist, 61,* 271–285.

Bettendorf, S. K., & Fischer, A. R. (2009). Cultural strengths as moderators of the relationship between acculturation to the mainstream U.S. society and eating- and body-related concerns among Mexican American women. *Journal of Counseling Psychology, 56*(3), 430–440.

Bronfenbrenner, U. (1977). Toward an experimental ecology of human development. *American Psychologist, 32,* 513–531.

Bronfenbrenner, U. (1979). *The ecology of human development.* Cambridge, MA: Harvard University Press.

Bronfenbrenner, U. (1986). Ecology of the family as a context for human development: Research perspectives. *Developmental Psychology, 22,* 723–742.

Falicov, C. J. (1998). *Latino families in therapy: A guide to multicultural practice.* New York: Guilford Press.

Gil, R. M., & Vazquez, C. I. (1996). *The Maria paradox: How Latinas can merge old world traditions with new world self-esteem.* New York: Berkley.

Lopez-Baez, S. (1999). Marianismo. In J. S. Mio, J. E. Trimble, P. Arredondo, H. E. Cheatham, & D. Sue (Eds.), *Key words in multicultural interventions: A dictionary* (p. 183). Westport, CT: Greenwood.

McNeill, B. W., Prieto, L. R., Niemann, Y. F., Pizarro, M., Vera, E. M., & Gomez, A. P. (2001). Current directions in Chicana/o psychology. *The Counseling Psychologist, 29,* 5–17.

Miville, M. L., Romero, L., & Corpus, M. J. (2009). Incorporating affirming, feminist, and relational perspectives: The case of Juan. In M. E. Gallardo & B. W. McNeil (Eds.), *Intersections of multiple identities: A casebook of evidence-based practices with diverse populations* (pp. 175–201). New York: Routledge.

Santiago-Rivera, A. L., Arredondo, P., & Gallardo-Cooper, M. (2002). *Counseling Latinas/os and la familia: A practical guide.* Thousand Oaks, CA: Sage.

Sue, D. W., & Sue, D. (2003). *Counseling the culturally diverse: Theory and practice* (4th ed.). New York: John Wiley & Sons.

Teyber, E. (2000). *Interpersonal process in psychotherapy* (4th ed.). Belmont, CA: Wadsworth/Thomson Learning.

Zuniga, M. E. (1992). Using metaphors in therapy: Dichos and Latino clients. *Social Work, 37*(1), 55–60.

PART III

Culturally Adapted
Counseling Skills for
Asian Americans and
Pacific Islanders

8 Working With Asian American and Pacific Islander Clients

Interdependent and Indigenous Approaches to Counseling

Christine J. Yeh

Overview

Asian Americans and Pacific Islanders (AAPIs) are the fastest-growing racial group in the United States and constitute 4.3% (13.8 million) of the U.S. population (U.S. Census Bureau, n.d.). The estimated number of Pacific Islanders living in the United States in 2005 was 517,600 (U.S. Census Bureau, n.d.). From 2000 to 2005, the Pacific Islander population grew by 12%, while one of the fastest growing groups in the United States was the Asian population, with a 20% increase (U.S. Census Bureau, n.d.).

More than 69% of Asian Americans are foreign born, and 79% speak a language other than English at home (Reeves & Bennett, 2004), whereas only 42% of Pacific Islanders are foreign born because of the large numbers of Native Hawaiians counted in this group (Harris & Jones, 2005). AAPIs are an incredibly heterogeneous group composed of East Asians (i.e., China, Taiwan, Japan, Korea), Southeast Asians (i.e., Vietnam, Laos, Cambodia, Thailand), South Asians (i.e., India, Pakistan, Bangladesh, Sri Lanka, Nepal, Bhutan, the Maldives), Filipino/as (i.e., from the Philippines), and Pacific Islanders and Native Hawaiians (i.e., Hawaii, Samoa, Guam; Liu, Murakami, Eap, & Nagayama Hall, 2008).

AAPIs represent a heterogeneous racial group with 66 different documented ethnicities: 32 Asian and 34 Native Hawaiian or other Pacific Islanders (U.S. Census Bureau, n.d.). Each of these groups has complex histories associated with immigration, family composition, refugee status, socioeconomic status (SES), education level, and acculturation (Liu et al., 2008). In spite of these vast within-group differences, there are many shared cultural values and norms that unite AAPIs, especially the values of collectivism (Yee, DeBaryshe, Yuen, Kim, & McCubbin, 2006), that have strong relevance in how we connect with them in counseling or therapy. In this chapter, I discuss interdependent and indigenous approaches to counseling by introducing the Asian American Skills Identification Stage Model (AA-SISM). The AA-SISM incorporates specific cultural values, histories, and priorities while also focusing on six main areas of the SISM: connecting with clients, assessment, facilitating awareness, setting goals, taking action/instigating change, and feedback and accountability (see Table 8.1). I believe these approaches collectively will raise the bar in terms of our notions of counselor competence (Parham, 2004).

Connecting With Clients

It has been well established in the research and theoretical writings on AAPIs that as a racial group, there is strong emphasis placed on collectivism (a term used interchangeably with *interdependence*; Yeh, Carter, & Pieterse, 2004; Yeh & Hwang, 2000). Yee et al. (2006) identified four main cultural themes for AAPIs: collectivism, relational orientation, family obligation, and familism. Specifically, the notion of *collectivism* underscores how the needs of the family are prioritized above the needs of the self. *Relational orientation* refers to defining oneself in terms of relations to others. *Family obligations* refer to strong ties that connect children and parents emotionally, behaviorally, and physically. Finally, *familism* "defines the family system as the most important social group that is hierarchical and central for culture and society" (Yee, Su, Kim, & Yancura, 2008, p. 298). Hence, as a result of the values of collectivism, AAPI clients become flexible and adapt to the needs and expectations of important others (including family and extended family, social groups, surrounding community, and educational and occupational relations). Further, research has revealed that AAPI youth try to negotiate both familial and societal expectations (Fuligni et al., 1999).

Shifts in self also serve the purpose of maintaining harmony in personal and family relationships (Yeh & Hunter, 2004). Given the strong cultural emphasis on collectivism in AAPI culture, counselors need to also be flexible and adapt to the cultural paradigm presented by the client. The AA-SISM identifies shifts in counselors' assumptions about what constitutes effective counseling. For example, many counselors may highly value and prioritize the egocentricity of self, whereas many AAPI clients may feel uncomfortable with such an individualistic orientation. For example, a client may spend much of a counseling session talking about the burdens of family obligations. A counselor may wish to redirect the focus to the client's own needs and wishes. This may be hard for the AAPI client to initially imagine or discuss

Table 8.1   Asian American Skills Identification Stage Model (AA-SISM)

Connecting With Clients	Acknowledge importance of maintaining harmony, shame and stigma, shifting selves
	Explore stereotypes
	Normalize the counseling process
	Negotiate the counseling environment
	Demonstrate achieved and ascribed credibility
	Use gift giving
	Save face
Assessment	Assess self as embedded in larger social and cultural context
	Examine influence of political history, acculturation, SES, immigration
	Conduct family and community genogram
	Explore holistic view of health, spirituality
	Examine complexity of language and translation issues
	Investigate preferred collectivistic coping styles
Facilitating Awareness	Reduce shame associated with emotionality
	Use creative approaches of deepening insight
	Explore reciprocity in client's social systems
Setting Goals	Develop collaborative goals with client's social systems
	Understand who is involved in the decision-making process
Instigating Change	Facilitate counselor and client change
	Negotiate changes at multiple systemic levels—ripple effect
	Facilitate consciousness raising and giving voice
	Examine role of fatalism and external locus of control
	Understand client's conceptualization of the healing process
Feedback/ Accountability	Use metaphors, storytelling, and written feedback
	Reframe the notion of feedback, practice
	Do not assume client will initiate the feedback process
	Structure the feedback routine
	Involve important others in client's social systems

due to the core values described above. Rather, using the AA-SISM approach, counselors may connect with their AAPI clients by listening to and appreciating their stories about their deeply rooted family obligations.

To suggest that AAPIs are only collectivistic is oversimplifying the diversity of their experiences and does not account for the complex blend of multiple social identities that influence their interactions (Chen, 2008). Specifically,

AAPIs belong to many social groups that are context dependent, including gender, religious affiliation, and sexual orientation, and they present themselves differently depending on the social setting (Chen, 2008; Yeh & Hunter, 2004). Depending on the setting, some identities may be more salient than others (Kwan, 2005). Hence, autonomous thinking and assertiveness may be culturally relevant in some domains but not others (Lewis-Fernandez & Kleinman, 1994; Rosenberger, 1992). Counselors need to be cognizant of how the nature of collectivism may, in fact, warrant situationally sanctioned moments of rugged individualism (Lin, 1988).

When making connections with AAPI clients, there are many important factors to consider. In particular, I recommend the following: Question your own assumptions and biases (Yeh & Pituc, 2008); understand and appreciate the role of cultural stigma and shame; demonstrate cultural credibility; negotiate what counseling looks like with the client; and offer a flexible and collaborative model of counseling in terms of the location and length of the visit.

The model minority stereotype and the great disparities in mental health care use among AAPIs have contributed to an inaccurate assumption that this racial group is free of stress and mental health concerns. Specifically, although there are many AAPIs who are academically and occupationally successful, many Asian ethnic groups are at great risk for serious social and psychological problems, such as poverty (Le, 2007; U.S. Census Bureau, n.d.), violence, depression, and suicide (Leong, Leach, Yeh, & Chou, 2007; Singh & Miller, 2004). For example, Asian immigrants aged 14 to 24 have higher suicide rates than whites, blacks, and Latinas/os, 18% of Asian immigrants live below the poverty line (U.S. Census Bureau, 2000), and Asian immigrant youth are found to be three times more likely to report depression (Schoen, Davis, & DesRoches, 1998; Schoen, Davis, & Scott Collins, 1997) than their black and white counterparts and experience racism, poverty-related stress, and alienation (Yeh, Kim, Pituc, & Atkins, 2008). AAPIs use counseling services less than their African American, Latino/a American, and white American counterparts and present with the highest levels of psychological distress at intake (Kearney, Draper, & Baron, 2005). Research has also found that even when faced with trauma and loss, AAPIs tend to avoid mental health services (e.g., Inman, Yeh, Madan-Bahel, & Nath 2007; Yeh, Inman, Kim, & Okubo, 2006). According to the National Latino and Asian American study), these statistics differ depending on generation and acculturation level, with more recent immigrants being less likely to seek professional mental health services (Abe-Kim et al., 2007). As a counselor, it is important to be aware of potential stereotypes and biases you may have about AAPIs (e.g., the client likely has concerns related to academic achievement) and be open to a variety of presenting concerns (e.g., racism, poverty, suicidality, sexuality, depression, acculturative stress).

Cultural stigmas may help to partially explain the low mental health utilization rates among AAPIs. For AAPIs, revealing personal problems traditionally only occurs within the bounds of the family and a close network of culturally similar friends (Uba, 1994). Sharing beyond these cultural in-groups is viewed as shameful and may reflect unfavorably on the family name and lineage. Specifically, in many Asian cultures, the notion of saving face is critical (D. Sue & Sue, 1987). According to Lewis-Fernandez and Kleinman (1994),

> [*face* is] an embodiment of social power that represents one's moral capital and one's prestige in the interpersonal field. To lose face is to lose one's ability to engage in reciprocal affective relationships guided by moral norms involving *renqing* (favor based on moral feelings); it is to be demoralized, bereft of *qi* (vital force), and quite literally faceless, unable to look directly at others. (p. 69)

Hence, when connecting with the client, the counselor must shift from primarily focusing on uncovering and revealing the emotional nature of self and instead protect the self from shame while also understanding the context in which the self is embedded.

Shame and stigma influence whether or not AAPIs go to counseling, how long they stay in counseling, and how they present their personal concerns. When AAPIs do engage in counseling, they have a tendency to terminate prematurely (Uba, 1994), primarily because they have had a shame-inducing experience. Since AAPIs also tend to wait until they are in a crisis to come to counseling (Lee, 1997), the initial connection becomes especially important in determining a client's commitment to counseling.

One way to decrease shame and build connections with AAPI clients is to establish ascribed and achieved credibility (S. Sue & Zane, 1987) as a way of building trust. Premature termination of therapy is not only a product of cultural shame, but intertwined with notions of cultural credibility. Sue and Zane assert that "lack of ascribed credibility (position or role assigned by others) may be the primary reason for underutilization of therapy, whereas the lack of achieved credibility (related to the counselor's skills) may better explain premature termination" (pp. 40–41). According to Lee (1997), establishing credibility involves using professional titles (such as Dr.); displaying diplomas and relevant certifications; and demonstrating confidence, maturity, and professionalism. Such displays of ascribed credibility decrease shame and offer hope to the client. Achieved credibility may be accomplished by conceptualizing the problem in a way that is congruent with Asian culture and by offering a "gift" (or direct benefit from treatment) to the client in the first session (S. Sue & Zane, 1987).

In the context of collectivism, the notion of gift giving is especially pertinent because many Asian cultures use this ritual to symbolize the importance and value of a relationship. Gifts are needed immediately when connecting with clients because AAPIs are often skeptical of Western forms of treatment. Gifts may include alleviating or reducing symptoms of depression or anxiety or offering a coherent explanation for a current crisis (S. Sue & Zane, 1987). In the context of our current model, gift giving is recommended as part of establishing connection, rapport, and trust. The gift in Asian culture also represents a commitment between two people, so by giving a gift to a client, you have also established a reciprocal obligation. Moreover, we recommend being explicit about giving something to the client, so that he or she may cognitively process this symbolic cultural gesture as part of formal relationship building.

The high priority of connecting with clients helps to provide a framework for how the initial sessions may look. Specifically, many AAPI clients are not familiar with the notion of counseling and may be embarrassed to ask questions about the counselor's role. To save face for the client, it is important to normalize the counseling process in a nonjudgmental way and to explain how counseling works. Initial sessions may also be longer than the typical 50-minute session, may involve the use of an interpreter, and may take place in the client's home or community. Although there is no set rule for what the sessions are like, it is important for the counselor to be flexible and adaptable in providing culturally congruent counseling. Moreover, verbal expression of feelings is just one way to make a connection. Some Asian clients may feel less shame if creative approaches to counseling are used, such as storytelling and drawing (Yeh & Huang, 1996).

Assessment

Racial biases have long been recognized in psychological assessment tools and diagnostic techniques (Malgady, 1996; Pavkov, Lewis, & Lyons, 1989; S. Sue, 1999; Thakker & Ward, 1998) and in particular with Asian and AAPI populations (Lewis-Fernandez & Kleinman, 1994; Yeh, 2000). Of particular concern in the AA-SISM is the emphasis on the individual's verbal articulation of cognitive, affective, and behavioral states; mind-body dualism; and the assumption of "culture as an arbitrary superimposition on a knowable biological reality" in current psychiatric assessments (Lewis-Fernandez & Kleinman, 1994, p. 67). Similarly, the importance of immigration status, generation, SES, spirituality, and cultural and familial context are largely ignored.

When doing an assessment with AAPI clients, counselors need to shift from the assumption that the self is a self-contained entity, composed of a unique configuration of internal characteristics that determine affect and behavior (Markus & Kitayama, 1991), and make an assessment from a multicultural and ecological worldview (Yeh & Kwan, 2009). Such a shift in perspective entails assessing family, peer, school, community, and cultural interactions. It also involves incorporating culturally valid aspects of the client's context and integrating a holistic perspective of health. D. W. Sue and Sue (2003) assert that assessments may include the family and community context. For example, a counselor may inquire, "How does your family see the problem" (p. 331)?

Assessments not only provide counselors with important background information, but they also have the potential to offer an avenue for clients to share their stories and feel validated and connected. For example, in Ecological Asset Mapping (Borrero & Yeh, in press), clients are asked to discuss their cultural and community strengths in the contexts of the various systems in which they interact. Given the within-group heterogeneity of AAPIs, assessing beyond just inquiring about individual symptomatology and standard intake information is especially pertinent (Lee, 1997). For example, to better understand familial dynamics, relationships, and multigenerational value systems, genograms are an effective tool in multicultural counseling (Adachi Sueyoshi, Rivera, & Ponterotto, 2001).

Genograms are especially useful because they encourage family participation (McGoldrick & Gerson,1985), are graphic and rely less on verbal articulation, and present information in an organized and structured format, which may be perceived by clients as a "gift." (Adachi Sueyoshi et al. 2001). Genograms may also reveal information about important extended family members, immigration stories, language use, acculturation, and how to deal with family ghosts (McGoldrick, 1998, 2004). The use of community genograms is also encouraged, which offer the wider context of community and culture (Rigazio-DiGilio, Ivey, Grady, & Kunkler-Peck, 2005).

AAPIs also include many refugee populations, in particular, the Hmong and Vietnamese. When working with Asian refugee clients, the context of the refugee experience is also critical in addition to familial, social, and community information. According to Prendes-Lintel's (2001) working model for counseling recent refugees, assessments should include inquiry about the history of the war experience, refugee experience, the first asylum, and the goodness of fit between refugee and community of resettlement. Given the traumatic nature of some of these experiences, counselors need to use their clinical judgment to gauge how to best time these questions so clients do not feel overwhelmed.

Traditional models of counseling, which highlight a strict dichotomy between the mind and body, have pathologized AAPI mental health patterns (Brislin, 1993). An alternative perspective, inclusive of Asian beliefs (Uba, 1994), conceptualizes healing from a holistic approach in which the mind, body, spirit, and universe are well integrated into one force (Yeh, Hunter, Madan-Bahel, Chiang, & Kwong, 2004). Given the mind-body connection in Asian cultures, the counselor needs to shift to a similar framework and take notice of the client's nonverbal cues, use of silence, gestures, changes in tone, and physical expressions (D. W. Sue & Sue, 2003). For example, for many Chinese American clients, a state of health exists when equilibrium is achieved between bodily functions and emotions, whereas illness refers to an imbalance in the system (Yeh, 2000). To interpret physical symptoms only as somatic manifestations of underlying emotional distress is to negate the legitimacy of cultural patterns of expressing emotion. Moreover, AAPIs are often characterized as alexythymic (unable to express affective states) when counselors attend to material that is primarily emotional versus symbolic or metaphoric (Yeh, 2000). In fact, for many AAPIs, expressing emotions may be viewed as a sign of weakness, and expressing physical symptoms is more socially acceptable (Leong, 1986). In addition, many English words used to express affective states do not exist in many Asian languages. Hence, counselors may need to shift their assessments to focus less on direct questions about emotions ("How are you feeling?") to more open questions ("Show me where you are experiencing that.").

Counselors should also consider the importance of spirituality and religion in their assessments of AAPI clients. For example, many Asian philosophical traditions emphasize fatalism, or the belief that things happen for a reason. Such a perspective encourages an external locus of control, a faith in a higher power, and a deep concern for meaning. These beliefs are in stark contrast to many of the values of Western approaches to counseling, which highlight an internal locus of control, autonomous decision making, and assertiveness (D. W. Sue & Sue, 2003). For example, Yeh, Inman, et al. (2006) explored the coping practices of AAPI family members who lost a relative in the 9/11 attacks and found that most of the participants exhibited fatalistic beliefs ("This was in God's hands," "It was part of a natural order"), and all but one participant reported an increase in religious activity, such as going to church and praying. When working with AAPI clients with fatalistic beliefs, counselors may need to shift from an egocentric view of self (What can we do to make you feel better? What action can you take to be in control of your life?) to a perspective that enables clients to explore the deeper meaning of an experience.

The findings from the 9/11 study are just one example of how AAPIs may cope with stress in culturally specific ways. Yeh, Arora, and Wu (2006) refer to this as collectivistic coping and include the use of indigenous healers, support from elders, intracultural coping, forbearance, fatalism, and family support. Assessments of AAPI clients may also include an understanding of their preferred coping styles as well as their preferences for indigenous practices and traditional medicine (Yeh & Kwong, 2008). Heppner et al. (2006) published a scale normed on 3,000 Taiwanese adults that measures several aspects of collectivist coping, including acceptance, family coping, religion and spirituality, avoidance and detachment, and private emotional outlets.

How clients express pain, or the meaning they make of events, is largely connected to the language that they use. Recent statistics indicate that in large metropolitan areas such as New York City, 96% of Asian Americans are immigrants or children of immigrants (Coalition for Asian American Children & Families, n.d.). Hence, it is likely that if you are not fluent in your client's preferred language you will need to use an interpreter at some point in your assessment. Even for clients who have learned to speak English, using phrases and words from their native language may offer important cultural insights, meanings, beliefs, and traditions (Yeh &

Inman, 2007). Moreover, there are many emotion words in other languages that have no accurate translation in English, which can pose challenges for counselors when trying to understand their clients. For example, Yeh and Inman discuss the complex meaning of certain words.

In Hindi, the word *mann* is often used interchangeably to refer to heart, mind, consciousness, and soul. Thus the phrase, "*mann nahi karta*" can mean "I don't feel like it because I am not interested," "my heart is not in it because of feeling sad," or "I am bored because I have nothing to do." Thus, in understanding the relevance of the phrase "*mann nahi karta*" it became relevant for us to consider the personal context within which it was being discussed. (p. 381)

Facilitating Awareness

A critical aspect of the AA-SISM is providing culturally relevant opportunities to facilitate client insight and awareness of the multiple forces that shape their physical, spiritual, and psychological experiences. Such forces may include interpersonal relationships, family dynamics, community and cultural contexts, racial histories, political climate, and personal values and beliefs. Helping clients understand how their lives are embedded within and across these various ecological social systems (Bronfenbrenner, 1979), and how these social systems interact reciprocally as acculturative contexts, offers a culturally meaningful lens for facilitating awareness. For example, after the Vietnam War, there was a large exodus of refugees from Vietnam, Cambodia, and Laos to the United States between 1975 and 1978. During this time, many families were separated and they faced drastic changes in cultural practices, poverty, and racism (Liu et al., 2008).

Data gathered from the assessment process can help to facilitate client awareness. Counselors may ask AAPI clients to discuss how environmental and interpersonal contexts shape their feelings and beliefs about race and ethnicity. This may be challenging for some AAPI clients who feel embarrassed about self-disclosure and discussing mental health concerns (Zhang, Snowden, & Sue, 1998). Given issues related to saving face and cultural shame, it will be important to offer multiple avenues for self-expression. Because some AAPIs may feel more comfortable using creative outlets for self-expression (Yeh & Huang, 1996; Yeh & Inose, 2002), counselors may use poetry, stories, or visual images such as photos and film clips to promote sharing and discussion. Perhaps through multiple avenues, clients can feel heard and understood by the counselor.

Because expression of emotion could potentially induce shame for many AAPIs, counselors must find ways to culturally adapt in their interactions with clients. For example, D. W. Sue and Sue (2003) suggest that if a client displays discomfort, the counselor should respond in an indirect manner and could say, "This situation would make someone uncomfortable" rather than, "You look uncomfortable" (p. 334). To facilitate client awareness, counselors must be flexible in their expectations of clients' comfort level, self-disclosure style (Gallardo, 2006), and willingness to introspect. According to Parham (2002), facilitating awareness involves assisting clients in understanding the impact of their past, present, and future life events and how their life stories influence their future actions. In order for clients to feel heard and understood, counselors must recognize the malleable and dynamic nature of AAPI identities and how they shift across relational and cultural domains (Yeh & Hwang, 2000).

Setting Goals

For many ethnic minority communities, and for AAPIs in particular, setting goals must be a collaborative process that may involve important others, family members, and people in the community. Because of the strong cultural emphasis on group cohesion, interpersonal relationships, and situated cultural identities, goals must be understood ecologically. Many AAPI clients may not feel comfortable articulating specific, individual goals for counseling and may prefer a clear directive plan with homework and specific instructions (S. Sue & Zane, 1987). Using the AA-SISM, we focus on priorities and considerations for goal setting with AAPI clients.

Counselors need to investigate how individual goals reciprocally impact the multiple systems in which AAPIs interact. How are decisions, priorities, and motivations shaped by others' involvement? What is the client's system of decision making, and who is involved in this process? Although many traditional forms of counseling highlight autonomous choice and individuation (D. W. Sue & Sue, 2003), the critical role of interdependence in the context of goal setting must be considered and must not be pathologized (Yeh & Hwang, 2000). It is especially critical, when setting goals, that the counselor be aware of potential biases regarding what constitutes a psychologically healthy goal.

For example, a young South Asian male college student may wish to temporarily drop out of school in order to help with the family business. Some counselors may feel strongly that a goal of the client's should be to stay in school and let the parents know he wants to live his own life, whereas the client and his family and extended family may see this as a family decision that reveals the client's personal maturity, filial duty, and a concern for helping the community. It is important, in this example, for both counselor and client to see both sides of the story and to see how the decision is situated in the larger cultural and familial context. Given the importance of incorporating meaningful contexts, counselors may ask the client, "How would achieving the different goals affect you, your family, friends, and social community" (D. W. Sue & Sue, 2003, p. 331)?

Taking Action/Instigating Change

For change to be effective in the therapeutic process, it must occur within the counselor as well as the client. Counselors must help to create ongoing conditions that foster positive change and growth while simultaneously making cultural shifts in the therapeutic alliance. When counselors are able to see and understand clients' goals as culturally situated, and they are able to facilitate awareness in the client, they must find ways to translate this process into change. For the AA-SISM, creating change in AAPI clients automatically has a ripple effect in the clients' social systems; taking action must be conceptualized holistically. Who is involved in this process of change? How can we foster collaborative changes?

In order to follow through in treatment with AAPI clients using the AA-SISM, counselors must be willing to change in a way that is culturally meaningful. AAPI clients typically do not have a strong focus on internal locus of control (D. W. Sue & Sue, 2003), so they may not feel they have the power or ability to change. In addition, many AAPIs have a strong belief in fatalism and often believe that things happen for a reason (Yeh, Arora, et al., 2006; Yeh, Inman, et al., 2006; Yeh & Kwong, 2008). AAPI clients may need to be educated about how to instigate change and their personal role in change. Similarly, the counselor needs to continue to be in close touch with her or his biases. Is she or he trying to initiate change for a client who is not ready?

Initiating client change can often induce shame among AAPI clients, and counselors may consider reframing this facilitative process. For example, Lee (1997) suggests that counselors may wish to use cultural terms to articulate client goals. If an AAPI male client who is a recent immigrant from Korea and a parent has a goal of addressing intergenerational conflict with his second-generation daughter, the counselor may frame the issue in terms of "making sacrifices to help children succeed in life" versus "compromising cultural traditions and traditional male parenting roles." By reconceptualizing and reframing client goals, the counselor may reduce embarrassment and foster greater compliance.

AAPI clients who live in poverty, such as many in the Samoan community, tend to think about taking action in terms of giving back to the next generation or making sure the younger generation does not also have to suffer (Borrero, Yeh, Tito, & Luavasa, 2010). This commitment to cultural generativity—or the passing along of cultural values and assets to the next generation—is commonly found in the Samoan community and a natural expression of their relational orientation (Borrero et al., 2010).

Counselors must seek to understand the client's conceptualization of healing. For example, in traditional Chinese medicine, healing is achieved when there is a balance in energies, or *qi*, within and outside the client. Other forms of healing, such as pranic healing, involve various natural forces (air, sun, ground, water, trees; Yeh, Arora, et al., 2006). Because change is meaningful at multiple levels for many AAPIs, counselors may seek to collaborate with indigenous healers and community leaders, as well as various stakeholders in the client's life, to increase opportunities for growth.

Feedback/Accountability

Throughout the counseling process, when using the AA-SISM it is important to continually assess whether we are making a meaningful difference to the client. In essence, counselors must be culturally accountable for the work they are doing with AAPI clients because it potentially shapes the lives of family members and important others.

Issues of accountability with AAPI clients may be complex at times because many AAPIs may not feel comfortable confronting or challenging the counselor if things are not going well. To this end, counselors need to be flexible in how they assess client progress and use creative outlets for evaluation such as metaphors, storytelling, and written feedback. For example, for AAPIs who are uncomfortable with direct communication, using a third party (such as a family member, community leader, or doctor) to communicate emotionally difficult material may be warranted. When using these additional resources, it is important to build trust and to offer avenues for critical feedback (offer words, phrases, suggestions).

In addition, counselors must always consider ways in which to be adaptive with AAPI clients. How can we restructure the process of accountability so it is culturally meaningful? Considering that confronting an authority figure is deemed disrespectful in many Asian cultures, the counselor may wish to frame the process of evaluation as "helping build trust and growth in the counselor" versus "are your needs being met?"

To encourage and facilitate ongoing and open feedback with AAPI clients, counselors should consider structuring the process, rather than waiting for the client to initiate it. For example, some counselors may state, "Please feel free to let me know whenever you have concerns about the counseling process." Although such a statement may be helpful to many clients, it does place the onus of responsibility on the client. For a client who is not familiar with counseling, it also may be too ambiguous. S. Sue (1998) emphasizes the importance of imposing structure and direction with many AAPI clients. For example, a counselor may wish to have a specific time allocated for feedback, such as the last 10 minutes of each session, and practice various ways in which feedback may be delivered and discussed (interview questions, written comments, quick survey, etc.). Alternatively, the counselor may assign the feedback as homework for the client.

Finally, in keeping with the strong emphasis on the relational orientation and collectivism among AAPIs, feedback may involve many people in the client's life, such as elders in the community, family members, and important relations. For example, in the Samoan community in San Francisco, elders are often asked to serve as a liaison for many different families and youth, to help bridge cultural and generational differences (Borrero et al., 2010). The counselor may ask the client whether his or her friends or family members have noticed any changes in the client's behavior, actions, beliefs, energy, spirit, and physical presence. If it is uncomfortable for the counselor to directly ask for feedback from the client, then he or she must be open to the various sources of feedback and make efforts to incorporate it in a culturally meaningful way.

References

Abe-Kim, J., Takeuchi, D. T., Hong, S., Zane, N., Sue, S., Spencer, M. S., et al. M. (2007). Use of mental health-related services among immigrant and U.S.-born Asian Americans: Results from the National Latina/o and Asian American Study. *American Journal of Public Health, 97*(1), 91–98.

Adachi Sueyoshi, L., Rivera, L., & Ponterotto, J. G. (2001). The family genogram as a tool in multicultural career counseling. In J. G. Ponterotto, J. M. Casas, L. A. Suzuki, & C. M. Alexander (Eds.), *Handbook of multicultural counseling* (2nd ed. pp. 655–672). Thousand Oaks, CA: Sage.

Borrero, N. E., & Yeh, C. J. (in press). Social class and school counseling: A collaborative asset-based approach. In W. M. Liu (Ed.), *The Oxford handbook of social class in counseling psychology.* New York: Oxford University Press.

Borrero, N. E., Yeh, C. J., Tito, P., & Luavasa, M. (2010). Alone and in between cultural worlds: Voices from Samoan students. *Journal of Education, 190*(3), 47–56.

Brislin, R. (1993). *Understanding culture's influence on behavior.* Fort Worth, TX: Harcourt Brace Jovanovich.

Chen, G. (2008). Managing multiple social identities. In N. Tewari & A. Alvarez (Ed.), *Asian American psychology: Current perspectives* (pp. 173–192). New York: Taylor & Francis.

Coalition for Asian American Children & Families. (n.d.). *Myths and facts.* Retrieved May 12, 2011, from http://www.cacf.org/resources_mythsfacts.html

Fuligni, A. J., Burton, L., Marshall, S., Perez-Febles, A., Yarrington, J., Kirsh, L. B., et al. (1999). Attitudes towards family obligations among American adolescents with Asian, Latin American, and European American backgrounds. *Child Development, 70,* 1030–1044.

Gallardo, M. E. (2006). Self-disclosure. In Y. Jackson (Ed.), *Encyclopedia of multicultural psychology* (pp. 418–420). Thousand Oaks, CA: Sage.

Harris, P. M., & Jones, N. A. (2005). *We the people: Pacific Islanders in the United States.* Census 2000 Special Report, CENSR-26. Retrieved May 12, 2011, from http://www.census.gov/prod/2005pubs/censr-26.pdf

Heppner, P. P., Heppner, M. J., Lee, D., Wang, Y., Park, H., & Wang, L. (2006). Development and validation of a collectivist coping styles inventory. *Journal of Counseling Psychology, 53,* 107–125.

Inman, A. G., Yeh, C. J., Madan-Bahel, A., & Nath, S. (2007). South Asian families: bereavement and coping post-9/11. *Journal of Multicultural Counseling and Development, 35,* 101–115.

Kearney, L. K., Draper, M., & Baron, A. (2005). Counseling utilization by ethnic minority college students. *Cultural Diversity and Ethnic Minority Psychology, 11*(3), 272–285.

Kwan, K.-L. K. (2005). Racial salience: Conceptual dimensions and implications for racial identity development. In R. Carter (Ed.), *Handbook of racial-cultural psychology* (pp. 115–131). New York: John Wiley & Sons.

Le, C. N. (2011). *Socioeconomic statistics and demographics.* Retrieved May 12, 2011, from http://www.asian-nation.org/demographics.shtml

Lee, S. (1997). Communication styles of Wind River Native American clients and the therapeutic approaches of their clinicians. *Smith College Studies in Social Work, 68*(1), 57–81.

Leong, F. T. L. (1986). Counseling and psychotherapy with AAPIs: Review of the literature. *Journal of Counseling Psychology, 33,* 196–206.

Leong, F. T. L., Leach, M., Yeh, C. J., & Chou, E. (2007). Suicide among Asian Americans: What do we know? What do we need to know? *Death Studies, 31*(5), 417–434.

Lewis-Fernandez, R., & Kleinman, A. (1994). Culture, personality and psychopathology. *Journal of Abnormal Psychology, 103,* 67–71.

Lin, N. (1988). Chinese family structure and Chinese society. Bulletin of the Institute of Ethnology. *Academia Sinicia, 65,* 59–129.

Liu, C. H., Murakami, J., Eap, S., & Nagayama Hall, G. C. (2008). Who are Asian Americans? An overview of history, immigration, and communities. In N. Tewari & A. N. Alvarez (Eds.), *Asian American psychology: Current perspectives* (pp. 1–29). New York: Taylor & Francis.

Malgady, R. G. (1996). The question of cultural bias in assessment and diagnosis of ethnic minority clients: Let's reject the null hypothesis. *Professional Psychology: Research and Practice, 27,* 73–77.

Markus, H. R., & Kitayama, S. (1991). Culture and the self: Implications for cognition, emotion, and motivation. *Psychological Review, 98,* 224–253.

McGoldrick, M. (1998). Introduction: Re-visioning family therapy through a cultural lens. In M. McGoldrick (Ed.), *Revisioning family therapy: Race, culture, and gender in clinical practice* (pp. 3–19). New York: Guilford Press.

McGoldrick, M. (2004). Echoes from the past: Helping families deal with their ghosts. In F. Walsh & M. McGoldrick (Eds.), *Living beyond loss* (2nd ed., pp. 310–339). New York: W. W. Norton.

McGoldrick, M., & Gerson, R. (1985). *Genograms in family assessment.* New York: W. W. Norton.

Parham, T. A. (Ed.). (2002). *Counseling persons of African descent: Raising the bar of practitioner competence.* Thousand Oaks, CA: Sage.

Parham, T. A. (2004). Raising the bar on what passes for competence. *The California Psychologist, 37*(6), 20–21.

Pavkov, T. W., Lewis, D. A., & Lyons, J. S. (1989). Psychiatric diagnosis and racial bias: An empirical investigation. *Professional Psychology: Research and Practice, 20,* 364–368.

Prendes-Lintel, M. (2001). A working model in counseling recent refugees. In J. G. Ponterotto, J. M. Casas, L. A. Suzuki, & C. M. Alexander (Eds.), *Handbook of multicultural counseling* (2nd ed., pp. 729–752). Thousand Oaks, CA: Sage.

Reeves, T. J., & Bennett, C. E. (2004, December). *We the people: Asians in the United States*. Census 2000 Special Report, CENSR-17, Retrieved May 12, 2011, from http://www.census.gov/prod/2004pubs/censr-17.pdf

Rigazio-DiGilio, S. A., Ivey, A. E., Grady, L. T., & Kunkler-Peck, K. P. (2005). *Community genograms: Using individual, family, and cultural narratives with clients*. New York: Teachers College Press.

Rosenberger, N. R. (1992). *Japanese sense of self*. Cambridge UK: Cambridge University Press.

Schoen, C. A., Davis, K., & DesRoches, C. (1998). *The health of adolescent boys: Commonwealth Fund Survey findings*. Retrieved May 12, 2011, from http://www.cmwf.org/publications/publications_show.htm?doc_id=221410

Schoen, C., Davis, K., & Scott Collins, K. (1997). *The Commonwealth Fund Survey of the health of adolescent girls*. Retrieved May 12, 2011, from http://www.cmwf.org/publications/publications_show.htm?doc_id=221230

Singh, G. K., & Miller, B. A. (2004). Health, life expectancy, and mortality patterns among immigrant populations in the United States. *Canadian Journal of Public Health, 95*(3), 114–121.

Sue, D. W., & Sue, D. (2003). *Counseling the culturally diverse: Theory and practice* (4th ed.). New York: John Wiley & Sons.

Sue, D., & Sue, S. (1987). Cultural factors in the clinical assessment of AAPIs. *Journal of Consulting and Clinical Psychology, 55*, 479–487.

Sue, S. (1998). In search of cultural competence in psychotherapy and counseling. *American Psychologist, 53*, 440–448.

Sue, S. (1999). Science, ethnicity, and bias: Where have we gone wrong? *American Psychologist, 54*, 1070–1077.

Sue, S., & Zane, N. (1987). The role of culture and cultural techniques in psychotherapy. *American Psychologist, 42*, 37–45.

Thakker, J., & Ward, T. (1998). Culture and classification: The cross-cultural application of the DSM-IV. *Clinical Psychology Review, 18*, 501–529.

Uba, L. (1994). *Asian-Americans: Personality patterns, identity, and mental health*. New York: Guilford Press.

U.S. Census Bureau. (2003). *Poverty: 1999*. Retrieved May 12, 2011, from http://www.census.gov/prod/2003pubs/c2kbr-19.pdf

U.S. Census Bureau. (n.d.). *National population estimates: National sex, age, race and Hispanic origin*. Retrieved May 12, 2011, from http://www.census.gov/popest/national/asrh/NC-EST2005-asrh.html

Yee, B. W., DeBaryshe, B., Yuen, S., Kim, S. Y., & McCubbin, H. (2006). Asian American and Pacific Islander families: Resiliency and life-span socialization in a cultural context. In F. T. L. Leong, A. G. Inman, A. Ebreo, L. H. Yang, L. Kinoshita, & M. Fu (Eds.), *Handbook of Asian American psychology* (2nd ed., pp. 69–86). Thousand Oaks, CA: Sage.

Yee, B. W., Su, J., Kim, Y., & Yancura, L. (2008). Asian American and Pacific Islander families. In N. Tewari & A. Alvarez (Eds.), *Asian American psychology: Current perspectives* (pp. 295–315). New York: Taylor & Francis.

Yeh, C. J. (2000). Depathologizing Asian-American perspectives of health and healing. *AAPI and Pacific Islander Journal of Health, 8*, 138–149.

Yeh, C. J., Arora, A. K., & Wu, K. (2006). A new theoretical model of collectivistic coping. In P. T. P. Wong & C. J. Wong (Eds.), *Handbook of multicultural perspectives on stress and coping* (pp. 55–72). New York: Springer.

Yeh, C. J., Carter, R. T., & Pieterse, A. L. (2004). Cultural values and racial identity attitudes among AAPI students: An exploratory investigation. *Counseling and Values, 48,* 82–95.

Yeh, C. J., & Huang, K. (1996). The collectivistic nature of ethnic identity development among Asian-American college students. *Adolescence, 31,* 645–661.

Yeh, C. J., & Hunter, C. D. (2004). The socialization of self: Understanding shifting and multiple selves across cultures. In R. T. Carter (Ed.), *Handbook on racial-cultural psychology* (pp. 78–93). New York: John Wiley & Sons.

Yeh, C. J., Hunter, C. D., Madan-Bahel, A., Chiang, L., & Kwong, A. (2004). Indigenous and interdependent perspectives of healing: Implications for counseling and research. *Journal of Counseling and Development, 82,* 410–419.

Yeh, C. J., & Hwang, M. (2000). Interdependence in ethnic identity and self: Implications for theory and practice. *Journal of Counseling and Development, 78,* 420–429.

Yeh, C. J., & Inman, A. G. (2007). Qualitative data analysis and interpretation in counseling psychology: Strategies for best practices. *The Counseling Psychologist, 35,* 369–403.

Yeh, C. J., Inman, A., Kim, A. B., & Okubo, Y. (2006). Asian American collectivistic coping in response to 9/11. *Cultural Diversity and Ethnic Minority Psychology, 12,* 134–148.

Yeh, C. J., & Inose, M. (2002). Difficulties and coping strategies of Chinese, Japanese, and Korean Immigrant students. *Adolescence, 37*(145), 69–82.

Yeh, C. J., Kim, A. B., Pituc, S. T., & Atkins, M. (2008). Poverty, loss, and resilience: The story of Asian immigrant youth. *Journal of Counseling Psychology, 55,* 34–48.

Yeh, C. J., & Kwan, K-L. K. (2009). Advances in multicultural assessment and counseling with adolescents: Community, ecological, and social justice approaches. In J. G. Ponterroto, J. M. Casas, L. A. Suzuki, & C. M. Alexander (Eds.), *Handbook of multicultural counseling* (3rd ed., 637–647). Thousand Oaks, CA: Sage.

Yeh, C. J., & Kwong, A. K. (2008). Asian American indigenous healing. In N. Tewari & A. Alvarez (Eds.), *Asian American psychology: Current perspectives* (pp. 561–575). New York: Taylor & Francis.

Yeh, C. J., & Pituc, S. T. (2008). Understanding yourself as a school counselor. In H. L. K. Coleman & C. J. Yeh (Eds.), *Handbook of school counseling* (pp. 63–78). Mahwah, NJ: Lawrence Erlbaum.

Zhang, A. Y., Snowden, L. R., & Sue, S. (1998). Differences between Asian and white Americans' help-seeking and utilization patterns in the Los Angeles area. *Journal of Community Psychology, 26,* 317–326.

9 Case Illustration: Culturally Adaptive Model of Counseling

Using a Multicultural Skills-Based Perspective in Working With a First-Generation Asian Indian American Elderly Female

Nita Tewari

Arpana Inman

In this chapter, we present and discuss the case of a first-generation Asian Indian American older female as a model for using the AA-SISM. We begin with a description of the case study, then we discuss the application of the AA-SISM for this particular client. The chapter is presented in dialogue format so that the psychologist and client voices are highlighted in this multicultural skills-based perspective.

Case Study

Mrs. Shah is a 71-year-old, married, Asian Indian, first-generation immigrant Hindu female. Having had an arranged marriage, in the 1960s she came to the United States from India with her husband, under the 1965 Immigration and Naturalization Act. The majority of the client's family of origin has remained in India. She travels to India every four years to see her siblings and relatives. She has two American-born children and three grandchildren also born in America. All live within close proximity to her.

Mrs. Shah has been a housewife for most of her married life and lives with her husband, whom she describes as a "workaholic" whom will never retire. She has had some college education.

Mrs. Shah is connected to a local senior center, where she attends yoga classes with a few of her friends. Mrs. Shah's friends have been increasingly concerned about her psychological and physical well-being because she spends most of her time alone due to her husband's work schedule. Over the past year, Mrs. Shah has had significant health issues, including diabetes, episodes of unconsciousness, and low iron levels in her blood. She has been taken to the emergency room three times and is reportedly "down" and unmotivated to participate in additional activities. Her friends and children see that she lacks the initiative to become involved in her children's and grandchildren's lives. Given the changes in her physical and mental health, one of her friends recommended that she see a psychologist through the senior citizen center to talk about her depression and overall health. Although she was resistant to the idea at first, Mrs. Shah's two friends accompanied her to see the African American female psychologist available on staff at the senior center. The following excerpts reflect the dialogue between Mrs. Shah and her psychologist, who used the AA-SISM to work with this particular client.

As with any client who presents to counseling, a psychologist must begin the assessment and exploration process by answering two questions that seek to identify the client's issues and practical skills: (1) What do I want to achieve therapeutically with my client? and (2) How can I achieve these goals using specific techniques? In the exploration of issues and the application of skills, the psychologist needs to place treatment within the context of the client's cultural characteristics and preferences (American Psychological Association [APA], 2005). The dialogue below illustrates such a culturally responsive process between the psychologist and the client. The client, Mrs. Shah, has informally visited with the psychologist once before at the senior citizen center.

Psychologist: Hello, Mrs. Shah. Did you make it to yoga class this week with your friends?

Mrs. Shah: No, I did not. My son was not feeling well, and he has a new baby. So, I went to his house, brought him lunch, and stayed until his wife came home from work. I took care of the baby so my son could sleep. Also, this week is very busy because it is *Diwali,* you know, the Festival of Lights, a major Hindu festival, so I've been busy cooking, cleaning, and preparing my home *Mandir* [Hindu place of worship where Ganesh, Lakshmi, and other statues of deities are kept]. I've invited my daughter's family over for *Diwali* dinner. My husband is very busy again this week, and I'm not sure he's going to be able to stay home all day on *Diwali.*

Using the AA-SISM, the psychologist explored Mrs. Shah's *ontology* and *cosmology* in the context of her Asian background. Although Asians and Asian Americans have differences between and within ethnic groups, there are significant similarities and ties among Asian racial groups (Tewari, Inman, & Sandhu, 2003). For an Asian American client who is exceptionally assimilated into American society and does not maintain traditional Asian worldviews, a culturally responsive psychologist may not need to explore the depth of this domain and its relevance to the client. However, given this conversation with Mrs. Shah, the psychologist needs to consider her multiple identities as a wife, mother, grandparent, and daughter, as well as explore her first-generation immigrant status, her connection to her family, her Indian cultural and religious values, and her gendered role in the family (e.g., Almeida, 1996; Dasgupta, 1998; Inman & Alvarez, 2009). Previous literature (Dasgupta, 1998) suggests that not only are women the bearers of tradition and the link between family members, but maintaining cultural and religious values are important ways of transmitting ethnic values in the Asian Indian community (Inman, Howard, Beaumont, & Walker, 2007).

Upon determining Mrs. Shah's ontology and cosmology, the psychologist continues to consider other issues in her life.

Psychologist: You must be looking forward to this special Hindu celebration this upcoming weekend.

Mrs. Shah: Yes, I am. In this country, my immediate family members are the only ones I have. I'm not sure how much my kids will do the Indian traditions and customs when I'm gone. When they were younger, I could push them and tell them what to do in the *puja* [Hindu prayers], but they are adults now, parents too, and have their own children; they're big. So, they need to decide what they want to do. I think it is important that they keep the Indian culture because their kids know less Indian culture than them. If I don't teach them, who will? I don't know if they have the time to do the celebrations themselves. This is the job of the mother and wife. My husband and I came to this country with very little, and we worked very hard to give our children good opportunities. They are successful, but they did not marry Indians; they married non-Indians. But, God and astrology say that when a child is born, their match is already made. My parents did not have the choices my kids have in who they married. My father asked me if I wanted to marry my husband, but I just respected whom my mother and father found for me, so we had an arranged marriage and did not disagree.

Given Mrs. Shah's strong cultural emphasis on family needs, attempts to socialize children to familial goals, and her recognition of traditional hierarchies, chances are Mrs. Shah follows the Asian worldviews of *axiology, epistemology,* and *praxis* (as presented in Chapter 1, this volume). An openness to exploring all five domains in understanding Mrs. Shah's culture is key to a successful therapeutic encounter in each session. There are many clues in the client's expression that leave room for questioning and for the further assessment of her culture and worldviews (Inman & Tummala-Narra, 2010).

The model presented by Gallardo and colleagues (Chapter 1) includes five domains and six primary issues that can be examined simultaneously during the therapeutic encounters. Early in the first session, the psychologist works toward connecting with the client. Irrespective of the modality of treatment, literature suggests that developing a strong therapeutic alliance is one of the key ingredients to effective treatment, as is the therapist's perspective on the therapy relationship (Baldwin, Wampold, & Imel, 2007; Wampold, 2001). As such, being aware of the stigma attached to seeking counseling (Inman, Yeh, Madan-Bahell, & Nath, 2007) and the need to maintain face in the community (Das & Kemp, 1997; Dasgupta & Dasgupta, 1996; Panganamala & Plummer, 1998), the psychologist acknowledged Mrs. Shah's shame in negotiating the counseling environment (Tewari, 2009). She recognized the value of privacy in Asian Indian culture (Inman & Tewari, 2003) and highlighted this, to make Mrs. Shah more comfortable. The psychologist further maintained harmony by shifting the conversation, as demonstrated below.

Psychologist: It must be kind of difficult for you to come and see a psychologist, even though you came here with your friend. I'm a complete stranger who wants to help and talk to you.

Mrs. Shah: Yes, but my friend thinks it will help.

Psychologist: I'm sure you've never been to counseling, and I bet in your culture men and women don't really see psychologists, so it must be a little embarrassing for you, too.

Mrs. Shah: [Silence]

Psychologist: But, I'm a professional, so whatever we discuss I won't share with your friends and family, unless there are specific reasons and circumstances for me to do so. I'm glad you are here, and we can talk about general things today. Do you come to the senior center a lot?

As the psychologist attempts to develop a relationship with Mrs. Shah, she needs to conduct an assessment, which occurs at multiple levels. Given the collectivistic notions of interdependence and relatedness within the culture

(Markus & Kitayama, 1991; Yeh & Hwang, 2000), the psychologist uses the client's relationships with her friends and children to examine her level of depression and the extent of the medical reasons influencing her lack of motivation and increasing physical inactivity. Relatedly, culturally appropriate methods of coping (Inman & Yeh, 2007; Yeh, Inman, Kim, & Okubo, 2006) need to be examined as a way to enter Mrs. Shah's life experience. Furthermore, stress tends to be the most pronounced at transition points in one's life cycle, when the individual and family have to redefine and realign themselves in relation to others in the family. Evaluating issues in terms of both the individual and family life cycle stages becomes important (Groth-Marnat, Beutler, & Roberts, 2001). Life cycle stages are further influenced by sociocultural contexts such as immigration, acculturation, gender, ethnicity, and age (Norcross, 2002). Thus, understanding how Mrs. Shah has been able to negotiate her multiple cultural identities and achieve the tasks within the context of the particular stages of her individual (aging) and family life cycles (grandparenting) in a foreign land becomes salient (Carter & McGoldrick, 1999). Throughout the first few sessions, the psychologist begins her assessment with conversations prompted by various questions.

Psychologist: Your friends really care about you. Do you know anyone who has seen a psychologist? What did your family do in India when someone was not feeling well? Did they believe in Ayurvedic medicine and homeopathic remedies? What do you do when you are not feeling well? Who do you speak to? What kinds of treatments do you use to help you deal with different stressors? Do you tend to follow more Western approaches to medicine? What changes have your friends noticed in you lately? How much do you children know about your health concerns? Would your children like to come in with you? You have indicated that you are away from your siblings and other family members. What has it been like to live away from your family of origin during the different transitions in your life (e.g., having children, being a grandparent in the United States, developing physical difficulties, getting older)? Whom do you speak to when you feel stressed about the different issues that are going on in your life?

Essentially, a culturally responsive psychologist must remain flexible in his or her questioning as the client's worldviews and culture becomes more apparent (Tewari, 2009). On the surface, Mrs. Shah might look as though she has one identity; however, she has multiple identities and roles that she negotiates daily and in different contexts. For example, she may be struggling with her increasing age and coming to terms with her elderly status. Moreover, on any given day, Mrs. Shah has to fluctuate between being medically challenged, a senior citizen, a long-distance sister, a wife, a mother, a grandmother, and an immigrant Indian woman. The potential losses that occur through aging, her physical disabilities, and their impact on her different roles and cultural identities need to be examined with sensitivity and respect (Inman, Yeh, et al., 2007).

Facilitating awareness of Mrs. Shah's multiple roles and identities is imperative in assisting her with maintaining and enhancing her psychological and physical functioning. Coming to terms with her increased dependence on her children, diminished control of her life's activities, and expectations about her aging can be saddening and increase her sense of loss (APA, 2004; Kim, 2009). Culturally responsive psychologists familiar with the challenges of aging and its impact on mental health can use creative approaches to foster deepening insight with elderly populations (Laidlaw & Pachana, 2009). Narrative therapy that encourages Mrs. Shah to share stories of her life changes, the connections she has developed through her immigrant experience, and the potential challenges and opportunities that have emerged in her life cycle can be therapeutic (Almeida, 1996; Semmler & Williams, 2000). Medically, Mrs. Shah has been diagnosed with Type 2 diabetes, seizures, arrhythmia, and low blood iron. Asian Indians, in particular, have a greater likelihood of being diabetic in comparison to other Asian subgroups (Mohanty, Woolhandler, Himmelstein, & Bor, 2005). Therefore, Mrs. Shah is at an increased risk for diabetes given her ethnicity (Oza-Frank, Ali, Vaccarino, & Narayan, 2009). Prior to these recent diagnoses, Mrs. Shah had been in very good physical and mental health.

For example, Mrs. Shah likes to cook and feed her children and grandchildren, yet her friends say that these activities have decreased. The psychologist can normalize her physical condition by providing her and her family members with some psychoeducational information on physical health and Asian Indians (Gallagher-Thompson & Coon, 2007). She may also discuss innovative Indian recipes, food preparation, and perhaps even suggest an Indian nutritionist to consult with, given her new diagnoses, as a starting point to talk about "more comfortable topics." Once the client "sees" the connection between her new health status, diagnoses, and the relationship to her psychological distress and change, then setting goals can be the focus in therapy.

Setting goals will require the psychologist to work in collaboration with Mrs. Shah and her social systems while also keeping in mind the mind-body-spirit interconnectedness and holistic views of health (Yeh, 2000). Mrs. Shah's vision of regaining her "normal life" may differ from the psychologist's vision of Mrs. Shah's psychological and physical levels of functioning. Further, given the client's collectivistic cultural values, decision making may be tied to intergenerational dependence and sharing between Mrs. Shah and her children (Lin, 2004). Therefore, the psychologist needs to be aware that Mrs. Shah may need the help of multiple family members in making progress toward stronger mental and physical health. In addition to having family and friends infused in the discussions related to Mrs. Shah's well-being, the psychologist may need to take on multiple roles, such as that of advocate or cultural broker (Inman, Yeh, et al., 2007; Sue & Sue, 2003). The psychologist should also work collaboratively with Mrs. Shah to identify and discuss different culturally grounded techniques or coping strategies (e.g., prayer, fatalistic thought processes) through which a healthier way of life may be experienced. Thus, within this context, with Mrs. Shah's permission, the psychologist contacted her daughter and son to determine Mrs. Shah's baseline of activity, ambition, and psychological strength. The psychologist found the children to be somewhat frustrated with their mother's acceptance of her health conditions (fatalism) and could not understand why their mother would not take control and greater initiative even though she was moving into the elderly stages of life.

Part of the psychologist's role in helping Mrs. Shah is incorporating strategies for assisting the children to shift their perspectives regarding their mother's traditional worldviews. In particular, the psychologist must serve as a cultural broker and provider of psychoeducational information, in order to assist the children to understand their mother's beliefs in fate, astrology, and other traditional cultural issues related to Indian women of Mrs. Shah's generation. Serving as a cultural broker and providing psychoeducational information about aging parents and having the ability to take initiative in times of uncontrolled health crises became important in this particular case.

At another point, the psychologist served as a social advocate for Mrs. Shah and contacted her health insurance agency to facilitate a consultation with a registered dietician knowledgeable about the nutritional values of Indian food. In each of these situations, the psychologist should also explore what Mrs. Shah's beliefs about fate, karma, and rebirth are, to determine goals and what is realistically obtainable for her. Exploration of these concepts will significantly impact the therapeutic phase of instigating change. Instigating change will be key in Mrs. Shah's movement toward accepting her physical situation and understanding the healing process. Given that health and well-being are seen from a holistic perspective, conceptualizing change from a mental, physical, and spiritual basis is most important (Hilton et al., 2001). Being taken to the emergency room several times by ambulance took an emotional toll on Mrs. Shah. Giving voice to such experiences (Almeida, 1996; Inman & Tewari, 2003), discussing the locus of control of the events (Knappe & Pinquart, 2009; O'Hea et al., 2009), and increasing Mrs. Shah's consciousness of the past year will contribute to her healing process (Inman & Yeh, 2007). Mrs. Shah will need the psychologist to take initiative in helping her to normalize the series of events as a natural part of one's life cycle. Furthermore, making connections between her physical health, emotional moods, and changes in physical and spiritual behavior can help Mrs. Shah conceptualize her healing process in a holistic manner in the future.

Feedback and accountability, the last or terminating phase of therapy, will also need to be addressed with Mrs. Shah, to determine the success of the therapeutic and change process. An illustration of feedback and accountability between Mrs. Shah and her psychologist is described below.

Psychologist: So, you made it through all these counseling sessions. You did great coming here, being on time, and talking to a complete stranger. All that you did was not easy since this was your first time meeting with a psychologist for counseling. Do you now have a better understanding of all that has happened in your life in the past year?

Mrs. Shah: Yes, I do. I didn't expect my life to change so much, and I did not know what to do. I never had so many health problems, and I kept burdening my children; I felt helpless. But what was good is that now I know my children want me to keep telling them what I am feeling, and they need to see that I want to keep living. They like it when I cook, go on walks, and see my friends. It makes them feel good, and it is good for me. I just know I am getting old but just have to be strong and keep living as long as I can. I'm taking my medicine, and I have to change what I eat even though I'm not used to all these new foods and changing my habits.

Acknowledging the insights and gains made in this context becomes an essential part of the feedback process. Encouraging Mrs. Shah to keep talking with her children and utilizing the cultural interventions in times of future setbacks are important ways to reinforce the gains made in therapy. Psychotherapy is a collaborative relationship that involves not only a mutual agreement of goals and tasks but also an emotional bond that helps bring about positive outcomes (APA, 2005). The psychologist ensured the gains made and highlighted the costs and benefits of psychotherapy (Haynes, Devereaux, & Guyatt, 2002).

Psychologist: Can you come by in three months and give me an update on how you are doing? It would be great if you could come with your friends so that I can see how you are doing. I'd love to hear about your new recipes, exercise plans, and medical doctor visits.

Mrs. Shah: Yes, I can come and give you an update. If my children are free, I can bring them so they can see the senior center and meet you. Okay, thank you, I liked talking to you; it was helpful.

Mrs. Shah clearly found counseling to be helpful but is limited in her expressiveness (verbally or in writing) in articulating her insight and elaboration on how counseling impacted her experience. In this case, the psychologist's best feedback mechanism is to see her in person for a follow-up to assess the degree of success in Mrs. Shah's physical activity, acceptance of medical conditions, and overall mental health. Feedback and accountability clearly vary between clients, and asking for Mrs. Shah's and her friends' reports offers an accurate assessment of her well-being post therapy (Chapter 1, this volume).

As illustrated in the case above, the culturally skilled psychologist needs to understand Mrs. Shah within the context of ontology, axiology, cosmology, epistemology, and praxis while attempting to engage in a thorough assessment of her issues. In providing treatment, she needs to reexamine traditional modes of therapy and expand her roles for therapy. Flexibility, openness, and some cultural awareness during the therapeutic encounters with Mrs. Shah are instrumental in using the AA-SISM. The psychologist's commitment to understanding Mrs. Shah's culture superseded her cultural competence; instead, the psychologist's continuous cultural responsiveness contributed to Mrs. Shah's return to therapy for the 10 sessions during which they worked together. An understanding of the five domains framework and the identification of six issues addresses the skills needed to guide multicultural relationships and multiple identities in therapy.

References

Almeida, R. (1996). Hindu, Christian, and Muslim families. In M. McGoldrick, J. Giordano, & J. K. Pearce (Eds.), *Ethnicity and family therapy* (pp. 395–423). New York: Guilford Press.

American Psychological Association. (2004). Guidelines for psychological practice with older adults. *American Psychologist, 59,* 236–260.

American Psychological Association. (2005). *Policy statement on evidence-based practice in psychology.* Retrieved May 13, 2011, from http://www.apapractice-central.org/ce/courses/ebpstatement.pdf

Baldwin, S., Wampold, B., & Imel, Z. (2007). Untangling the alliance-outcome correlation: Exploring the relative importance of therapist and patient variability in the alliance. *Journal of Consulting and Clinical Psychology, 75,* 842–852.

Carter, B., & McGoldrick, M. (1999). *The expanded family life cycle: Individual, family and social perspectives* (3rd ed.). Boston: Allyn & Bacon.

Das, A. K., & Kemp, S. F. (1997). Between two worlds: Counseling South Asian Americans. *Journal of Multicultural Counseling and Development, 25,* 23–33.

Dasgupta, S. D. (1998). Gender roles and cultural continuum in the Asian Indian immigrant community in the United States. *Sex Roles, 38,* 953–974.

Dasgupta, S. D., & Dasgupta, S. (1996). Public face, private space: Asian Indian women and sexuality. In N. B. Maglin & D. Perry (Eds.), *"Bad girls" "good girls": Women, sex, and power in the nineties* (pp. 226–243). New Brunswick, NJ: Rutgers University Press.

Gallagher-Thompson, D., & Coon, D. W. (2007). Evidence-based psychological treatments for distress in family caregivers of older adults. *Psychology and Aging, 22,* 37–51.

Groth-Marnat, G., Beutler, L. E., & Roberts, R. I. (2001). Client characteristics and psychotherapy: Perspectives, support, interactions, and implications for training. *Australian Psychologist, 36,* 115–121.

Haynes, R. B., Devereaux, P. J., & Guyatt, G. H. (2002). Clinical expertise in the area of evidence-based medicine and patient choice. *Evidence-Based Medicine Notebook, 7,* 1–3.

Hilton, B. A., Grewan, S., Popatia, N., Bottorff, J. L., Johnson, J. L., Clarke, H., et al. (2001). The desi ways: Traditional health practices of South Asian women in Canada. *Health Care for Women International, 22*(6), 553–567.

Inman, A. G., & Alvarez, A. N. (2009). Individuals and families of Asian descent. In D. C. Hays & B. T. Erford (Eds.), *Developing multicultural counseling competency: A systems approach* (pp. 246–276). Boston: Pearson Merrill Prentice Hall.

Inman, A. G., Howard, E. E., Beaumont, L. R., & Walker, J. (2007). Cultural transmission: Influence of contextual factors in Asian Indian immigrant parents' experience. *Journal of Counseling Psychology, 54,* 93–100.

Inman, A. G., & Tewari, N. (2003). The power of context: Counseling South Asians within a family context. In G. Roysircar, D. S. Sandhu, & V. B. Bibbins (Eds.), *Multicultural competencies: A guidebook of practices* (pp. 97–107). Alexandria, VA: Association for Multicultural Counseling and Development.

Inman, A. G., & Tummala-Nara, U. (2010). Clinical competencies working with immigrant communities. In J. Cornish, B. Schreier, L. Nadkarni, & E. Rodolfa (Eds.), *Handbook of multicultural counseling competencies* (pp. 117–152). Hoboken, NJ: John Wiley & Sons.

Inman, A. G., & Yeh, C. J. (2007). Asian American stress and coping. In F. T. Leong, A. Ebreo, L. Kinoshita, A. G. Inman, L. H. Yang, & M. Fu (Eds.), *Handbook of Asian American psychology* (2nd ed., pp. 323–340). Thousand Oaks, CA: Sage.

Inman, A. G., Yeh, C. J., Madan-Bahel, A., & Nath, S. (2007). Bereavement and coping of South Asian families post 9/11. *Journal of Multicultural Counseling and Development, 35,* 101–115.

Kim, S. H. (2009). Older people's expectations regarding ageing, health-promoting behavior and health status. *Journal of Advanced Nursing, 65*(1), 84–91.

Knappe, S., & Pinquart, M. (2009). Tracing criteria of successful aging? Health locus of control and well-being in older patients with internal diseases. *Psychology, Health & Medicine, 14*(2), 201–212.

Laidlaw, K., & Pachana, N. A. (2009). Aging, mental health, and demographic change: Challenge for psychotherapists. *Professional Psychology: Research and Practice, 40*(6), 601–608.

Lin, L. W. (2004). Intergenerational interdependence: Mid-life couples' help exchange in a three-generational model. *Family and Consumer Sciences Research Journal, 32*(3), 275–290.

Markus, H. R., & Kitayama, S. (1991). Culture and the self: Implications for cognition, emotions, and motivation. *Psychological Review, 98,* 224–253.

Mohanty, S. A., Woolhandler, S., Himmelstein, D. U., & Bor, D. H. (2005). Diabetes and cardiovascular disease among Asian Indians in the United States. *Journal of General Internal Medicine, 20*(5), 474–478.

Norcross, J. C. (Ed.). (2002). *Psychotherapy relationships that work: Therapist contributions and responsiveness to patient needs.* New York: Oxford University Press.

O'Hea, E. L., Moon, S., Grothe, K. B., Boudreaux, E., Bodenlos, J. S., Wallston, K., et al. (2009). The interaction of locus of control, self-efficacy, and outcome expectancy in relation to HbA1c in medically underserved individuals with type 2 diabetes. *Journal of Behavioral Medicine, 32*(1), 106–117.

Oza-Frank, R., Ali, M. K., Vaccarino, V., & Narayan, K. M. (2009). Asian Americans: Diabetes prevalence across U.S. and World Health Organization weight classifications. *Diabetes Care, 32*(9), 1644–1646.

Panganamala, D. R., & Plummer, D. L. (1998). Attitudes towards counseling among Asian Indians in the United States. *Cultural Diversity and Mental Health, 4,* 55–63.

Semmler, P. L., & Williams, C. B. (2000). Narrative therapy: A storied context for multicultural counseling. *Journal of Multicultural Counseling and Development, 28*(1), 51–62.

Sue, D. W., & Sue, D. (2003). *Counseling the culturally diverse: Theory and practice* (4th ed.). Hoboken, NJ: John Wiley & Sons.

Tewari, N. (2009). Seeking, receiving and providing culturally competent mental health services: A focus on Asian Americans. In N. Tewari & A. N. Alvarez (Eds.), *Asian American psychology: Current perspectives* (pp. 575–606). New York: Routledge/Taylor and Francis.

Tewari, N., Inman, A. G., & Sandhu, D. S. (2003). South Asian Americans: Culture, concerns and therapeutic strategies. In J. Mio & G. Iwamasa (Eds.), *Culturally diverse mental health: The challenges of research and resistance* (pp. 191–209). New York: Brunner-Routledge.

Wampold, B. E. (2001). *The great psychotherapy debate: Models, methods and findings.* Mahwah, NJ: Lawrence Erlbaum.

Yeh, C. J. (2000). Depathologizing Asian-American perspectives of health and healing. *Asian American and Pacific Islander Journal of Health, 8,* 138–149.

Yeh, C. J., & Hwang, M. (2000). Interdependence in ethnic identity and self: Implications for theory and practice. *Journal of Counseling and Development, 78,* 420–429.

Yeh, C. J., Inman, A. G., Kim, A. B., & Okubo, Y. (2006). Asian American families' collectivistic coping strategies in response to 9/11. *Cultural Diversity and Ethnic Minority Psychology, 12,* 134–148.

Case Illustration: A Culturally Adaptive Conceptualization for 1.5-Generation Southeast Asian Americans

10

Jorge Wong

Kao Chiu Saechao

Introduction

The SISM presented in this volume encompasses multiple aspects of an individual's sociocultural identity, cultural ideological development, and the transcendence of culturally inherited and accepted interaction norms. Parham's (2002) Skills Identification Model offers skills that operationalize the clinical applications of this model. By referencing these two models conceptually and practically, a clinician working with Asian American clients can develop culturally responsive conceptualizations and effective interventions for working with Asian Americans. In this chapter, we present a case study of an Asian American family receiving services from a publicly designated culturally specific mental health service provider (i.e., counselor or psychologist) in order to highlight these particular concepts and skills.

Fictitious names have been assigned to protect the identity of the individuals who graciously allowed their case to be used for the enrichment of future clinicians and educational purposes. Informed consent for the use of this case for educational purposes was given and signed by adult participants and parents/legal guardians of all minor participants. The fictitious names assigned to protect confidentiality are Anh (the father), Bich (the mother), Chris (the son), Dan (the therapist), Elena (the clinical supervisor), Frank (social worker), and Gia (social worker). The parents are unmarried, financially unstable, and young.

Reason for Referral

Chris is a 10-year-old, second-generation, obese Vietnamese American boy who is in the fourth grade. He was referred to mental health services at a local linguistically and culturally specific community mental health center. He was referred by the County Social Service Agency's (SSA) Department of Family and Children Services (DFCS), due to a reported case of physical and emotional abuse. Chris appeared at school with a handprint across his face and reported to school staff that his father punished him because he had received a "bad note" from school.

This note addressed to the parents stated that Chris was not attending in class, was talking excessively, and was not following the teacher's directions. Chris also reported that his father disciplined him by having him stand facing the wall with his arms folded for a three-hour period. The school became alarmed and, as mandatory reporters, school staff reported the incident to Child Protective Services (CPS). This report was the second of its kind by the school to CPS, the first having been made seven months prior on a related suspicion of physical abuse, which was investigated and deemed unfounded.

After this second incident, Chris was removed from his home and placed temporarily at a Children's Shelter, where all minors are placed during these investigations. Once the investigation was completed and allegations confirmed, Chris was placed in the care of his mother, who had to reside with her family without contact from his father. Weekly supervised visits with his father were scheduled during this time.

After Chris was removed from home and was required to live with the maternal side of the family, he began to display increased problem behaviors at home and school. At home, his explosive and aggressive behaviors would be directed toward himself and others whenever his immediate needs were not met to his satisfaction, and his frustration tolerance levels were depleted. Chris's mother, Bich, reported he would hit himself on the leg and/or face when frustrated and angry when he would "not get his way," and at other times, he would physically assault and aggressively push his mother when he had difficulty with parental directives (e.g., unwillingness to complete homework or follow through with mother's directives to stop playing video games, general demands for a snack before a meal). Bich also shared that Chris once stole money to purchase a video game that she had initially refused to purchase.

Chris was suspended from school on three occasions. The first occasion, Chris punched a female student in the face due to a verbal altercation between the two. During the second incident, Chris brought "nunchucks" to school, which the school considered to be a deadly weapon. On the last occasion, Chris was caught attempting to set a fire in the boys' bathroom by burning toilet paper in the garbage can. Bich felt hopeless and helpless about her parenting Chris as a result of these compounded behavioral outbursts. In the past, when Chris was living with both parents, it was his father, Anh, who would be the disciplinarian at home, and Bich was not involved, or at the time minimally involved, in this disciplining process because she saw herself to be the nurturing parent in the dyad.

During the family's initial contact with social services, a culturally and linguistically matched Vietnamese male social worker, Frank, was assigned to the family, as is customarily done by the SSA, without consideration of additional factors (Chow, 1999; Sue, 1998) that could influence their professional relationship, such as whether he was the best fit to manage this case, whether he had preconceived notions of what Vietnamese parenting styles should be like in the United States, whether he considered his potential countertransference toward these Vietnamese parents, and whether this child abuse case was the culmination of current psychosocial stressors. This was an example of a praxis violation dictating the interpersonal and familial obligations that culturally bind parenting practices.

Frank works at SSA and was assigned to work with Vietnamese families due to his linguistic and cultural expertise with this population. Of particular interest is that Frank, Anh, and Bich were all foreign born. Frank and Anh immigrated to the United States during their mid-teenage years. Bich immigrated to the United States at a much earlier age and was placed in elementary school upon arrival.

After a month of interactions, Anh and Bich both felt Frank was being critical and passing unsolicited cultural judgments about their parenting skills. Statements made by Frank such as "You are in America now, not in Vietnam anymore! You know you are not supposed to hit your kids!" were understood by the parents to mean "You are not good enough parents because you are too young, not financially stable, and not married." Anh and Bich were experiencing cultural stigma (Rasinski, Viechnicki, & O'Muircheartaigh, 2005), in which attitudes and beliefs are reflected in the language used to communicate. They both felt misunderstood and accused of being poor parents with weak cultural values and skills, which made them lose face and feel ashamed in front of Frank. These feelings of shame and stigma were exacerbated by the fact that their community is very small and tightly knit, and confidentiality is viewed as a Western concept.

Anh and Bich requested to be reassigned to another social worker after feeling offended by Frank. This surprised Frank, especially since Frank, Anh, and Bich were close in age and ethnicity and had similar immigration histories. There were also unspoken assumptions of cultural understanding and acceptance as to how parenting has been practiced in the Vietnamese culture for centuries.

The new social worker, Gia, was not Vietnamese. Gia's ethnocultural background provided further assurance to Anh and Bich that confidentiality would not be breached in the Vietnamese community. Anh had a different reaction to Gia and did not feel threatened or embarrassed by her. Gia was an outsider and from the majority Eurocentric culture. Gia did not project stigmatizing intracultural discrimination toward them as young, unmarried parents working on their early careers, nor did she attribute negative qualities to their individual personal characteristics. Due to this position, she was perhaps less critical in applying the laws and expectations established by the SSA. In contrast, Frank had been very rigid in his application of these expectations, which then contributed to the clients' feeling cultural suspicion and paranoia, social stigma, and disapproval. This pairing made Anh and Bich feel more reassured of the process, particularly because Gia was also close in age to them.

Court-Ordered Parenting Classes

Anh and Bich were both ordered by the court to attend parenting classes. Anh was able to better comply with this order. His employment consisted of audiovisual equipment installation projects and all-around handyman work on an occasional basis. Bich was less able to abide by this condition because her employment was more professional, and scheduling difficulties made it more difficult, especially because she did not want to disclose to her employer the reasons for her needing to take so much time off. Bich's additional economic challenges stemmed from her being the primary source of and stable income in their family. When asked about the effectiveness of the parenting classes, Anh responded, "It's okay", and said they were time consuming. Bich had not completed her mandate, and Gia was assisting in finding a more appropriate schedule for her attendance.

Referral to Mental Health Services

Previous literature on Asian Americans' underuse of psychological services has associated it with unfamiliarity with services and cultural stigmas (Snowden & Cheung, 1990; Sue, Fujino, Hu, Takeuchi, & Zane, 1991). Chow (1999) suggests that linguistically and culturally appropriate community-based service providers offering psychological counseling in the client's primary language are typically more successful in increasing the use of counseling. In addition,

Asian American children who received services at ethnic-specific centers were less likely to drop out of services after the first session, they used more services, and they functioned better when they finished therapy (Yeh, Takeuchi, & Sue, 1994). In addition, Southeast Asians have shown higher rates of counseling use at intake than more established East Asian groups (Akutsu, Tsuru, & Chu, 2004). Chris and his family had been referred to a nonprofit community agency designated as a culturally specific provider for Asian Americans by the County's Mental Health Department. Chris and his family had no contact with therapy or counseling prior to this referral.

Case Assignment

The American Psychological Association' (APA; 2005) defines "clinical utility" as applicability, feasibility, and usefulness of the intervention in the local or specific setting where it is offered. Hence, to maximize the psychological utility of cases, supervisors need to determine the best therapist and client match, in order to increase the clinical utility. Roland (2006) describes how Asian American clients' hierarchical perspective affects the therapeutic relationship to a considerable degree. Asian American clients observe the social etiquette of formal hierarchical expectations (related to age and gender), in which they are supposed to show deference, respect, and obedience to the superior, keeping disagreements and any negative feelings to themselves (Roland, 2006).

Specifically, there is a deep-seated, culturally internalized reciprocity in the hierarchical relationship. The client displays deference and respect and expects the superior to be responsible and nurturing, and each maintains and enhances the esteem of the other. There is an expectation of a close "we" relationship. In this particular case, Elena (the clinical supervisor) assigned the case to Dan (the therapist) based on several factors. First, Chris had a negative experience with his father disciplining him; hence, Dan could offer a positive corrective experience if Chris worked with a male role model. In addition, all parties were fluent English speakers and there was a parallel "1.5-generation" relationship between the parents and the therapist, which could potentially decrease the formal, hierarchical cultural expectations. Finally, although Dan is not Vietnamese, he is still of Southeast Asian descent, and his area of specialty is pre-teen Asian Americans.

Intake Assessment

Presenting problem: Chris was referred by CPS for physical and emotional child abuse and mental health services. He exhibits externally focused aggressive behaviors, including hitting his mother, not following parental directives, frequent temper tantrums, and he hits himself on the leg and/or face whenever frustrated or angry. He is also disrespectful to female teachers at school and uses profane language.

Psychosocial stressors: Financial pressures on the family are a reminder of the social role reversal (Gold, 1992; Zhou & Bankston, 1998) that many Vietnamese families experience when they live in the United States, where the men lose their higher social roles and status as the family head of household and primary financial supporter and the women have increased social and financial opportunities to become significant financial contributors to the family system. This axiological reversal presents itself within the family system as an unspoken and shameful phenomenological burden. Anh did not have stable employment or a steady income to support the family, while Bich was more acculturated and beginning her professional healthcare career. This divergent vertical disparity between the parental and gender opportunities was clear evidence of an axiological clash.

Chris's behavioral and academic challenges at school are a constant source of parental discord. Family conflicts stemming from the parental relationship instability, differing parenting values and practices, and their potential separation were all too real. Chris was the only child living in a multigenerational home of his maternal grandparents and mother during this time of parental separation. Mandated parenting classes were conflicting with parents' work schedules.

Medical history: No known or reported significant medical conditions or allergies affecting Chris's daily activities, except that he is obese.

Mental health history: No prior contacts or services received from mental health services prior to this current referral. Parents denied family history of mental illness in their families.

Substance abuse history: None reported per client and/or parents.

Cultural factors: Both parents are of the 1.5 generation, which Rumbaut (1991) defines as those individuals who arrived in the United States between the ages of 5 and 12: They are marginal to both the old and new world and are fully part of neither one of them. The current home in which Chris resides is intergenerationally mixed with three generations. The family has no common or consistent religious affiliation; they have attended both Buddhist and Catholic events. Paternal grandparents are more devout Buddhist and do not speak English, and at times Chris is disrespectful to them.

Contact with Social Services: Initially, a Vietnamese male social worker was assigned to work with the family as a cultural match. After a month of working together, Anh and Bich requested to be reassigned to another social worker due to the Vietnamese social worker critically accusing them of poor parenting skills. A second social worker was assigned to the case, and this time it was an American woman of European decent. Anh and Bich did not have issues with this assignment as they both speak English fluently (although Anh speaks with a noticeable accent).

Family history: Chris's parents are unmarried, 1.5-generation Vietnamese. Anh and Bich have been cohabiting for 11 years and have been living with the paternal grandparents in a multigenerational home. Chris was born soon after the parents began their romantic relationship. They all lived together prior to Chris's removal from the home by CPS. Chris is an only child. Chris's mother came with her family to the United States during her early adolescence, as part of the 1980s second wave of refugees. Chris's father came with his family in the early 1990s as part of the third wave of immigrants from Vietnam. Both parents are fluent in Vietnamese and English and have no religious affiliations. Chris's paternal grandparents are monolingual Vietnamese and Buddhist. Chris's maternal grandparents are also monolingual Vietnamese but Catholic. Anh is presently 28 and Bich 27 years old. They met in high school and began a long-term romantic relationship. Bich graduated high school and went on to pursue a healthcare profession. Anh did not complete high school and became an independent contractor installing home entertainment systems. During the weekends, both parents joined forces in a small retail operation at a local outdoor market. The family struggles financially due to Anh's unstable employment situation. This financial stress challenged Anh's cultural perception as the head of household, resulting in marital discourse, disagreement, and inconsistent parenting styles and poor self-efficacy.

School history: Chris was suspended from school on three occasions during the same academic year. The first suspension, in March, was for bringing nunchucks, the martial arts weapon popularized by Bruce Lee in the movies, to school. The second suspension, in May, resulted from punching a girl in the face because she was verbally insulting him. The third suspension, in September, resulted from attempting to set fire to rolls of toilet paper in the boys' bathroom at school.

Initial Session

During the initial session, Bich and Chris met Dan. Dan discussed the limits of confidentiality and professional ethics surrounding the therapy sessions. This information helped to ease Bich's initial concerns and Bich felt comfortable and reassured discussing the friction she and Anh initially had with Frank, the parent and child dynamics, and the challenges associated with disciplining Chris with differing parenting styles. Anh subscribed to disciplining Chris in the same manner his parents disciplined him in Vietnam, an intergenerational transmission of parenting (Ho, 1990). Bich believed in nonviolent parenting and not physically disciplining Chris because she believed it led to child abuse. Simultaneously, she firmly believed that physically disciplining Chris was the only way that he would listen and obey parental authority. When further queried about violence in the family, Bich reported that she had experienced domestic violence in her relationship with Anh: "I don't think Chris was affected because it all happened when [Chris] was not around." Bich also disclosed feelings of helplessness, worthlessness, and often self-deprecation as a parent, spouse, and adult when she compared herself with other Vietnamese parents who blamed their children for their woes.

Near the end of the initial session, Bich asked Dan, "You're not Vietnamese . . . what are you?" Dan disclosed that he was Lao-Mien. Bich sighed and showed relief that Dan was not Vietnamese. Dan was in the same age group as Bich; he was also 1.5 generation, and he was going to serve as the cultural ambassador and bridge the gap between the parents and Chris. Bich's transference was appeased, and she was better able to relate to Dan and not see him as a judgmental representative of the social services system criticizing her parental skills, marital status, and acculturation level as 1.5 generation.

Course of Therapy

Dan educated Bich about the therapeutic process, demystified the stigma related to mental health services, and focused on developing culturally responsive interventions aimed at intergenerational relationships, as suggested by Ying and Han (2007) and Dan's clinical supervisor Elena. A few months later, Anh was allowed by the court to join in the family treatment. He initially joined very hesitantly because he did not see the usefulness of this process. As part of the Intensive Outpatient Services (IOP), Dan explained that home/school/community treatment modalities were customarily offered in community-based IOP. Home visits were not welcomed by Bich and Anh, and they only agreed to office and school-based sessions.

Dan's Southeast Asian cultural insights and his own lived experiences served as the cultural facilitator to build a bridge between Chris and his parents. He understood Anh's traditional Vietnamese belief that "one can be proud if one can swallow the bitterness without complaining" (*Ethnic Communities*, 2006). Dan empowered Anh to consider learning new parenting skills aligned with the Buddhist concept of "impermanence." This change of perspective would bring a positive and strengths-based change to his role as a father and his adherence to a traditional view of parenting. As Anh became more accepting of this conceptual approach, he was more able and willing to adopt a nonviolent parenting style. He was also able to accept Chris's negative behavior in class not as an indirect rejection or disapproval of his parenting, but as a family system imbalance. Anh felt supported and understood by Dan in his struggles as a father raising an Asian American son. Anh was appreciative of being able to widen his repertoire of parenting skills and accepted this self-cultivated (*Ethnic Communities*, 2006) change en route to becoming a better parent. Dan was also able to assist Bich in decreasing her fatalistic and guilty perception of herself as a "bad parent" by encouraging her to learn more nonviolent parenting skills as part of her parenting strategies.

Dan also worked to empower Bich to recognize her personal and cultural strengths and assume responsibility as an equally contributing parent. As she gained more self-confidence in her role as a parent, her locus of control changed from externally focused to internally focused. She was able to begin redefining herself and embracing efficacious Western ideas of effective parenting. Her newfound confidence as an able parent enabled her to increase her parental effectiveness and build on her new identity. Incorporating Western views of parenting enabled her to begin distancing herself from traditional patriarchal parenting and gender roles. It enabled her to bridge biculturally acceptable parenting practice and effectively match an Asian American parenting style to her Asian American son. Bich was encouraged by Dan and by Anh to partake in a more balanced and harmonious system of parenting. Through introspection, she was able to realize and accept that she possessed many strengths that had enabled her to complete her education and professional training, gain steady employment, develop professional goals, and show motivation to improve herself. These same qualities would serve her to become a resourceful, resilient, nurturing, and capable young mother.

Over the course of a year, Dan was able to educate, model, and rehearse live these new parenting concepts and skills. Bich and Anh were assigned to spend more positive, reinforcing, and quality time with Chris (e.g., Anh helped Chris with his homework, went on neighborhood outings with him, and offered desired rewards once he was able to successfully complete set weekly behavioral and scholastic goals; Bich was able to set limits with Chris, communicate effectively, and present a consistently united parental front when addressing Chris). Dan was able to accomplish these changes with both parents because they had a collective understanding of how to achieve family harmony.

Conclusion

The APA's (2002) *Guidelines on Multicultural Education, Training, Research, Practice, and Organizational Change for Psychologists* states that all individuals exist in social, political, historical, and economic contexts, and psychologists are increasingly called upon to understand the influence of these contexts on individuals' behavior. The SISM presented in this book encompasses multiple aspects of an individual's sociocultural identity, cultural ideological development, and the transcendence of culturally inherited and accepted interaction norms. This case illustrates the importance of cultural responsiveness when working with Asian Americans, the importance of cultural matching (Yeh et al., 1994), the significance of linguistically and culturally appropriate service providers (Chow, 1999), and the relevance of recognizing the success of Southeast Asians in entering community-based services and completing intakes (Akutsu et al., 2004). This case also illustrates the complex interplay between the technical skills a clinician is required to master and the use of personal history and identity in order to successfully engage and produce significant clinical and practical outcomes with Asian American clients in a multicultural and multiethnic community mental health setting. Culturally responsive clinicians working with Asian Americans are most effective when they possess sound clinical skills and knowledge, culturally and historically relevant knowledge of their client population, a confident self and cultural identity, ascribed credibility from their role as professional healthcare providers, and often their own lived experiences. It is the mastering of this constant and dynamic fluctuation between these multiple dimensions in the clinical setting that makes being an effective, culturally responsive clinician a developmental process and enlightened goal for clinicians to achieve.

References

Akutsu, P. D., Tsuru, G. K, & Chu, J. P. (2004). Predictors of nonattendance of intake appointments among five Asian American client groups. *Journal of Consulting and Clinical Psychology 72*(5), 891–896.

American Psychological Association. (2002). *Guidelines on multicultural education, training, research, practice, and organizational change for psychologists.* Retrieved May 13, 2011, from http://www.apa.org/pi/oema/resources/policy/multicultural-guidelines.aspx

American Psychological Association, Presidential Task Force on Evidence-Based Practices. (2005). *Report.* Retrieved May 13, 2011, from http://www.apa.org/practice/resources/evidence/evidence-based-report.pdf

Chow, J. (1999). Multiservice centers in Chinese American immigrant communities: Practice principles and challenges. *Social Work, 44,* 70–81.

Ethnic communities of Santa Clara County. (2006). San Jose, CA: Santa Clara Valley Health and Hospital System, Santa Clara County Mental Health Department.

Gold, S. J. (1992). Cross-cultural medicine a decade later: Mental health and illness in Vietnamese refugees. *West Journal of Medicine, 157,* 290–294.

Ho, C. K. (1990). An analysis of domestic violence in Asian American communities: Multicultural approach to counseling. *Women and Therapy, 9,* 129–150.

Parham, T. A. (2002). *Counseling persons of African descent: Raising the bar of practitioner competence.* Thousand Oaks, CA: Sage.

Rasinski, K. A., Viechnicki, P., & O'Muircheartaigh, C. (2005). Methods for studying stigma and mental illness. In P. W. Corrigan (Ed.), *On the stigma of mental illness* (pp. 45–65). Washington, DC: American Psychological Association.

PART IV

North American Indian and Alaska Native Communities

Moving Beyond the Surface Level

11

Working With North American Indian and Alaska Native Clients

Understanding the Deep Culture Within

Joseph E. Trimble

Non-Native mental health counselors who work with North American Indians and Alaska Natives must understand the extraordinarily diverse demographic and individual identity characteristics of the groups that make up North America's indigenous populations. These populations are no doubt more diverse than those that make up the rich tapestry of national and ethnic groups in European countries. Native North American Indians reside in all of Canada's provinces and in all of the U.S. states. In the United States, about 60% of them reside in urban areas, with the remainder living in rural villages and small rural communities and on reservations (U.S. Census Bureau, 2006). An unknown number follow traditional lifestyles, and countless others embrace the values and lifestyles of the common North American culture (Herring, 1990; Trimble, 1981; Trimble & Gonzalez, 2008). The extraordinary variation in lifestyle orientations and physical appearance among the Native populations presents a daunting challenge for anyone who tends to view American Indians as a homogeneous group.

Indeed, the tendency of non-Natives to view American Indians and Alaska Natives in a collective manner has been a source of considerable concern among scholars (Trimble & Dickson, 2005); that is, there is the tendency to gloss over the rich cultural heterogeneity that exists in numerous tribal and linguistic groups by referring to them with a sweeping label. It may well be the major reason so many non-Natives experience difficulty understanding the complexity of the varied lifeways and thoughtways of Native North American Indian populations.

In the past four decades, scholars and practitioners have published more than 150 articles related directly or indirectly to the provision of counseling and psychotherapeutic services to Indians; more than 40% of these articles have been published in the past five years alone (Herring, 1999; Trimble & Bagwell, 1995). A theme occurs repeatedly in the Indian and Native literature: Counselors of Indian and Native clients must be adaptive and flexible in their personal orientations and in their use of conventional counseling techniques. Additionally, one finds that numerous scholars, mental health specialists, and practitioners provide insights, observations, and recommendations for a variety of settings and situations. After poring over the publications, invariably questions arise as to what is the best and most culturally respectful way to deliver counseling services to North America's indigenous populations.

Considering the range of individual differences between Indians and Natives who subscribe closely to tribal worldviews and those who marginally identify as Indian or Native, how can a counselor provide effective and culturally resonant mental health services to members of these populations? Is there a common set of procedures and strategies available that are known to be effective? What does a conventionally trained counselor need to know about facilitating positive relationships with Indian and Native clients? Many counselors have been unsuccessful with them, and not because of a lack of effort and concern. Counselors may be unsuccessful in working with Indian and Native clients for a number of different reasons: The counselor may lack basic knowledge about the client's ethnic and historical backgrounds; the client may be driven away by the professional's counseling style; the client may sense that his or her worldview is not valued; the client may feel uncomfortable talking openly with a stranger; or the ethnic background of the counselor may create client apprehension.

To put the questions, considerations, and concerns in a culturally resonant perspective, use of the Skills Identification Stage Model (SISM) is appropriate and relevant to the overarching theme of this book. In this section, the model is referred to as the American Indian and Alaska Native Skills Identification Stage Model (AIAN-SISM). Resources and information are provided for the core components: connecting with clients, assessment, facilitating awareness, setting goals, taking action and instigating change, and feedback and accountability (see Table 11.1).

Connecting With Clients

North American Indians and Natives often view traditional healers as wise and knowing; thus, it is possible that they will view counselors in a similar way (Gone, 2010; Mohatt & Eagle Elk, 2000; Reimer, 1999; Trimble, 2010c).

Table 11.1 American Indian and Alaska Native Skills Identification Stage Model (AIAN-SISM)

Connecting With Clients	Review purpose, goals, and approaches of counseling.
	Discuss counseling arrangements and negotiate conditions such as time, setting, etc.
	Accept long periods of silence.
	Establish perceived levels of ethnic identity and acculturative status with client.
	Discuss trust and trustworthiness.
	Acknowledge historical trauma conditions.
	Value and use humor.
Assessment	Recognize that client may have different views of conventional psychological diagnostic categories.
	Provide opportunity for client to discuss tribal and own history.
	Family and friend relationships may be a source of the problem; discuss and map relationships.
	Recognize that formal testing may be suspect.
	Use projective techniques such as "draw-a-person" procedure. Create a list of current stressful life situations—then create one for how client copes effectively with the situations. Identify and discuss unrealistic coping patterns.
	Perform content analysis of client's spoken or written words.
Facilitating Awareness	Discuss values and beliefs and client's commitment to them.
	Recognize that client may not be in harmony with his or her world.
	Identify presenting problem and client (or other) responsibilities.
	Promote the concept of mindfulness and deep openness to truth.
Setting Goals	Recognize that gender makes a difference in client goals.
	Acknowledge the value of traditional healing ceremonies and accommodate client's interests.
	Relational counseling approaches should be considered.
	Recognize that goal setting will involve a context and others, especially kin.
	Identify steps to achieving harmony, balance, and connectedness with the world.
Instigating Change	Be open to use of family members, friends, and coworkers to promote change.
	Provide occasions for anger to be discussed and vented.
	Understand and implement the importance of gradual pacing of sessions.
Feedback/ Accountability	Use storytelling, legends, and inspirational writings.
	Use behavioral records of positive client changes.
	Have client summarize main points of each session in writing/dictation—3" × 5" card.
	Provide occasions to discuss letting go of control and options.
	Summarize each session and open sessions with summaries of previous sessions.

Consequently, Indians and Natives may view counselors as helpers and "may seek advice regarding medical problems, spirituality, financial concerns, or the problems of other members of the family" (Helms & Cook, 1999, p. 188). Counselors, therefore, should anticipate that they may be expected to fulfill multiple roles that go beyond the provision of mental health services.

Providers of traditional helping services in Indian and Native communities most often exemplify empathy, genuineness, availability, respect, warmth, congruence, and concreteness, characteristics that are likely to be effective in any therapeutic treatment setting, regardless of the provider's theoretical orientation or counseling style (Reimer, 1999). Effective counseling with Indians and Natives begins when a counselor carefully internalizes and uses these basic characteristics in counseling settings.

Traditional counseling sessions conducted in health clinics tend to create high levels of apprehension and anxiety for traditional Indians and Natives. Clients may be wary of the possibility that someone at the clinic will recognize them and therefore may be reluctant to seek counseling. Consequently, the counselor should consider alternative sites for sessions that are familiar and comfortable for the client. Possibilities include conducting some sessions in the client's residence, at a comfortable and peaceful spot in his or her neighborhood or community, or in settings where the client feels relaxed and connected with the environment around him or her. A few counselors who work effectively with Indian and Native clients use a "walk and talk approach". Sessions occur during hikes in a forested area, along the wash of a river, or along a beach; sessions often continue when the couple rests and sits on beached logs, on fallen trees, on large boulders, or in a comfortable or spiritual place where the client feels the need to pause and reflect on the discussion. In essence, the counselor should be flexible in choosing the site that best accommodates the client's need to be in a setting that allays fears and apprehensions about the presenting problem and the counseling process.

Other ways in which counselors can work to be effective with Indian and other Native clients have been identified, including building trust and nurturing trustworthiness; in general, both are highly correlated with client self-disclosure. Self-disclosure typically is not consistent with traditional Indian and Native communication styles; nonetheless, trust building is essential, especially if a non-Indian counselor wants to establish mutual respect and rapport with an Indian client on a one-to-one basis (Lockhart, 1981). LaFromboise and Dixon (1981), for example, found that Indian students clearly rated simulated interviews more positively when the counselors in the interviews, regardless of their own ethnicity, enacted trustworthy roles. Trustworthiness appeared to be enhanced for these researchers' respondents when the counselors used culturally appropriate communication styles and trust behaviors. But establishing trust may take several sessions; hence, the counselor must be willing to be patient; trust will occur on the client's terms and from his or her cultural worldview.

Non-Native counselors must be aware of the possibility that cultural differences derived from personal experiences with people from other cultural groups may be the Indian or Native client's main presenting problem. A client's culturally grounded problems thus add to the number of conventional counseling circumstances and approaches that one must consider. The addition of the culturally grounded problem may create an awkward situation for the counselor, to the extent that the client's cultural history and worldview may become of more interest than the client's presenting problem; in this instance, the counselor may act more like an ethnographer than a mental health specialist. In most cases where this has occurred, the Indian or Native client will recognize this untoward development and terminate the counseling arrangement without the counselor knowing the true reason behind the client's decision.

Although the counselor could become absorbed and enchanted with the client's cultural and tribal background, one must seek to promote a culturally affirmative environment that leads to a positive counseling outcome for the client. Creating and sustaining an enriching affirmative environment means that the counselor recognizes and supports the position that cultural and environmental factors influence the client (Darou, 1987; McCormick, 1996; Trimble & Gonzalez, 2008; Witko, 2006). Framed in a synergetic counseling paradigm, Herring (1999) maintains that the initial session should be devoted to demonstrating content knowledge of the client's cultural background and include such factors as an awareness of tribal heritage and levels of identity, family influences, educational background, residential effects on socialization, and experiences with different healing traditions.

Providing counseling services to Indian and Native clients requires careful thought and planning. Initial sessions are vitally important in establishing rapport and building trust. If the sessions are conducted in a culturally affirmative environment, a counselor increases the likelihood that the client will stay with the sessions until some reasonable level of positive outcomes has been achieved (Trimble, 2010c). Part of that planning should involve an assessment of the biases and myths that have been perpetrated about non-Indian counselors within the Indian and Native community from which clients will be drawn. Biases and myths vary from one community to the next; hence, counselors would be wise to examine these at all levels (Peregoy, 1999). Informal ethnographic interviews with community members represent one way to gather information on these biases. When the informal interviews are conducted, non-Indian counselors are likely to discover that community members believe, among other things, that (1) "outsiders" tend to interpret behavior and emotions in terms of norms and expectations not shared by the tribal community and (2) counselors will attempt to convert Indians to a "better" culture or try to get them to act and think according to the outsiders' worldview (Anderson & Ellis, 1995).

To enhance a culturally affirmative environment, non-Native counselors should recognize that many Indians and Natives, especially those from communities that are more traditional, are not familiar with the principles and practices associated with self-disclosure (Good Tracks, 1973; Herring, 1999;

LaFromboise, Trimble, & Mohatt, 1990; Lee, 1997; Peregoy, 1993; Trimble & Gonzalez, 2008; Trimble & Thurman, 2002). LaFromboise and Bigfoot (1988), for example, suggest that the counselor devote early sessions to explain what self-disclosure is and provide clients the opportunity to role-play and practice the process. Furthermore, the counselor should provide some information on what counseling is, what it can achieve, and what the client would have to do in order for the sessions to be beneficial; in essence, many traditional Indians and Natives may not have a concept of what counseling, from a mental health perspective, means and entails in the non-Native world (Peregoy, 1993, 1999).

Non-Native counselors who work with Indians and Natives must be aware of the histories, traditions, customs, and ceremonial events of the tribes, communities, villages, and locales where the mental health services will be provided (LaFromboise, Berman, & Sohi, 1994; Trimble & Hayes, 1984). Indigenous worldviews grounded in historical tradition, legends, folkways, and daily experiences define community life and shape individual beliefs, behaviors, and emotions (Nebelkopf & Phillips, 2004). Moreover, counselors must be keenly aware that many Indians and Natives continue to experience various degrees of individual and community trauma as a consequence of European contact, a "wound to the soul of Native American people that is felt in agonizing proportions to this day" (Duran & Duran, 1995, p. 27; Duran, 2006). The counselor must recognize and understand that historical trauma is caused by centuries of incurable and untreated diseases, forced relocation, unemployment, economic despair, poverty, forced removal of children to boarding schools, abuse, racism, loss of traditional lands, betrayal, and broken treaties, among other nefarious and noxious events. For decades, those directly affected by the trauma kept the debilitating and horrific experiences to themselves. But with the encouragement of many concerned mental health practitioners, family members, and community leaders, the once muted voices and repressed traumatic experiences are being brought out into the open with more frequency. In many instances, the horrific stories, experiences, and the effects they have had on Indian and Native people have been shared privately and consequently passed down from one generation to another. Each generation then internalizes the stories and the effects they have had on their kin, to the extent that often the offspring are negatively influenced by the effects the memories and experiences have had on their elders. The passing of trauma and its effects to subsequent generations leads many of them to acquire the guilt, anger, frustration, and fears experienced by their elders (Brave Heart & DeBruyn, 1998; Duran, 2006; Duran & Duran, 1995; Gone, 2009; Morrissette, 1994; Weaver & Brave Heart, 1999). Duran specifically draws attention to the personally debilitating effects of internalized oppression and how it influences the mental health of many Indian and Native clients; counselors are encouraged to use a culturally tailored approach grounded in the client's cultural background to effectively deal with the problem.

Counselors interested in and committed to working with indigenous peoples must recognize and honor the significance of spirituality (Duran, 2006; Gone, 2010; Olson, 2003). In his formative book *Spirit Matters,* Lerner (2000) says,

> Understanding the spiritual realm of human needs, and how the world gets distorted when our spiritual needs are thwarted, can provide us with a much deeper understanding of what's going on in this world and in our personal lives as well. (p. 1)

For many indigenous people, spirituality is about feeling and being connected—connected to friends, family, community, and the world around them. For client and counselor, a belief in and commitment to spirituality promotes and strengthens certain values that are related, in many ways, to values and beliefs about multiculturalism—embracing these values strengthens connectedness. Spirituality is an intense experience of harmony, but many Indian and Native clients experience identity through a sense of isolation and loneliness. Due to a variety of circumstances, clients believe they are disconnected from others and the world that brings comfort to them. The feeling of disconnectedness contributes to the feeling and belief that they are losing their identity; they may even believe that they have lost their identity entirely through soul loss or a related mystical or magical intervention.

Merely acknowledging the meaning and importance of spirituality is not sufficient to establish deep-level, relational trust and rapport with the client (Mohatt, 1988). If necessary, the counselor should be willing to assist the client in exploring the meaning of spirituality and its purpose in his or her current life situation; in fact, it may be that clients are struggling with spiritual beliefs even to the extent that they believe they may have violated certain facets of spiritual practices and beliefs (Duran, 2006; Gone, 2010).

Assessment

Use of psychological tests to assess and measure an Indian or Native's psychological well-being or mental health status has generated considerable discussion and debate in recent decades. Well-meaning and informed critics argue that many of the existing standardized psychological tests that presume universal or culture-general features are not useful for meaningful application to culturally unique populations (Dana, 2000). Several cross-cultural psychologists contend that "comparing elements from differing societies leads to inadmissible distortions of reality" (Kobben, 1970, p. 584). Part of the problem stems from the possibility that the tests and measures are not culturally resonant with the population or ethnic group of interest. In effect, test developers appear to give little serious attention to issues of cultural measurement equivalence (Trimble, 2010b). Any psychological test's content, format, and metric style must be congruent with and comparable within and across the cultural groups selected for study.

Achieving cultural measurement equivalence requires that common measurement and assessment processes exist with an ethnocultural group. The principle holds that a universal process must be developed to demonstrate and assess ethnocultural group comparability. Consequently, to achieve functionality, two or more behaviors must "pre-exist as naturally occurring phenomena" that are related or identical to a similar problem or circumstance; the behaviors serve a similar function for all groups involved in the comparison test findings (Berry, 1969; Trimble, Helms, & Root, 2003; Trimble, Lonner, & Boucher, 1983). Conceptual and stimulus equivalence exists when the meaning of stimuli, concepts, methods, and so on are similar or identical for the culturally different respondents. Linguistic equivalence is similar, although the emphasis is placed on the linguistic accuracy of item translations. Unfortunately, few researchers have actively sought to develop psychological measures that fit the basic criteria for cultural measurement equivalence with Indian and Native populations (Allen & Walsh, 2000). Conventional standardized measures and tests typically used to assess mental health and psychological characteristics, therefore, must not be used at all or used with extreme caution, unless the test developer has validated the measure and corresponding scales' measurement equivalence with North America's indigenous people (Trimble, 2010a).

Lonner (1976) and Lonner and Ibrahim (2002) point out that most multicultural counselors and psychotherapists do not routinely use mental health tests in their client sessions.

> The difficulties associated with their use across cultures will serve only to reinforce their preference to use the interview, medical reports, academic records, or other means to develop a dossier of information for the mutual benefit of this professional interaction. (Lonner, 1976, p. 298)

If counselors who work with Indians and Natives use any assessment tool or mental health test at all, they tend to use measures of depression. Use of standardized depression measures, such as the Center for Epidemiological Studies Depression Scale (CES-D), the Diagnostic Interview Schedule for Children (DISC), or the Minnesota Multiphasic Personality Inventory (MMPI), dominate the small literature in the field on the use of diagnostic instruments to assess Indian and Native mental health status. (Dinges, Atlis, & Ragan, 2000). Research findings from the use of the three measures are mixed and uneven as they often depart from norms. Many of the research problems and findings derive from the fact, certainly among more traditional Indians and Natives, that there is the tendency to somaticize psychological complaints, which often belies the intent, approach, and themes of certain psychological tests; the client's tendency to rely on somatic explanations can come out in the initial sessions, and if that's the case, it assists in defining a counseling strategy.

There are a few workable alternatives to the conventional use of standardized tests and measures that are worthy of consideration. Because of the collective, familial orientation of most indigenous people, use of genograms in the early sessions is worthy of consideration. Typically, genograms enable a counselor to map and illustrate family patterns, the extent of the history of relationships, and their connections with the client's perceived problems. Using summary illustrations, results from genograms often serve to illuminate clients' understanding and the influence that repetitive family relationships and dynamics have had in their lives (McGoldrick, 1998, 2004; McGoldrick & Gerson, 1985; Rigazio-DiGilio, Ivey, Grady, & Kunkler-Peck, 2005).

Counselors also should consider using projective tests, such as the Tell-Me-A-Story Test (TEMA; Costantino & Malgady, 2000), the Draw-A-Person Test (French, 1993), and the Once-Upon-A-Time Test (Fagulha, 2000). These assessment procedures have been used with other ethnocultural groups with success, although there is no documentation of their use with Indians and Natives. Nonetheless, the cited projective tests are known to resonate with the deep cultural thoughtways of indigenous people because they rely on storytelling and use of culturally specific metaphors, and therefore create opportunities for self-expression and reflection that might not arise during the sessions.

Finally, Herring (1999) recommends use of a synergetic form of assessment, which is "a creative synthesis and a selective blending of the unique combinations of diverse assessment techniques" (p. 43). Herring's model creates a blend of assessment tools that fits with the counselor's assessment preferences and honors and shows respect for the client's lifeways and thoughtways. The model also provides the counselor with the opportunity to understand how clients construct their worldview and ascribe meaning to its dimensions and elements.

Facilitating Awareness

Many traditional Indians and Natives who experience behavioral, cognitive, and emotional problems may actually be waiting for something outside themselves to take care of them. The belief is lodged in the folk wisdom that something outside them contributed to their uncomfortable and distressing feelings, so the resolution is thought to lie somewhere outside and around them. Such individuals contend that hope and patience will bring about positive change, and if it doesn't, they believe they haven't been patient enough. Others may believe that their problems were caused by some violation of a cultural norm or are a form of punishment brought on by a transgression that disturbed the harmony and balance of the world around them. Others might believe they have little to no control over what happens to them, so consequently they have no idea why others say they are acting differently or strangely.

There are other explanations for one's decline and "troubles in the head" that often reflect the degree to which a client has knowledge of his or her mental health and what typically occurs in counseling sessions. Beyond ignoring the problem or having little or no understanding of it, most traditional Indian and Native clients are likely to have an explanation for their "strange" thoughts and behavior; in effect, they may be well aware of their circumstances. Apparent client idleness, therefore, may not be due to a client's lack of interest or evidence of irresponsible behavior. In essence, there are seemingly countless tribal-specific normative styles that are used by traditional clients to deal with problematic and stressful life situations (Heilbron & Guttman, 2000). Facilitating client awareness of problems begins with the counselor recognizing the possibility that the client already has the explanation and solution at hand. Therefore, opportunities should be created to allow clients to express themselves, that is, if they believe the counselor will listen with understanding ear and open mind.

Use of a mindful approach can facilitate an understanding of the client's presenting problem as well as promote the counselor's willingness to consider the deep cultural factors that influence it. According to Langer (1997), "A mindful approach to any activity has three characteristics: the continuous creation of new categories; openness to new information; and an implicit awareness of more than one perspective" (p. 4). To create an atmosphere filled with mindfulness, counselor and client must agree to the three characteristics. The client's culturally grounded explanations for the presenting problems may be at odds with the real-life circumstances that contribute to them. And if that's the case, the counselor and client should consider alternative explanations. Langer points out that "we discover that by reviewing the same information through several perspectives, we actually become more open to that information" (p. 133).

Numerous cross-cultural counselors and psychotherapists indicate that traditionally oriented Indian and Natives are not comfortable with open and frank discussions with strangers about their personal problems, much less with someone from a non-Indian or non-Native ethnocultural group (Herring, 1999; LaFromboise et al., 1990; Matheson, 1986; Peregoy, 1999; Sage, 1997; Trimble & Gonzalez, 2008). Self-disclosure achieved through a continuous conversation about one's personal experiences and the factors that contribute to the problems may be unacceptable. Use of self-disclosure as a counseling technique, therefore, may have to be negotiated. Additionally, the counselor may have to resort to an assortment of counseling strategies to assist the client in learning how to be a client whose ultimate goals could be personal insight, partial or complete acceptance of responsibility for the problem, and the awareness that he or she has the power to bring about positive change.

Counseling, whatever form it takes, is predicated on the principle that people learn from the experience. The learning outcomes depend a great deal on the nature and quality of the relationship forged between the client and the counselor; for the relationship and the outcomes to be positive, the partners must negotiate the conditions under which client and counselor awareness occur.

Setting Goals

Counselor and client relationships are dictated by the time frames and settings in which counseling occurs. Consequently, organizational and temporal constraints on the relationship will influence client and counselor goals as well as the outcomes. For many Indian and Native clients, goals may have to be framed in the short term, as past experiences suggest this is more practical than laying out long-term strategies (Herring, 1999; Sue & Sue, 1999). Counselors can begin this process by helping the client identify and acknowledge a part of the problem that can be dealt with in the short term; that is, identifying a part of the problem for which there may be an obvious or clear-cut solution, such as what to do with an employer, transportation needs, child care, or problems with school attendance. Once a goal is identified, reasonable solutions can be worked out that could assist in leading to the identification of other achievable goals for which there may be uncomplicated solutions. Through this process, the counselor and client may be able to move closer to identifying and setting goals that get closer to the core of the presenting problem.

For many Indian and Native clients, the counseling process is a narrative. Through a storytelling medium, the client's problems and circumstances are described, often in great detail. Indian and Native women and men, however, may differ considerably in what they choose to emphasize in the narrative (Malone, 2000; Portman & Garrett, 2005). Women may choose to focus on their emotions and how events and relationships affect their feelings about the problems that surround their lives (LaFromboise et al., 1994). Men, on the other hand, may choose to deal strictly with factual or descriptive information. The effects of the events and relationships on them typically are not captured with emotionally laden words. In effect, according to Mio, Barker-Hackett, and Tumambing (2006), "women tend to internalize their disorders, whereas men externalize their disorders" (p. 239). Furthermore, the authors claim that because many women believe they have less power over their lives, they may "live with profound feelings of sadness, loss, low self-esteem, guilt, hopelessness, and self-blame" (p. 238). Men tend to avoid the expression of feelings in counseling sessions. Expressions of anger, rage, and frustration, however, may be exceptions to this general pattern. Nonetheless, the tendency for gender content differences in a counseling narrative will greatly influence the goal setting process and the identification of the actions necessary for positive client outcomes.

Harmony, balance, and close spiritual connections with relationships and the environment are strong values and beliefs for seemingly countless Indian and Native clients (J. Garrett & Garrett, 1998; M. Garrett, 1999; Gone, 2010; Reimer, 1999; Trimble & Gonzalez, 2008). A client's conviction and the corresponding nagging feeling that his or her actions created a disruptive imbalance can be sufficiently overpowering to forge a foreboding sense of helplessness and hopelessness. Use of conventional counseling strategies and techniques may be woefully insufficient to assist the client in removing the portentous cloak of disrupted balance and disharmony. If and when the client reveals this feeling and belief, the counselor might consider discussing the circumstances with a traditional healer, preferably one who is a member of the client's Indian tribe or Native village; indeed, the client should be asked for permission to seek out the consultation.

Counselors also should consider working with "community caretakers" who can be found in most, if not all, Indian and Native communities. Many work in tribal government offices, local health care authorities such as the Indian Health Service or urban Indian and Native mental health centers, and in law enforcement. Communities often have local support groups that deal with a variety of personal and community problems such as mental health, substance abuse, domestic violence, and educational development. In many instances, the groups base their relational approach on a self-help orientation in which group members cooperate in promoting positive growth and development. Client participation in local self-help groups can provide them with a sense of purpose as well as assist them in identifying effective coping styles for dealing with problematic life events by working closely with others who may be experiencing similar problems (Lieberman, Borman, & Associates, 1979).

There is a growing tendency for counselors to establish working relationships with traditional healers (Moodley & West, 2005). Such collaboration can take several forms: (1) support for the use of traditional healing as an effective treatment system; (2) actively referring clients to indigenous healers; or (3) actively working with healers. Often clients will choose to work simultaneously with traditional healers and counselors. Such arrangements influence counseling goals, especially if the healer and counselor are communicating with one another.

There is a growing trend for counselors working with Indian and Native clients to incorporate spirituality in counseling sessions. According to a few multicultural counselors, such approaches have achieved a modest degree of success. J. Garrett and Garrett (1998), for example, describe the use of the "sacred circle" and its related symbolism in an "inner/outer circle" form of group therapy and how the Indian and Native perspective can facilitate client progress through use of short-term client goals. Using a variant of process-oriented training that is grounded in spirituality, Lewis, Duran, and Woodis (1999) found that the technique enabled counselors to enter into a non-Western-based reality with their clients, thus enhancing their sensitivity to and respect for Indian and Native worldviews; the achievement of the sensitivity can be a laudable relational goal.

_____ Taking Action and Instigating Change

Change can only occur if clients are willing to acknowledge that they are, at a minimum, responsible for taking the positive steps to achieve counseling goals; that is, with a counselor's guidance, clients come to realize they have the power, control, and responsibility to initiate personal change as well as manage certain environmental factors that contribute to their presenting problem. To initiate the process, the counselor should assist the client in identifying troubling or problematic factors and circumstances that appear to be within reach. Put another way, the client would be asked to identify and describe personal and environmental stressors. Counselors can facilitate the process by having the client narrow the stressors to single descriptors, to allow for the discussion of the various ways that clients cope with each of them, especially those that appear to be counterproductive. In turn, this permits the counselor and client to identify as well as negotiate constructive coping strategies. To assist in organizing coping skills, Moos (1986) suggests that they can be framed according to three domains:

1. Appraisal. Focused coping occurs when the client attempts to find meaning in a problematic life situation. Properly guided appraisal and reappraisal discussions can be viewed as a coping style because they provide the client with the opportunity to view the problem from slightly different mindful perspectives.

2. Problem. Focused coping provides the client with the opportunity to confront the problem and its plausible sources. The confrontation can facilitate the client's plan for dealing with the problem and its sources.

3. Emotion. Focused coping "aims to manage the feelings provoked by the crisis and to maintain emotional equilibrium." (p. 14)

When experiencing problematic life events, some traditional Indian and Native clients believe that the problems will eventually fade away if one is willing to be patient and endure occasional emotional shock and psychological distress. Others believe if they work harder and longer at something or engage in busywork, the problems will decrease gradually in intensity and eventually disappear. In effect, a fatalistic orientation to one's problems is the dominant coping strategy and thus negatively influences the possibility of one taking actual control and power in bringing about constructive change.

To shift the locus of evaluation away from a fatalistic orientation, an approach worth considering is use of a "mirroring technique." Inviting family members or trusted community members into selected counseling sessions can facilitate the effectiveness of the technique. With the assistance of co-counselors, the client's discussions and enactments of the stressors and their compounding problems can be "mirrored" or "reflected" back to the client. In effect, after the client describes his or her feelings and thoughts, others "mimic" or "mirror" the descriptions, enabling the client to experience what he or she presents to others. The technique can assist client and counselor to identify client insights and possible sources of resistance. Potential sources of change can flow from the experience and guide the apprehension and fulfillment of client goals.

Use of cognitive-behavioral counseling strategies that emphasize self-appraisal and the meaning of events through an emphasis on self-efficacy can be useful for Indian and Native clients (McDonald & Gonzalez, 2006). Emphasizing self-efficacy can be viewed as a positive coping strategy and thus lead the client to influence and control positive movement toward change. An emphasis on the clients' belief that they can take charge of their life circumstances and their presenting problem facilitates counseling goals.

By gaining personal strength from a strong belief in self-efficacy, the client would be able to more easily identify goals and the coping styles necessary to work toward them. With the counselor's guidance and encouragement, clients can identify the most efficacious tasks that will lead to effective adaptations to client life stressors. Moos (1986) recommends that the client and counselor work through the following tasks to achieve identifiable goals:

1. Establish the meaning and understand the personal significance of the situation.

2. Confront reality and respond to the requirements of the external situation.

3. Sustain relationships with family members and friends as well as with other individuals who may be helpful in resolving the crisis and its aftermath.

4. Maintain a reasonable emotional balance by managing upsetting feelings aroused by the situation.

5. Preserve a satisfactory self-image and maintain a sense of competence and mastery. (p. 11)

Feedback and Accountability

Although feedback and accountability occurs last in the AIAN-SISM list, it's something that should occur throughout the counseling process. Indian and Native clients unfamiliar with the possibility that counseling will involve many sessions may not attend scheduled sessions if feedback is not provided all along. Similarly, clients must be held accountable, and therefore responsible, for following through on negotiated agreements; in some instances, Indian and Native clients have been known to hold counselors responsible for the absence of change in their lives and thus terminate the relationship.

Indian and Native grounded feedback procedures can take many useful forms. However, the most useful approach is for the client and counselor to summarize the events, dialogue, and agreements at the end and the beginning of each session. Some multicultural counselors ask clients to summarize the main points on small 3" x 5" cards or notepaper. Counselors review the summaries for clarification and accuracy and then give the written material to the clients, with the instructions that they review it before their next session. In subsequent summaries, clients can jot down noticeable and positive emotional, cognitive, and behavioral changes that have occurred. Use of this technique serves to sustain the narrative, the process of self-discovery, confidence, self-mastery, and hope.

Use of counseling feedback strategies and techniques that resonate with Indian traditions and customs can be effective. Herring (1994) and Herring and Meggert (1994) recommend that counselors use humor, especially in the forms of storytelling, story reading, puppetry, and games. Dufrene and Coleman (1994) and Appleton and Dykeman (1996) note the importance of art for Indian and Native clients and its role in promoting well-being and healing. Humor and art are very much a part of many traditional healing practices; thus, these recommendations make good sense because they tie counseling procedures to the clients' traditions and customs.

Occasionally, with the assistance of local "community caretakers" and family members, counselors may want to weave traditional healing approaches in with conventional techniques to effect a positive outcome and promote accountability. Simms (1999) describes the use of a blended counseling approach that combined an integrated relational behavioral-cognitive strategy with traditional healing approaches, including talking circles, sweats, and participation in cultural forums; each of these approaches involved the constant use of feedback. The client that Simms describes was experiencing cultural identity, self-confidence, and academic problems that could not be resolved through the use of a straightforward conventional counseling technique.

J. Garrett and Garrett (1998) describe the use of the "sacred circle" and its related symbolism in an "inner/outer circle" form of group therapy and how the Indian and Native perspective can facilitate client progress and facilitate feedback. Using a variant of process-oriented training that is grounded in spirituality, Lewis et al. (1999) have found that the technique can enable therapists to enter into a non-Western-based reality with their clients, thus enhancing their sensitivity to and respect for Indian and Native worldviews. Moreover, Tafoya (1989) advocates the use of a traditional Sahaptin legend as a paradigm for the way many Indians and Natives view the core elements of family therapy, specifically relationships, responsibilities, learning, and teaching. He recommends that counselors working with Indians and Natives recognize and value the significance of the circle as a model for relationships; he also suggests that counselors avoid the use of direct, confrontational questioning; respect individual clients' life choices; and strive to achieve rapport with clients by openly expressing respect for culturally different worldviews.

Incorporating traditional spiritual and healing methods such as the sweat lodge and talking circles can facilitate counselor effectiveness and client retention and progress, under controlled circumstances (Colmant & Merta, 1999). Decisions to use such techniques must be made with a strong degree of caution. LaDue (1994) strongly recommends that non-Indian counselors abstain from participating in and using such practices, asserting that they should not promote or condone the stealing and inappropriate use of Indian and Native spiritual activities. Doing so may invoke ethical considerations, as Indian and Native spiritual activities and practices are the sole responsibility of acknowledged and respected healers and elders.

Conclusion

While the AIAN-SISM highlights specific skills that can be implemented where appropriate, in the process of culturally attending to the needs of American Indian and Alaska Native clients in therapy, the process by which counselors choose to understand and extend their efforts to learn about the culture is more critical. The case examples in the following chapters illustrate evidence-based practices within an AIAN-SISM framework. Consistent with the EBPP definition, the authors have outlined any available research within the context of their clients' presenting problems, included their own clinical expertise and experience in their work, and placed culture as primary to their work with these cases.

References

Allen, J., & Walsh, J. A. (2000). A construct-based approach to equivalence: Methodologies for cross-cultural multicultural personality assessment research and assessment. In R. H. Dana (Ed.), *Handbook of cross-cultural and multicultural personality assessment* (pp. 63–85). Mahwah, NJ: Lawrence Erlbaum.

Anderson, M., & Ellis, R. (1995). On the reservation. In N. Vacc & S. DeVaney (Eds.), *Experiencing and counseling multicultural and diverse populations* (pp. 179–197). Muncie, IN: Accelerated Development.

Appleton, V., & Dykeman, C. (1996). Using art in group counseling with Native American youth. *Journal for Specialists in Group Work, 21,* 224–231.

Berry, J. (1969). On cross-cultural comparability. *International Journal of Psychology, 4,* 119–128.

Brave Heart, M. Y. H., & DeBruyn, L. (1998). The American Indian holocaust: Healing unresolved grief. *American Indian and Alaska Native Mental Health Research, 8*(2), 56–78.

Colmant, S., & Merta, R. (1999). Using the sweat lodge ceremony as group therapy for Navajo youth. *Journal for Specialists in Group Work, 24,* 55–73.

Costantino, G., & Malgady, R. G. (2000). Multicultural and cross-cultural utility of the TEMAS (Tell-Me-A-Story) test. In R. H. Dana (Ed.), *Handbook of cross-cultural and multicultural personality assessment* (pp. 481–513). Mahwah, NJ: Lawrence Erlbaum.

Dana, R. H. (Ed.). (2000). *Handbook of cross-cultural and multicultural personality assessment.* Mahwah, NJ: Lawrence Erlbaum.

Darou, W. G. (1987). Counseling and the northern Native. *Canadian Journal of Counselling, 21,* 33–41.

Dinges, N., Atlis, M. M., & Ragan, S. L. (2000). Assessment of depression among American Indians and Alaska Natives. In R. H. Dana (Ed.), *Handbook of cross-cultural and multicultural personality assessment* (pp. 623–646). Mahwah, NJ: Lawrence Erlbaum.

Dufrene, P., & Coleman, V. (1994). Art and healing for Native American Indians. *Journal of Multicultural Counseling and Development, 22,* 145–152.

Duran, E. (2006). *Healing the soul wound: Counseling American Indians and other native peoples.* Williston, VT: Teachers College Press.

Duran, E., & Duran, B. (1995). *Native American postcolonial psychology.* Albany: State University of New York Press.

Fagulha, T. (2000). The Once-Upon-A-Time Test. In R. H. Dana (Ed.), *Handbook of cross-cultural and multicultural personality assessment* (pp. 515–536). Mahwah, NJ: Lawrence Erlbaum.

French, L. A. (1993). Adapting projective tests for minority children. *Psychological Reports, 72,* 15–18.

Garrett, J., & Garrett, M. (1998). The path of good medicine: Understanding and counseling Native American Indians. In D. R. Atkinson, G. Morten, & D. W. Sue (Eds.), *Counseling American minorities* (5th ed., pp. 183–192). New York: McGraw-Hill.

Garrett, M. (1999). Understanding the "medicine" of Native American traditional values: An integrative review. *Counseling and Values, 43*(2), 84–98.

Gone, J. P. (2009). A community-based treatment for Native American historical trauma: Prospects for evidence-based practice. *Journal of Consulting & Clinical Psychology, 77*(4), 751–762.

Gone, J. P. (2010). Psychotherapy and traditional healing for American Indians: Exploring the prospects for therapeutic integration. *The Counseling Psychologist, 38*(2), 166–235.

Good Tracks, J. G. (1973). Native American noninterference. *Social Work, 17,* 30–34.

Heilbron, C., & Guttman, M. (2000). Traditional healing methods with First Nations women in group counseling. *Canadian Journal of Counselling, 34,* 3–13.

Helms J. E., & Cook, D. (1999). *Using race and culture in counseling and psychotherapy: Theory and practice.* Boston: Allyn & Bacon.

Herring, R. D. (1990). Understanding Native American values: Process and content concerns for counselors. *Counseling and Values, 34,* 134–137.

Herring, R. D. (1994). The clown or contrary figure as a counseling intervention strategy with Native American Indian clients. *Journal of Multicultural Counseling and Development, 22,* 153–164.

Herring, R. D. (1999). *Counseling with Native American Indians and Alaska Natives: Strategies for helping professionals.* Thousand Oaks, CA: Sage.

Herring, R. D., & Meggert, S. S. (1994). The use of humor as a counselor strategy with Native American Indian children. *Elementary School Guidance and Counseling, 29,* 67–76.

Kobben, A. (1970). Comparativists and non-comparativists in anthropology. In R. Naroll & R. Cohen (Eds.), *A handbook of method in cultural anthropology* (pp. 581–596). New York: Natural History Press.

LaDue, R. (1994). Coyote returns: Twenty sweats does not an Indian expert make. *Women and Therapy, 5*(1), 93–111.

LaFromboise, T., Berman, J., & Sohi, B. (1994). American Indian women. In L. Comas-Diaz & B. Greene (Eds.), *Women of color: Integrating ethnic and gender identities in psychotherapy* (pp. 30–71). New York: Guilford Press.

LaFromboise, T., & Bigfoot, D. (1988). Cultural and cognitive considerations in the prevention of American Indian adolescent suicide. *Journal of Adolescence, 11*(2), 139–153.

LaFromboise, T., & Dixon, D. (1981). American Indian perceptions of trustworthiness in a counseling interview. *Journal of Counseling Psychology, 28,* 135–139.

LaFromboise, T., Trimble, J. E., & Mohatt, G. (1990). Counseling intervention and American Indian tradition: An integrative approach. *The Counseling Psychologist, 18*(4), 628–654.

Langer, E. J. (1997). *The power of mindful learning.* Cambridge, MA: Perseus.

Lee, S. (1997). Communication styles of Wind River Native American clients and the therapeutic approaches of their clinicians. *Smith College Studies in Social Work, 68*(1), 57–81.

Lerner, M. (2000). *Spirit matters.* Charlottesville, VA: Hampton Roads.

Lewis, E., Duran, E., & Woodis, W. (1999). Psychotherapy in the American Indian population. *Psychiatric Annals, 29,* 477–479.

Lieberman, M. A., Borman, L. D., & Associates. (1979). *Self-help groups for coping with crisis: Origins, members, processes, and impact.* San Francisco: Jossey-Bass.

Lockhart, B. (1981). Historic distrust and the counseling of American Indians and Alaskan Natives. *White Cloud Journal, 2*(3), 31–43.

Lonner, W. J. (1976). Psychological tests and intercultural counseling. In P. Pedersen, W. J. Lonner, J. Draguns, & J. E. Trimble (Eds.), *Counseling across cultures, revised and expanded edition* (pp. 273–298). Honolulu: University Press of Hawaii.

Lonner, W. J., & Ibrahim, F. A. (2002). Appraisal and assessment in cross-cultural counseling. In P. Pedersen, J. Draguns, W. Lonner, & J. E. Trimble (Eds.), *Counseling across cultures* (5th ed., pp. 355–379). Thousand Oaks, CA: Sage.

Malone, J. (2000). Working with Aboriginal women: Applying feminist therapy in a multicultural counseling context. *Canadian Journal of Counseling, 34,* 33–42.

Matheson, L. (1986). If you are not an Indian, how do you treat an Indian? In H. P. Lefley & P. B. Pedersen (Eds.), *Cross-cultural training for mental health professionals* (pp. 115–130). Springfield, IL: Charles C Thomas.

McCormick, R. (1996). Culturally appropriate means and ends of counseling as described by the First Nations people of British Columbia. *International Journal for the Advancement of Counseling, 18*(3), 163–172.

McDonald, J. D., & Gonzalez, J. (2006). Cognitive-behavior therapy with American Indians. In P. A. Hays & G. Y. Iwamasa (Eds.), *Cognitive-behavior therapy with culturally diverse people* (pp. 23–46). Washington, DC: American Psychological Association.

McGoldrick, M. (1998). Introduction: Re-visioning family therapy through a cultural lens. In M. McGoldrick (Ed.), *Re-visioning family therapy: Race, culture, and gender in clinical practice* (pp. 3–19). New York: Guilford Press.

McGoldrick, M., & Gerson, R. (1985). *Genograms in family assessment.* New York: W. W. Norton.

Mio, J. S., Barker-Hackett, L., & Tumambing, J. (2006). *Multicultural psychology: Understanding our diverse communities.* Boston: McGraw-Hill.

Mohatt, G. V. (1988). Psychological method and spiritual power in cross-cultural psychotherapy. *Journal of Contemplative Psychotherapy, V,* 85–115.

Mohatt, G., & Eagle Elk, J. (2000). *The price of a gift: A Lakota healer's story.* Lincoln: University of Nebraska Press.

Moodley, R., & West, W. (2005). *Integrating traditional healing practices into counseling and psychotherapy.* Thousand Oaks, CA: Sage.

Moos, R. H. (Ed.). (1986). *Coping with life crises: An integrated approach.* New York: Plenum Press.

Morrissette, P. (1994). The holocaust of First Nations people: Residual effects on parenting and treatment implications. *Contemporary Family Therapy, 16,* 381–392.

Nebelkopf, E., & Phillips, M. (Eds.). (2004). *Healing and mental health for Native Americans: Speaking in red.* New York: Altamira.

Olsen, M. J. (2003). Counselor understanding of Native American spiritual loss. *Counseling and Values, 47,* 109–117.

Peregoy, J. J. (1993). Transcultural counseling with American Indians/Alaskan Natives: Contemporary issues for consideration. In J. McFadden (Ed.), *Transcultural counseling: Bilateral and international perspectives (pp. 163–192).* Alexandria, VA: American Counseling Association Press.

Peregoy, J. J. (1999). Revisiting transcultural counseling with American Indians and Alaskan Natives: Issues for consideration. In J. McFadden (Ed.), *Transcultural counseling* (2nd ed., pp. 137–170). Alexandria, VA: American Counseling Association.

Portman, T. A., & Garrett, M. T. (2005). Beloved women: Nurturing the sacred fire of leadership from an American Indian perspective. *Journal of Counseling and Development, 83*(3), 284–291.

Reimer, C. S. (1999). *Counseling the Inupiat Eskimo.* Westport, CT: Greenwood.

Rigazio-DiGilio, S. A., Ivey, A. E., Grady, L. T., & Kunkler-Peck, K. P. (2005). *Community genograms: Using individual, family, and cultural narratives with clients.* New York: Teachers College Press.

Sage, G. (1997). Counseling American Indian clients. In C. C. Lee (Ed.), *Multicultural issues in counseling: New approaches to diversity* (2nd ed., pp. 35–52). Alexandria, VA: American Counseling Association.

Simms, W. (1999). The Native American Indian client: A tale of two cultures. In Y. Jenkins (Ed.), *Diversity in college settings: Directives for helping professionals* (pp. 21–35). New York: Routledge.

Sue, D. W., & Sue, D. (1999). *Counseling the culturally diverse: Theory and practice* (3rd ed.). New York: John Wiley & Sons.

Tafoya, T. (1989). Circles and cedar: Native Americans and family therapy. *Journal of Psychotherapy and the Family, 6*(1–2), 71–98.

Trimble, J. E. (1981). Value differentials and their importance in counseling American Indians. In P. B. Pedersen, J. G. Draguns, W. J. Lonner, & J. E. Trimble (Eds.), *Counseling across cultures* (Rev. ed., pp. 203–226). Honolulu: University of Hawaii Press.

Trimble. J. E. (2010a). Bear spends time in our dreams now: Magical thinking and cultural empathy in multicultural counselling theory and practice. *Counselling Psychology Quarterly, 23*(3), 241–253.

Trimble, J. E. (2010b). Cultural measurement equivalence. In C. S. Clauss-Ehlers (Ed.), *Encyclopedia of cross-cultural school psychology* (pp. 316–318). New York: Springer.

Trimble, J. E. (2010c). The virtues of cultural resonance, competence, and relational collaboration with Native American Indian communities: A synthesis of the counseling and psychotherapy literature. *The Counseling Psychologist, 38(2),* 243–256.

Trimble, J. E., & Bagwell, W. (Eds.). (1995). *North American Indians and Alaska natives: Abstracts of psychological and behavioral literature, 1967–1995.* Washington, DC: American Psychological Association.

Trimble, J. E., & Dickson, R. (2005). Ethnic identity. In C. B. Fisher & R. M. Lerner (Eds.), *Applied developmental science: An encyclopedia of research, policies, and programs* (pp. 412–415). Thousand Oaks, CA: Sage.

Trimble, J. E., & Gonzalez, J. (2008). Cultural considerations and perspectives for providing psychological counseling for Native American Indians. In P. B. Pedersen, J. G. Draguns, W. J. Lonner, & J. E. Trimble (Eds.), *Counseling across cultures* (6th ed., pp. 93-111). Thousand Oaks, CA: Sage.

Trimble, J. E., & Hayes, S. A. (1984). Mental health intervention in the psychological contexts of American Indian communities. In W. A. O'Connor & B. Lubin (Eds.), *Ecological models: Applications to clinical and community mental health* (pp. 293–321). New York: John Wiley & Sons.

Trimble, J.E., Helms, J. E., & Root, M. P. P. (2003). Social and psychological perspectives on ethnic and racial identity. In G. Bernal, J. E. Trimble, A. K. Burlew, & F. T. L. Leong (Eds.), *Handbook of racial and ethnic minority psychology* (pp. 239–275). Thousand Oaks, CA: Sage.

Trimble, J. E., Lonner, W. J., & Boucher, J. D. (1983). Stalking the wily emic: Alternatives to cross-cultural measurement. In S. Irvine & J. Berry (Eds.), *Human assessment and cultural factors* (pp. 259–273). New York: Plenum Press.

Trimble, J. E., & Thurman, P. (2002). Ethnocultural considerations and strategies for providing counseling services to Native American Indians. In P. B Pedersen, J. G. Draguns, W. J. Lonner, & J. E. Trimble (Eds.), *Counseling across cultures* (5th ed., pp. 53–91). Thousand Oaks, CA: Sage.

U.S. Census Bureau. (2006). *Statistical abstract of the United States: 2006.* Washington, DC: U.S. Government Printing Office.

Weaver, H. N., & Brave Heart, M. Y. H. (1999). Examining two facets of American Indian identity: Exposure to other cultures and the influence of historical trauma. In H. N. Weaver (Ed.), *Voices of First Nations people: Human services considerations (pp. 19-33).* New York: Haworth.

Witko, T. M. (Ed.). (2006). *Mental health care for urban Indians: Clinical insights from Native practitioners.* Washington, DC: American Psychological Association.

12

Case Illustration: The Treatment of PTSD With a Laguna Pueblo Woman

Implementation of the AIAN-SISM

Jeff King

Maria was a 35-year-old Laguna Pueblo woman who was referred by an Arizona Victims' Assistance program. Maria had witnessed a robbery and shooting. The robbers followed her to her apartment and shot her in the face. The bullet went through her left cheek and lodged itself in her right cheek bone. Maria was referred for posttraumatic stress related to this incident. However, there were many more issues Maria was dealing with that needed to be part of our therapeutic journey.

Maria had been diagnosed previously with bipolar disorder and was taking prescribed medication for this. Her primary features from the bipolar condition were pronounced mania that often included intense rage and violent behaviors. Complicating her condition were other significant traumas throughout her life.

Maria was born on the reservation in poverty conditions. She witnessed a good deal of violence among both family and community members. Further, she did not know her father and her mother was a chronic alcoholic. Maria was also raped at age 13 by a maternal uncle. This was not reported to any authorities, which further compromised her ability to trust family or anyone else.

During her teens she was a rough and tough sort of adolescent, her anger fueling many fights and social conflicts. She became pregnant at age 16 and subsequently raised her son at her mother's house. During this time, she continued to live a wild life, including significant alcohol abuse and violent behavior. She married an ex-soldier who was extremely violent and possessive. She recalled that it "was like being held prisoner in my own home." She was not allowed friends or visitors, except maybe her mother. Once Maria tried to escape and was severely beaten by her husband. Over the course of the relationship, she was beaten many times. The physical results of these beatings were a fractured eye socket (she saw double and triple out of this eye), both shin bones broken (one had a rod inserted by doctors that had become problematic and caused her chronic pain), punctured ear drums, and fractured fingers.

She was finally able to escape and get into a victim relocation program and was able to relocate to a major city in the southwest. She had been in this program for several years when the shooting incident occurred. As if this was not tragic enough, her 14-year-old son had committed suicide seven months earlier, back on her reservation.

Maria did not expect much from the therapeutic relationship because her previous attempts at counseling had yielded very little positive change. She was pleased to have been referred to an Indigenous American counselor and expressed some encouragement that she "might be understood better."

Theoretical Orientation: Traditional/Culturally Responsive

The theoretical orientation utilized in this case is linked more with a newly emerging North American Indigenous peoples' psychology. North American Indigenous Psychology (NAIP) is the study and practice of what comprises the well-being of Indigenous peoples. It is primarily rooted in the worldviews of indigenous peoples and thus acknowledges and respects the history, beliefs, traditions, and spirituality of each tribe/nation it serves. NAIP applies itself in such a manner that the persons served become more fully who they are meant to be as tribal members (cultural beings). In this context, it understands both well-being and ill-being as it relates to each person, family, and tribe/nation according to their worldview, values, beliefs, and lifeways.

A broader definition of this type of approach, while utilizing theories and techniques developed within Euro-American science, recognizes the inherent racism and limitations of these approaches. It broadens the psychological approach to healing by acknowledging the spiritual realm; the importance of traditional healing practices; ceremony; and the sacredness of place, person, and life. It may incorporate these aspects into counseling, study, or intervention, depending on permission or invitation by the person/family/tribe.

Model Implementation and Treatment Implications

Because of historical trauma suffered by Indigenous people and how that has affected individual views of psychological treatment, the foremost concern in the beginning of treatment was building trust. Thus, it was important to identify myself by letting her know my name, tribal affiliation, clan, and township. Maria provided identification about herself in a similar manner. It is a way of introduction that the other can feel, "Now I know who you are." Comfort level is increased at this point and there is the beginning of a sense of safety in being able to fully tell your story. Family and life history are shared as well, and this serves to provide context for the specific issue(s) to be addressed through therapy. In congruence with the NAIP approach, this style of introduction and storytelling communicates to clients that they will be understood and related to in a manner that is consistent with who they are as a tribal person. This is usually a very different experience than what they are accustomed to in their encounters with social services, and in some ways provides a healing aspect to past treatments that required them to adapt to Euro-American systems of care.

Case Conceptualization

Case conceptualization from an Indigenous perspective often is premature. The focus is not on analyzing or coming up with a diagnosis for the person. Rather, it is more focused on the unfolding story and the information provided therein. If anything, the case conceptualization was viewed as that of two people journeying together and exploring what has happened and what is to happen.

Because of the comfort level and feeling understood as a cultural person, Maria felt free to open up about her "gifts." One of these gifts was her ability to see into the future. She described many events where she predicted who was going to visit or what was going to happen to another person and how they came true. This would not necessarily have been something she would have told a doctor who was not sensitive to her culture. However, it figures quite centrally in her view of what happened and actually provided her with a sense of hope around her future and her healing from this trauma.

The day before this shooting, Maria had a premonition that she was going to die. This frightened her and she sought help from both a medicine man and a priest. They both prayed for her and the medicine man conducted a ceremony for her protection. Maria believes that it was the prayers and ceremony that lowered the aim on the man's gun from her temple to her cheek. She felt the Creator had answered these prayers and honored the ceremony performed for her. We used this notion of "being helped spiritually" as a framework for her treatment.

However, in the course of our therapy, Maria, in one of her manic rages, assaulted her boyfriend with a baseball bat and broke one of his legs. He filed charges and she was placed in jail. The critical point here was to ensure that she was able continue her medications while incarcerated. I, along with her Victims' Assistance caseworker, accompanied her to her hearing before the judge. We both recommended that Maria receive psychiatric inpatient care rather than jail time, stating that her bipolar condition was a significant causal factor in her rage and subsequent assault.

The judge went along with our recommendations and Maria was hospitalized. (The judge had to suspend her sentence and finagle her case so that she was sent to the hospital. This was the first time he had done this for a case like hers.)

Maria was frightened about going into the psychiatric hospital, asking, "Isn't that where they send the crazy people?" We told her this was a chance for her to get a full psychiatric evaluation and receive the medications she needs with monitoring so she could reach a point of emotional and psychological stability. When being admitted to the hospital, she told the intake worker, "I know you." The intake worker was a bit startled, but checked on Maria's history and replied, "No, you've never been here before." Maria replied, "I've seen you before and I know that doctor over there and that worker over there. I know this place." The intake worker insisted Maria had not been at the hospital previously. Maria explained this event to me later, and I understood that she had a déjà vu experience, which was likely related to her premonition ability. However, this experience served to reassure her that she was supposed to be in this place, helped calm her down, opening her up to benefiting from the treatment afforded her during her stay.

Hospital staff allowed me to visit her once weekly, and we were able to go out on the grounds where we would smudge (a cleansing procedure) with sage and then talk about what she was getting from her treatment.

Interestingly, since this was a state hospital, she had a thorough physical examination where they were able to discover injuries that had not been treated or had not properly healed. They told Maria that they would repair her eardrums, fix her shattered eye socket, address the injured shin bone with the inserted rod and the associated chronic pain, and quite possibly remove the bullet in her jaw. Further, hospital personnel were able to enroll her in Medicaid and get her social security disability compensation. Of course, this news was exciting for her and confirmed her premonition that she was supposed to be there.

After she was released from the hospital, she was able to find affordable housing within the limits of her social security income. Our therapy continued and began to go deeper now that there was a greater degree of stability in her life. We began to see many self-sabotaging patterns in her life and discovered they were related to her son's suicide. Although not a conscious decision, she had determined that she would never allow good to come into her life. For her, this was a way to remain connected to her son. She believed that if she were to allow good into her life, she would be betraying him by allowing her life to be better than his. We were able to explore this in terms of the many things that had come into her path (e.g., her death premonition saving her life, the judge's type of sentencing being unprecedented, all the good that came out of her contact with the state hospital, her getting medical and financial help) as an indication that it was meant to be that her life was to be better. A good portion of our therapy was working on being able to honor her son while at the same time permit herself to get better as a person. She grasped the idea easily because it fit with her experience, but found the emotional work of internalizing this more difficult. Over time, she was able to emotionally accept that getting better as a person did, indeed, honor her son and would help keep her out of trouble (something she had not experienced for many, many years). Concurrently, more good things were occurring in her life and remaining there. This was quite different from the early therapy in which good things would happen and yet she would sabotage any chance of them remaining in her life.

Therapy continued for a number of months, with deliberate slow progress in allowing greater stability and internalized good feelings about herself. Her surgeries were also ongoing. She had her ear drums fixed, had surgery on her eye socket and leg, and even had the bullet removed. Maria was getting her life back. I was honored to be a part of her journey.

Additional Clinical Considerations

The inclusion of the spiritual realm as offering meaning and healing was essential for Maria. It is hard to imagine her accepting the help that came into her life without her personal connection to her spiritual life. These things were already in place for her, even though her life was in shambles. Honoring her connection and culture allowed her to follow a path of healing that caused things to fall into place for her. These same processes gave her the ability to look deep within herself to discover the origin of her self-destructive behaviors and internalized negative self-perceptions. The work was not easy; it took great courage to continue to face these challenges, but Maria hung in there.

Within an NAIP approach, healing and wholeness stem from a central connection to spirit and culture. Most, if not all, tribes embrace this concept. Thus, therapy aligned with these core elements is not so much preformulated, as in a treatment plan, but rather accepts the idea that the things necessary for healing will unfold in their time. For the therapist, it is simply recognizing this process or force and paying attention, along with the client, to what it is saying. Life events are interpreted through this lens, and strength and hope are derived from the messages contained in these life events, dreams, premonitions, visions, and so on.

Identification of the Author's Personal Dimensions of Diversity and Worldview

I am a tribally enrolled member of the Muscogee (Creek) Nation of Oklahoma. My father's ethnicity was Euro-American. Growing up, our family was more connected to my mother's side of the family and our tribal heritage. My learning has been threefold: the academic pursuit of information, the participation in tribal/indigenous communities, and the clinical knowl-edge derived as a practitioner. These converging dimensions have led to an approach to psychotherapy that has been illustrated in this chapter. I do not believe that expertise comes from academic studies or necessarily being a clini-cian. Rather, I strongly believe (and my clients have taught me) that there is a healing process woven into the fabric of the universe, and we can learn its processes. My journeying with clients in their healing has allowed me to dis-cover some of the patterns and principles of this healing process. There is much to communicate about what all this means, but suffice it to say that the healing process manifests itself through culture, through the individual's own experience, and through the clinician's own life processes. It uses whatever means are available. It is up to the person to pay attention to his or her healing and learn to hear it, to see it, and to trust it. Once this healing begins, wonder-ful things typically occur.

Clinical and Therapeutic Recommendations _____

Therapy consisted of a number of approaches: relationship building, cultural identification with values and cultural practices, storytelling, his-tory gathering, boundary setting, visualization, dream interpretation, and spirituality in perspective taking, all tenets highlighted by the AIAN-SISM. In an Indigenous worldview, however, these disparate notions are easily accepted (e.g., what I do in the physical world affects what I am able to do in the spirit world). In contrast to a Euro-American worldview, there is much more room for mystery, and the analytical/logical under-standing of events and perceptions is not necessary. In fact, logic may get in your way. In other words, in an Indigenous approach, healing may often come in ways not understood by the conscious mind; however, Indigenous people accept this and feel comfortable with not knowing and simply accepting.

Overall, beneath her significant traumas, my client was a woman who held to her traditional ways, and thus therapy would need to respect, honor, and build on this outlook. Obviously, if she were more assimilated to main-stream culture in its outlook, therapy would have been very different. Given her ties to culture, traditional spirituality needed to be an integral part of our therapy because it formed the core principles by which she lived her life. My role as counselor was to align myself with her journey and be a helper along the way. Thus, my conceptualization evolved along the way. However, it was clear that she had significant resources in her traditional spirituality and sense of community, family, and friends. Furthermore, she had unique gifts of exquisite sensitivity and openness to the spirit world. These strengths were built on and trusted to guide the course of therapy. There was no predetermined plan for therapy but rather a trusting of Maria's spiritual process to bring to the sessions the necessary life situa-tions, dreams, images, and insights to show what the next steps would be.

Conclusion

Maria was a Laguna Pueblo woman who experienced significant and complex trauma, both recent and chronic. Furthermore, her bipolar condition was exacerbated by those traumas. A typical Euro-American therapeutic approach would have perhaps been helpful to Maria, but it would have been limited in its ability to fully comprehend her difficulties from a tribal or traditional viewpoint. Additionally, a Euro-American approach would have lacked the ability to connect and build upon her spirituality, strengths, gifts, and the healing process as manifested through her cultural outlook. Using an NAIP approach, these facets could be incorporated into the treatment. Of necessity, the therapeutic relationship dynamics were different than standard psychotherapy, and the process of therapy was changed significantly as well. The results were remarkable and beyond what any treatment plan could have envisaged. However, the most important aspect of this approach was that the client did not have to move away from her cultural bearings in order to get better. A truly culturally competent approach would be that clients receive help according to their beliefs and values, and thus, when treatment is completed, they feel even more connected to who they are as cultural beings.

Additional Clinical Considerations

Tribes have always had their healers. These healers have actively sought to understand the causes or reasons for ill health or being out of balance. Thus, psychotherapy has manifested itself in many forms in many tribes. A "best practices" psychotherapy used in tribes must be seen as an art and not as a technique. If one utilizes a theory and the techniques contained therein, one is acting as a technician, not an artist. Healing in Indian Country is an art. The focus must be on the healing process as it manifests itself within the particular individual and as part of the tribal culture. Healing wears the costume of culture, and we as clinicians must learn to recognize it in its culturally congruent form. Our therapy must be adapted to the culture to the extent that when the therapeutic process is completed, clients feel even more fully the cultural beings they are. In this context, they believe the healing is theirs, not the therapist's. Effective practice in Indian Country is one in which the history of the tribe is known, felt, and honored because the worldview of the tribe is understood and taken into account in the counseling process. Consequently, the background factors of historical trauma, the dynamics of racism, white supremacy, and oppression are, in effect, reversed in the therapy room (if that is where you decide to meet) and in the healing process. This conceptualization is a very different way of approaching psychotherapy. However, if we are serious in our efforts to provide best practice, or evidence-based practices, in Indian Country, the hard work of changing our own views about psychology and healing must be undertaken. It is not that these efforts have been made and have failed. It is that we have not given serious and respectful attention to cultural foundations of healing.

13

Case Illustration: The Throw-Away Boy

The Case of an Eastern Woodlands American Indian Adolescent

Gayle Skawennio Morse

Angela M. Enno

Jake was 16 years old when he was first seen on the sex offender unit of a maximum-security adolescent residential treatment facility for adjudicated sex offenders. Jake was remanded to the residential treatment facility after he forcibly raped a 45-year-old woman. A requirement for his eventual release was successful completion of group and individual sex offender cognitive behavioral treatment. During the initial assessment, prior to his court date in the criminal justice system, Jake was diagnosed with Conduct Disorder, adolescent onset. The diagnosis was based on the circumstances surrounding his crime, including a three-day drug binge Jake engaged in prior to the rape and his apparent lack of remorse at the time of assessment.

Jake was born on a reservation to teenaged American Indian parents. He has had only supervised visits with them since their parental rights were revoked early in Jake's life. Jake has been institutionalized since he was an infant. He was first removed from his parents at three months of age, when he was discovered in an infant car seat in a smoky bar near closing time. He had a severely infected diaper rash. His parents underwent parenting classes and regained custody of Jake. He was permanently removed from their care a year later when it was discovered he was being neglected and also used for sexual favors so his parents could obtain drugs. Jake was subsequently placed in a series of foster homes. Jake's mother maintained minimal contact with him, but his father's whereabouts were unknown. When Jake was eight years old, the tribe requested he be placed in a foster home closer to the reservation. This was granted and he lived there until he was remanded to the court for his crime.

While living at the foster home, Jake experienced little supervision from his foster parents, who were both employed. There were seven other foster children in the home, and there were often inappropriate sexual interactions between the foster children and extended family members. Jake noted that there was often "weed" available and there were few rules in the home. He did not do well in school but indicated that he enjoyed history and gym. His foster parents made only minimal and haphazard efforts to help Jake remain connected to his tribal community.

Jake initially came to treatment for mandated individual sex offender treatment. He was not interested in treatment and did not think it would be beneficial for him. However, he was interested that he had a "Native Counselor" from his tribe and was pleased to learn that if he completed treatment successfully, he would be released sooner than his sentence mandated.

Theoretical Orientation

Evidence-based practice has determined that cognitive behavioral therapy works best for sex offenders. However, despite the requirement for cognitive behavioral sex offender treatment, it quickly became apparent that Jake had other issues and problems needing treatment, such as posttraumatic stress disorder and possible reactive attachment disorder. Realizing that Jake's situation was multifaceted and multileveled, as well as anchored in conditions similar to many Native people, the therapist quickly changed to a focus more in keeping with his tribal belief system. This orientation suggests that each individual is the expert regarding himself or herself. The treatment provider in this model must pay attention to what the client knows and focus on and respect what he or she presents. The client's ability to choose to participate is paramount to the success of the treatment. Second, the therapist must trust that the client already innately has the tools that will help him or her heal and find a unique position in the world. At the same time, clients learn to trust that the therapist has additional beneficial skills to help them find their way. Third, the therapist must recognize the shared equity or reciprocal relationship between helper and helpee: Both gain from the therapeutic relationship. Finally, it is essential to empower both client and therapist to grow in their current life stage. The helper needs to continue to grow spiritually in order to continue to be an effective helper, and the helpee needs to continue to grow and heal, to find his or her position in the world and grow into his or her current life stage and potential. This orientation recognizes, and is based on, the historic information of Jake's ancestors and their joys and trials as well as the need to restore the spirit of each person.

It was important that Jake's treatment be rooted in an understanding of his cultural and historical context as an American Indian. As Duran and Duran (1995) assert, treatment of American Indian people that stems exclusively or primarily from perspectives in Western psychology is responsible for the frequent failure of the mental health system to adequately treat American Indian clients. Contemporary psychological theory and interventions are grounded in the logical positivistic frameworks of thought that gave birth to colonization and forced assimilation of Native peoples. Duran and Duran argue that the use of such treatment methods without positioning them within the theoretical context of indigenous thought represents neocolonization of our American Indian clients. Such clients are not to be blamed when the cultural paradigm of Western psychology is inadequate to address their suffering. Rather, the responsibility falls on the clinician, trained in Western psychology, to take an American Indian worldview in assessing and treating American Indian clients and to use Western psychological methods only as they are appropriate to the clients' cultural frameworks. The Western psychological worldview should not be considered more valid than traditional knowledge of healing. Thus, an attachment perspective was taken in Jake's treatment, in part because it is consistent with a Native worldview as to the importance of an individual's place in the community, his or her ability to choose, and the intertwining of spirituality with mind and body.

Jake's suffering was considered from a collectivist, rather than an individualist, perspective. It was understood that Jake's conduct problems were rooted in a disruption of his connections to family and tribe. From a Native perspective, Jake's ability to connect with and to be supported and taught by his elders was paramount to his well-being. Because of the illness in his family, he did not have the opportunity to understand this interconnectedness and to regard himself within the context of his tribal identity. Jake needed to learn about who he was as an American Indian: that his place in this world existed relative to his family and tribe. Once his ability to relate in this way was restored, Jake could find healing in his ability to relate to others.

Jake's treatment was provided with careful consideration of his tribe's traditional thought regarding an individual's ability to choose. Jake was welcomed to view his treatment from a perspective that he was comfortable with and to express his desires and expectations for the treatment he would receive. He preferred the term *meetings* over *sessions*, and he wanted to learn about traditional ways. Jake's treatment conformed to his desires and expectations, bringing in Western psychological interventions only as they were acceptable to him. As treatment progressed and his cultural identity was adequately addressed, Jake was able to benefit from the integration of both indigenous and Western systems of healing.

Model Implementation
and Treatment Implications

It is important to note the inherent difficulties of counseling in a setting that does not adequately support or facilitate mental health counseling. In a prison, there is no right to privacy. Cameras record interactions between those in the therapeutic dyad, and there is clear distinction between us (the inmates) and them (the staff). Further, this particular young man also had some problems that would predict a poor prognosis if we were following a more Western counseling model. First, although Jake was motivated to leave the institution and therefore willing to participate at a minimal level, he was mandated for treatment and did not think it was worthwhile. Second, his relationships with the expected caretakers in his life have all been based on mistrust, lack of nurturance, and pain, which made building a trusting relationship a difficult task.

Treatment began with dialogue and meetings designed to create rapport, trust, and respect. He initially agreed to meet only because he was mandated but then agreed to continue meeting if he could be taught about "Indian ways." He developed a plan together with the therapist, who also had him verbalize his expectation of their "meetings," as he preferred to call them. He dictated a summary of each meeting, and the therapist read them back to him at the beginning of the next meeting.

The initial phase of treatment consisted of creating a timeline drawing of his life from birth to the present and learning basic words in his traditional language. Eventually, additional meetings were arranged with the only available Native spiritual leader who had chaplain privileges in the facility. Although the chaplain was from a different tribe, he agreed to tell Jake traditional stories that coordinated with his life events or problems, to help him develop new ways of problem solving. This phase of building trust took place over a six-month period.

Phase 2 began with the rudiments of respect beginning to emerge as Jake recognized that the counseling sessions were actually helpful for his well-being, and he began to participate willingly and actively. Treatment consisted of a continuation of his life timeline as he examined his life and the events that may have influenced his behavior and his understanding of interpersonal relationships. He also continued dictating the session notes, reading them at the beginning of the next session, and meeting with the chaplain (American Indian spiritual leader) once a month.

During this time, contact with his birth mother played a role in his therapeutic breakthrough. He shared with his unit staff that he wished his mother would call him. They frequently pointed to her irresponsibility and lack of parental rights as the reason she did not call, and Jake seemed to feel obligated to defend her. She eventually wrote him a note, indicating that she would call if only she had some money. Jake saved his small work stipend for six months and sent her $50. She never called. Several months later, he brought this up in a "meeting." When the therapist defended his mother and commented that his mother had many problems that might have made it difficult for her, Jake was finally able to tearfully verbalize his anger and sadness about the lack of love, lack of protection, and lack of connection with her, for which he yearned. He stated, "She was never there for me and I don't think she ever will be!" They then talked about what loving someone should look like. This event was a pivotal moment for Jake: He allowed himself to be angry with his mother and thus began potential healing and moved into Phase 3 .

Phase 3 began with a new interest in how counseling could possibly help him. This phase continued with his life timeline and expanded to include his active learning of healthy interpersonal interactions. They focused on continuing to build trust and respect while moving into the next two modes of growth. Jake began to recognize that he was able to benefit from both the counseling sessions and his relationship with his counselor as he developed effective ways of coping and developing healthy relationships. These emerging skills also helped to empower him toward continued growth.

Case Conceptualization

The conceptualization of this case occurred over time as Jake began to open up. His story unfolded over a two-year period as he began to trust, and eventually respect, his counselor and himself. Jake's case was conceptualized from an attachment perspective, drawing on the work of Bowlby (Solomon & George, 1999). His conduct problems were viewed as stemming from the psychological impact of sexual abuse and neglect he endured at the hands of his biological parents. Under this conceptualization, it was hypothesized that as an infant, Jake made appraisals about himself and his caregivers that would form the fabric of his attachment style and unconsciously impact the way he interpreted and responded to other attachment-relevant stimuli. As an infant, Jake experienced psychological distress, sometimes as a result of typical infant needs and experiences (e.g., needing to be fed, have his diaper changed) and other times as a result of sexual abuse and neglect. When infants experience intense negative affect in response to their physiological and emotional needs, they may not learn the self-soothing skills they might have learned from their caregivers. In essence, they have lost an opportunity to find their unique position in the world.

Because as an infant Jake had not yet developed the capacity to meet his own basic needs or to cope with intense affect, he was dependent on his caregivers to provide basic care and emotion regulation. When such ruptures in this system occur regularly, the infant's needs for safety, food, hygiene, and emotion regulation go unmet, and an insecure attachment is likely to develop. His tribal tradition suggests that without a secure attachment, it was nearly impossible for Jake to find his place in the world, thus thwarting his ability to know how he could benefit from or contribute to his community. In other words, the lack of secure attachment to his caregiver then generalized to his community, where he was not able to develop secure attachments to potential tribal caregivers.

In Jake's case, it is possible that the sexual abuse coupled with the neglect resulted in the development of a disorganized attachment. Because of the abuse and neglect, Jake internalized a self-representation that he was unacceptable and unworthy of care and protection. Further, he was unable to develop the capacity for emotion regulation because his parents regularly failed to attend to his distress and modulate it through caregiving and through their own sympathetic emotional responses. Thus, he also internalized representations of his parents as neither desirous, nor able, nor available to provide care and protection for him. These representations became a sort of template for the way Jake would interpret and interact with the world around him. This made it difficult for him to not only get the help he needed in order to heal, but also to be able to make use of the help that was available.

Because of his natural infantile dependency, Jake experienced his parents as the source of resolution for his stresses, as every infant does. However, he also experienced them as a significant and chronic stressor, creating inherent conflicts, which led to the development of a disorganized attachment style. The natural need for attachment and the conflicting experience of caretakers as inadequate and distressing could have supported the development of an approach-avoid attachment. This may have made it difficult to engage in therapy, initially.

According to Solomon and George (1999), the behavioral manifestations of a child's disorganized attachment often include sudden, out-of-context, angry, defiant behavior. Mash and Barkley (1998) outline the interpersonal deficits that are often associated with disorganized attachments: difficulty interpreting others' emotions, lack of self-control, aggressiveness, social avoidance, peer rejection, depression, low self-esteem, and posttraumatic stress disorder. Also included are aggression, destructive behavior, juvenile crime, violence, and lack of empathy. Thus, it is not difficult to conceive that Jake's conduct problems stemmed from the disorganized attachment style he developed in response to the sexual abuse and neglect inflicted on him as a helpless infant.

Solomon and George (1999) also discuss other impacts of child sexual abuse. Notably, this includes a pattern of problems with sexuality in which a child may become hypersexual, expose himself or herself in public, and/or go on to victimize others. Children who go on to victimize others, as Jake did, often have traits consistent with disorganized attachments, such as lack of interpersonal skills, friends, interests, and empathy. They are typically impulsive and compulsive and most have endured not only sexual abuse, but other forms of maltreatment. This is certainly true in the case of Jake. It is theorized that these children victimize others in order to reenact their own victimization in a way that allows them to gain mastery over the situation, rather than remaining in the helpless position of victim. This perspective may help us gain some insight into how Jake came to rape another person after being sexually abused himself.

In addition, the behavioral manifestations of disorganized attachment may also include a pattern of behaving in a controlling way toward the attachment figure(s). The child may attempt to exercise control over the parent by acting as that parent's caregiver, or he or she may attempt control by being punitive toward the parent. Although we don't know how Jake interacted with his parents because he was removed from the home at such a young age, we can see a controlling punitive pattern of interaction toward other adults he encountered in childhood and adolescence, including the adult woman that he raped as well as his initial need for control in his therapy session.

It was important to consider Jake's conduct problems in light of his early experiences and to understand that there was much more amiss in his life than just the problematic behaviors he exhibited. First and foremost, Jake's need to develop trusting, safe attachments had to be addressed. Once this was developed, he needed to learn to regulate intense negative affective states and to interact interpersonally in appropriate ways. Furthermore, he needed to develop a new way of responding to his environment that was not based on his long-held negative representations of self and attachment figures. If his conduct problems were not addressed within this context, his treatment may have failed to reduce the likelihood of recidivism.

One way in which the treatment addressed Jake's conduct problems was discussed above. As noted, Jake was welcomed to define the therapeutic relationship and therapeutic encounter in terms he was comfortable with (e.g., using the term *meeting* instead of *session*). He dictated the treatment summaries at the end of each meeting and reviewed them at the beginning of the next. As Mash and Barkley (1998) explain, abused and neglected kids often approach adults fearfully. The authors recommend that the child be given greater control over what happens in sessions, in order to foster a greater sense of safety and trust in the therapeutic dyad. This may also serve to counter internalized representations of the self as helpless. This is also true with our tribal beliefs, in that we believe in trusting the Spirit to bring the true individual into the present. Thus, we honor the process as it manifests itself in the individual's choices.

Unfortunately, therapy ended before completion due to Jake's aging out of the residential treatment center. He had to complete his treatment in an adult prison. However, he did have some skills to take with him, and additional therapy was recommended in his transfer plan, so it is hoped that he was able to continue his growth.

Additional Clinical Considerations

Clearly, Jake needed additional therapy in order to continue his growth toward appropriate and healthy interpersonal attachments, and it is hoped he continued this in the next phase of his incarceration. The question remains as to how Jake can learn normal, healthy behavior in an abnormal setting.

A second point is the importance of a cultural lens in conceptualizing and developing an effective treatment. Jake was ultimately able to connect to treatment due to a cultural viewpoint that was consistent with the problems he was experiencing. Further, the cultural view was geared to his growth and ability to function effectively as a community member in harmony with his cultural background, which was useful in engaging a reluctant client.

Authors' Personal Worldview

Both authors are American Indian and consider the individual in the context of his or her group relationship, mutual trust, respect, and the understanding that each person must choose his or her path and destiny, as indicated by the AIAN-SISM.

Angela M. Enno is a first-degree descendent of the Turtle Mountain Chippewa of the Northern Plains and was raised in a rural, non-reservation community in Utah, on the other side of the country from Jake's tribe. Thus, Gayle Skawennio Morse provided the expertise as it related to the client's specific tribe's worldview and customs. Ms. Enno favors a contextual paradigm in case conceptualization, choosing to view the client's situation with a broader scope: understanding contextual factors before ascribing client difficulties to purely individual pathology. In Jake's case, both authors viewed his situation in the context of his early attachment experiences as well as his identity as an American Indian tribal member, and they used this information to inform an understanding of how his conduct problems developed in context.

References

Duran, E., & Duran, B. (1995). *Native American postcolonial psychology.* Albany: State University of New York Press.

Mash, E. J., & Barkley, R. A. (Eds.). (1998). *Treatment of childhood disorders.* New York: Guilford Press.

Solomon, J., & George, C. (Eds.). (1999). *Attachment disorganization.* New York: Guilford Press.

PART V

Middle Eastern Americans

Challenging Misperceptions and Widening the Lens

14 Middle Eastern Americans in Therapy

An Application of the SISM

Maryam Sayyedi

Noha Alshugairi

Metra Azar-Salem

The heterogeneity of Middle Eastern Americans (MEAs) as a population challenges adherence to any specific therapeutic guidelines. However, being collectivistic, MEAs share characteristics with other collectivistic ethnocultural communities in the United States. It is this shared experience that justifies cross-application of culturally responsive models in therapy with the MEA population. Parham (2002) proposes six stages in the Skills Identification Model to organize culturally responsive therapeutic encounters for African American clients. In this chapter, we demonstrate the utility of this model, now called the Skills Identification Stage Model (SISM), in organizing the therapeutic encounters with MEAs.

Although there are shared values and characteristics among ethnocultural communities in the United States, MEAs can be distinguished as newcomers to psychotherapy and counseling. MEAs also have become more visible and the focus of negative attention since the 9/11 tragedy. MEAs have attracted the attention of the political sciences for decades, but as newcomers to therapy they have not yet aggregated a substantial body of research evidence addressing their mental health or help-seeking experiences in therapy. The dearth of research on MEAs, which suffers from weak methodology and poor sampling practices, is scattered across disciplines and tends to engender stereotyping rather than foster an appreciation of the complexity and heterogeneity of the ancient and diverse cultures of MEAs. The help-seeking behaviors of MEAs also have been curtailed by their own cultural stigmas against therapy and by their experiences of discrimination and negative media attention (Marvasti, 2005).

As Middle Eastern therapists, our first responsibility is to raise the cultural awareness of the readers, who may be biased by misinformation and negative stereotyping rooted in the unbalanced foreign policies of our time. An understanding of the geopolitical characteristics and complexity and heterogeneity of the Middle East as a cultural area is crucial for the development of any culturally responsive practice in counseling or therapy with MEAs.

This chapter's main focus, however, is to delineate the SISM in counseling and therapy with MEAs. The discussion offered here may better describe MEAs who recently immigrated and not those who assimilated as second or third generation within the MEA community. Toward this end, we have drawn from our own lived experiences as MEAs, years of clinical experience with this population, and the sparse body of research literature.

The SISM has been utilized to organize therapeutic encounters, and the suggestions offered for implementation within each stage of this model should be conceptualized contextually rather than literally. We firmly believe that therapy should be informed by each MEA client's unique cultural identifications. From our perspective, therapy is ultimately a unique, dynamic, and reflexive interpersonal discourse between a therapist and a client who manifest intersections of multiple identities and cultural affiliations. We also believe that cultures are ever evolving through contact with each other and are shaped by individuals' ultimate goals of survival, adaptation, and belonging.

The limits of multiculturally informed therapy are based on the therapist's level of cultural awareness and how the therapist's awareness of his or her own cultural biases may inform his or her practice. Although we have identified ourselves as MEA therapists, we are acutely aware of how our unique cultural worldviews are informed by our unique developmental histories, immigration histories, and level of acculturation. In our encounters with MEAs, we remain acutely aware of our cultural identification and consider each client to be a unique portal or gateway to unique and different experiences of our shared culture.

Given our diverse Middle Eastern backgrounds (i.e., nationalities, ethnicities, religious identification, and level of acculturation), we debated which classification to choose in order to honor the heterogeneity of our group. We wanted to encompass all of our experiences without privileging a particular subgroup (e.g., Muslims, Arabs, Iranians, Afghanis). In the end, we felt that the term *Middle East,* in spite of its shortcomings, remains the best description of that particular area of the world.

The following brief authors' biographies provide an example of the heterogeneity of the MEA population while underscoring the supremacy of personal history over cultural global history. Maryam Sayyedi is a 48-year-old, Iranian American, married female who immigrated to the United States at 17 and has raised two first-generation Iranian American children who are now 18 and 25. She is a clinical psychologist by education, specializing in child psychology and neuropsychology. She also teaches as an adjunct faculty at California State University, Fullerton. Noha Alshugairi is a 47-year-old, Arab American Muslim, married female who immigrated to the United States at 22 and has raised four children who are now 23, 22, 20, and 18. She is a marriage and family therapist intern in private practice. Metra Azar-Salem is a 30-year-old, Afghan American Muslim whose parents immigrated to the United States from Afghanistan when she was two years old. She is married and the mother of three young boys. She is a candidate for a doctoral degree in psychology and is completing her predoctoral internship at a private Islamic elementary school and at Omid Multicultural Institute for Development.

Middle East: A Cultural Area

Both Gregg (2005) and Rassam (1995) argue that despite the ethnic and religious diversity, the Middle East is a "culture area" that shares a vision of life that guides the values, concepts, and traditions of its people. Both scholars attribute this cultural cohesion to three main factors. First, the people of the region share an arid and semiarid geography in addition to sharing three distinct ways of life: nomadism, peasant agriculture, and urban commerce. Second, Arabic is the official language for written and verbal communication in all countries of the Middle East, with the exception of Turkey, Iran, Afghanistan, and Israel. Third, the Islamic worldview, if not the faith itself, has been adopted by the majority of people in the area, due to rule by various Muslim dynasties from about 690 AD to 1920 AD.

It is this shared worldview that enables researchers to study this heterogeneous group collectively. Variations within the main themes of this cultural area are inadvertently present due to differences in languages spoken, local customs, geopolitical significance, socioeconomic status, educational levels, religious affiliation, gender discourse, urbanization, and immigration history. According to Rassam (1995), the two most important cultural markers of individual identity in the region are language and religion.

Definitions

Although *Middle East* was a colonial term and fraught with a long history of Western geopolitical meddling and influences (Esposito, 2004; Shabbas, 2006), it is the classification that has become most salient and most discriminated against (Marvasti, 2005). At its most encompassing, the term *Greater Middle East* describes an area that stretches from Pakistan in the East to Morocco in the West. On the other hand, there are those who limit the Middle East to an area that includes only the Arab countries of Asia in addition to Turkey, Persia, and Egypt. Hence, whenever this area is studied it is imperative to define which countries are included in the definition. For the purposes of this chapter, we have chosen the latter definition: Egypt, Arab countries of Asia (Saudi Arabia, Yemen, Oman, United Arab Emirates, Qatar, Bahrain, Kuwait, Iraq, Jordan, Lebanon, Syria), Israel, Afghanistan, Turkey, and Iran. We believe this definition to be the most widespread classification of that area.

It is important to note that although Westerners identify people who live in the Middle East as "Middle Easterners," natives of that area of the world rarely see themselves as such. Throughout history, they have defined themselves depending on their geopolitical situation of the time. Today, they identify with their countries of citizenship.

History and Languages

The Middle East is a region steeped in ancient history and traditions (Rassam, 1995). This is an area that historians call "the cradle of civilizations." Today's Egypt was home to the pharaohs and their pyramids, and today's Iraq was the seat of the Assyrians, Sumerians, and Babylonians, who established the first human civilizations. The longstanding history of this area ensured a constant influx of people and ideas that, over the years, resulted in four major cultural heritages, as reflected by their spoken languages: Arabic, Persian, Turkish, and Hebrew. Other distinct cultural groups within the area include Kurds, Armenians, Druze, Circassians, and the Berbers, who each have their own unique languages.

Religious Diversity

This region is the birthplace of the three monotheistic religions (Judaism, Christianity, and Islam), yielding a unique mosaic of religious diversity. As such, until only recently, this region continuously had people of all three faiths coexisting peacefully, even when the area was ruled by Muslims for more than a thousand years (Rassam, 1995).

Accordingly, before the establishment of the State of Israel in 1948, large Jewish communities lived in all countries of the Middle East, with the exception of Saudi Arabia and the Gulf States (Rassam, 1995). They tended to speak the dialect or language of the country they lived in and adopted local customs and traditions. In the 1950s, the massive emigration of Jews to Israel from Europe and North America led to a decrease in the Jewish communities across the Middle East, while dramatically increasing the Jewish concentrations in the newly established State of Israel.

On the other hand, it is important to understand and appreciate that the Christian groups of the Middle East are distinct from their counterparts in the West in their hierarchy, rites, and ceremonies (Rassam, 1995). The schism between Eastern and Western Christianity occurred following the religious controversies of the fifth and sixth centuries. Accordingly, while Catholicism and Protestantism spread in Europe and eventually the New World, Eastern Churches were able to maintain their traditions in the Middle East under the tolerant Muslim rule. The Copts of Egypt represent the largest Christian community of the Middle East, while in Lebanon, the Maronites represent the second-largest Christian group. There are also Christians who follow the Greek Orthodox Church, the Assyrian Nestorian church, and the Chaldean church.

When we discuss Muslims in the Middle East, it is essential to make some distinctions between various terms that have become synonymous due to media bias. The terms *Arab, Middle Eastern*, and *Muslim* have been used interchangeably by individuals who have a limited knowledge of the Middle East. Although the words are related, they do not represent the same group of people (Shabbas, 2006). *Arabs* are those who speak Arabic. Arabs could be Muslims, Christians, or Jews. They are the largest ethnic group in the Middle East but are not the only group. Turks, Iranians, and Israelis, in addition to the other aforementioned cultural groups, are all from the Middle East.

Muslims are those who have adopted Islam as their creed; they reside all over the world. Hence, Muslims are ethnically diverse. Of all the world's 1.6 billion Muslims (Kettani, 2010), only about 15–20% are Arabs (Shabbas, 2006). In fact, the majority of Muslims reside outside the Middle East. Accordingly, a Middle Easterner is not necessarily an Arab, as the Middle East is not an area populated by Arabs and Muslims only, and the majority of Muslims are non-Arabs and non–Middle Easterners.

Besides the three monotheistic traditions, the Middle East is home to other religious groups. These include Zoroastrians, Baha'is, Druze, Alawis, Zaidis, and the Yazidis.

Middle Eastern Americans

Following this brief introduction about the Middle East, it becomes clear that Middle Eastern Americans encompass many ethnic groups, speak different languages, and espouse different religions. The most recent figures on the major groups of Middle Eastern Americans estimate that there are about 1.5 million Arab Americans, 414,000 Iranian Americans, 169,000 Turkish Americans, and 142,000 Israeli Americans (U.S. Census Bureau, 2006). Arab Americans were evenly distributed among the four regions of the United States, while Iranian Americans were predominantly found in the

Western regions. Israeli Americans were concentrated in the Northeastern regions, with moderate numbers in the Southern and Western regions, while the majority of Turkish Americans were in the Northeastern and the Southern regions of the United States. The census data reported here is a gross underestimation of these populations in the United States. For example, the Iranian population is estimated to be one million by the Interest Section of the Islamic Republic of Iran, in Washington D.C., which handles the affairs of immigrants from Iran (Sayyedi, 2004). The reasons are not systematically studied; however, the general understanding among people from the Middle East is that governments cannot be trusted, thus cooperating with the census is discouraged. There is a fear that by being identified as someone from the Middle East, one may be at risk of harassment by the authorities. The cultural distrust in the central governments of their countries of origin and the unfavorable policies of the United States toward the Middle East might have created a general cultural, healthy paranoia toward participating in the census, hence the underestimation of the statistics.

In a more detailed report by the U.S. Census Bureau (2003), 48% of all Arab Americans were found to live in five states: California, Florida, Michigan, New Jersey, and New York. Michigan was the state with the highest proportion of Arabs, and New York City had the largest population of Arab Americans. The three largest Arab groups, Lebanese (37%), Syrian (12%), and Egyptian (12%), constituted 61% of all Arab Americans. There were no similar reports on other Middle Eastern Americans.

Immigration History

Middle Eastern Americans immigrated to the United States in three main waves that tended to reflect the political situation of the Middle East at the time. The first wave occurred between 1890 and 1940 and included Arab Christians from Syria and Lebanon who were seeking better economic opportunities and Armenians who were escaping the massacres and genocide by the Turks (Abudabbeh, 2005; Dagirmanjian, 2005). The second wave took place following World War II (1940–1945) and during the establishment of the State of Israel (1948). The second wave included Iranians and Muslim Arabs who were college educated or were seeking a college education (Abudabbeh, 2005; Jalali, 2005). It included Armenians who came from various Armenian Diaspora communities in the Middle East and elsewhere (Dagirmanjian, 2005). The second wave also saw the first group of Israeli immigrants (Ziv, 2005). The last wave of immigration began in 1967 following the Arab-Israeli war and included different groups coming to the United States in response to various political unrests in the area: the 1975–1990 Lebanese civil war, the 1979 Iranian revolution, the 1988 earthquake in Soviet Armenia, the 1990 conflict between Soviet Armenia and Soviet Azerbaijan, and the 1991 Gulf war (Abudabbeh, 2005;

Dagirmanjian, 2005; Jalali, 2005). In general, the second wave of immigrants were more educated and better equipped to adapt to living in the United States than the first and third wave of immigrants (Abudabbeh, 2005; Dagirmanjian, 2005; Jalali, 2005). The different waves of immigrants might have acculturated at different speeds and along different paths. However, there are no studies that systematically have explored such variations. Few have focused on the influence of the most pervasive shared cultural values of the Middle East or the level of psychological adjustment to acculturation stress for different immigrant groups from the Middle East.

Worldview

The centrality of family and kinship systems, code of honor, social hierarchy and status, language, and spirituality in Middle Eastern identity have been addressed in studies focusing on adjustment issues related to immigration and in guidelines for providing mental health services to Arab Americans (Erickson & Al-Timmi, 2001; Nobles & Sciarra, 2000; Read, 2003), American Muslims (Abdal-Ati, 1977; Carolan, Bagherinia, Juhari, Himelright, & Mouton-Sanders, 2000; Hassouneh-Phillips, 2001; Hedayat-Diba, 2000; Hodge, 2005; Waugh, Abu-Laban, & Qureshi, 1991), and specific nationalities such as Iranian Americans (Badal, 2001; Famili, 1997; Ghaffarian, 1998; Jalali, 2005) or more recent immigrant groups of Afghanis (Omeri, Lennings, & Raymond, 2006) and Iraqis (Jamil, Nassar-McMillan, & Lambert, 2007).

Centrality of Family and Kinship Systems. The family unit is the cornerstone of the community for Middle Eastern Americans (Abudabbeh, 2005; Dagirmanjian, 2005; Jalali, 2005; Ziv, 2005). Relationships within the family unit follow a hierarchical structure that demands unequivocal respect for the parents and the elders. Although the family unit tends to be patriarchal in nature, with fathers holding the final authority, there is a great deal of variation in power differentials in immigrant families, with the modern nuclear families now becoming more egalitarian. Family membership may be extended to very close friends and even members of the community (e.g., calling the best female friend of one's mother "Aunt" or best male friend of one's father "Uncle"). Children are loved and cherished by all within the kinship system, particularly when very young, and are expected to take on the responsibility for their parents as the latter grow old. The parenting style is primarily authoritarian yet warm, and contrary to the authoritarian style of parenting recognized by Western culture, it is not a negative parenting style (Ben-Arieh & Khoury-Kassabri, 2008; Rudy & Grusec, 2006).

Code of Honor. The code of honor describes a complex set of rules determined by one's social group and governs behaviors and expectations in all domains. The code of honor is not limited to sexual conduct between the sexes (Abudabbeh, 2005). It also includes guidelines on how to treat elders, strangers, guests, and enemies; how to protect one's own; how to be responsible and accountable; and how to work hard for the educational and economical advancement of one's family (Gregg, 2005). The edicts of this code vary from one group to another within the Middle Eastern community. It is also changing due to the impact of immigration, acculturation, urbanization, and separation from the extended family system (Erickson & Al-Timmi, 2001; Nobles & Sciarra, 2000).

Social Hierarchy and Status. Maintaining social decorum and a veneer of prosperity and success that represents a higher socioeconomic status establishes respect for one's family and fosters a duality in personal representations. This edict emphasizes the demarcations between the "public" and "private" selves and varies across socioeconomic strata, with those from more affluent backgrounds feeling more pressured to present a "public self" congruent with their pre-immigration affluent family status. The goal of demonstrating this "public self" is to regain social status here in the United States. Similarly, the choice of language (i.e., formally educated vs. informally; personal or national language vs. English) influences social boundaries and determines the level of trust and intimacy in interpersonal engagements (Erickson & Al-Timmi, 2001; Jalali, 2005; Nobles & Sciarra, 2000). Certain professionals (e.g., medical doctors) and those with higher education are given a higher status in the community and society. Hence, there is pressure on MEA children to succeed academically and pursue professions in medicine, law, and engineering. This pressure also explains the success of the general MEA population in sciences, medicine, and academic positions.

Language. Language has had a special place in MEA cultures: It is not representational or objective but it is transformative, with the intention of deepening connections and enhancing emotional processing. Although the style of communication underlines deference, status, and the nature of interpersonal relationships, its content can be vague, figuratively rich, poetic, and emotionally expressive. Its purpose is to reaffirm the importance of the present and the unpredictability of the future. It is tentative and relies on rhetoric and generalities rather than objective, systematic accurate analysis. It lends itself best to story and drama, rather than scientific discourse. For some Middle Eastern Americans, preserving and teaching children one's native language has been another way of maintaining one's heritage and identity. Their pride in their group identity and their need to distinguish themselves from others in the larger American community spurs them to ensure that their descendants learn the ethnic language. For Arab Muslims in particular, preserving the Arabic language is seen as a sacred religious duty. Because the Muslims' holy book, the Quran, was revealed in Arabic, learning the language becomes a commitment to the faith.

For some Iranians, the language preference and practices have become a measure of acculturation experiences. Some Iranians, not wanting to be readily identified as a Middle Eastern immigrant and desperate to assimilate, have abandoned the native language and do not even speak Farsi at home or have abandoned teaching their children to speak Farsi (Mobasher, 2006).

Religion and Spirituality. Spirituality and Judeo-Christian-Islamic values are inherent in Middle Eastern Americans' view of the world. A deeply rooted belief in creationism and the supreme power of an omnipotent God permeates all experiences, from those that are highly private to those that are highly public. What Westerners may view as fatalism and predetermination is an affirmation on the part of Middle Eastern Americans of their belief in the direct influence of God in their daily lives. Nonetheless, this belief manifests itself when they are faced with events that are beyond their control, such as an earthquake. In all other areas of their lives they believe in their own direct power to change the course of events and situations. Their belief in the divine also imbues them with an internal compass to do good in life, which is seen as a temporary sojourn.

However, religious identities, while complex, may manifest differently in different individuals and tend to be more persistent and stable than ethnic or national identities. For some, identifying with one's creed has provided an opportunity to transcend nationality and ethnicity to unite with those of the same faith across the globe; their personhood is shaped by their faith and its practices rather than by their national fervors or the secular aspects of their cultural heritage. Some Middle Eastern Americans identify themselves as Christian or Jew or Muslim, and their faith has supremacy over the geography, language, and ethnic practices unique to their country of origin. On the other hand, for the secular members of the Middle Eastern communities, particularly those who are disenchanted with what appears to be faith-based conflicts and wars or who have experienced displacements and prejudice by theocracies (e.g., Iranians), the secular classification and nationalistic fervor takes precedence over faith.

The centrality of family and kinship systems, code of honor, hierarchy and social status, language, and spirituality transcend diverse cultures of the Middle East, but there is a great deal of individual variation. Immigration history, generation status, gender, and other demographics add more definition to an individual's identity against the backdrop of their Middle Eastern classification. Each individual or family or couple in therapy or counseling is a unique window to a complex and ever-changing representation of their global culture. The uniqueness is informed by the individual's developmental history as well as the unique course of ethnic identity development in the United States. Therapists' knowledge of the global characteristics delineated here, and the level of appreciation they may be able to demonstrate in relating to MEA clients, will significantly impact the quality of the therapeutic endeavor and its continuity as organized by the SISM.

MEA Skills Identification Stage Model _____

The MEA Skills Identification Stage Model (MEA-SISM) discussed in this chapter organizes the general therapeutic encounter, but the unique aspects of each encounter will need to be co-created by each therapist and each client. Furthermore, the six skills identified by Parham (2002) are presented here in a linear format (see Table 14.1), but they do not need to be applied linearly. It is a well-known trade secret that the demarcation between assessment and treatment (i.e., instilling change) is elusive at best and fictitious at worst. Regardless of theory and therapeutic inclinations, the process of assessing the client's problems and difficulties is not separated from the interventions and therapy because the therapist needs to constantly gauge the client's responses. In fact, it is through the process of inquiry and assessment that the client may develop a better understanding of the nature of his or her problems or identify hidden strengths. In such instances, assessment is the intervention. Also, connecting is not limited to the first encounter in therapy; it is a stream of client-therapist relational experiences that runs through the entire course of therapy. It goes through ebbs and flows and needs sustained and conscious effort on the part of the therapist to maintain its collaborative and positive course throughout the therapeutic encounter.

Connecting _____

Most MEAs are not familiar with the concept of individual therapy; it is often considered a last resort, and even then, most MEA clients seem to approach therapy with a great deal of reservation and skepticism. The therapist's warm, friendly, respectful demeanor will be crucial but not sufficient in establishing a connection. A professional ambiance, as reflected by professional attire, cleanliness and organization of the office, and inviting and comfortable decoration, may seem superficial to some, but it furthers the process of connecting with the therapist. The overall professional ambiance reflects the therapist's professional prosperity, which seems to overcome the client's skepticism and legitimize the profession of psychotherapy or counseling. In fact, perhaps implicitly, it facilitates the therapeutic connection by instilling hope in the MEA client, who tends to equate prosperity with professional competence. Any experiences that verify the credibility of the therapist will enhance the client's belief in the legitimacy of the process.

Although the therapist's education and years of experience and the presence of framed diplomas on the office walls symbolically attest to the therapist's credibility, it is the therapist's humility, warmth, and caring demeanor that seals the connection and, over time, will promote him or her to the status of a trusted and wise member of the kinship system. For most acculturated MEA clients, therapists are considered a "healthcare" provider. Psychiatry is an established profession in Middle Eastern countries, but there

Table 14.1   Middle Eastern American Skills Identification Stage Model (MEA-SISM)

Connecting With Clients	Therapist's attire and office should project professionalism, cleanliness, and prosperity, with diplomas and credentials framed and available for client's scrutiny.
	Language, when English, should reflect the warmth, friendliness, and availability of the therapist, yet not imply informality.
	Professional demeanor (e.g., using surnames of the client), particularly for older clients, is necessary.
	Allow for nontraditional therapy time.
	Educate client about the process; emphasize the confidential nature of the process.
	Offer positive self-disclosure to instill hope and foster trust.
	Use of a close and trusted relative as an interpreter can be tolerated, but do not use children as interpreters. If a member of the community is used for interpretation, he or she should be allowed some time to develop rapport with the client and to ensure client's confidentiality.
	Be open to discussing your education, training, and experience, and do not challenge their inquiry.
	The therapist's warm and personable demeanor foster trust.
	Don't ask the client to educate you about the culture. More acculturated clients expect a universal treatment and may not appreciate the cultural emphasis by the therapist.
Assessment	Educating the client about the purpose of the assessment is indispensable.
	Assess the presenting problems first, then assess history of immigration, generation status, and ethnic identification.
	ICD-10 and *DSM-IV-TR* are frequently utilized in technologically advanced and modern societies within the region.
	Clients are open to share cultural experiences only in the context of being a unique window to their cultures.
	Somatic idioms often reflect mental anguish and distress and should not be misinterpreted as somatization.
	Natural and supernatural (will of God or evil eye) may comprise client's view of his or her problems and should not be challenged.
	Externalizing is done to ward off shame and is not to be mistaken for shirking personal responsibility.
Facilitating Awareness	Provide a great deal of validation and normalization to ameliorate the shame associated with seeking help.
	Integrate a developmental and systemic exploration to enhance insight.
	Help client understand the influence of or the process of acculturation as a stressor toward a bicultural ethnic identity development.

(Continued)

Table 14.1 (Continued)

	Explore the distance between the private and public senses of self and ways that the client can differentiate without damaging significant relationships.
	Explore the wants, needs, and the guilt associated with the individuation process.
	Help the client negotiate individual goals within the interpersonal network.
	For children and adolescents, educate parents regarding developmental challenges and ethnic identity development.
Setting Goals	Client expects that the therapist, as an expert, will set the goals. Educate the client regarding the collaborative nature of therapy and goal setting.
	For children and adolescents, parents should be involved closely in the process.
	Individual adult clients should be given a choice of the extent to which they want to involve their family system.
	Immediate concerns have priority: "solving tangible problems," "ameliorating symptoms." First set concrete and easily attainable goals, then focus on loftier goals of personal development.
	Account for gender, socioeconomic status, faith practices, level of acculturation, and generational status in goal setting.
Instigating Change	Teach skills; advocate or be a cultural liaison to facilitate adaptation.
	Educate the client regarding psychological factors and influence of culture in the process of change.
	Package insight from a developmental and social learning perspective to provide rationale for change.
	Recognize holistic approaches and incorporate spirituality and alternative medicine as well as pharmacotherapy, day programs, hospitalization, and rehabilitation.
	Cautiously explore fatalism and external locus of control, as well as negotiating the distance between the private and public selves.
Feedback/ Accountability	Direct feedback is not culturally condoned, even when solicited by the therapist.
	Educate the client about the process and discuss different roles that the therapist can play in providing the therapeutic service.
	Assess for progress and utility of previous interventions on session-by-session basis to evoke accountability in the process.
	Use of metaphors, stories, poems, and indirect communications allow for more uncomfortable or undesirable feedback to be communicated more easily.
	Appropriate use of humor often softens the sharp edges of honest feedback.

is a great deal of stigma associated with seeking psychiatric services. Personal issues, crises, and hardships are brought to a wise family elder or a very close and trusted friend for problem solving or support. The therapist should, therefore, be able to negotiate his or her role to encompass both aspects of the MEA cultural expectations.

The therapist should be able to shift and transition between his or her position as a competent mental health professional who understands the etiology of the symptom manifestations and a wise, close relative who caringly can advise the client and solve his or her problems. The therapist's personable, warm, and caring approach, in concert with timely self-disclosures, destigmatizes and ameliorates the experience of shame and transforms the therapist from a professional to a member of the client's inner, more intimate circle of trust. The self-disclosures should not compromise the therapist's competence or expertise, however, but rather normalize the experience of emotional hardship in dire situations.

The therapist should not question or deflect the client's attempts to maintain familial attachment in the therapy room, but should remain vigilant to maintain professional boundaries. For example, although the therapist may graciously accept reasonable inexpensive gifts of flowers or homemade pastries, the therapist needs to apologetically and graciously decline invitations to family dinners or social events outside the office. For therapists of a different cultural background than that of the client, there might be exceptions to this rule that need to be carefully assessed on a case-by-case basis and executed with utmost sensitivity, for example, when the therapist's participation in a family event or a cultural event may be considered a gesture of embracing the client's culture to enhance the therapeutic relationship. However, for therapists with the same cultural background as the client, declining such invitations will maintain stronger professional boundaries. Given the diffuse nature of boundaries in more traditional and collectivistic cultures, it would be difficult to maintain healthy therapeutic boundaries once the therapist is not symbolically represented as a member of the client's family or clan but, in fact, is experienced as a close relative. When professional boundaries are diffused, the client may not feel safe and may fear disclosure or breach of confidentiality, particularly when the therapist is a member of his or her community.

Another boundary issue in therapy is the standard therapy time. For MEA clients, time is a relative and fluid construct. The therapist should be willing to modify the standard therapy time and extend it when necessary, at least for the first encounter or until the client is educated regarding the structure of the therapy hour. The education may also extend to defining the therapist's role and the nature of the therapeutic relationship.

An indispensible strategy for developing therapeutic relationships and connecting with MEA clients while maintaining healthy professional boundaries is to educate the client about the nature of therapy and your role as a therapist. The better a therapist can convey the nature of the therapy experience, therapist's role, rationale for assessment, and rationale for treatment, the stronger the client's trust in the process of therapy and the stronger the therapeutic connection. Without a strong therapeutic connection, the assessment process will become a futile practice of obtaining vague and irrelevant information as the MEA client remains elusive in the assessment process. Although not systematically studied, it has been our experience that the client's level of openness in disclosing pertinent personal history, at least for most MEA clients, seems to be directly associated with the client's trust in the therapeutic connection and the client's understanding of the therapist's role.

Conducting Culturally Relevant Assessment

Cultural paranoia of mainstream systems, fear of stigma of mental illness, and skepticism about the efficacy of Western psychotherapy or counseling impede and complicate the assessment process with MEA clients. In some situations, ironically, the paranoia of seeking help is more palpable with MEA therapists. MEA clients may fear that the MEA therapist will inadvertently breach confidentiality because they tend to encounter the therapist more readily within their own small communities. On the other hand, for some, the fear of negative political sentiments toward the Middle East leaves them with no option but to seek MEA therapists, or those who are at least more knowledgeable about the culture and less negatively biased. The discrimination and frustrations that most Middle Eastern immigrants experience in their process of immigration or in establishing legal residency maintains a general distrust in all systems. Given the level of discrimination in mainstream institutions, some clients may dread the therapist's seemingly innocuous question, "What is the origin of your name?" or "Where are you from?" Thus, ironically, the assessment should not always start with the obvious or the most salient inquiry into the client's cultural background. The unfamiliar context of talk therapy should first focus on the client's primary concerns, demonstrating the therapist's ability to understand the client's concerns and expectations of the profession as a healthcare service. Only later in that process, and within the context of obtaining relevant background history to further facilitate the therapist's understanding of the problem, can the therapist approach the client's immigration history and acculturation experiences.

For the more acculturated and educated client, the assessment may focus primarily on the presenting problem and clarify the nature of stressors and the dynamics of the client's relationships. For the less acculturated or the less familiar with the therapy process, the assessment becomes the orientation process, a goal-directed conversation during which the therapist demonstrates his or her ability to understand the client and the nature of his or her problems.

Another factor influenced by the level of the client's acculturation process is the way psychological distress is communicated. How a client expresses or may manifest his or her psychological distress (i.e., idioms of distress) varies across cultures, with the more traditional cultures relying more on somatic idioms to express psychological distress. MEA clients who are less educated, older, and less acculturated tend to express psychological distress using somatic idioms (Omeri et al., 2006; Rouhparvar, 2001; Torres, 2001).

The inclination of those clients to use somatic idioms does not mean that they are somatizing their psychological conflicts; it is rather how those psychological distresses are communicated or symbolized by organs that are symbolically associated with specific psychological or emotional distress. Therapists should not pathologize such cultural expressions as somatization or conceptualize it as a lack of psychological mindedness. Those somatic idioms have been embedded in a rich cultural history and are metaphorically representational of the nature of the client's conflicts. The lack of psychologically based expressions of the problem does not necessarily imply a lack of awareness of one's internal conflicts. One's "heart" hurting or one's "nerves" malfunctioning may relate to difficulties with grief and stress-related anxiety problems, respectively.

The native languages of MEAs are figurative and rich with metaphors; they are also indirect and highly subjective. The figurative nature of the language discourages direct communication or recounting one's psychological problems in factual or concrete details. Clients should be given the time to tell their story their way. They may use rich imagery, maybe even resorting to reciting poems to enhance the impact of their story on the therapist, or they may go into a fable to address a moral conflict. However, when time is limited and crisis management is needed, the therapist needs to be more systematic and directive in the initial course of assessment, behaving somewhat similar to a physician but with a great deal of kindness and empathy. Although some therapists may disagree with using a medical model to approach the assessment process, in working with MEA clients, it has been our experience that they respond positively because they often tend to approach the medical field seeking help for psychological issues.

Furthermore, the therapist needs to be aware that the client's exaggerations, repetitions, and emphatic expressions in communicating his or her hardships are a cultural manner of communication that relies on evoking feelings of sympathy and an empathic response, rather than promoting accuracy to evoke understanding (Nobles & Sciarra, 2000). Usually the older and less acculturated members of the culture implement this manner of communication to establish a culturally sanctioned "sick role" within a larger system of care. The assignment of the sick role to older patients mobilizes the family system of care. It is within that system of care that change can develop meaningfully.

The importance of the therapist's emotional understanding of the client's psychological woes and hardships calls for the therapist's timely expressions of empathy woven skillfully throughout the process of gathering relevant history and other pertinent information. It is the timely expressions of empathy that enhance the process of connection and assessment.

In addition to demonstrating an emotional understanding of the client's hardships, the extent to which the therapist can formulate relevant inquiries exploring the nature of the client's problems will enhance the client's understanding of therapy as a collaborative process of exploration and problem solving. Ultimately, this transforms the "assessment" process into an introduction to the process of therapy. The relevance of the inquiries, and the ease by which the therapist can unearth the unexpressed emotions and issues, increases the client's level of trust in the process of therapy and the therapist's competency in helping the client with his or her problems.

In deepening the client's understanding of the presenting problem, the therapist can be trusted with pertinent background history. The client comes to understand that the inquiry or assessment is, in fact, a crucial part of the treatment process, and secrecy or repression of information may hinder the treatment process. A sensitive aspect of the process of gathering relevant information has to do with the client's immigration history.

Immigration History

Immigration history is a sensitive and crucial area of assessment, as most clients may fear the immigration office and not trust the therapist's promise of confidentiality. If a client does not voluntarily start with his or her immigration history, it would be best to allow some time in therapy for the trust to develop before such information is obtained. Those who may still be in the process of establishing legal residency or asylum are apprehensive of the Homeland Security Office and its connections to other institutions and organizations. Furthermore, many Middle Eastern countries have been under dictatorial and oppressive political hegemonies, and many MEA clients may have experienced the pressures of the omnipotent dictatorial regimes and feared secret service surveillances of all citizens. Therefore, based on those negative experiences in their country of origin, they have learned not to trust authorities of any kind in any situation. Therapists who are part of a clinic, county organization, or institution may not be trusted until they earn the trust of the client by educating the client about their role and the significance of maintaining confidentiality in the therapeutic relationship. Thus, not trusting the therapist, who as a professional is a member of the mainstream institution, particularly during the assessment process, is not an exaggerated and deviant response, but rather an adaptive trait that should be respected.

In some situations, and depending on the quality of the therapeutic connection, clients may openly and willingly share their immigration history and the history of their acculturation experience, but embellish it with dramatic editorials and perhaps some strategic half-truths to protect self and others involved. The immigration history, including (1) nationality or country of origin, (2) impetus for immigration, (3) age at the time of immigration, (4) the presence of trauma prior and post immigration, (5) level of hardship experienced during immigration, and (6) language fluency at the time of immigration, highlights factors that may facilitate or hinder the acculturation process or the level of acculturative stress experienced by the client and the client's family. Furthermore, the presence of a support network of friends and relatives upon arrival in the United States often has a major impact on the adjustment experience, and the nature of this support network should be fully evaluated when interventions are planned and utilized throughout the course of treatment.

Through the assessment process, and as therapy unfolds, the therapist allows the client to witness firsthand how the client's past and present experiences co-create and maintain the life of the problem. Using an assessment of the client's expectations for self and others, the reality of their relationships, and the cultural dynamics, the therapist takes the first step toward intervention. The first component according to the SISM, with which we agree, is to facilitate the client's awareness regarding the nature of the problem, the client's resiliency, and his or her choices.

Facilitating Awareness

MEAs vary greatly in terms of their "readiness for insight"; therefore, the process of facilitating awareness may develop at different stages of the therapeutic relationship and not necessarily at any specific time. Overall, the locus of control is more likely to be external, and the client's experiences of shame may preclude the deepening of the insight. Yet, by clarifying the client's expectations for self and others, in relationship to the expectations of the client's internalized significant others, the therapist may facilitate the client's awareness of the private versus public self.

Therapists should be aware that for most MEA clients, there is a great deal of anxiety associated with rendering the "private" sense of self publicly. In the presence of a therapist, whom they respect or hope to please or impress as a significant other in their lives, the unveiling of the private self may become an arduous, if not improbable, event. The MEA client approaches all social engagements with the "public" persona, even within the safety of the therapy room. The client's willingness to challenge his or her unrealistic expectations of self and others may be misperceived by the client as a betrayal of significant others, with whom she or he needs to maintain connections. Given that one's identity is so closely tied to the family system, abrupt separations may result in more anguish, rather than growth, for some MEAs.

With the less acculturated clients, the therapist may have to first enhance the client's awareness regarding his or her sense of agency by highlighting the client's resiliency and adaptability manifested during the immigration process. The therapist should be cautious with challenging the client's tendency to maintain an external locus of control or be fatalistic and should realize that self-efficacy and agency are applied indirectly by MEA clients in order not to rupture connections.

Enhancing the MEA client's awareness of the nature of his or her experiences and problems, while challenging, is not impossible. The challenge lies within the domain of attention. The client's attention needs to shift from focusing on others' behaviors to focusing on the self. The process of changing the client's focus of attention from others to the self is a gradual and slow process, which we have noticed is enhanced when the MEA client is educated regarding the basics of the Cognitive-Behavioral Therapy (CBT) model. The MEA client's understanding of how thoughts and feelings are related to and influence one's behaviors has been helpful in increasing the client's self-awareness without shaming him or her. The MEA client learns to become aware of his or her thoughts, feelings, and actions by realizing that he or she cannot control others' feelings and thoughts, but only his or her own. The awareness of one's own thoughts and feelings and behaviors leads to the discussion of taking responsibility for one's actions and thoughts and feelings and not blaming others. Furthermore, the therapist then has the opportunity to differentiate between the truth or reality of an event and how the client's misinterpretations, faulty assumptions, and faulty processing of information may influence his or her feelings, behaviors, adjustment, and adaptation. In our experience, regardless of the level of acculturation, MEA clients have responded well to CBT interventions focused on raising their self-awareness and shifting the MEA clients' external locus of control to take responsibility for their own well-being and adjustment.

Once MEA clients develop awareness and understanding of their own role in maintaining the life of a problem or ways of coping, then the therapy can become more focused on setting attainable goals. The MEA clients need some direction in identifying and setting reasonable goals, while understanding their own role in attaining those goals with the therapist acting as a guide, mentor, and support system.

Setting Goals

The therapist can educate MEA clients about the different roles she or he can play in helping them reach their goals. Given that MEA clients prioritize maintaining interdependence and relatedness to their family and significant others over individuation and independence, setting therapeutic goals may involve negotiating with other members of the client's kinship system. For example, in the case of children and adolescent clients, parents should be closely involved and are a vital part of the goal-setting process. For women in dissatisfied marriages or relationships, it is imperative to involve the partners or spouses, even the most unwilling ones. Many of the MEA women come to therapy presenting with chronic marital discord and dissatisfaction as a result of feeling trapped and experiencing a low sense of agency due to their lack of financial independence. Often they are unable to bring their spouse into therapy and feel helpless in changing their status due to their devotion to their role as mothers. Unless there is domestic violence, the therapist should at least have an inquiry session with the client's spouse to develop a better understanding of the dynamics of the relationship and the client's marital struggles.

Without an objective assessment of the marital discord, the therapist may unwittingly take the client's views and perceptions as the truth or reality, which ultimately derails the therapy from its goal of helping the client to increase a sense of agency and independence. Such a bias is more prominent in working with MEA female clients when the therapist is not an MEA therapist. The non–Middle Eastern therapists may unwittingly be influenced by biases toward MEA males as oppressive and violent, as well as the bias of considering MEA women to be second-class citizens with no authority of their own. In our experience, these biases leave therapists wanting to rescue the female clients and may result in promoting the client's dependency on the therapist while hindering the female client's personal growth, or worse, may result in prematurely supporting the female clients to get a divorce. Such a knee-jerk reaction of most non–Middle Eastern therapists interferes with the development of awareness and personal growth in MEA female clients presenting with marital issues.

Women who seek individual therapy for marital discord are often elated to know that you may be able to bring the reluctant husband into the therapy process, even if it is under the auspices of helping the wife to set goals for her own therapy. Such an encounter helps the male partner to develop an understanding of his wife's struggles in their marriage and realize how he is playing a major role in the process. Under the auspices of setting goals to help the wife reach her potential, the therapist will have the chance to cajole the husband into couples therapy, or at least assess the spouse's level of adjustment and potential for improving the relationship. The indirect, perhaps even manipulative, approach described here may not sit well with feminist therapists; however, at least in our experience, it has been a safe and effective way of helping the female MEA client to set realistic goals for her therapy, with or without the continued participation of her spouse. It also allows the therapist to assess the potential and motivation for change in the relationship. Another MEA client group requiring special attention in setting goals is the MEA elderly.

For elderly MEA clients, who may be experiencing a great deal of grief due to immigrating at a later stage of life and becoming dependent on their adult children residing in the United States, setting goals often may involve their adult children. For most elderly MEA clients who immigrated at a later stage of their lives, a strong family system and connections help maintain their special and revered status as the elders of the family. Additionally, it is also consistent with the culture of their countries of origin, where the respect of one's adult children is culturally sanctioned and guaranteed. However, in the United States, those cultural privileges often are compromised or threatened due to acculturation gaps between the elderly parents and their adult children who are active members of the mainstream society and perhaps adhere to more mainstream, modern values. However, depending on the level of acculturation and the influence of the kinship system in the individual's life, the goal-setting process may vary drastically from one elderly MEA client to the next. Many elderly clients struggle with grief issues related to displacement and being homesick, which, depending on their support system here in the United States, may or may not be easily resolved with time. For some, it may even accentuate or exacerbate a culturally sanctioned form of fatalism, resulting in withdrawal and depressed mood. For those elderly MEA clients, setting goals may become a process of reviewing their lives with the focus on their accomplishments rather than losses. In these cases, goal setting may be more of a private event, in order to empower clients and not to compromise their status of power and reverence in the family.

In working with MEA clients in therapy, we have realized that we are navigating uncharted territory and have developed heightened sensitivity not to take any intervention or experience for granted, so that we can carefully track those experiences that may eventually help us chart the therapy domain of working with MEA clients. It is based on these careful observations that we have learned to periodically invite the client and/or the client's family to recalibrate the goals to enhance the therapeutic outcomes. We are continually assessing and reassessing the client's response to therapy as it relates to reaching the client's short-term and long-term goals. MEA clients are also outcome oriented because they are new to the process of therapy and are therefore pragmatic and concrete when it comes to evaluating their therapeutic experience or results. The recalibration of goals often requires direct solicitation of feedback from the client regarding the client's progress. Given that the MEA client may not readily express his or her disappointment in the therapy process, or avoids confronting the therapist directly, recalibrating goals and evaluating outcomes become a process rather than an event. Therapists should encourage the client's active and continued participation in therapy, through education about the rationales for treatment or through exploration of the client's progress. For any intervention to be effective and any change to manifest, MEA clients should be highly motivated to not only participate in setting direction (i.e., goals) for the therapy process, but also realize what change entails.

Taking Action and Instigating Change

Some MEA clients approach the individual therapy process to enhance personal growth or to overcome chronic interpersonal conflicts, but they are reluctant to involve any significant others in their process. For those clients, expectations for therapy should be clearly mapped at the outset, in order to maintain their collaboration and active participation. Helping the clients to clearly articulate their expectations, definition of personal growth, or understanding of what they believe will improve their relationship experiences becomes a crucial part of the therapeutic experience and may take several sessions. Those clients are often more acculturated and may take more responsibility for changing their interpersonal as well as intrapersonal experiences. They may also be more willing to stay in therapy longer to achieve those goals. For most MEA clients we have encountered, however, the therapeutic actions and interventions may focus on tangible or short-term goals such as ameliorating symptoms, managing stress, and providing social resources and referrals. In our experience, the therapist should be able to provide the MEA client with tangible and timely results before expecting a longer-term engagement in therapy for deeper and longer-lasting psychological transformations or change.

In addition to the quality of change that the clients may expect in therapy, in working with the MEA clients, therapists may face other challenges influencing the change process. Instigating change by promoting self-efficacy should be balanced with the MEA client's cultural practice of fatalism, surrendering to the will of God (forces beyond one's control), or the belief that the future is only known by the omnipotent God. Another cultural value, the centrality of kinship systems and nuclear family, promotes the individual's accountability to others more than to oneself; thus, it may be critical to discourage any change that may compromise the kinship system.

To instigate change, the therapist should be cognizant of the MEA client's anxiety and guilt associated with rupturing attachment ties and breaking from or challenging the kinship system. For those clients who are tangled in unhealthy and abusive relationships, cognitive restructuring and remapping of their relationship schema may create new ways of relating to self and others. Most important, this may only be considered within a strong therapeutic relationship with the therapist and with mobilization of alternative support systems in place. In those cases, the therapeutic relationship provides a safe docking and refueling station for the MEA client in her therapeutic journey of leaving the abusive relationship behind. The therapeutic relationship also provides a model for the client to experience a healthy, respectful relationship with a significant adult (i.e., the therapist), who is often adopted by the client as a kinship member during the course of therapy, particularly in long-term therapies.

The utility of interventions that may resolve the MEA client's intrapersonal issues—often related to negotiating one's autonomy while maintaining familial bonds—has not been fully explored. Most guidelines for treatment support an active and direct role for the therapist, who facilitates problem solving or improving communication skills to enhance the familial connections, particularly those connections that are at risk to be ruptured due to different speeds of acculturation across different generations of a family.

In response to the aforementioned challenges, the authors have developed an integrated model of therapy, combining a systemic worldview, attachment theory, and cognitive-behavioral approaches in instigating change with the MEA client population. In order to instigate change, the therapist needs to not only become familiar with the complex hybrid psychology of immigrant families, but also be practical and able to integrate myriad interventions, theories, and possibly even opposing worldviews into an integrated model that provides a level of flexibility and broad-based perspective often lacking in a single theoretical orientation.

Culturally Based Rituals for Change

Most culturally based rituals associated with the MEA population appear to be faith based or involve a significant spiritual component. For some it may involve consulting with the imams, rabbis, or clergy, or cultural rituals such as sacrificing a chicken or a sheep to feed the poor, whose prayers are then expected to ward off calamities or the effects of the "evil eye." When dealing with those with more modern religious affiliations, particularly modern Muslims born and raised in the United States, the therapist's knowledge of Islam and its mandates is imperative, and making a referral to a practicing Muslim therapist is prudent and necessary. Islam is a way of life and not just a faith; therefore, a practicing Muslim therapist is in a more advantageous position to help the client who has a strong belief in the practice of his or her Islamic faith, particularly when there is a conflict arising from the client's difficulty with negotiating experiences outside or contradictory to the mandates of his or her faith. It is prudent to make a referral to a practicing Muslim therapist after consultation with the client and assessment of the client's expectations of the therapist or therapy. The client can make an informed decision as to whether a referral to a Muslim therapist may be in his or her best interest. It is the ethical standard of care, if not legally mandated, that the therapist be aware of his or her own cultural biases in working with any client of any cultural background, in order to make the appropriate referrals and/or seek supervision, training, and education to work with clients of different cultural backgrounds.

For the secular MEA clients, the alternative practices in medicine, particularly adherence to herbal medicine, as well as a healthy diet and regular exercise, often are considered before the client agrees to enter modern forms of therapy or start pharmacotherapy. Pharmacotherapy to ameliorate tension and sooth the nerves (*Aa'sab*) or to ameliorate panics and rumination should be considered when the MEA client is not committed to talk therapy or prefers an integration of modern and traditional interventions (Froggett, 2001).

Feedback and Accountability

The client will avoid confrontations or direct feedback to the therapist who becomes part of the client's larger kinship system. Educating the client about the collaborative nature of the therapeutic process is essential to ensure open communication about the client's experiences in therapy. The collaborative nature of therapy may be foreign to MEA clients who expect the therapist to be an expert. The expert should not need to consult with the client; a competent expert should be all-knowing. The adherence to social hierarchies and acceptance of the power differential in the therapeutic relationship may further hamper the client's willingness to openly share his or her feedback directly. However, some clients use humor and other indirect communications (i.e., telling a story, using metaphors) to share their dissatisfaction with the therapy progress or lack of improvement in their condition. Positive experiences are often shared directly with a great deal of gratitude and may even be accompanied by a nice gift from the client.

Early in the therapeutic relationship, the MEA client prefers the therapist to have more control over the course of therapy. Over time, the therapist may need to directly involve the client in goal setting and providing feedback. For most MEA clients, the exploration of obstacles in their way of reaching therapeutic goals may require that clients share their experiences of the therapist and therapy. On the other hand, for more acculturated and affluent MEAs, such solicitation may not be necessary as they are open to express their dissatisfaction or skepticism. In those situations, the therapist's awareness of how social status and power are played out in the MEA community may help the therapist explore the client's expectations without negative stereotyping or bias.

In conclusion, we would like to reiterate that our impressions and arguments offered here are only to provide a cultural overview, or perhaps a cultural backdrop, against which therapy with each MEA client can be viewed and evaluated. The goal of this chapter was to demonstrate the application of the MEA-SISM in organizing counseling or therapy with MEA clients who are considered newcomers to therapy. Given the dearth of research and evidence-based outcomes, effective therapy with MEA clients within the current political context will depend on how well the therapist can overcome his or her own misperceptions, biases, and misjudgments about this population. Given the broad brush stroke we implemented to depict the vast cultural heritage of Middle Eastern Americans, the pertinent details should be collaboratively and painstakingly drawn within each unique client-therapist encounter. It is the nature of those unique details that renders the practice of culturally responsive therapy an art form rather than a scientific discourse.

The two case studies in the following chapters will demonstrate the utility of the MEA-SISM in practice. The first case is about an Iranian American adolescent boy who presented with Attention Deficit Hyperactivity Disorder and Oppositional Defiant Disorder. The second case is about a young Middle Eastern couple who presented with discord and marital dissatisfaction.

References

Abdal-Ati, H. (1977). *The family structure in Islam*. Burr Ridge, IL: American Trust.

Abudabbeh, N. (2005). Arab Americans: An overview. In M. McGoldrick, J. Giordano, & N. Garcia-Preto (Eds.), *Ethnicity and family therapy* (pp. 423–437). New York: Guilford Press.

Badal, A. (2001). A qualitative case study of the psychosocial effects of acculturative stress and forced displacement of Assyrian-Iranian refugees living in the United States. *Dissertation Abstracts International, 61*(12B), 6696.

Ben-Arieh, A., & Khoury-Kassabri, M. (2008). Attitude toward and understanding of children's rights among middle school students in Jerusalem: The role of family values and patterns, nationality and religion. *American Journal of Orthopsychiatry, 78*(3), 359–368.

Carolan, M. T., Bagherinia, G., Juhari, R., Himelright, J., & Mouton-Sanders, M. (2000). Contemporary Muslim families: Research and practice. *Contemporary Family Therapy, 22,* 67–79.

Dagirmanjian, S. (2005). Armenian families. In M. McGoldrick, J. Giordano, & N. Garcia-Preto (Eds.), *Ethnicity and family therapy* (pp. 437–451). New York: Guilford Press.

Erickson, C. D., & Al-Timmi, N. (2001). Providing mental health services to Arab Americans: Recommendations and considerations. *Cultural Diversity and Ethnic Minority Psychology, 7*(4), 308–327.

Esposito, J. L. (Ed.). (2004). *The Islamic world past and present.* New York: Oxford University Press.

Famili, A. C. (1997). The relationship among acculturation, acculturative stress and coping processes in Iranian immigrants. *Dissertation Abstracts International, 58*(3B).

Froggett, L. (2001). From rights to recognition: Mental health and spiritual healing among older Pakistanis. *Psychoanalytic Studies, 3*(2), 177–186.

Ghaffarian, S. (1998). The acculturation of Iranian immigrants in the United States and the implications for mental health. *Journal of Social Psychology, 138,* 645– 654.

Gregg, G. S. (2005). *The Middle East: A cultural psychology.* Oxford: Oxford University Press.

Hassouneh-Phillips, D. S. (2001). Marriage is half of faith and the rest is fear Allah. *Violence Against Women, 7,* 927–946.

Hedayat-Diba, Z. (2000). Psychotherapy with Muslims. In P. S. Richards & A. E. Bergin (Eds.), *Handbook of psychotherapy and religious diversity* (pp. 289–314). Washington, DC: American Psychological Association.

Hodge, D. R. (2005). Social work and the House of Islam: Orienting practitioners to the beliefs and values of Muslims in the United States. *Social Work, 50,* 162–173.

Jalali, B. (2005). Iranian families. In M. McGoldrick, J. Giordano, & N. Garcia-Preto (Eds.), *Ethnicity and family therapy* (pp. 451–468). New York: Guilford Press.

Jamil, H., Nassar-McMillan, S. C., & Lambert, R. G. (2007). Immigration and attendant psychological sequelae: A comparison of three waves of Iraqi immigrants. *American Journal of Orthopsychiatry, 77*(2), 199–205.

Kettani, H. (2010, January). *2010 world Muslim population.* Paper presented at the 8th Hawaii International Conference on Arts and Humanities, Honolulu, Hawaii.

Marvasti, A. (2005). Being Middle Eastern American: Identity negotiation in the context of the war on terror. *Symbolic Interaction, 28,* 525–547.

Mobasher, M. (2006). Cultural trauma and ethnic identity formation among Iranian immigrants in the United States. *The American Behavioral Scientist, 50*(1), 100–117.

Nobles, A. Y., & Sciarra, D. T. (2000). Cultural determinants in the treatment of Arab Americans: A primer for mainstream therapists. *American Journal of Orthopsychiatry, 70*(2), 182–191.

Omeri, A., Lennings, C., & Raymond, L. (2006). Beyond asylum: Implications for nursing and health care delivery for Afghan refugees in Australia. *Journal of Transcultural Nursing, 17*(1), 30–39.

Parham, T. A. (2002). *Counseling persons of African descent: Raising the bar of practitioner competence.* Thousand Oaks, CA: Sage.

Rassam, A. (1995). Introduction to the Middle East. In D. Levinson (Ed.), *Encyclopedia of world culture* (Vol. IX, pp. xxxix). Boston: G. K. Hall.

Read, J. G. (2003). The sources of gender role attitudes among Christian and Muslim Arab-American women. *Sociology of Religion, 64*, 207–222.

Rouhparvar, A. (2001). Acculturation, gender, and age as related to somatization in Iranians. *Dissertation Abstracts International: Section B. Sciences and Engineering, 61*(8B), 4426.

Rudy, D., & Grusec, J. E. (2006). Authoritarian parenting in individualist and collectivist groups: Associations with maternal emotion and cognition of children's self-esteem. *Journal of Family Psychology, 20*(1), 68–78.

Sayyedi, M. (2004, November/December). Psychotherapy with Iranian-Americans: The quintessential implementation of multiculturalism. *The California Psychologist, 37, 12-13.*

Shabbas, A. (2006, February). *The Arab world and Islam colloquium.* Colloquium conducted at California State University, Fullerton.

Torres, S. (2001). Understanding of successful aging in the context of migration: The case of Iranian immigrants in Sweden. *Aging and Society, 21*(3), 333–355.

U.S. Census Bureau. (2003). *Report on Arab population released by Census Bureau.* Retrieved September 10, 2009, from http://www.census.gov/Press-release/www/releases/archives/census_2000/001576.html

U.S. Census Bureau. (2006). *Population by selected ancestry group and region: 2006.* Retrieved May 15, 2011, from http://www.census.gov/compendia/statab/2009/tables/09s0051.xls

Waugh, E. H., Abu-Laban, S. M., & Qureshi, R. B. (Eds.). (1991). *Muslim families in North America.* Edmonton Alberta, Canada: University of Alberta Press.

Ziv, A. (2005). Israeli families. In M. McGoldrick, J. Giordano, & N. Garcia-Preto (Eds.), *Ethnicity and family therapy* (pp. 680–689). New York: Guilford Press.

15 Case Illustration: The Case of Kian

Application of the MEA-SISM

Maryam Sayyedi

Noha Alshugairi

Metra Azar-Salem

Kian, a 14-year-old Iranian American boy, and his parents came to therapy to seek help for Kian, who was at risk of expulsion from his middle school. He was defiant toward his teachers, assistant principal, and his parents, particularly his mother. He presented with a somewhat depressed mood, felt unjustly treated, and expressed a great deal of contempt for authority, particularly that of his parents. Kian and his parents immigrated to the United States in 1989, when he was two, in order to escape religious persecution. His parents were able to seek asylum and establish their life in a large community of Baha'i Iranians in the United States. Both parents were educated in Iran and from a middle-class background. In the United States, Kian's father managed to complete his master's degree in engineering and owned an engineering consultation firm. His mother worked in a pharmacy as an assistant, although she was a pharmacist in Iran. Both parents were fluent in English and believed that over the last 12 years, they had acculturated to some extent but still identified themselves as Iranians and not as Iranian Americans. Their kinship system was composed of a handful of close friends and a few distant relatives who resided on the East Coast. Kian's parents had divorced when he was 12 and sought therapy for him at that time. They believed that the therapist was not culturally competent because he did not involve them in his therapy, and Kian had to educate him about the Iranian culture rather than focus on dealing with the divorce. The father was skeptical about the process of therapy and proclaimed emphatically that it did not help save their marriage. Apparently, they were in couple's therapy with an Iranian marriage and family therapist for two years before they divorced.

Kian believed that his parents were unreasonable and demanding. He also believed that his parents did not know him and wanted to ruin his life. His parents wanted him to become a lawyer or an engineer, and Kian was interested in music and aspired to become a disc jockey. He did not have any interest in school work, did not turn in homework, and was failing his classes. He admitted that he had a hard time paying attention in class and had serious problems with many of his teachers, whom he thought discriminated against him for being Iranian. His school was predominantly Latina/o Americans with a minority of white Americans and a handful of students with Asian and Middle Eastern backgrounds. His close friends were mostly Latina/o, and he felt culturally more compatible with Latinas/os than with other Middle Easterners or Asians. He had no white friends.

Beginning Sessions: Making Connections

The parents came for the initial session without Kian, as I had requested when they made their appointment on the phone. I met with them first to allow them to freely express their concerns, and also to not subject Kian to their criticisms in front of another adult (i.e., me, the therapist). Iranian parents often freely share their disappointments with other adults, as shaming has been a culturally condoned method of discipline. Given that I see my role as a cultural attaché who helps the teenage client and his parents to communicate across their generational and cultural divide, I would rather not start the relationship in a negatively charged environment. Seeing the parents alone also allows me to shower them with my attention and respect, recognizing their importance in their adolescent's life, yet not alienating the adolescent client in that process of joining with his parents. Kian might have misperceived my culturally expected deference to his parents as an alliance with his parents, which in turn would have compromised my connection with him.

In making the connection with them, I validated and normalized their frustration and skepticism. I also self-disclosed that I was the mother of two teens, and I realized how difficult it was to raise children here in the United States without much support from an extended family system, which often is readily available to the parents in Iran. Although I readily connected with them as a parent, to establish the legitimacy of my profession as a child clinical psychologist required that I educate them about the process of assessment, the nature of therapy, my role, and the client's developmental challenges. The session lasted an hour and a half, and I made sure that they left with some tangible information about their teenage son's course of development and the nature of his defiant behaviors. I had the parents take the children's symptom checklist home to complete before our next session, which I had scheduled to see their son alone. The parents completed their higher education in the United States, so I knew they were able to complete the questionnaires; nevertheless, I went over the instructions and answered their questions about the rationale and purpose of the assessment. I also had them take similar behavioral checklists to the client's teachers because his problems were also school-based. I gave them the checklists at the end of the session after giving them ample time to report on their son's issues at home and school. While I went over the checklists with the client's mother, his father glanced at my framed diplomas and, in a casual tone (so as not to offend me), inquired about my education and training. His mother acknowledged that my office location was ideal, and she liked the view from my office. The father also expressed his relief that based on our "short" visit he felt reassured by the information I had provided regarding teenage development and the course of therapy. He also glanced at the behavioral checklist and indicated that he appreciated my thorough approach. They also openly appreciated my willingness to involve them in the assessment and help them as a family. We exchanged warm and pleasant compliments as I reciprocated their compliments (a cultural ritual) by validating their competency as parents seeking professional help. I also appreciated them as parents for wanting to do the best for their child regardless of their disagreements and conflicts with each other. The exchange of compliments and pleasantries that transpired at the end of the session shifted the relationship just slightly toward a more intimate social relationship. Eventually, over time, our interactions became more casual; they combined humor and skepticism to provide feedback regarding therapeutic results, implicitly holding me accountable for Kian's therapeutic progress.

During the next two sessions after the initial intake with the parents, I met with Kian to complete my assessment of his school problems and issues with his parents. Making a connection with him was not easy; he had an oppositional streak and was not motivated to be in therapy. However, when I self-disclosed my immigration history, he softened and was willing to participate more actively in the interview process. I shared with him that I was 17 when I came to the United States and had my share of troubles with authority and discrimination during the 1980s hostage crisis (American Embassy staff were accused of being CIA spies in Iran and were kept as hostages by the militant revolutionary students for more than a year during President Carter's administration). I also shared that when I attended junior high in Iran, I could not get along with my mother or my teachers. Self-disclosure and my genuine interest in learning about his likes and dislikes, as well as his DJ aspirations, facilitated a tenuous connection and enabled me to obtain his assent for formal assessment of his inattention problems and school failures.

Middle Sessions: Assessment, Facilitating Awareness, and Setting Goals_____

Of the 10 sessions that followed, I devoted two sessions with Kian to completing formal assessment of his difficulties with inattention, impulsivity, and difficulties in reading and writing. Although most standardized assessments are not normed on Iranian Americans, some still can be utilized and the results are interpreted with caution. The intelligence tests, in particular, are highly sensitive to language abilities and can render biased and unreliable results when used to assess children with English as a second language. However, although Kian was more fluent in English than Farsi, his overall intellectual functioning was evaluated by a nonverbal (i.e., not culturally biased) intelligence test. On the Achievement test, grade-equivalent norms were used because he was primarily educated in the United States. Furthermore, the results of the Reading and Comprehension as well as Oral Expression tests, which could have been biased due to his somewhat bilingual status, were analyzed with caution.

He reportedly was gifted in math and did okay in sciences. He was at risk of expulsion mostly due to his acting-out behaviors and being oppositional in language arts and history; both classes rely heavily on language abilities. Academically, he was labeled as an underachiever by his parents and teachers. But his poor grades were not due to lack of comprehension or language difficulties. He intermittently obtained high grades on his tests while consistently failing to submit homework assignments.

The formal assessment entailed a nonverbal test of intellectual functioning, a formal achievement test, a computer test of Attention Deficit Hyperactivity Disorder (ADHD), and completion of self-report measures of ADHD by his parents, teachers, and the client. The results supported a diagnosis of ADHD, Predominantly Inattentive Type, and relative weaknesses in reading fluency and comprehension. I met with the client and his parents on the fifth session to share the results of the assessment, to initiate educational interventions and referrals, and more important, to allow the client and the family to experience tangible and positive outcomes of their engagement in the assessment process. This experience mitigated their skepticism concerning the therapy process and enhanced their commitment to the longer-term therapy needed to improve Kian's mood, self-esteem, and relationship with them.

The remaining five sessions were focused on further assessment, facilitating the client's awareness of the nature of his conflicts with authority, and setting short-term and long-term goals with Kian and his parents. He soon realized that he had been angry at his parents for their divorce. He asked, "It is okay if they disappoint me, but not okay for me to disappoint them?" He also believed that his parents were not consistent or truthful because they promised a lot and never delivered. He did not want to succeed because he did not want them to take credit for his academic success; he was acutely aware of how Iranian families and friends of his parents bragged about their children's academic success or achievements. Later on in therapy, Kian realized that he also underachieved to avoid his fear of failure.

Taking Action and Instigating Change

Collaboratively, Kian and I explored his choices and options for negotiating between cultural expectations for academic success and his individual aspiration to become a DJ. He was painfully aware that in his small kinship network of family and close friends, disc jockeying was frowned upon and not respected as a profession; everyone had commented that he could pursue it as a hobby, but not a profession. He was quite aware of cultural sanctions against some professions, as well as how Iranians respected and valued those with higher levels of education and professional status. He had made his "private" aspirations and sense of self "public" and was challenged by the "public" pressure to conform and abandon his "private" aspirations in order to regain public respect and acceptance.

Kian attended weekly individual therapy sessions and worked with a private tutor to help him with school assignments. I wrote a letter to his school and was able to secure some academic support by invoking the provisions of a 504 educational plan. I also met with his parents and discussed issues pertinent to parenting teenagers with ADHD who manifest their dissatisfactions and unhappiness in oppositional and defiant behaviors. Kian's parents were worried about him getting into so much trouble with the teachers and school personnel, as his behaviors were a reflection of their parenting and were shaming them in their community of friends and family.

My therapeutic recommendations for meeting in conjoint or family sessions were, however, deflected and resisted by Kian. During the course of the individual therapy sessions, I educated Kian about the rationale for combining the individual and family therapy approaches. He also was educated about cognitive-behavioral therapy as well as the importance of his relationships with his parents, peers, and the larger culture in developing a positive ethnic identity and good self-esteem.

Kian kept a thought diary and began to identify his automatic thoughts in response to any encounter with family or friends that left him feeling slighted, criticized, or rejected. He realized that it was his misperceptions and irrational processing of information that led him to feel put down or disrespected or controlled, to which he reacted with defiance and contempt. He became mindful of the automaticity of his negative thinking and began to challenge his negative thoughts. He learned to ask others for clarification and not make assumptions or mind read.

Kian soon became quite an expert in exploring his own thoughts and the associated feelings. He became less oppositional and guarded in therapy as he began to practice his skills in solving his issues with his friends. As his grades improved, he was able to negotiate with his parents for more privileges and outings with his friends. He learned that his oppositional behaviors stemmed from the feeling of victimization that he often experienced in significant relationships because he expected disappointments.

Although he reported a positive relationship with me and felt understood, his relationship with his mother deteriorated; he was becoming more aggressive toward her. When I insisted on family sessions with his parents, Kian expressed anxiety because he anticipated the sessions would become yelling contests and would not be helpful. Yet, despite his reluctance to focus on his relationship with his parents, he began to take more responsibility for his actions. He also learned that by acting responsibly in his school work, he was able to secure more respect from his parents and have more freedom to spend time with his friends. He was doing better in school, getting help from his tutor, and he began to turn in all his assignments.

Eventually, a conjoint therapy session with the client and his father revealed that his mother was demanding and did not leave him alone when he was upset and needed time to cool down. He seemed to do better in his relationship with his father, who seemed to choose his battles with Kian more wisely and allowed him to cool down when he was upset. Kian and I spent six more session focusing on anger management and his relationship with his mother. He eventually began to share how his mother continuously put him down in front of her close female friends (i.e., aunts), or how she always expressed her disappointment in him by comparing him to his aunt's children, who were doing well in school. His mother also blamed him for her stress-related back problems, headaches, and insomnia, and had told him on several occasions that he was the reason for his parents' divorce. Unfortunately, however, Kian's positive relationship with me negatively impacted his relationship with his mother; he was relying on "splitting," where I became the "good" mother and he began to distance himself from the "bad mother," his own mother. I had to prepare Kian for conjoint sessions with his mother and make an attempt to repair their relationship. He understood that respect for and deference to one's mother was unconditional based on the culture, there were culturally sanctioned ways of communicating respectfully, and respect had a significant impact on Iranian parents. He was also reassured prior to the conjoint sessions that my role was to help him communicate more effectively and to help his mother to understand him better.

Final Sessions: Feedback and Accountability

His mother came to the first conjoint session after four months of my work with Kian in individual therapy. The one family meeting we had was in Week 5, to review the results of the formal assessment and set therapeutic goals. Although the father had at least one conjoint session, Kian's mother was coming back to therapy after four months. She greeted me very formally and seemed guarded. My awareness of cultural sanctions against direct confrontation led me to be readily apologetic for not having had the opportunity to involve her sooner. I had to first show my respect for her to empower her as a parent, given Kian's exaggerated alliance with me. She remarked that she was very busy herself and seeing that Kian was doing better in school she was reassured that the therapy was helping him. I validated her and took responsibility for not keeping in touch with her as I had promised earlier in the therapy process. I also empowered her by acknowledging her important role in the client's life, while indicating how hard Kian had worked to prepare for that meeting.

I started the session by reviewing the basic rules of communication and safety, then identified my role as a facilitator and the goal for that session. Kian's mother agreed to allow Kian to share his thoughts and feelings without interrupting him. The goal was to develop mutual respect and understanding. A lofty goal, particularly for one session, but both agreed to be civil if nothing else, and they agreed to meet at least a few more sessions if we needed to. I then directly solicited his mother's feedback regarding her expectations. She indicated that Kian, as her only child, was the most important thing in her life and she came to the session for him and was willing to hear him out. She then sighed and stated, "Let's hear what he has to say first." Kian glared at her and seemed very tense. To facilitate an emotional connection, I had him open the communication with his poem that he composed over a month of therapy for this particular occasion. His poem described a boy who dreamt to be an artist, only waking up to realize he had no talents of any kind. He dreamt of ways to make his mother proud, only waking up to realize he was empty handed and had nothing to offer. His mother became emotional and tearful, and I could hear in Kian's voice that he struggled to keep his tears back in his throat.

When he finished his poem there was a long pause, which I had to interrupt in response to Kian's pleading with his eyes for me to do something. I cleared my throat, as I was emotional as well, and acknowledged his courage to share his deep feelings. I modeled mirroring and a validation process for his mother, who was struggling to hold back her tears. Kian's mother wiped her tears and indicated that she has always been proud of him and moved to sit closer to him on the couch. Kian did not expect that reaction from his mother; he was ready to deflect one of her usual sarcasms. I reflected on the process of their emotional communication through a poem. Kian shared his disbelief and stated that he was expecting to be teased or put down for making such an attempt. His mother hugged him and indicated that she always had encouraged him, knowing how talented he is, but that he is the one who keeps rejecting her. As I had promised Kian, I had to politely redirect his mother to reflect his feelings, as I earlier demonstrated, then share her own feelings, thoughts, and reactions.

It took us six more conjoint sessions before Kian and his mother were able to communicate their feelings about their relationship better, particularly about the divorce. His mother learned also to use more humor in her communications with him and not always lecture him or use sarcasm. We never had a family session. Kian did not get expelled; he finished the year with a C+ average and became motivated to take a writing class that summer. His parents were not able to dissuade him from his interest in becoming a DJ, but they agreed not to pressure him to become a lawyer or an engineer as long he did better in school and planned to attend a four-year university, not a junior college.

The parents expressed their appreciation by sending flowers to the therapist's office. Kian's mother called a few years later to report that Kian was accepted at the University of California in Irvine in the engineering department. He was interested in obtaining his bachelor's degree in acoustics and sound engineering. I did not hear from Kian, and I still wonder whether he was forced to abandon his dream of becoming a famous DJ or he eventually grew out of it. Or perhaps, the course of development eventually surrendered to the cultural edicts, and he learned to keep his true aspirations private.

16

Case Illustration: The Case of Mena and Ahmad

Application of the MEA-SISM

Maryam Sayyedi

Noha Alshugairi

Metra Azar-Salem

M ena and Ahmad came to therapy to work on issues they were struggling with in their 13-year marriage. They were arguing daily, Mena had frequent anger outbursts, and they disagreed on the parenting of their five-year-old daughter. Both felt distressed and expressed helplessness. They did not want to divorce or separate but believed that the home environment and their relationship with each other were unbearable. Ahmad was 35 years old at the time of therapy and Mena was 33. Ahmad was born in Palestine and his family immigrated to Lebanon as Palestinian refugees. His father was from a working-class background, and as refugees they had a lower socioeconomic status through all of his childhood years. His kinship system was composed of 13 siblings, uncles and aunts, and other displaced Palestinian families that grew close over the years in Lebanon. Ahmad reports that although he experienced poverty as a child, he remembers these years as happy, joyful, and stable. He immigrated to the United States when he was 18 years old on a student visa to attend a local state university.

Mena and her family left Iran when she was six years old, and after many stops in Europe, they finally immigrated to the United States when she was eight years old. As immigrants, they struggled with the stress of having to learn the English language, experienced financial hardship, and experienced family conflicts related to different rates of acculturation. Their kinship system included the maternal aunt's family and cousins who lived nearby. They also had a few Iranian friends who were close to them during those difficult years of adjustment to the new country. Mena reported that her parents' marriage was dysfunctional and that her mother was the victim of domestic violence. Mena ran away from home as a teenager and lived with several boyfriends until she met her current husband at age 19. She claimed that Ahmad was what saved her and guided her back to her faith and the Islamic way of living. After they were married, due to financial instability and hardship, both were unable to finish their college degrees. Mena had aspirations of becoming a dentist, and Ahmad always wanted to become a college professor. At the time of therapy, they ran an Internet business.

Beginning Sessions: Connecting With Clients and Assessment

Connecting with Middle Eastern American (MEA) clients is a crucial phase of the therapeutic process. For many Muslim clients from this population, coming to therapy is a foreign process fraught with anxiety and skepticism. I therefore devote a great deal of attention to returning their initial phone calls for appointments in a timely manner. On the phone, I respond kindly and with patience, addressing their inquiries about the fees, my credentials and background, and whether or not I will be able to help them.

As a Muslim therapist with knowledge of their religious identification as Muslims, I greeted them with the Islamic greeting to lessen their anxiety and to join with them. For non-Muslim therapists, a courteous greeting would suffice. Depending on the level of religiosity of the client, I would wait to see whether she or he extends her or his hand to shake. Some religious men and women in the Islamic faith choose not to shake hands with the opposite gender. A nice smile and eye contact would be appropriate in these instances. For the non-Muslim therapist, the rules of confidentiality are the same, although certain cultural sensitivities need to be addressed, especially concerning gender relations. As mentioned previously, some Muslim men and women prefer not to make any physical contact with the opposite gender, and this should be noted as culturally appropriate behavior. Also, personal space is to be respected and regarded as sacred space; thus, infringement of that space is an infraction of the boundaries.

I thoroughly reviewed the limits of confidentiality and reassured them that if I encountered them in the community (e.g., the mosque) I would allow them to approach me and would not approach them, to maintain their confidentiality. Given that the people in the community know me as a therapist, and knowing the couple's concerns about confidentiality, I devoted ample time to this matter. They understood that if they preferred not to greet me or show acquaintance, I would not be offended; greetings and social courtesies are very important to Muslims, particularly when you encounter people in the mosque or other parts of the community.

Clarifying and delineating boundaries directly are pertinent to the process of connecting with MEA clients, given the newness of therapy and therapists' roles in their cultural socialization processes. When using the language and self-disclosure to further our connections, I took their age and education, as well as levels of acculturation, into account and tried to join them by introducing myself first. Given Mena and Ahmad's young age, and the fact they are of the same generation as I am, I maintained a friendly demeanor in my introduction of my background. I introduced myself and briefly educated them about the agenda for the first few meetings and how I conduct therapy with couples. I self-disclosed about my roles as a mother and wife, and shared my Middle Eastern background as well. I also tried to match their style of communication and use their terminology for expressing their difficulties, in order not to pathologize. Mena and Ahmad were fluent in English, although Ahmad had a heavy accent and spoke slower. While maintaining a professional decorum, I tried to evoke an atmosphere of a friendly and safe encounter, to lessen the power differential in the room so that they felt a sense of comfort in the therapeutic process.

Knowing that the standard therapy time may be too short for some clients, I allocated 90 minutes. However, as a couple they needed more time to share their histories. We planned on two individual sessions to follow the intake session. For this couple, I ensured that each client had an equal opportunity to express his or her issues in his or her own way while making meaning of their situation. Toward the end of our first session, the couple became relaxed and seemed to have overcome their skepticism. They spontaneously provided feedback that they felt comfortable and were hopeful that they had made the right decision to seek help. They were very appreciative of the fact that I was a practicing Muslim therapist and felt I could better understand their lifestyle.

The assessment phase with Mena and Ahmad was very detailed and thorough. I handed them some simple informal questionnaires I have devised for assessment of couples at the end of their first session and asked them to bring them to the next session. The questionnaire is not a formal assessment instrument, but it identifies a couple's satisfaction in different domains (e.g., time spent together, friendship). For the next two sessions, I met individually with them. Once I gained an understanding of their general marital issues and screened their mental health status and overall adjustment, I gathered more information about their immigration histories, Muslim identity, family support system, social support networks, kinship ties, their experiences of acculturation, and ethnic identity.

In my assessment interview with Ahmad, several dominant themes were apparent. He had a difficult immigration experience when his family first had to leave Palestine and become refugees in Lebanon; Ahmad was only six years old at the time. Immigration to the United States was another difficult experience for Ahmad. At age 18 he had to abandon his parents, his 13 brothers and sisters, and the families he grew up so closely with in Lebanon to come to the United States.

He was awarded a scholarship that enabled him to help his family financially, and he accepted the opportunity but paid a great price by separating from his support system, leaving his entire family and kinship system behind in Lebanon.

The sacrifices he had made, however, did not culminate in a university degree and the respect that it would have earned him. Instead he had to abandon his education to make a living, and now being married he was struggling to work full time and had his educational goals on hold indeterminately. Later it became evident that his feelings of failure and shame were closely associated with his struggles to complete his degree program. Almost daily, he felt judgment and criticism from his wife with regard to his lack of educational and professional status. Ahmad also felt he had let his family down, both his nuclear family and his family of origin. Ahmad reported that his stereotypical Middle Eastern features and darker complexion and his heavy Arabic accent furthered his sense of inadequacy after the 9/11 tragedy, as he had been experiencing more discrimination. He stated he felt everyone sees him as "guilty" and untrustworthy. He hated the palpability of the racism that he felt in the mainstream culture. He stated that he was a very moderately practicing Muslim and that this labeling and association with violence or terrorism had negatively affected his psyche and his ethnic identity. The insecurities permeated all his relationships, particularly his relationship with his wife, whom he believed did not respect him either.

I saw Mena in an individual session as well because gathering her full immigration history and developmental history was not possible during the intake session. Mena's family immigrated to the United Sates when she was eight years old. Her parents adapted quickly to American culture, as most secular Iranians do, and maintained a bicultural status. They did not practice their faith, and their children were allowed to associate freely with the dominant culture. Mena was the oldest of three children. She reports that she was the overly responsible child. She was always responsible for taking care of her younger siblings, filling out legal documents for her parents, and running the family business as she got older. Her parents, she reported, had a very dysfunctional marriage. Her father was violent toward her mother and exerted unrelenting control over everyone in the family, particularly the females.

As a teenager, she rebelled and finally ran away from home at age 17. She believed that she adopted the American culture of individualism and autonomy fully and disappointed her parents by not meeting their expectations for doing well in school and pursuing higher education. She lived with many boyfriends and worked at different jobs until she met her husband at age 19. He was 21 years old at the time. After a brief courtship, they married when Mena was almost 21 and Ahmad was 23. Mena attributed her returning to Islam to her positive experiences with her husband when they were dating. They both reported that since they married they have been truly practicing Muslims, and now "Muslim American" is their primary identification.

Gathering such information through a detailed assessment is crucial to my approach in providing therapy for couples who are from different nationalities in the Middle East. During the assessment process, they warm up to the therapy process as a collaborative exploration of their inter- and intrapersonal experiences. During this discourse, religion often becomes the point of convergence, as our Islamic identity enables us to reach each other across geographical boundaries and national identities representing MEAs.

After assessing for their adherence to Islamic practices and faith, I freely utilize the Islamic practices and beliefs in all aspects of working with couples, given that Islam provides the context and the rituals for improving one's daily life. Mena and Ahmad had created a Muslim American culture of their own that left behind many of the cultural practices of their parents. When I inquired about how their faith and its practices impact their own relationships as well as their relationships with their parents, Mena reported that her parents never accepted Ahmad because of his Arab heritage. Her parents always wanted her to marry an Iranian man who was from their own cultural background. A long history of rebellion against the Islamic faith and Arabs exists among some Iranian dissidents in the United States. This was a source of family conflict for many years when Mena married Ahmad. She also converted from the Shi'ite sect of Islam practiced in Iran to the Sunni sect that her husband practiced. The schism between Sunni and Shi'ite Islam originated in a political disagreement during the first century of Islam about who had the right to be Caliph (Islamic leader) after the death of the Prophet Muhammad. Today, 85% of Muslims are Sunni and 15% are Shi'ite. Practically, the Shi'ites give infallible status to their Imams and spiritual leaders, and they also rely on historical events that define the majority of their religious commemorations and practices. The Sunni majority does not have an infallible religious leader system because most of their rulings are derived from the Quran and statements of the Prophet Muhammad. Mena and Ahmad were the quintessential heterogeneity characterizing MEA clients.

When working with minorities in general, and MEAs in particular, I conduct a thorough assessment of their experiences of discrimination to provide them with a safe place to process such experiences. Mena also had experienced discrimination. After 9/11, she had a difficult time finding a job. She had been wearing the Muslim *hijab* (headscarf) for three years. But after 9/11, because she could not find work she removed it. She believed that discrimination against her faith affected their financial opportunities negatively. She had also experienced discrimination within her own culture because she married someone of Arab descent. Her parents have rejected her husband, and when she wore her *hijab* and began to practice her faith more publicly, she had negative experiences within her own Iranian community.

To get a clear picture of the cultural practices they adhere to, I asked both to share with me their values that comprised the core of their experiences. In this conversation, I allowed them to remain the experts of their experiences. I took a curious stance and asked questions only for clarification. As this was their first therapy experience, they shared that it does not feel "normal" to share their views on their own culture and practices they adhere to. I assured them that I was listening to collect data that would perhaps help me better understand them as a couple. It is not uncommon that MEA clients will not be accustomed to therapy or sharing personal experiences and views about themselves. It was against their worldview that we discussed and explored their styles of parenting, communication, dealing with conflict, household responsibilities, and finances in order to facilitate awareness. Sharing these private conversations with an outsider is something uncommon to the MEA population. Assuring confidentiality in the initial session is very crucial for this process to take place. Throughout this session, I remained very empathetic and curious and allowed them to be authors of their own experience.

Middle Sessions: Facilitating Awareness, Setting Goals, Instigating Change

For the next three sessions after the individual assessment sessions, I saw the couple together and shared with them my observations and impressions. I normalized and validated their need to seek therapy and praised them for doing so. I educated them on the process of acculturation and immigration and its effects on family life and marriage of immigrant families. I explained the dynamics of systems of relationships and how the Middle Eastern culture thrives on all systems working together toward the betterment of the system. The clients also needed to understand how the stress of immigration and acculturation shaped their early development and their identity development, as well as their relationship. I facilitated their awareness and insight into more systemic issues while encouraging them to reflect on how, individually, they contributed to the life of their problems. An important area needing immediate therapeutic attention was their parenting practices. By associating their parenting practices with their own early experiences with their parents, they gained insight into their problematic approaches. We spent a few sessions on how they could negotiate parenting strategies, and I helped them learn positive parenting strategies.

During these parenting training sessions (i.e., therapy sessions reconceptualized as such), they discussed their different styles of parenting and how this consistently resulted in conflicts for the couple. We all agreed that the old system was not working and that a new parenting system was needed. I recommended several parenting books, and we used them in therapy to come up with their new parenting styles. We set up a new system for their parenting strategies, which included family meetings, discipline guidelines for both to adhere to when needed, and also an underlying mission statement that would be the goal of all their parenting practices. We took time to role-play different scenarios and how they would use the different techniques if the scenarios were to come up with their daughter. We also established that criticism of the other parent would not be allowed in front of the child. They both agreed that a 10-minute session every evening would be used to recap how they interacted as parents that day. Ahmad preferred e-mailing as a method to communicate with Mena regarding their new parenting strategies. Once the couple knew what their goals were as parents, it was easier for them to delineate what changes they had to make to reach those goals.

The nature of their conflicts and how it tied to their feelings of inadequacy, feelings of failure, and unresolved anger was also discussed. They were very open to receiving my professionally grounded impressions as feedback, and we collaboratively set goals in the sessions that followed parenting training. The impetus and primary goal for many MEA couples is to work on their relationship for the sake of their children, and this couple was highly motivated to do so. They wanted to improve their marriage so they could ultimately become better parents.

The issue of parenting took precedence because it enhanced their self-awareness and awareness of their own attachment issues. They identified individual goals as well. Mena wanted to deal with her anger, while Ahmad wanted to be able to emotionally connect with Mena and learn how to overcome his feelings of inadequacy. Both also wanted to use spirituality in therapy and work toward enhancing this aspect of their lives. They both came up with a plan to attend more events at their local mosque and listen to and study more the Quran, the Muslim holy book. They both expressed that they were very close spiritually when they met, and now they had spiritually grown apart. Muslims pray five times a day, and they agreed to save the last prayer of the night as a special time they would pray together.

The strength of the therapeutic relationship kept the couple committed to therapy, and they attended their sessions regularly. The strength of our relationship stemmed from a combination of several items. I spent a lot of time establishing trust and confidentiality with this couple. Another key factor to building this strong therapeutic relationship was normalizing their experiences. Many MEA clients feel that they are the only ones going through this experience. There is much shame attached to having marital problems or difficulties with their children. As a shame-based community, this population does not encourage sharing problems or issues outside your most immediate circle of friends and family. I was able to share the fact that many MEA families have similar struggles, which relieved them and engaged them in the therapeutic process. As a therapist, I also used a lot of self-disclosure to gain their trust and to normalize the struggles they were having. The four sessions that followed the parenting sessions focused on learning about the nature of their issues and discussion of options or interventions to resolve those issues.

I offered them an integrative therapeutic rationale incorporating developmental, systemic, and cognitive-behavioral theories, which also organized our therapeutic efforts to initiate the change and reach our therapeutic goals. Knowing this population, I wanted to approach their circumstances in a holistic manner. Knowing that spirituality and family play a big role in their lives, I wanted to educate them on the importance of systems working well together. When I described the systemic nature of problems and how we are all connected to the different systems we are a part of, they became aware of the changes that were needed in each system. They understood in this session that in order for them to function well, the system as a whole needed to change. This was culturally appropriate for this population, in that MEA clients rely on and value community, systems, and the interdependence of families. Explaining the developmental stage their daughter was in really helped them conceptualize where she was and what behavior they should expect from her. Finally, explaining the cognitive-behavioral therapeutic approach and how it could help them in therapy moved them from shame and skepticism to a sense of action and responsibility for their own lives.

In the next four sessions, both worked individually and collaboratively in therapy on their individual goals. For Mena, we brainstormed areas she would like to further explore through journaling. Themes that came up in our session included her childhood experience as a new immigrant in the United States, her relationship with her father, and what success and failure meant to her as a parent. Within these topics she also included which pieces of her culture she wanted to incorporate in her child's upbringing as well as how much of the American culture she wanted to adopt in her parenting practices. A lot of her journaling involved revisiting her childhood memories and writing letters to those she never clearly expressed herself to. Culturally, in the MEA population, "talking back" to parents is considered very disrespectful, and journaling allowed her to openly express her feelings and thoughts about her parents. This process was very instrumental in initiating change for her as she gradually gained more insight into her own emotional and cognitive processes.

Because Mena and Ahmad were very new to the therapeutic process, many of our sessions consisted of psychoeducation. Before we were able to begin cognitive-behavioral therapeutic techniques, I had to teach the clients about this theory and what it can potentially do for them. We went through many thought records and examples, so they could learn how to use thought records themselves. Both of these clients were fluent in English, and their level of acculturation enabled them to understand and use these tools in therapy. By keeping thought records and journaling, Mena was able to identify her family schema, her automatic thoughts, and how she continued to think and react in ways that she had as a child with her father. The cognitive-behavioral approach really enhanced her ability to recognize her distorted ways of thinking and connect this to her problematic behaviors. As we looked at distorted ways of thinking, Mena and Ahmad were able to add a few cognitive distortions specific to their cultures. We explored ways in which the MEA population may have its own cognitive distortions. Once again, each culture within the MEA population is distinct, so I allowed them to come up with their own distortions from the specific cultures they grew up in. This adjustment to the "traditional" methods of using cognitive distortions in therapy added to their comfort and understanding of the cognitive-behavioral approach to therapy.

Externalizing Mena's anger and putting her in control of her emotions deepened her insight and motivated her to change. Processing her experiences of discrimination, and recognizing her parents' discrimination against her husband as an Arab, helped her realize how she had internalized their bigotry. She also realized that she was getting angry with her husband because of her unfulfilled expectations of her father.

For Ahmad, facilitating change involved normalizing and validating his feelings of abandonment and isolation as well as being emasculated by his wife's disrespect. He realized that he missed his family of origin and was longing to be with them in Lebanon. He had to process his feelings of displacement at multiple levels. Under all of his self-directed anger and daily criticisms and undermining by Mena, he had buried his sense of masculinity, pride, and honor as an Arab man. Her family never accepted him and always saw him as "less than" their family. He labeled himself a Palestinian refugee, but he realized that moving away from this label while still contributing to his new family and his family of origin helped him strengthen his lost sense of identity. He also benefited from journaling his thoughts and feelings related to experiences of rejection and demoralization in different aspects of his life. Spirituality and religion, which he turned to in times of sadness and difficulty, were labeled by the larger society as "fanaticism" and "violence." Themes that came up during his journaling experience included marginalization as a Muslim man, his lack of control over his financial burdens, and his spiritual journey that had come to a halt due to 9/11. A great resource in his life was his religion, and after the events of 9/11 he felt ashamed of what had happened and this affected his level of spirituality. There were many feelings of shame, abandonment, and just anger that arose from the writing experience and the discussion of these experiences in therapy. Exploring his pain with those realities facilitated awareness of how his exaggerated need for control, as a reaction to perceived oppression, played out at his own home. The only place he could exert any control or power was in his home. His internal conflicts stemmed from discrimination, refugee status, and low economic standards, which made him feel emasculated and disempowered. The therapy had to focus on empowering him and facilitating awareness of his resiliency and strengths that helped him survive as a young man in a foreign country. Some of these sessions were conducted privately and some with Mena. I find that men in the MEA community have never had this venue to share and explore their feelings, and thus I wanted him to do this in private so that he did not feel judged or labeled by Mena. Toward the end, he felt comfortable sharing these experiences with her in the room, and this really facilitated a different level of empathy from Mena toward Ahmad. It was very eye-opening for Mena to bear witness to some of the conversations that took place in therapy.

Mena explored her displaced anger with her father and his domestic violence. She recognized she was rebelling against her husband's exaggerated need for control in the same way she did with her father. She recognized that her expectations of her husband were rooted in her need for protection and acceptance from her father. The change began to impact the nature of their relationship as they realized how they could help each other heal from the wounds of their early hardships. As a result of my being sensitive to their individual experiences of oppression, cultural practices, and diverse family-of-origin issues and facilitating their insight regarding those issues, Mena and Ahmad became appreciative of the complexity of their problems and aware of their strengths.

However, they initiated change by using their strengths, which included their social networks, their mosque, and their reliance on God. Exploring how their private identity as a couple was greatly influenced by their public identity as Muslims enabled them to further understand the impact of religion and ethnicity on their relationship. As we combined journaling, exploring their childhoods, and looking at cognitive distortions in the realm of their specific cultures and their immigrant experiences, we were able to facilitate a level of awareness that they had not experienced before. During their therapeutic experience, they also became more God conscious in their lives, which facilitated growth and a sense of spiritual revival. Being able to really dissect their identities as individuals, as a couple, as immigrants, as parents, and as Muslims in their public lives helped them design a new system of communication and connection with each other. A new sense of attachment and interdependence began to form between the couple. Once each really heard the other in therapy and really empathized with the experience of the other, they were able to understand and fulfill their roles in a more cohesive way. The therapeutic journey for each of them was not just working on their couple issues with me: As they were sharing stories of their different cultural and immigration experiences, they were processing their own experiences. During these sessions, the skill of listening and validating was practiced because both Ahmad and Mena were not used to this form of communication.

Last Sessions: Feedback and Accountability

Compassion and cultural sensitivity unfolded through my invitations to discuss their cultural, familial, and religious beliefs. Without that feedback, I might have been swayed by my own culturally ingrained assumptions as an MEA therapist. This is a hazard that can be avoided only by opening the therapeutic communication and discourse to allow clients to inform me of their experiences of therapy. I had to solicit feedback directly; otherwise, these clients would have remained passive and soon would have been disenchanted, leaving therapy while feeling misunderstood and unassisted. Disclosure of my knowledge of the MEA community, my levels of religiosity, and my reservations regarding working within my own community assisted me in soliciting feedback. I was very clear early on in therapy that this is their process, and the only way I can assist them is if they teach me and inform me of what they consider their cultural norms. The MEA community, I find in my experience, appreciates direct interactions rather than attempts to indirectly solicit information. Of course, all this direct communication was rooted in the foundations of compassion, honesty, and my true desire to help them. Once they knew they were not just another client to me and that I truly cared about their well-being, our therapeutic relationship began.

In our last few sessions, many words of appreciation were exchanged. We ended therapy in a very different environment than when we started. As I recall, our first sessions were hostile, angry, and difficult sessions. Now our last sessions were filled with humor, love, and connection. Mena expressed appreciation for my being a "role model" for her. She expressed that this experience gave her insight into her own life, and my sharing pieces of my life really encouraged her to create change in her own. They were both very appreciative of my self-disclosure and recognized that it inspired them in several of our sessions together. I continue to see them occasionally at community events or the mosque, and they always make an effort to express their appreciation whenever they see me.

PART VI

Where Do We Go From Here?

Education, Training, Practice, and Research Implications

17

So What Should I Actually Do?

Developing Skills for Greater Multicultural Competence

Rebecca L. Toporek

As a counselor educator and instructor of multicultural counseling courses, one of the biggest challenges I see for students and curriculum is the practical aspect of multicultural competence. Possibly the most frequently used model of cultural competence is the tripartite model of multicultural competence. The tripartite model identifies the need for awareness of counselor attitudes and beliefs; awareness of clients' worldview; and culturally relevant interventions (D. Sue, Arredondo, & McDavis, 1992). Over the past 20 years, there has been an increase in the development of activities and curriculum to assist students and practitioners in developing greater multicultural self-awareness (e.g., Bieschke, Gehlert, Wilson, Matthews & Wade, 2003; Pedersen, 2003; Roysircar, Gard, Hubbell, & Ortega, 2005). There is also considerable literature and research aiding in understanding culture-specific information regarding a range of cultural groups (e.g., Santiago-Rivera, Arredondo, & Gallardo-Cooper, 2002; D. W. Sue & Sue, 2008). Several documents have augmented the literature in practice and provide concrete and specific guidelines and recommendations (American Psychological Association [APA], 2002; Arredondo et al., 1996). Yet an area that continues to be identified as needing attention is that of skill development (Pieterse, Evans, Risner-Butner, Collins, & Mason, 2009; Priester et al., 2008). Further, as communities become increasingly diverse and there is greater acknowledgment of the complexity of cultural identity, it is clear that counselors need to have a wider repertoire of skills that allows them to be more flexible and relevant.

This chapter is designed to address training issues specifically related to developing skills for multicultural competence. As such, I will touch briefly on some of the challenges of facilitating the development of cultural competence that I have observed as an educator. These experiences have helped me to shape and reshape my approach to teaching and the application of the Skills Identification Stage Model (SISM). The main objective of this chapter is to share some of the ways that I have attempted to facilitate skill development in each component of the model as well as share some specific exercises and activities. Several documents provide a useful backdrop for integrating the SISM into training.

Multicultural Competence and Training in Counseling and Psychology

When Sampson (1993) wrote his criticism regarding the inadequacy of counseling and psychology to address advances of the multicultural movement, he asserted that attention given to training programs had merely added to traditional training and interventions rather than truly changed the structure of training, practice, and research. Almost 20 years later, programs continue to struggle with a patchwork of multicultural training, and the majority of programs rely on one course to provide the bulk of multicultural training (Pieterse et al., 2009; Priester et al., 2008). The findings from Priester and his colleagues and Pieterse and his colleagues indicate that the focus of most multicultural training has been on raising awareness and imparting culture-specific information and that ethnicity and race tend to dominate training. Examples include writing a self-awareness paper and cultural immersion exercises. Both studies also concluded that the focus on raising awareness and increasing culture-specific knowledge seems to have left skill building with minimal attention.

As someone who teaches a graduate-level multicultural counseling course, I am not surprised by these findings. Most students come to our program with a wide range of awareness and knowledge of oppression, cultural values, biases, and other aspects critical to multicultural counseling and therapy. Thus, awareness is addressed first as the foundation on which cultural information can be integrated and interpreted appropriately. I integrate skill building implicitly throughout this process (e.g., dyad interviews, self-disclosing, case conceptualization). Yet students often express a desire for more attention to skill building, suggesting that they are not necessarily aware that they are building skills through the awareness and knowledge acquisition process. This has led me to two conclusions. First, multicultural counseling skill building must be done throughout the curriculum, including in practicum courses. Second, despite attention to multicultural aspects in case conceptualization, consultation, treatment planning, and assessment, it is possible that a structural shift that integrates specific multicultural microskills and concrete behavior would be helpful. It is critical for training programs to provide multicultural development throughout the curriculum, including skills-based courses.

In my work as an educator, I observe that counseling trainees experience a tremendous amount of growth in their awareness of their own worldviews and the assumptions they make given their cultural frame. They anxiously and excitedly research various cultural groups that are prevalent in their field sites and their communities. As models of learning indicate, when we begin to learn a new task, we tend to focus on concrete actions and observable behaviors. As we develop, we are better able to synthesize our observations and our understanding of the complexities present and adjust our approach, depending on the needs of the situation. Our repertoire broadens, and we have the ability to adapt our base set of skills and behaviors according to unexpected demands. The focus on cultural self-awareness is essential in helping trainees understand their presence as a tool and the significance of their worldview in shaping the way that they use themselves. Similarly, their increased comprehension of the sociopolitical context within which they, and their clients, have existed also provides an important frame for beginning to assess and understand the complex variables in practice.

Students often experience difficulty in translating their awareness and knowledge into concrete action in practice. In training, we spend a fair amount of time talking about and practicing implementing culture-specific knowledge and self-awareness into the counseling and therapy work. We watch multi-cultural demonstration videotapes, do role plays, and engage in activities to understand the skills that are useful in culturally diverse settings. Yet students continue to call for more specificity and more tangible guidance. "What would I actually do if I were a multiculturally competent counselor?"

What Should I Actually Do? Helping Students Develop Culturally Adaptive Skills

As noted above, the process of developing skills has often been the least attended area of multicultural counseling training. The SISM provides specific areas that can be integrated into training. As a foundation, it is essential that the relevance of culture be recognized throughout the training program, rather than relegating it to a multicultural counseling course. The repertoire of possible learning activities is expansive, as is the potential to be creative. I will describe just a few activities in each of the components of the model. Although these merely scratch the surface of skill development, I hope that they provide some stimulus for generation of new approaches.

Connecting With Clients

In this component of the SISM, practitioners are encouraged to identify and demonstrate a number of behaviors that can communicate an understanding of the client's history, norms, identity and beliefs, and circumstances, with culture as an integral force. It is important to reiterate that the practitioner may not be aware of the client's salient identity during the early stages of the relationship. The complexity and fluidity of identities means that the practitioner should be cautious about assuming that a client would feel more comfortable with traditional ethnic practices. Hence, there are a number of strategies that can be useful in helping students begin the process of connecting with clients generally as well as assess cultural identity. One of the first areas of skill is attending to and setting the context of counseling and therapy. There are several goals in setting the context, such as gathering information regarding the client's salient identities and developing hypotheses about culturally adaptive ways to proceed.

The Introduction. The introduction is an opportunity for students to practice being observant and mindful, which leads to greater awareness of their client. This is an activity that can be useful at the beginning of a semester-length class. Students greet each other and introduce themselves individually very briefly, describing a little about themselves and their background. After each introduction, students are instructed to write down observations regarding the interaction:

- What did they notice about the person they just met?
- Was a handshake or other form of touch used? If so, how did the handshake feel (soft, forceful, etc.)?
- How close were the two individuals physically?
- Where were the other person's eyes focused?
- What does the student know about herself or himself in terms of tendencies and beliefs about handshakes, physical proximity, eye contact and other aspects of introductions?
- What tentative hypotheses might they consider about that interaction?
- Were there ways in which the student's behavior influenced the way the person interacted with him or her?
- Are there contextual or socialization cues that predetermine how students interact with one another? Has the student modified his or her own behavior to adapt to these perceived expectations?

It is recommended that this process continue for at least three cycles of introductions, to provide students with opportunities to compare and contrast. In addition, students may find that they modify their behavior after each introduction, given that they have become more self-observant and possibly more self-conscious. In the early stages of a class, it is helpful to ask students to reflect and share observations of themselves rather than observations of others. Although this is a simple exercise, it can be very revealing and bring up feelings of vulnerability. The central objective of this activity is to help students begin to be mindful of very simple ways that they, and their clients, communicate from the very beginning. It is important to note students' considerations of the contextual cues they may have used in determining their own behavior, for example, cues to approach or pull back. It is useful to have a discussion regarding how their socialization into the culture of higher education may have created some common behavior in the exercise, as well as to contrast this with their hypotheses about clients' experience entering counseling or therapy.

Setting the Context. A second activity for connecting with clients is helping students develop their ability to talk about the process of counseling or therapy in a way that also enables them to assess clients' cultural perspectives and familiarity with counseling and therapy. The importance of discussing the process of counseling and therapy with clients is not new and is often addressed as an issue of informed consent. Yet using culturally adaptive skills shifts this intervention from simply informing the client about the "rules" of counseling and therapy, and instead provides opportunities to learn about the client as well as demonstrate culturally appropriate behaviors. A number of authors in this book provide specific information that can be helpful in this regard. For example, Parham (Chapter 2, this volume) describes the importance of creating a culturally appropriate ambiance when working with African American clients. In addition to the model and information presented in this book, there are a number of resources that can be helpful for this process, two of which are Hays (2008) and McAuliffe (2008).

The constructs of credibility and gift giving, as discussed by S. Sue and Zane (1987), have been wonderful foundations for approaching multicultural counseling and therapy within a concrete framework. Discussions regarding credibility can provide an opening to talking about students' fears and anxieties about how clients may perceive them across a number of identity dimensions. Gift giving can involve a range of items or behaviors, including tangible and concrete items such as food, tea, an anchor object, or informational materials. Gifts can also be intangibles such as words of hope. As Sue and Zane noted, "Giving is the client's perception that something was received from the therapeutic encounter" (p. 40). The discussion about gifts and the broad possibilities for what might constitute a gift in the eyes of clients emphasizes the importance of demonstrating cultural sensitivity.

Assessment

Teaching assessment skills begins with teaching a complex understanding of assessment. The importance of multiple sources of data, cultural equivalence in assessment, inclusions of the clinical interview as a credible method, and strengths assessment are critical foundations. Often students tend to view effective assessment as only including objective measures. Basic assessment courses should provide students with a basic understanding of reliability and validity, including cultural validity. Further, training programs should also be sure that cultural equivalence is adequately addressed (Helms, 1992; Lonner, 1981). Trainees need to be informed about different aspects of cultural equivalence, such as psychometric equivalence, functional equivalence, and linguistic equivalence. Beyond familiarity with these forms of cultural equivalence, it is important to understand how to assess instruments and protocol for cultural equivalence. Similar to activities that help trainees evaluate validity, examination of various aspects of cultural equivalence can be integrated.

Multicultural intake interviews such as the Career-in-Culture interview (Ponterotto, Rivera, & Sueyoshi, 2000) as well as the Person-in-Culture interview (Berg-Cross & Chinen, 1995) provide basic guidelines for students to practice asking about clients' cultural context. One way to use these tools is to have students role-play a counseling or therapy session in which they attempt to use questions from the Career-in-Culture or Person-in-Culture interviews. Students often find this difficult and stumble through feelings of being invasive, irrelevant, and awkward. After this first round of role plays, I ask students to work with their partner to examine some of the questions and consider what the goal of each question might be. In other words, what information might be obtained from asking such a question? For example, one of the questions suggested by Ponterotto and his colleagues asks clients about their religious background. If students have not had exposure to the relevance of religion or spirituality in their training program, they may have difficulty understanding the importance of this information. Talking in groups or pairs about the meaning of this information can help them to more clearly understand how the question can lead to clients' expectations, sources of strength, beliefs about human nature, and other topics that can be central to the counseling and therapy work. Students may find this book helpful because it articulates five domains of information that represent elements of culture at the deep structure level (ontology, cosmology, axiology, epistemology, and praxis). I ask students to consider alternative ways of inquiring, given the range of contexts in which they might be practicing. This encourages students to consider ways of inquiring that contribute to a smoother flow of interview. It is also important at this point to ask students to reflect on their discomfort. Do they have fears about what clients might think about them? Do they have difficulty articulating to clients how culture is relevant in counseling or therapy? I share that one of the ways that I have adapted questions about practices and beliefs is to ask clients what their family believes, then what their community believes, and then whether they have experienced any conflict or difference between these two or, more commonly, any conflict or difference between what their family or community believes and what the larger society seems to believe. I share this with students because it can be helpful in acknowledging cultural complexities and the potential for commonalities and differences in individual beliefs, family beliefs, and cultural beliefs. As noted earlier, it is important to use these types of exercises in a wide variety of counseling classes, including practicum, multicultural counseling, career counseling, ethics, developmental foundations, and assessment. In addition to these resources, McAuliffe (2008) and Rodriguez and Walls (2000) provide guidelines for culturally relevant inquiry.

Another activity I have used focuses on identifying client strengths that may be useful in the counseling and therapy process. In his demonstration of

Africentric counseling, Parham (1999) asks the client to honor and consider ancestors that he would like to call into the room to be present during their work together. I have suggested to students that this may be a way to help clients feel a sense of strength during counseling or therapy and may even be expanded into a discussion with the client to identify specifically the strengths they associate with those whose spirits they chose to bring to counseling/ therapy. It sometimes helps students to consider using a more general phrase to begin, such as "a person who gives you strength: ancestor, role model, or loved one." In counseling/therapy, the client and counselor/therapist can discuss those qualities and how those qualities may also reflect aspirations the client may have for himself or herself. Incidentally, I have also used this exercise with students at the beginning of class sessions in which I anticipate demanding emotional challenges, such as difficult dialogues. When I use this in class, I begin the exercise by asking the students to close their eyes. I then say something to the effect of, "I would like you to think about one or two people who give you strength: ancestors, role models, fictional or real, alive or passed on. Visualize that person and feel the strength and warmth that he or she brings to you; invite him or her into the room. I will be asking a lot of you today and I am expecting that you will push yourself beyond your comfort zone. Allow his or her strength to help you maintain your sense of strength, integrity, and compassion for yourself and your colleagues." I then ask them to write the name of the person on the board if they choose, or alternatively, I may ask them to draw a picture of the person and include symbols or words that reflect the strength that person's image brings. I also suggest that the strength may not necessarily be represented by a person but may be represented by a particular spiritual belief they have.

Facilitating Client Awareness

A significant objective of the SISM is to describe the process of assisting clients to broaden their perspective of their problem and context. Raising awareness of the influence of the social system and structural barriers can help shift the blame from the client (or clients blaming themselves), thereby allowing clients to identify strengths and capacities to change the way they respond to the world (traditionally the goal of psychotherapy) as well as change the way they can work toward addressing challenges in their environment. Two models have been helpful for me when teaching counselors to implement this process in counseling: psychotherapy as liberation (Ivey, 1995) and the American Counseling Association Advocacy Competencies (Lewis, Arnold, House, & Toporek, 2002).

Counseling from a liberation approach is informed by liberation theory (Freire, 1972), liberation psychology (Martín-Baró as cited in Martín-Baró, Aron, & Corne, 1994; Watkins & Shulman, 2008), and Ivey's (1995) description of psychotherapy as a tool for liberation. Ivey contended that the practice of counseling ought to help clients increase their understanding of themselves in relation to themselves, but also in relation to their context. This approach emphasizes the potential for helping clients understand that their current conditions are integrally connected to current and historical contextual variables. Similarly, Duran, Firehammer, and Gonzalez (2008) describe how they "analyze and help clients deconstruct their cultural history in ways that liberate them from the traumatic and oppressive conditions that brought them to their present situation" (p. 289). When facilitating students' understanding of and skills in using this approach, a foundational exercise is to facilitate their understanding of themselves and their cultural and historical context first, in order for them to be able to implement this with clients. One way this can be done is by using an ecological cultural genogram (see Figure 17.1). This reflects an important aspect of the Personal Dimensions of Identity noted by Arredondo and her colleagues (1996), which includes the influence of historical context on one's identity. In the first part of the exercise, students examine their identities and experiences within each of the ecological regions. This is followed by an examination of their ancestors, either through interviews or research. It is important to note here that instructors must be sensitive to students who are adoptees, former foster youth, refugees, and others who have limited access to ancestor information or for whom the information may bring traumatic memories. It has been useful to have students who are in these situations examine the greatest influences in their life and their ecological context. When students are able to identify the significance of cultural and historical forces on their beliefs, coping styles, resources, and other aspects of daily living, they are better able to help clients see themselves in a cultural context.

The other model that is an exceptional teaching and practitioner tool is the ACA Advocacy Competencies (Lewis et al., 2002). This model provides guidance to counselors regarding understanding and intervening in partnership with clients and on behalf of clients at individual levels (empowerment and client advocacy), community or school levels (community collaboration and systems advocacy), and societal levels (public information and social/political advocacy). The application of this model is elaborated extensively in a special section of the *Journal of Counseling and Development* (Toporek, Lewis, & Crethar, 2009) and the *ACA Advocacy Competencies: A Social Justice Framework for Counselors* (Ratts, Toporek, & Lewis, 2010).

Setting Goals

Helping students develop skills to partner with clients in setting goals holds exciting potential for positive action. Traditional goal-setting models can be helpful, yet they tend to encompass several assumptions that may limit their usefulness, such as presumed superiority of linear processes. To understand skills and behaviors that may be useful in collaborative goal-setting

Figure 17.1 Ecological Cultural Genogram

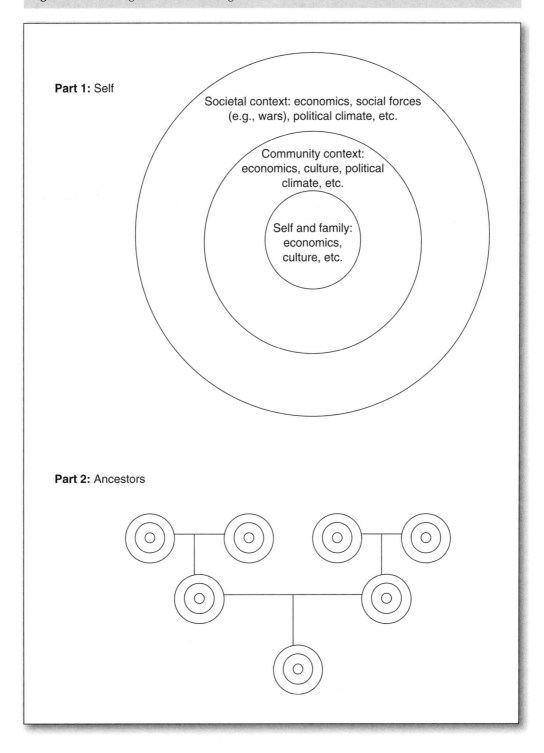

processes, it is important for students to begin to distinguish between linear and spatial or circular processes. As noted earlier, the students in my program tend to come from communities and cultural backgrounds that encompass a range of cognitive styles. Yet, by the time they get to graduate school, they have been socialized in a traditional educational system that tends to reward linear thinking and decision making over other means. By teaching students about the different ways of looking at problems, experiences, and decisions and validating their cultural ways of viewing the world, we can come closer to helping them do the same with their clients. Similarly, examining the Western reliance on the individual and devaluation of the collective in decision making presents another opportunity for helping students to reclaim and, in some cases, expand accepted ways of defining and setting goals.

In counseling/therapy with individuals who have limited economic means, many of the action-oriented models inadequately address systemic and practical barriers faced by clients. To adjust for that, I find it useful to spend some time working with clients to articulate practical and daily needs in light of long-term goals and to build this into the goal-setting process. The process then integrates an exploration of supports and alliances as well as subgoals that may include establishing stronger supports. This process is outlined in the social justice career counseling model (Toporek & Chope, 2006) and can be very useful in counseling beyond career goals. One benefit of this model in training students is that it provides very concrete areas for consideration that can be developed collaboratively with clients. In addition, the counselor and client can begin anywhere in the model, depending on where the client is at the time of goal exploration, thus encompassing linear, spatial, and circular ways of moving through the process.

Instigating Change

The tools described in the section on client awareness and setting goals can be instrumental in helping students understand how to work in partnership with clients to instigate change. The ACA Advocacy Competencies, the ecological genogram, and the social justice career counseling model all facilitate awareness and understanding of contextual variables and can be followed by attention to identifying which of these areas the client may act upon. It is useful to help students to work on enhancing their ability to work in partnership with clients rather than define the goals for clients. At times, students (and even experienced practitioners) may share a client's sense of being overwhelmed by contextual and systemic forces and feel a lack of skills or resources for addressing systemic issues. Some of the steps in the social justice career counseling model can be helpful in addressing the sense of being overwhelmed, such as the process of identifying supports as well as allies. At other times, the counselor feels more sense of righteousness and motivation to change the system than the client does. For example, in a situation in which the client has been the victim of harassment, the counselor or trainee may feel especially strongly that the client should confront the offender or the system in which the offense occurred. However, this may not be the approach that is culturally congruent with the client, or the repercussions may be significant, and thus the client prefers to choose another path. Helping trainees to recognize when their motivations and beliefs are overpowering those of the client is essential. Goodman and her colleagues (2004) provide a great discussion of the tension that can arise in such a situation.

Feedback/Accountability

The process of sharing power with clients (Goodman et al., 2004) can be greatly enhanced by integrating methods for obtaining feedback from clients regarding their experience in counseling. There are multiple ways for students to develop skills in this area, including indirect and direct assessment methods. Building in check-ins throughout the treatment plan is a useful process for longer-term counseling or therapy. For one-session counseling/therapy, check-ins may be built in after establishing the goal for the session, during the counseling/therapy process, and then toward the end of the session. There are several important factors that should be considered, including the congruence between the language of the counselor/therapist and the language of the client, cultural norms regarding direct and indirect communication, and the power differential in the counseling relationship. Beyond having students practice direct check-ins, I find that the following activities can help them develop skills for this process.

Reaction observation is an activity in which students watch demonstration videotapes and record and then discuss their observations of the clients' behaviors and responses at various points in the counseling/therapy process. This is a good activity for feedback and accountability in the moment, rather than feedback regarding the longer-term counseling/therapy process, relationship development, or treatment plan. There are a number of demonstration videotapes that are particularly good for this, and I have found that it is most helpful to use tapes that involve real clients because their behavior is most genuine. The introductions activity described earlier in this chapter provides a good foundation for students in observing nonverbal behaviors that can help them in this activity. This activity can be adjusted for the developmental level of the students. For example, if the students are more advanced, as in an advanced practicum class, I may play a long section of the videotaped counseling/therapy session and ask students to record instances of client reactions to something the counselor did or said. These could be positive or negative. They are to record the client behavior or vocalization, the trigger (what the counselor did just prior to the reaction), and the counselor's response (or lack of response) to the client behavior. Students then identify and discuss their observations in a small group. The discussion should include their observations;

their interpretation of the observation; discussion regarding their own cultural lens in interpreting; and consideration of hypotheses regarding the client's reactions, such as the extent to which the reaction reflects clinical issues and the extent to which it may reflect counselor behavior. I modify this activity for less advanced students by playing a video demonstration and intentionally stopping and prompting group discussion at specific points in the tape.

Cultural impasses provide an excellent opportunity for students to practice noticing and then coping with situations in which the feedback they receive, either directly or indirectly, is negative. Cultural impasse has been described by Liu and Pope-Davis (2005) as a situation in which culture is used inappropriately in counseling or therapy, resulting in stalls or problems in the therapeutic relationship. I extend this definition to include any stalls or problems in the counseling relationship due to cultural misunderstandings. The videotape exercise noted above can be helpful in training students to recognize possible impasses. Role plays can allow students to practice what they might do to address such an impasse. For the role play, I provide students with a vignette in which they are counseling a client who becomes upset with them due to some aspect of cultural difference or assumed similarity. If the client is culturally different from the counselor, often the impasse reflects an outburst from the client about his or her perceptions of counselor assumptions and the counselor misunderstanding him or her. If the client is culturally similar along one dimension (e.g., ethnicity), I then ask the role-play client to identify another aspect of identity in which he or she is culturally different from the counselor. For example, sexual orientation, religion, gender, disability, age, or socioeconomic status can all be salient dimensions of one's identity that are important for students to be aware of and are often areas that may not be attended during the counseling/therapy process. Once identified, a potential conflict then arises out of presumed similarity and important differences. There are several resources and readings that I have found to be very useful in helping students to understand this concept. The qualitative study by Pope-Davis and his colleagues (2002) presented a number of examples of cultural impasses and how they affected clients' experiences and ratings of counseling and therapy. In addition, Choudhuri (2005) and Lee (2005) present great narratives of their experiences with cultural impasses. The key skills I want students to develop through these activities include recognizing that they will make mistakes, taking a nondefensive posture, recovering from their mistakes or perceived mistakes, and really listening to and observing the client.

Learning Activities and Resources for Use Across the Model

In addition to the specific activities described above, there are a number of learning tools and activities that can be useful in helping students develop skills across different components of the SISM. The ways that these activities are framed and debriefed can be customized to highlight any of the above components of the model. In addition to numerous videotaped counseling demonstrations and autobiographical documentaries, there are two other activities that I have found to be useful: difficult dialogues and role-play demonstration and critique.

I use the term *difficult dialogues* to describe events or discussions designed specifically to facilitate communication between participants with divergent viewpoints, with the goal of increased understanding and community building. For example, in one assignment, students find and present news articles about topics relevant to course objectives. Often when students present, they choose news items or events that they have positive or negative feelings about. Students in the class are invited to comment and query the presenter. At times, this raises differences of opinion, feelings of offense, or other issues that then need to be addressed in dialogue. When used in the context of multicultural counseling training, difficult dialogues provide opportunities for students to practice empathy and listening skills in situations where they may disagree with the speaker. Although students need to be clear about the difference between their behavior as a participant and their behavior in a counseling/therapy session, it does provide a good opportunity to practice their communication skills in a potentially heated situation. I have used this most often in courses that involve 25 or fewer graduate students, and thus will be framing my discussion with that type of group in mind. Other literature regarding difficult dialogues may be helpful for readers who work with community members, undergraduate students, and larger groups (see Frank, 2006; D. W. Sue, Lin, Torino, Capodilupo, & Rivera, 2009; Walsh, 2007). In their study of students' reflections on their experience of difficult dialogues in the classroom, Sue, and her colleagues (2009) found that participants indicated that professors' behavior strongly influenced the process of the discussion and that strategies reported to be helpful included "legitimizing the discussion on race, validating feelings of the participants in class, willingness to accept a different racial reality from students of color, comfort in addressing race and racism, and using a direct approach in managing the discussion" (p. 188).

Extended *role-play demonstration and critique* is an activity that I use to help students examine and consider the client, the counselor/therapist, and cultural impasses. Although I like to use videotaped demonstrations, I find that students tend to be very critical of the counselor and distance themselves from the process. In my experience, they tend to be more constructive when I act as the counselor in the role play and clearly frame the role play as an exercise in observing the client's reactions, potential difficult points, possible alternative directions, and other observations. I emphasize that this role play is not intended to be an expert demonstration; rather, it is the contrary. I tell them that I anticipate making some missteps and that I know that there will be areas that they should be able to identify where I, the counselor, could have done something differently. I conduct this session much as I would any counseling or therapy session and don't necessarily try to make errors. What is most important in this role play is that they observe how the role-play client reacts to my interactions. Approximately two weeks before the role play, I solicit a volunteer from the class to play a client in a 30-minute role play. I also ask the "client" to try to show once or twice that he or she is displeased, angry, or uncomfortable with my interactions. Thomas and Schwarzbaum (2006) present lengthy narratives from individuals providing a relatively thorough picture for the role-play client. During the class session, we demonstrate a 30-minute improvisational counseling session followed by a short debriefing between the student and myself in front of the class. I then facilitate a discussion of students' observations of verbal and nonverbal interactions in the role play. It often feels like students start off gently, possibly to protect my feelings. They begin with positive observations, identifying specific things I may have done to address cultural components in the session. Gradually, one or two students will note times when the "client" seemed less than positive about a reflection or question I asked. If students seem too hesitant to move toward constructive and critical observations, I will suggest a few. For example, I might say, "At X point, I was hoping to get at Y aspect; however, I noticed that when I asked that question the client withdrew. What makes me think he withdrew? What behavior did I observe? How could I have done that differently?"

In addition to these activities, a number of authors have provided resources and guidelines for experiential learning aimed at increasing awareness, cultural empathy, and knowledge, as well as skills (e.g., Alberta & Wood, 2009; Arthur & Achenbach, 2002; Hays, 2008; Kim & Lyons, 2003; McAuliffe, Grothaus, Paré, & Wininger, 2008; Nwachuku & Ivey, 1992).

Assessing Competence and Skill

> Latina/o-centered therapists should consider redefining what progress means in therapy from a Latina/o-centered frame of reference; how culture may change the way progress unfolds in treatment; and how to achieve change within the individual's local, cultural context and standards, and not by a generic standard typically used to measure effectiveness therapeutically. (Chapter 5, this volume)

There is currently a move in the field of professional psychology to develop a more concrete system for benchmarking readiness for practicum, readiness for internship, and readiness for entry to practice (Fouad et al., 2009). This model supports the necessity of multicultural competence in practice and assessment as a component of trainee evaluation. However, the benchmarks and behavioral anchors provide minimal guidance regarding definitions that would assist in the development of pedagogical approaches to facilitating the acquisition of these competencies. Clearer articulation of measurable markers of multiculturally relevant and adaptive skills is needed.

One method of assessing multicultural competence that has been recognized as a promising and comprehensive approach is Coleman's (1996) multicultural competence portfolio model. Within Coleman's portfolio framework, the instructor and student collaboratively determine goals by specifying the desired skills and knowledge needed for a particular counseling or therapy context. Throughout the training process, the student identifies and includes concrete products that demonstrate the accomplishment of those skills and knowledge. Such demonstrations may include research papers, case conceptualizations, self-reflection papers, videotaped demonstrations, and other evidence relevant to the established goals. As noted by Coleman and his colleagues, this approach is flexible and can be adapted to any developmental level, ranging from undergraduate to professional, and can easily use the already articulated multicultural counseling competencies (Arredondo et al., 1996; D. Sue et al., 1992) to serve as performance objectives.

Additional Considerations: Authenticity and Multicultural Ethics

I teach in a very ethnically and socioeconomically diverse program. Students represent a wide array of backgrounds and experiences. One of the challenges that arise in multicultural counseling training is that students often have difficulty translating and adapting culture-specific models and demonstration videos when they represent a cultural identity that is different from the culture-specific approach or actor. On more than one occasion, students have asked how they might apply Africentric counseling, for example, in a genuine way, given that they may not be African American themselves or feel personally and spiritually congruent with the demonstrator. The value of authenticity, which is highlighted in multicultural counseling, requires an ability to understand how and when to utilize culture-centered models when they do not represent the culture of the counselor. In learning the material presented in the SISM, students can begin to explore where boundaries may be in terms of authentically implementing culturally specific behaviors and ways in which they may adapt the information presented as necessary. Culturally sensitive authenticity is a delicate skill that is enhanced with experience as well as a level of confidence in one's ability to respond to testing by the client and impasses. It is also more likely that students will be able to be more authentic when they have a genuine respect for and understanding of the client's experience and perspective, as well as a willingness to accept that there may be times when they are not the ideal counselor for the client; for example, given an immersion racial identity status.

In addition to difficulties applying self-awareness and knowledge in the moment with clients, students often have difficulty discerning the complexities of ethical and professional issues in multicultural counseling. For example, there are a number of approaches that are discussed in multicultural counseling that diverge from traditional counseling and psychotherapy, such as appropriateness of dual relationships, management of boundaries, the use of self-disclosure, client advocacy, and the extent to which a therapist should be directive. Students, particularly students of color, often find this divergence welcoming and more congruent with their cultural values. Yet the complexities of applying this divergent approach in a professional manner are often difficult for students to grasp. It is important, in addition to basic skill building, to explicitly provide students with an opportunity to explore and practice multiculturally adaptive ways of addressing these ethical challenges. Many of the exercises described earlier can integrate aspects of ethical practice to address these challenges. In addition, Gallardo, Johnson, Parham, and Carter (2009) provide useful recommendations for bridging traditional ethics with culturally responsive behavior in therapy and counseling.

Conclusion

A central function of training in counseling and psychology is socialization into the field. Students entering the field have a range of motivations and prior exposure to the field, including being told that they are "good at helping people," being encouraged early on by significant help givers (e.g., college counselors), or having personal experience with therapy. Their knowledge of the field, and hence their expectations of training, is shaped by these early experiences. In the process of training, educators introduce a broader understanding of the field, introduce a new language, and reinforce shared values and goals; in other words, they socialize trainees into a new culture and paradigm. Thus, for most trainees, it is likely that the inclusion of culturally responsive practice is not any stranger than the paradigm that has traditionally been taught. It is more likely that this paradigm is strange for faculty who were socialized into the field during a time when the paradigm of the field was lacking the recognition of cultural factors and sociopolitical context that influence clients and communities. The Skills Identification Stage Model provides educators and students with a framework for enhancing their ability to provide students with appropriate and effective multicultural training and skill development.

References

Alberta, A. J., & Wood, A. H. (2009). A practical skills model for effectively engaging clients in multicultural settings. *The Counseling Psychologist, 37*(4), 564–579.

American Psychological Association. (2002). *Guidelines on multicultural education, training, research, practice, and organizational change for psychologists.* Retrieved May 16, 2011 from http://www.apa.org/pi/oema/resources/policy/multicultural-guidelines.aspx

Arredondo, P., Toporek, R., Brown, S., Jones, J., Locke, D., Sanchez, J., et al. (1996). Operationalization of multicultural counseling competencies. *Journal of Multicultural Counseling and Development, 24*(1), 42–78.

Arthur, N., & Achenbach, K. (2002). Developing multicultural counseling competencies through experiential learning. *Counselor Education and Supervision, 42*(1), 2–14.

Berg-Cross, L., & Chinen, R. T. (1995). Multicultural training models and the person-in-culture interview. In J. G. Ponterotto, J. M. Casas, L. A. Suzuki, & C. M. Alexander (Eds.), *Handbook for multicultural counseling* (pp. 333–356). Thousand Oaks, CA: Sage.

Bieschke, K. J., Gehlert, K. M., Wilson, D., Matthews, C. R., & Wade, J. (2003). Qualitative analysis of multicultural awareness in training groups. *Journal for Specialists in Group Work, 28*(4), 325–338.

Choudhuri, D. (2005). Oppression of the spirit: Complexities in the counseling encounter. In S. K. Anderson & V. A. Middleton (Eds.), *Explorations in privilege, oppression, and diversity* (pp. 127–136). Belmont, CA: Brooks/Cole.

Coleman, H. (1996). Portfolio assessment of multicultural counseling competency. *The Counseling Psychologist, 24*(2), 216–229.

Duran, E., Firehammer, J., & Gonzalez, J. (2008). Liberation psychology as the path toward healing cultural soul wounds. *Journal of Counseling & Development, 86*(3), 288–295.

Fouad, N., Grus, C., Hatcher, R., Kaslow, N., Hutchings, P., Madson, M., et al. (2009). Competency benchmarks: A model for understanding and measuring competence in professional psychology across training levels. *Training and Education in Professional Psychology, 3*(4), S5–S26.

Frank, J. (2006, August). *Guidelines for sponsoring community dialogues on mapping a culture of peace.* Presentation at the National Coalition for Dialogue and Deliberation Conference. Retrieved May 16, 2011 from http://www.thataway.org/exchange/files/docs/Guidelines_Comm_Dlogs.doc

Freire, P. (1972). *Pedagogy of the oppressed.* New York: Penguin Books.

Gallardo, M., Johnson, J., Parham, T., & Carter, J. (2009). Ethics and multiculturalism: Advancing cultural and clinical responsiveness. *Professional Psychology: Research and Practice, 40*(5), 425–435.

Goodman, L., Liang, B., Helms, J., Latta, R., Sparks, E., & Weintraub, S. (2004). Training counseling psychologists as social justice agents: Feminist and multicultural principles in action. *The Counseling Psychologist, 32*(6), 793–837.

Hays, P. A. (2008). *Addressing cultural complexities in practice: Assessment, diagnosis, and therapy* (2nd ed.). Washington, DC: American Psychological Association.

Helms, J. E. (1992). Why is there no study of cultural equivalence in standardized cognitive ability testing? *American Psychologist, 47*(9), 1083–1101.

Ivey, A. (1995). Psychotherapy as liberation: Toward specific skills and strategies in multicultural counseling and therapy. In J. G. Ponterotto, J. M. Casas, L. A. Suzuki, & C. M. Alexander (Eds.), *Handbook of multicultural counseling* (pp. 53–72). Thousand Oaks, CA: Sage.

Kim, B., & Lyons, H. (2003). Experiential activities and multicultural counseling competence training. *Journal of Counseling & Development, 81*(4), 400–408.

Lee, L. J. (2005). Taking off the mask: Breaking the silence—The art of naming racism in the therapy room. In M. Rastogi & E. Wieling (Eds.), *Voices of color: First-person accounts of ethnic minority therapists* (pp. 91–115). Thousand Oaks, CA: Sage.

Lewis, J., Arnold, M. S., House, R., & Toporek, R. L. (2002). *ACA advocacy competencies.* Alexandria, VA: American Counseling Association.

Liu, W., & Pope-Davis, D. (2005). The working alliance, therapy ruptures and impasses, and counseling competence: Implications for counselor training and education. *Handbook of racial-cultural psychology and counseling, Vol. 2: Training and practice* (pp. 148–167). Hoboken, NJ: John Wiley & Sons.

Lonner, W. J. (1981). Psychological tests and intercultural counseling. In P. B. Pederson, J. G. Draguns, & J. E. Trimble (Eds.), *Counseling across cultures* (pp. 275–303). Honolulu: East-West Center & University of Hawaii.

Martín-Baró, I., Aron, A., & Corne, S. (1994). *Writings for a liberation psychology.* Cambridge, MA: Harvard University Press.

McAuliffe, G. (2008). *Key practices in culturally alert counseling: A demonstration of skills* [DVD]. Thousand Oaks, CA: Sage.

McAuliffe, G., Grothaus, T., Paré, D., & Wininger, A. (2008). The practice of culturally alert counseling. In G. McAuliffe & Associates (Eds.), *Culturally alert counseling: An introduction* (pp. 570–627). Thousand Oaks, CA: Sage.

Nwachuku, U., & Ivey, A. (1992). Teaching culture-specific counseling using microtraining technology. *International Journal for the Advancement of Counselling, 15*(3), 151–161.

Parham, T. A. (1999). *Innovative approaches to counseling African descent people* [DVD #501]. Hanover, MA: Microtraining Associates.

Pedersen, P. B. (2003). *A handbook for developing multicultural awareness* (3rd ed.). Alexandria, VA: American Counseling Association.

Pieterse, A., Evans, S., Risner-Butner, A., Collins, N., & Mason, L. (2009). Multicultural competence and social justice training in counseling psychology and counselor education: A review and analysis of a sample of multicultural course syllabi. *The Counseling Psychologist, 37*(1), 93–115.

Ponterotto, J. G., Rivera, L., & Sueyoshi, L. A. (2000). The career-in-culture interview: A semi-structured protocol for the cross-cultural intake interview. *The Career Development Quarterly, 49*(1), 85–96.

Pope-Davis, D. B., Toporek, R. L., Ligiero, D., Ortega, L., Bashshur, M. L., Brittan-Powell, C. S., et al. (2002). A qualitative study of clients' perspectives of multicultural counseling competence. *The Counseling Psychologist, 30*(3), 355–393.

Priester, P., Jones, J., Jackson-Bailey, C., Jana-Masri, A., Jordan, E., & Metz, A. (2008). An analysis of content and instructional strategies in multicultural counseling courses. *Journal of Multicultural Counseling and Development, 36*(1), 29–39.

Ratts, M. J., Toporek, R. L., & Lewis, J. A. (Eds.). (2010). *ACA advocacy competencies: A social justice framework for counselors.* Alexandria, VA: American Counseling Association.

Rodriguez, R., & Walls, N. (2000). Culturally educated questioning: Toward a skills-based approach in multicultural counselor training. *Applied & Preventive Psychology, 9*(2), 89–99.

Roysircar, G., Gard, G., Hubbell, R., & Ortega, M. (2005). Development of counseling trainees' multicultural awareness through mentoring English as a second language students. *Journal of Multicultural Counseling and Development, 33*(1), 17–36.

Sampson, E. (1993). Identity politics: Challenges to psychology's understanding. *American Psychologist, 48*(12), 1219–1230.

Santiago-Rivera, A. L., Arredondo, P., & Gallardo-Cooper, M. (2002). *Counseling Latinos and la familia: A practical guide.* Thousand Oaks, CA: Sage.

Sue, D., Arredondo, P., & McDavis, R. (1992). Multicultural counseling competencies and standards: A call to the profession. *Journal of Counseling & Development, 70*(4), 477–486.

Sue, D. W., Lin, A. I., Torino, G. C., Capodilupo, C. M., & Rivera, D. P. (2009). Racial microaggressions and difficult dialogues on race in the classroom. *Cultural Diversity and Ethnic Minority Psychology, 15*(2), 183–190.

Sue, D. W., & Sue, D. (2008). *Counseling the culturally diverse: Theory and practice* (5th ed.). Hoboken, NJ: John Wiley & Sons.

Sue, S., & Zane, N. (1987). The role of culture and cultural techniques in psychotherapy: A critique and reformulation. *American Psychologist, 42*(1), 37–45.

Thomas, A. J., & Schwarzbaum, S. (2006). *Culture and identity: Life stories for counselors and therapists.* Thousand Oaks, CA: Sage.

Toporek, R. L., & Chope, R. (2006). Individual, programmatic, and entrepreneurial approaches to social justice: Counseling psychologists in vocational and career counseling. In R. L. Toporek, L. H. Gerstein, N. A. Fouad, G. S. Roysircar, & T. Israel (Eds.), *Handbook for social justice in counseling psychology: Leadership, vision, and action* (pp. 276–293). Thousand Oaks, CA: Sage.

Toporek, R., Lewis, J., & Crethar, H. (Eds.). (2009). Special section: Advocacy competence. *Journal of Counseling and Development, 87*(3).

Walsh, K. C. (2007). *Talking about race: Community dialogues and the politics of difference.* Chicago: University of Chicago Press.

Watkins, M., & Shulman, H. (2008). *Toward psychologies of liberation.* New York: Palgrave Macmillan.

18

Multicultural Counseling in a Multitheoretical Context

New Applications for Practice

Jeff E. Harris

W hen conducting counseling or psychotherapy with clients from diverse ethnocultural groups, it is essential to consider how their cultural background will impact the therapeutic process. Using the Skills Identification Model originally developed by Parham (2002), the authors of earlier chapters in this book have done an admirable job of describing ways that culture can be addressed throughout the process of psychotherapy. By identifying culture-based skills for four distinct groups and throughout six stages of psychotherapy, the Skills Identification Stage Model (SISM) has become a powerful tool for guiding counselors and psychotherapists through the process of working with culturally diverse clients (Chapter 1, this volume). This chapter is designed to build on the strengths of the ideas presented in earlier chapters and to expand the definition of multicultural counseling in three ways.

First, this chapter will provide an ideographic method for addressing culture in counseling and psychotherapy when clients' cultural identity does not easily fit within one of the four most prominent groups in the United States. This idiographic approach describes culture-centered skills that explore identity and the impact of culture beyond ethnicity and race. For example, these culture-centered skills are useful for looking at the intersection of ethnicity with other aspects of identity such as gender, sexual orientation, socioeconomic status, disability, and religion. Within the multicultural movement, there is a delicate

AUTHOR'S NOTE: Correspondence concerning this book chapter should be addressed to Jeff E. Harris, Department of Psychology and Philosophy, Texas Woman's University, P.O. Box 425470, Denton, TX 76204–5470. E-mail: jharris18@twu.edu.

balance between understanding groups of people and recognizing the individuality of each person. Ridley (2005) described the distinction between a *nomothetic* perspective, focusing on "the prominent characteristics of the group to which an individual belongs" (p. 86), and an *idiographic* perspective, providing a method to "understand the personal meaning that the client holds as a *particular person*" (p. 86). This delicate balance was acknowledged earlier in this book when Gallardo (Chapter 5, this volume) spoke of Latina/o clients and suggested that "we can no longer assume that to know one means we understand all." Both nomothetic and idiographic ideas are essential to understanding how individuals are shaped by cultural forces within social groups. Earlier chapters in this book are fine exemplars of a nomothetic approach, which is most helpful when ethnocultural identity is salient in counseling and when a client closely identifies with a single group. When a client does not closely identify with a single group, or when the impact of ethnicity intersects with other aspects of identity, an idiographic approach may be more useful.

Second, this chapter will introduce an integrative multicultural approach focusing on the ways that culture interacts with other dimensions of human functioning like thoughts, actions, feelings, interpersonal patterns, and social systems. These multicultural adaptations of established interventions can be used to modify evidence-based treatments to be more sensitive to culture and to be more applicable to diverse populations. Modified strategies from five theoretical approaches will be introduced here: (a) cognitive, (b) behavioral, (c) experiential, (d) interpersonal, and (e) systemic. This chapter will describe the way that both idiographic and integrative approaches can be used to complement the nomothetic skills described in earlier chapters.

In this way, a distinction will be made between three methods of encouraging the use of multicultural skills within counseling and psychotherapy. These three approaches to multicultural practice are summarized in Table 18.1 along with quotes from the American Psychological Association's (APA; 2003) multicultural guidelines. The first and most prominent method involves describing *group-specific strategies* for distinct ethnocultural communities, which enables counselors and therapists to meet cultural expectations for clients from these groups. Five sets of group-specific strategies have been described in earlier chapters in this text (Chapters 2, 5, 8, 11, and 14). The second approach entails the identification of *culture-centered skills* that can be used across groups to build a multicultural foundation and establish a cultural focus based on an idiographic understanding of each client. Six clusters of culture-centered skills will be described later in this chapter. The third method involves the description of *multicultural adaptations of established interventions* that address the interaction between culture and other dimensions of functioning and combine multicultural ideals with emphases from other theories. Five clusters of multicultural adaptations will be described later in this chapter.

A third theme in this chapter is related to the *application* of multicultural counseling rather than its *content*. Instead of focusing primarily on how ethnicity impacts clients' identities and expectations for treatment, this chapter

Table 18.1   Three Types of Multicultural Skills Suggested by the APA Multicultural Guidelines

Group-Specific Skills

Different sets of skills are developed for clients from different groups and backgrounds.

- "Cross-culturally sensitive practitioners are encouraged to develop skills and practices that are attuned to the unique worldviews and cultural backgrounds of clients by striving to incorporate understanding of a client's ethnic, linguistic, racial, and cultural background into therapy" (APA, 2003, p. 391).

Culture-Centered Skills

These general skills view clients culturally and explore contextual influences.

- "We use the term culture-centered throughout the guidelines to encourage psychologists to use a 'cultural lens' as a central focus of professional behavior. In culture-centered practices, psychologists recognize that all individuals, including themselves, are influenced by different contexts, including the historical, economic, sociopolitical, and disciplinary" (APA, 2003, p. 380).

Multicultural Adaptations

Established interventions are modified to consider cultural interactions with other dimensions.

- "It is not necessary to develop an entirely new repertoire of psychological skills to practice in a culture-centered manner. Rather, it is helpful for psychologists to realize that there will likely be situations where culture-centered adaptations in interventions and practices will be more effective" (APA, 2003, p. 390).

will highlight the way that stressful cultural encounters may actually result in *cultural adjustment disorders* that are related to psychological problems and psychiatric diagnoses. Cultural experiences—such as immigration, discrimination, cultural violence, or changes in status—often result in psychological problems like depression or anxiety. If psychological problems are closely related to stressful cultural encounters and have an impact on identity development, then it may be helpful to address culture in treatment. This recognition of cultural encounters as the source of problems suggests an expanded role for the use of multicultural strategies. Multiculturalism is not just a lens for understanding clients based on their background; it can be used to appreciate how cultural experiences may result in symptoms that bring clients into treatment. This chapter will conclude by proposing that multicultural strategies may be effective in treating psychological problems that result from stressful cultural encounters.

Three Historical Phases Within the Multicultural Movement

In order to understand how the three approaches to multicultural practice summarized in Table 18.1 are related to one another, it may be helpful to describe their historical development. Each of these approaches to multicultural skills has grown out of the wider multicultural movement, and all three approaches represent different ways culture has been applied to new areas over time. Three phases of historical development have inspired the recognition of different types of multicultural skills.

Phase 1: Educating Counselors About Racial-Ethnic Differences

The multicultural counseling movement grew out of the realization that clients from some racial/ethnic groups were not benefiting from counseling as much as Euro-American clients. In the late 1970s, some counselors and psychotherapists began to recognize that "counseling has failed to serve the needs of minorities, and in some cases, proven counterproductive to their well-being" (Atkinson, Morten, & Sue, 1979, p. 11). This conclusion was based on the observation that non-white clients were receiving different diagnoses and treatments than white clients. Euro-American counselors were misunderstanding the cultural norms of clients from different cultures and were assuming that mental health should look the same for all people. The first historical phase in the multicultural movement involved educating Euro-American counselors and therapists, helping them understand culturally different clients, and encouraging them to adjust treatment based on cultural awareness and knowledge.

Derald Wing Sue's *Counseling the Culturally Different* was first published in 1981 and described the way the profession was embedded in white, middle-class values that may conflict with the values of other ethnocultural groups. In order to become culturally skilled, counselors and therapists were encouraged to be more aware of sociopolitical forces; understand barriers including culture, class, and language; and emphasize cultural identity in counseling. Separate chapters were used to describe the cultural values and historical experiences of four groups: Asian Americans, blacks, Hispanics, and American Indians. These chapters concluded with implications for counseling clients from each group. For example, counselors and psychotherapists were encouraged to recognize that Asian clients with traditional values may experience shame and guilt when admitting that a problem exists. Counselors were reminded that many black clients may view counseling as an instrument of oppression and believe that counseling should promote self-identity (Sue, 1981). These implications for counseling represented an early example of group-specific skills and fit the definition provided in Table 18.1. Other writers have used a similar approach in order to tailor counseling to the cultural expectations of Native Americans (Herring, 1999), Asian Americans (Hong & Ham, 2000), Latinas/os (Santiago-Rivera, Arrendondo, & Gallardo-Cooper, 2001), and African Americans (Parham, 2002). Earlier chapters in this text are extensions of this work on identifying group-specific skills (Chapters 2, 5, 8, 11, and 14).

Phase 2: Broadening the Scope of Multiculturalism

The second historical phase in the multicultural movement involved broadening the definition of culture. In 1990, Paul Pederson described multiculturalism as a fourth force in counseling—complementing psychodynamic, behavioral, and humanistic movements—and suggested a new definition of culture:

> By defining culture broadly—to include demographic variables (e.g., age, sex, place of residence), status variables (e.g., social, educational, economic), and affiliations (formal and informal), as well as ethnographic variables such as nationality, ethnicity, language, and religion—the construct "multicultural" becomes generic to all counseling relationships. (p. 7)

This broader definition of culture resulted in the recognition that counselors and psychotherapists need to be responsive to other dimensions of clients' identity beyond race or ethnicity. A contemporary example of the broad definition of culture is seen in the work of Pamela Hays (2008), who described a framework for considering the complexity of cultural influences that uses the acronym ADDRESSING to remember 10 salient aspects of cultural identity. This framework suggests that cultural influences include age, developmental disabilities, acquired disabilities, religion and spiritual orientation, ethnic and racial identity, socioeconomic status, sexual orientation, indigenous heritage, national origin, and gender.

The first edition of Sue's (1981) classic text was described earlier as an example of educating counselors and therapists about racial/ethnic differences. This popular book is in its fifth edition and is now called *Counseling the Culturally Diverse* (Sue & Sue, 2007). This recent edition has clearly embraced a broader definition of culture in tune with changes in Phase 2 of the multicultural movement. Sue and Sue explored the similarity between racism, sexism, and heterosexism. In addition to the four prominent groups explored in the first edition, there are also chapters on counseling multiracial individuals, Arab Americans, Jewish Americans, immigrants, and refugees. In addition to addressing ethnic and racial differences, there are additional chapters on counseling sexual minorities, older adults, women, and individuals with disabilities. Instead of assuming that all counselors and psychotherapists are white, there is even a chapter titled "Minority Group Therapists: Working With Majority and Other Minority Clients" (Sue & Sue, 2007).

Using a broad definition of culture introduces a level of complexity that makes it more difficult to identify group-specific skills. If we recognize that each client has a unique identity that is composed of multiple facets, it becomes more difficult to identify a set of skills for specific groups. A counselor or therapist might wonder, "Should I use skills that match the client's ethnicity, gender, sexual orientation, religion, or his or her social class?"

An alternative that is more consistent with the broad definition of culture is to identify culture-centered skills that can be used across groups and enable counselors and therapists to understand the intersection of multiple cultural influences that shape a unique identity for each individual. The APA (2003) multicultural guidelines described a cultural focus in this way:

> We use the term culture-centered throughout the guidelines to encourage psychologists to use a "cultural lens" as a central focus of professional behavior. In culture-centered practices, psychologists recognize that all individuals, including themselves, are influenced by different contexts, including the historical, economic, sociopolitical, and disciplinary. (p. 380)

Culture-centered skills offer systematic ways to translate theory into practice by describing specific strategies for ensuring that psychotherapy appropriately incorporates culture at all levels and phases of the therapeutic process. These strategies encourage an idiographic view of clients, rather than relying on a nomothetic perspective. Six clusters of culture-centered skills will be introduced later in this chapter.

Phase 3: Addressing Culture in Evidence-Based Practice

The third historical phase in the multicultural movement involved addressing culture in evidence-based practice. Psychology and other social service disciplines have increasingly recognized that practice should be based on science and that research should be used to test counseling and psychotherapy theories and methods. One early effort in this area was the list of empirically supported treatments published by the Society of Clinical Psychology (Division 12 of the American Psychological Association). Dianne Chambless chaired a task force that published criteria that made a distinction between "well-established treatments" with strong research support and "probably efficacious treatments" with moderate research support. When lists of empirically supported treatments were first published, more cognitive and behavioral treatments met the criteria for strong research support compared to treatments based on other theories (Task Force on Promotion and Dissemination of Psychological Procedures, 1995). Since this time, three important changes have occurred related to evidence-based practice. First, researchers have been more successful in demonstrating the efficacy of a wider variety of theoretical approaches. For example, Hayes and Sahl (2011) have now identified 12 empirically supported treatments for depression that include cognitive, behavioral, experiential, interpersonal, psychodynamic, and integrative approaches. Second, the definition of evidence-based practice in psychology has been expanded to recognize the relationship between research evidence, clinical expertise, and client characteristics (APA, 2005). Third, there is recognition that scientific evidence supports the idea that culture impacts clients and their experience with psychotherapy. For example, the APA (2005) *Policy Statement on Evidence-Based Practice in Psychology* recommends that psychological services should be responsive to "sociocultural and familial factors (e.g., gender, gender identity, ethnicity, race, social class, religion, disability status, family structure, and sexual orientation)" as well as "environmental context (e.g., institutional racism, health care disparities)" (p. 2).

One reaction to the publication of lists of empirically supported treatments was the observation that these treatments had been developed and tested predominantly with Euro-American clients. Therefore, it was not clear whether these treatments would work equally well with other cultural groups. Lau (2006) described two situations in which it may be particularly important to adapt evidence-based practices for the specific needs of particular cultural groups. First, some mental health problems are closely related to the sociocultural context of a particular group. In this case, adaptation may involve "*contextualizing content,* such that the adapted intervention accommodates the distinctive contextual factors related to the presenting problem in the target community" (p. 300). Second, some cultural groups may respond poorly to certain treatments because the methods do not fit cultural expectations, and participants may drop out of treatment because they do not feel engaged. In this case, adaptation is geared toward *enhancing engagement:* "The main challenge is to design adaptations that increase engagement . . . without undermining the therapeutic value of the original intervention" (p. 300). In the context of Lau's recommendations, the culture-centered skills (defined in Table 18.1 and described later) may be useful in enhancing engagement, whereas the multicultural adaptations (also defined in Table 18.1 and described later) represent examples of contextualizing content. One difference is that the skills described in this chapter are general skills for adapting established treatments to be more sensitive to culture, rather than creating adaptations for a particular cultural group. The APA (2003) multicultural guidelines described multicultural adaptations in the following way:

> It is not necessary to develop an entirely new repertoire of psychological skills to practice in a culture-centered manner. Rather, it is helpful for psychologists to realize that there will likely be situations where culture-centered adaptations in interventions and practices will be more effective. (p. 390)

The five clusters of multicultural adaptations that will be introduced later in this chapter represent strategies drawn from established theoretical traditions that have been adapted to take culture into account.

Multicultural Counseling
in a Multitheoretical Context

How does multicultural counseling relate to other theories of psychotherapy? Different writers have proposed different answers to this question. Pederson (1990) described multiculturalism as a fourth force in counseling and psychotherapy, complementing the three traditional forces of psychodynamic, behavioral, and humanistic psychotherapy. In contrast, Sue, Ivey, and Pederson (1996) described multicultural counseling as a metatheory describing the way that Western psychotherapy theories and indigenous helping models all represent different worldviews. The advantage of viewing multiculturalism as a metatheory is the recognition that each model of counseling or psychotherapy is embedded in the culture in which it was developed. The disadvantage is that viewing multicultural counseling as a metatheory may make it harder to translate it into distinct strategies or to know when to use multicultural interventions rather than skills drawn from another theory.

Multitheoretical psychotherapy (MTP; Brooks-Harris, 2008) suggests that multicultural counseling is one of seven theoretical approaches that focus on different dimensions of human functioning. This viewpoint is more similar to Pederson's (1990) "fourth force" perspective and less consistent with Sue et al.'s (1996) "metatheory" position. MTP views multicultural counseling as a theoretical approach that focuses on culture and identity, parallel to the way cognitive therapy focuses on thoughts or systems theory on social groups like families. This focus on cultural contexts is seen as complementary to, rather than competing with, other theories focusing on other dimensions. Counselors and therapists are encouraged to develop the ability to view their clients from more than one perspective and to develop multicultural skills that can be combined with interventions drawn from other theories.

MTP is organized around a multidimensional model of human functioning (Brooks-Harris, 2008) displayed in Figure 18.1. In the center of the figure are three concurrent dimensions: thoughts, actions, and feelings. These are in the center of the figure to suggest that, for the most part, people are always thinking, acting, and feeling. These concurrent dimensions are seen as highly interactive and influence one another in a fluid, multidirectional manner. Surrounding these concurrent dimensions are four contextual dimensions: biology, interpersonal patterns, social systems, and cultural contexts. All four of these contextual dimensions shape the way people think, act, and feel. In some situations, the influence of one contextual dimension may be more obvious than another. For example, when someone has been diagnosed with a medical illness, the impact of biology on functioning may be particularly salient. In contrast, when someone moves to a new country, the way culture impacts one's thoughts, actions, and feelings may be more obvious. MTP recommends that counselors and psychotherapists survey all seven of these dimensions and identify with their clients those that are most relevant to understanding and resolving a

Figure 18.1   A Multidimensional Model of Human Functioning

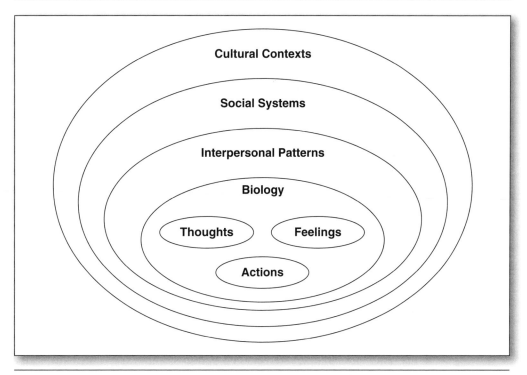

Source: Adapted from *Integrative Multitheoretical Psychotherapy* by J. E. Brooks-Harris (2008). Reprinted with permission.

particular problem (Brooks-Harris, 2008). As a result of this process of integrative treatment planning, culture may be a focal dimension with some clients but may remain in the background with others.

One important application of the multidimensional model is that it can be used to organize different approaches to counseling and psychotherapy. The result is the multitheoretical framework (Brooks-Harris, 2008) depicted in Table 18.2. Each of seven theoretical approaches is seen as focusing on a different dimension. Multicultural counseling and feminist therapy have been combined because of their common emphasis on cultural contexts and identity development. This combination is consistent with a broad definition of culture (Hays, 2008; Pederson, 1990) that recognizes sex and gender as salient aspects of cultural identity. MTP describes 12 to 16 key strategies for each theoretical approach to counseling. Fourteen key strategies drawn from multicultural-feminist psychotherapy were described in the MTP text (Brooks-Harris, 2008). More information about MTP can be found at www.multitheoretical.com.

Two implications from MTP will be highlighted in this chapter. First, it is important for counselors to acquire skills that enable them to directly focus on culture and to understand the cultural identities of their clients. This implication corresponds to the culture-centered skills described in Table 18.1. The 14 multicultural-feminist key strategies described in Chapter 10 of the MTP text

Table 18.2   A Multitheoretical Framework for Psychotherapy

Theoretical Approaches	Focal Dimensions
Cognitive	Thoughts
Behavioral	Actions
Experiential-Humanistic	Feelings
Biopsychosocial	Biology
Psychodynamic-Interpersonal	Interpersonal Patterns
Systemic-Constructivist	Social Systems
Multicultural-Feminist	Cultural Contexts

Source: Adapted from *Integrative Multitheoretical Psychotherapy* by J. E. Brooks-Harris (2008). Reprinted with permission.

(Brooks-Harris & Savage, 2008) offered a place to start for psychotherapists to acquire basic culture-centered skills. The second implication is that culture often interacts with other dimensions. For example, culture directly shapes thoughts, actions, and feelings. Culture also interacts with other contextual dimensions like biology, interpersonal patterns, and social systems to shape current functioning. This implication corresponds to the multicultural adaptations described in Table 18.1. Multicultural adaptations focus on the interaction between culture and other dimensions of functioning. For example, cognitive-multicultural skills focus on the interaction between culture and thoughts. Five clusters of multicultural adaptations will be described later.

Identifying Key Strategies for Multicultural Counseling

While I was working at the University of Hawaii at Manoa, I invited a group of colleagues and graduate students to help me identify an expanded catalog of culture-centered skills and a second catalog of multicultural adaptations. Both of these efforts were presented at the annual APA convention in Honolulu in 2004 (Altschul, 2004a; Brooks-Harris, 2004a). These two catalogs of skills correspond to the second and third types of multicultural skills highlighted in Table 18.1.

Culture-Centered Skills

A catalog of culture-centered skills divided into six clusters is presented in Table 18.3 (Altschul, 2004a). This catalog represents an expansion of the 14 multicultural-feminist key strategies described in the multitheoretical

Table 18.3   Six Clusters of Culture-Centered Skills

Becoming Aware of Your Own Worldview

OW1. Learning About Your Own Culture
OW2. Understanding Your Personal Worldview
OW3. Appreciating Your Own Multiple Identities
OW4. Presenting Options With Limited Bias
OW5. Accepting Responsibility and Tolerating Ambiguity
OW6. Recognizing Limits of Your Competence

Creating a Culturally Sensitive Therapeutic Relationship

TR1. Viewing Psychotherapy as a Cultural Encounter
TR2. Affirming Client's Uniqueness and Diversity
TR3. Orienting Client to Psychotherapy
TR4. Creating a Culturally Appropriate Collaborative Alliance
TR5. Anticipating and Responding to Client's Internal Dialogue
TR6. Illuminating Differences and Similarities

Understanding the Client's Worldview

CW1. Learning About the Historical Context of the Client's Culture
CW2. Exploring the Current Context of the Client's Culture
CW3. Viewing Clients as Individuals
CW4. Appreciating the Client's Multiple Identities
CW5. Understanding the Client's Worldview
CW6. Clarifying the Impact of Culture on Current Functioning

Facilitating Cultural Identity Development

ID1. Assessing Identity Development
ID2. Acknowledging Differences in Cultural Worldviews
ID3. Helping Clients Recognize Beliefs and Values
ID4. Processing Encounters With Oppression or Difference
ID5. Embracing Culture, Exploring Identity, and Cultivating Pride
ID6. Internalizing Culture and Valuing Others

Responding to Societal Structures and Values

SS1. Examining Social Oppression
SS2. Considering Systems of Privilege
SS3. Identifying Social Messages
SS4. Exploring Moral, Ethical, and Spiritual Values
SS5. Facilitating Movement Toward Social Action
SS6. Supporting Informed Choices

Utilizing Complementary Roles Beyond Psychotherapy

CR1. Educating About Options
CR2. Consulting About Change
CR3. Advocating for Environmental Change
CR4. Integrating Spiritual Awareness
CR5. Facilitating Indigenous Support and Healing
CR6. Seeking Consultation With Cultural Experts

textbook (Brooks-Harris, 2008). The first three clusters are considered foundational and should be used to understand every client. The last three clusters may or may not be applicable for a particular client, depending upon this individual's concerns, situations, and goals.

Becoming Aware of Your Own Worldview (OW). The first cluster of culture-centered skills recognizes that counselors and therapists are influenced by culture as much as clients and encourages awareness that may help prevent bias (Buhin, 2004). Unlike most of the other skill clusters (described later) that are likely to be used in verbal interactions with clients, some of these skills are seen as precursors to good multicultural counseling and may develop as part of academic classes, experiential learning, or clinical supervision (Chapter 17, this volume). Awareness-oriented skills like learning about your own culture (OW1) and understanding your personal worldview (OW2) may be necessary so that more applied skills like presenting options with limited bias (OW4) can be implemented with more success. If counselors become aware of their own identity, they can be more effective when exploring the culture and identity of their clients. For example, if a therapist who values autonomy and individuality were providing career counseling for a client from a collectivist culture, the counselor's awareness of her own values would help her avoid imposing personal values when the client expresses a desire to identify career choices that would be acceptable to his family. This therapist might tell her supervisor, "I think my client should feel free to follow his own dreams, but I know that might not fit his culture." All of these skills enable counselors to understand their own role in the complex cultural encounter that occurs in each therapeutic relationship.

Creating a Culturally Sensitive Therapeutic Relationship (TR). The second cluster of skills describes strategies that can be used to customize the relationship between counselor and client based on cultural expectations (Hamada, 2004). This cluster of skills is closely related to the process of "connecting with clients" described by Gallardo, Parham, Trimble, and Yeh (Chapter 1, this volume). Skills related to creating a culturally sensitive relationship include orienting clients to psychotherapy (TR3) in order to correct misperceptions and creating a culturally appropriate collaborative alliance (TR4), recognizing that some clients may want a more formal and prescriptive relationship whereas other clients may desire an informal collaboration. When cultural differences exist in the relationship, it may be particularly helpful for counselors to anticipate and respond to clients' internal dialogue (TR5) or illuminate differences and similarities (TR6). For example, it may be helpful for a female therapist to ask a male client, "How has it felt to talk to a woman about your aggressive history with your girlfriend?" All of these skills allow the therapeutic relationship to be custom-tailored for each client with the cultural context in mind.

Understanding the Client's Worldview (CW). The third cluster of culture-centered skills focuses on exploring history, appreciating multiple identities, and clarifying the impact of culture on functioning (Altschul, 2004b). This process of exploration includes considering membership in ethnocultural groups and identifying the way the worldview associated with different groups may impact counseling or psychotherapy (Chapter 1, this volume). When clients' identities do not closely match a single group membership, or when identity is impacted by factors beyond ethnicity, it may be necessary to explore worldview in a more ideographic manner. In these cases, these six skills enable counselors and therapists to view clients as individuals who have developed within a particular cultural context. This process may involve learning the historical context of clients' culture (CW1) outside a counseling session as well as exploring the current context of clients' culture (CW2) directly during a counseling session. For example, a counselor might explore the cultural context by saying, "You mentioned that your family immigrated from Mexico when you were 10. What led to the immigration" (Altschul, 2004b)? Appreciating clients' multiple identities (CW4) reminds counselors and psychotherapists that each person contains many facets. Together, the skills in this cluster are designed to help counselors understand each client as an individual with a complex and unique identity.

Facilitating Cultural Identity Development (ID). These skills look at the way identity develops over time and view counseling as a process that can help clients develop more positive views of themselves and their cultures (Brooks-Harris, 2004b). These strategies may be most useful for clients working through a process of identity development. This process often begins by assessing identity development (ID1) using a model that fits the client's identity. For example, for a lesbian client exploring her gay identity, it may be helpful to use Cass's (1979) model to determine whether the client is experiencing identity confusion, comparison, tolerance, acceptance, pride, or synthesis. Helping clients develop their own identity may sometimes involve processing encounters with oppression or difference (ID4). For example, a counselor or therapist might ask, "How did you feel when your girlfriend told you her father did not approve of your relationship because of racial differences?" These skills enable psychotherapists to focus on identity development and help clients move toward awareness and integration.

Responding to Societal Structures and Values (SS). The fifth cluster describes strategies that are particularly useful when clients are facing experiences of discrimination or other encounters that make them aware of society as a whole (Savage, 2004). This cluster includes skills that examine social oppression (SS1) as well as consider systems of privilege (SS2). An important outcome of helping clients identify social messages (SS3) is that counselors can support informed choices (SS6) about which roles to embrace and which to discard. For example, a therapist might help a gay client explore family values about marriage by saying, "It sounds like you and your partner are considering a commitment ceremony, though your parents are against it. How does their opinion affect you?" The skills in this cluster are designed to encourage a sense of intentionality and choice.

Utilizing Complementary Roles Beyond Psychotherapy (CR). The last cluster of skills encourages a broader definition of the helping role (Nacapoy, 2004) that may include educating about options (CR1) or consulting about change (CR2). These skills enable counselors to explore areas such as advocacy (CR3) and spirituality (CR4) that might have been defined as "out of bounds" for psychotherapists and counselors in the past. Facilitating indigenous support and healing (CR5) may include integrating cultural practices that support therapeutic change. For example, a therapist might say to a Buddhist client, "We've been talking about addressing your anxiety through meditation. Do you think it would be helpful to talk to your priest about your anxiety?" These skills enable counselors to broaden their repertoire and scope in order to perform a more comprehensive helping role. The way that a counselor or psychotherapist explores issues related to spirituality or indigenous support should be closely informed by an understanding of the worldview associated with ethnocultural group membership (see Chapter 1, this volume).

Multicultural Adaptations

Table 18.4 lists a catalog of multicultural adaptations divided into five clusters (Brooks-Harris, 2004a). Each of these groups of skills focuses on the way culture interacts with a different dimension of functioning. These strategies are most useful when culture is a salient dimension in counseling and when cultural experience or identity is impacting thoughts (cognitive-multicultural strategies), actions (behavioral-multicultural strategies), or feelings (experiential-multicultural strategies). These skills are also useful when culture interacts with interpersonal patterns (interpersonal-multicultural strategies) or social systems (systemic-multicultural strategies).

Cognitive-Multicultural Strategies (CM). The first cluster of skills addresses the interaction between culture and thoughts (Jennette, 2004). These skills are drawn from well-established treatments like Beck's (1967/1970) cognitive therapy but have been modified to address thinking in its cultural context. Many traditional interventions focus on identifying cognitive errors that result in illogical thinking. The first multicultural adaptation from this cluster is understanding cognitions in their cultural context (CM1) and recognizes that a particular thought may be adaptive in one cultural context but maladaptive in another. For example, thinking that "I should not show any signs of competition" may help people adapt to one culture but may hold

Table 18.4   Five Clusters of Multicultural Adaptations

Cognitive-Multicultural Strategies

CM1. Understanding Cognitions in Their Cultural Context
CM2. Identifying Culturally Sensitive Alternative Cognitions
CM3. Exploring Cultural Schemas
CM4. Testing Hypotheses About Culture
CM5. Educating About Cross-Cultural Variations
CM6. Facilitating Cultural and Cognitive Flexibility

Behavioral-Multicultural Strategies

BM1. Understanding Actions in Their Cultural Context
BM2. Illuminating Cultural Reinforcement
BM3. Setting Culturally Appropriate Goals
BM4. Prescribing Actions Within the Cultural Context
BM5. Exposing Clients to Multicultural Experiences
BM6. Providing Cultural Skills Training

Experiential-Multicultural Strategies

EM1. Attending to Feelings Within the Cultural Context
EM2. Promoting Culturally Appropriate Growth
EM3. Communicating Respect, Empathy, and Positive Regard
EM4. Clarifying Self-in-Relation
EM5. Integrating Cultural Parts of Self
EM6. Examining Freedom, Choice, and Responsibility With Cultural Sensitivity

Interpersonal-Multicultural Strategies

IM1.   Recognizing How Interpersonal Relationships Are Shaped by
         Cultural Contexts
IM2.   Honoring Resistance That May Be Culturally Appropriate
IM3.   Understanding Past Interpersonal Conflicts Within the Context of Culture
IM4.   Understanding the Therapeutic Relationship as a Cultural Exchange
IM4a. Cultural Transference
IM4b. Cultural Countertransference
IM5.   Helping Clients Adapt to Cultural Changes

Systemic-Multicultural Strategies

SM1. Understanding Family Structures Within Cultural Contexts
SM2. Identifying Culturally Influenced Family Expectations
SM3. Detecting Multigenerational Patterns Within Varied Cultural Contexts
SM4. Illuminating Cultural Values That Are Transmitted Through the Family
SM5. Encouraging Change Within Families That Fits Cultural Contexts

them back in another context. Other skills in this cluster enable psychotherapists to explore cultural schemas (CM3) or test hypotheses about culture (CM4). Together, these skills explore the way culture shapes thinking
and encourages clients to use their cognitive resources in support of cultural
adaptation.

Behavioral-Multicultural Strategies (BM). The next cluster of strategies looks at the way culture shapes behavior (Oliveira-Berry, 2004). These skills use traditional behavioral concepts like reinforcement, exposure, and skills training but apply them to the cultural context. For example, illuminating cultural reinforcement (BM2) enables counselor and clients to recognize the way culture influences behavior by reinforcing some actions and extinguishing or punishing others. For example, while exploring relationship choices, a therapist might ask, "Were cultural factors, such as sharing similar ethnic backgrounds or having similar views regarding marriage and family, an influence in your decision to become involved with this person?" (Oliveira-Berry, 2004). Other skills in this cluster focus on exposing clients to multicultural experiences (BM5) and providing cultural skills training (BM6). All these skills enable counselors to help clients choose actions that help them adapt to cultural contexts and experiences.

Experiential-Multicultural Strategies (EM). The third cluster examines the way culture shapes feelings and other parts of human experience (Wagner, 2004). These skills are drawn from traditional humanistic and experiential approaches, like client-centered therapy (Rogers, 1957) and gestalt therapy (Polster & Polster, 1973), but have been modified to address cultural identity. This cluster starts by encouraging counselors and psychotherapists to attend to feelings within the cultural context (EM1) and to promote culturally appropriate growth (EM2). One of the more advanced skills in this cluster, integrating cultural parts of self (EM5), is drawn from gestalt therapy but is adapted here to describe the experience of bicultural individuals or people who have moved from one cultural context to another. For example, when an immigrant client is experiencing a conflict between her American side and her Chinese side, it may be helpful to create contact and dialogue between these two parts of the same individual. Together, these skills encourage counselors to foster phenomenological awareness while recognizing that experience is always grounded in its cultural context.

Interpersonal-Multicultural Strategies (IM). The fourth cluster explores relationships within a cultural context (Hanawahine, 2004). These interventions are drawn from traditional psychodynamic and interpersonal therapies but have been adapted to focus on the way culture shapes interpersonal patterns. This focus starts by recognizing how relationships are shaped by culture (IM1) and understanding past conflicts within the context of culture (IM3). At a more advanced level, understanding the therapeutic relationship as a cultural exchange (IM4) highlights the role of both cultural transference and cultural countertransference. Many of the interpersonal perceptions that are examined and modified in psychotherapy are the result of cultural expectations, and exploring transference within culture can result in insight and healing that enables clients to view others in a more adaptive manner. For example, a counselor or therapist might explore cultural transference in the following way: "I noticed you had a strong reaction to the suggestion I made to you at the end of our last session. From what I've learned about you, questioning me about something I may say that you don't agree with would be culturally inappropriate for you. Can we explore together those feelings by taking a look at the cultural influences impacting your reactions?" (Hanawahine, 2004). This cluster of skills enables counselors and clients to understand and change interpersonal patterns in a way that is sensitive to cultural influences.

Systemic-Multicultural Strategies (SM). The final cluster of multicultural adaptations includes skills that focus on the interaction between culture and social systems (Castagnini, 2004). These skills acknowledge that families are the primary conduit for cultural learning and that culture has a profound influence on the experience of one's family of origin. This cluster encourages counselors and psychotherapists to understand family structures within cultural contexts (SM1) and to identify culturally influenced family expectations (SM2). Based on a clear cultural understanding of the family, counselors and therapists will be better prepared to encourage change within families that fits cultural contexts (SM5). For example, when working with parents who are feeling protective of their teenaged daughter, a counselor might say the following: "Perhaps Maria is upset because she is not able to go out with her friends and be social. I understand you are concerned about her safety, but it seems as if you are comfortable with her being at church. Is it possible for Maria to go to church functions when she has some free time? That way you know where she is and she is still able to go out and have some fun with her friends" (Castagnini, 2004). Each of these skills encourages psychotherapists to help promote adaptation to social systems and cultural contexts. All the skills summarized in Tables 18.3 and 18.4 represent theoretical constructs that have not yet been tested empirically. Future research will be necessary to determine whether counselors or therapists can learn to use these strategies and whether their use enhances the efficacy of psychotherapy when culture is a salient dimension in counseling.

_____ A New Application for Multicultural Counseling

Mental Health: Culture, Race, and Ethnicity concluded,

> Racism and discrimination are stressful events that adversely affect health and mental health. They place minorities at risk for mental disorders such as depression and anxiety. Whether racism and discrimination can by themselves cause these disorders is less clear, yet deserves research attention. (U.S. Department of Health and Human Services, 2001, p. 10)

This connection between stressful cultural events (like racism and discrimination) and mental health problems (like depression and anxiety) suggests a new application for multicultural counseling. This chapter is proposing the following hypothesis: When psychological problems are related to cultural experiences or identity, then treatment will be more effective if multicultural skills are used. This strategy of treating the effects of stressful cultural encounters goes beyond the traditional effort to understand cultural differences between counselor and client and to adapt counseling to the identity of clients. Multicultural treatment related to stressful cultural events may involve the combined use of all three types of multicultural skills highlighted in Table 18.1.

Stressful Cultural Encounters

One of the ways the multicultural counseling literature has recognized the impact of stressful events related to racism and discrimination is to describe the way certain encounters in one's life may impact the development of cultural identity. William Cross (1971) was the first psychologist to describe stages of black identity development. Cross's model described the way identity could be changed by certain types of encounters:

> Because the person's ongoing identity will defend against identity change, the person usually has to experience some sort of encounter that has the effect of "catching the person off guard." The encounter must work around, slip through, or shatter the relevance of the person's current identity and worldview and, at the same time, provide some hint of the path the person must follow in order to be resocialized and transformed. (Cross, 1995, p. 105)

Before such an encounter, African Americans may possess anti-black attitudes they learned from mainstream American culture. After an encounter, individuals may immerse themselves in African American culture and emerge with a new identity (Cross, 1971, 1995).

A *stressful cultural encounter* is being described here as a way to link three related concepts: (1) the encounter stage of identity development, following Cross's (1971, 1995) description; (2) the psychiatric diagnosis of adjustment disorders; and (3) acculturation difficulties, including culture shock. Stressful cultural encounters frequently result in psychological problems like anxiety and depression. These encounters may occur when people face cultural stressors, such as (a) moving from one culture to another (e.g., immigration, international studies); (b) discrimination, oppression, prejudice (e.g., sexual harassment, racism); (c) moving between two cultural contexts with conflicting values or norms (e.g., a lesbian who is "out" to her friends at college but is "closeted" with her family, a Native American who works in the city but returns to the reservation on weekends); (d) changes in patterns of minority/majority status or privilege (e.g., a Euro-American moves from Iowa to Hawaii and feels less white privilege in a more diverse culture, an African American moves from Atlanta to Maine and feels isolated from his racial community); (e) cultural stressors (e.g., poverty, refugee experience, illegal immigration); and (f) cultural violence (e.g., sexual assault, hate crimes). Multicultural counseling strategies are ideally suited for the treatment of stressful cultural encounters. When psychiatric symptoms that impair functioning are related to experiences with oppression or difference, it may be helpful to acknowledge the role of stressful cultural encounters and use multicultural skills to promote positive adjustment and help reduce negative symptoms.

Encounter Stage. Describing stressful cultural encounters as a multicultural construct builds an important bridge between the fields of multicultural counseling, traditional treatment of psychological problems and psychiatric disorders, and cross-cultural communication. Many cultural identity development models describe an encounter stage in which individuals have an experience that changes the way they understand their own identity. Cross (1995) pointed out that an encounter might be either negative (a racist event) or positive (exposure to powerful cultural-historical information). The encounter stage creates dissonance and confusion about how people from oppressed groups define themselves (Helms, 1995).

Adjustment Disorders. According to the *Diagnostic and Statistical Manual of Mental Disorders (DSM-IV-TR)*, adjustment disorders represent "a psychological response to an identifiable stressor or stressors that result in the development of clinically significant emotional or behavioral symptoms" (American Psychiatric Association, 2000, p. 679). Adjustment disorders can result in symptoms of depression or anxiety (or both) that impair social, occupational, or academic functioning. Depressed mood associated with adjustment can be displayed by tearfulness and feelings of hopelessness. Anxiety that results from adjustment can result in nervousness, worry, jitteriness, or fear. The *DSM-IV-TR* recognizes that adjustment disorders are reactions to stressful events, rather than medical diseases with a biological origin. Although the *DSM-IV-TR* acknowledges that an "individual's cultural setting should be taken into account" (p. 681) when diagnosing an adjustment disorder, it does not address the role that cultural encounters may play in the development of these symptoms. The assumption being made in this chapter is that many of the examples of stressful cultural encounters listed earlier are likely to result in adjustment problems and symptoms like anxiety or depression.

Culture Shock. Culture shock is a term used to describe the anxiety and feelings of disorientation felt when people have to operate within an entirely different cultural or social environment, such as a foreign country. "In a multicultural context, culture shock is a more or less sudden immersion into a nonspecific state of uncertainty where the individuals are not certain what is expected of them or what they can expect from the persons around them" (Pederson, 1995, p. 1). This process can occur when a person has to adjust to a new role, a new identity, or an unfamiliar social system. The process of cultural adjustment can result in affective stress, cognitive changes in identity, and the behavioral need to learn new skills (Ward, Bochner, & Furnham, 2001).

This chapter is proposing that stressful cultural encounters, adjustment disorders, and culture shock are closely related constructs that should be considered together. One way of thinking about this relationship is to hypothesize that stressful cultural encounters often result in cultural adjustment disorders. This relationship is depicted in Figure 18.2, with relevant examples of both encounters and psychological problems that may result. *Cultural adjustment disorder* is being proposed here as a construct that describes the psychological symptoms (e.g., anxiety, depression, disturbance of conduct, a mixture of these symptoms) that often result from stressful cultural encounters. At a low level of intensity, this may take the form of culture shock with transient feelings of uncertainty or disorientation. When encounters are more stressful, it is more likely that individuals will display symptoms that meet criteria for an adjustment disorder (American Psychiatric Association, 2000). In response to extremely stressful encounters, individuals may display psychiatric symptoms consistent with more serious or long-lasting problems, including anxiety disorders such as posttraumatic stress disorder (PTSD) or social phobia, or mood disorders such as major depressive disorder. If any of these disorders are closely related to stressful cultural encounters and have an impact on identity development, then it will be helpful to address culture in treatment. For example, when a female client develops symptoms of PTSD after being sexually assaulted by a male, then her gender identity may be impacted in a way that impairs her social functioning. In this case, treatment may be more effective if multicultural skills are used to explore the impact of the assault on the development of her cultural identity as a woman and if thoughts and feelings are explored in the context of the assault as a stressful cultural encounter. Treatment of cultural adjustment disorders should involve the intentional application of different types of multicultural skills.

The multicultural treatment of symptoms related to stressful cultural encounters was demonstrated in a recent training video (Brooks-Harris & Hamada, 2007). Both clients featured in this video met diagnostic criteria for an adjustment disorder as a result of moving from one cultural context to another and encountering a different set of cultural beliefs and norms. The first client was a Native Hawaiian and Filipina American female experiencing anxiety as a result of moving from Hawaii to Illinois and encountering a new cultural context in a predominantly white graduate school department. As the only woman of color in the engineering department, her change in status made her feel vulnerable to both social isolation and discrimination. The

Figure 18.2   The Relationship Between Stressful Cultural Encounters and Cultural Adjustment Disorders

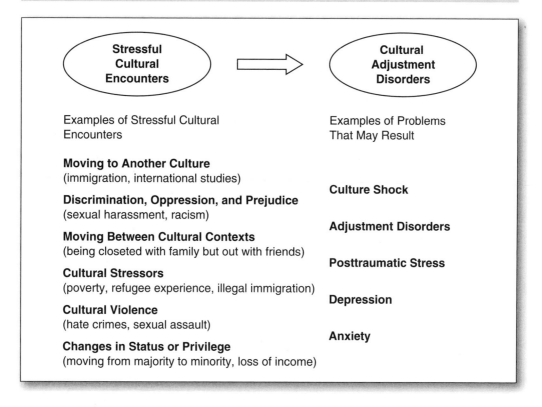

Examples of Stressful Cultural Encounters

Moving to Another Culture
(immigration, international studies)

Discrimination, Oppression, and Prejudice
(sexual harassment, racism)

Moving Between Cultural Contexts
(being closeted with family but out with friends)

Cultural Stressors
(poverty, refugee experience, illegal immigration)

Cultural Violence
(hate crimes, sexual assault)

Changes in Status or Privilege
(moving from majority to minority, loss of income)

Examples of Problems That May Result

Culture Shock

Adjustment Disorders

Posttraumatic Stress

Depression

Anxiety

second client was a Cuban American woman experiencing symptoms of depression as a result of moving from Florida to Hawaii and encountering a new cultural context living on a military base and being expected to play the role of military wife. Her Cuban values made her feel out of place and, as a result, she was isolating herself and questioning her self-worth. The use of multicultural skills enabled psychotherapists to address culture as a central part of treatment.

Should a Multicultural Treatment Manual Be Developed and Tested?

In order to test the effects of different forms of psychotherapy, treatment manuals have been developed to ensure that all clients in each research group are receiving equivalent treatment. One of the first psychological treatments to be tested in this way was described in *Cognitive Therapy of Depression* (Beck, Rush, Shaw, & Emory, 1979). Since then, dozens of treatments have been described in manual form so they can be tested in controlled research. Some researchers consider randomized clinical trials to be the most powerful way to test the causal efficacy of a particular treatment (e.g., Hollon, 2006). Randomized clinical trials involve taking a large group of clients with the same diagnosis and assigning them to different treatments (or to a placebo or control group) and measuring which group of clients shows the most improvement.

If researchers want to demonstrate the efficacy of multicultural counseling as a psychotherapeutic treatment, should it be described in the form of a treatment manual and tested using clinical trials? Some multicultural counselors and therapists see clinical trials based on treatment manuals as a rigid and technical method that is more easily applied to other theoretical approaches. These counselors may prefer to view multiculturalism as an esteemed system of values, beyond the reach of empirical scrutiny. Proposing the development of a multicultural treatment manual may be controversial. However, if multicultural counseling were to be manualized and tested in clinical trials, many of the ideas presented in this chapter could be used to develop a multicultural treatment manual. There are two possible avenues for the development of this type of scholarship. First, the strategies described in this chapter (and in earlier chapters in this text) could be used to create a stand-alone treatment manual for cultural adjustment disorders. Second, multicultural skills could be used to augment an existing treatment that has already been empirically supported (Lau, 2006).

Treating Cultural Adjustment Disorders

The first approach to developing a multicultural treatment manual would involve describing multicultural counseling as a treatment for cultural adjustment disorders that may result from stressful culture encounters, as summarized in Figure 18.2. The group-specific skills described in earlier chapters of this text could be used to adapt the treatment to the cultural context of clients from distinct racial or ethnic groups. The culture-centered skills identified in Table 18.3 would be used to understand clients and explore how their identities may have been impacted by stressful cultural encounters. The multicultural adaptations introduced in Table 18.4 could be used to examine ways that stressful encounters have impacted different dimensions of clients' lives and to encourage positive adaptations in response to stressful encounters. A clinical trial would involve identifying clients experiencing the results of stressful cultural encounters and experiencing a particular set of symptoms, such as adjustment disorder with anxiety. Half the clients would receive a standard treatment for anxiety that has been empirically supported. The other half would receive treatment that has been developed to address the role of culture and includes the multicultural skills described throughout this book. The following hypothesis could be tested: When psychological symptoms result from stressful cultural encounters, the use of multicultural strategies will result in more positive outcomes, compared to traditional treatments that do not address culture. In addition to testing the effect of treatment on traditional measures of anxiety, it may also be helpful to test cultural identity development. This type of research may also test the hypothesis that using multicultural skills to treat cultural adjustment disorders would result in positive movement through stages of cultural identity development.

Adapting Existing Treatments

The second approach to developing a multicultural counseling treatment manual is to take an existing treatment that has received empirical support and to add the skills described in this book in order to increase sensitivity to culture. Barrera and Castro (2006) described a method for conducting research to test the effectiveness of these types of multicultural adaptations. In the context of their analysis, a stressful cultural encounter can be considered a *unique mediator* and a cultural adjustment disorder may be a *unique outcome*. The multicultural skills described in Tables 18.3 and 18.4 would represent a *unique adaptive element* that could be used to augment an evidence-based treatment. Outcome research could be used to test whether the addition of multicultural strategies would enhance the effectiveness of standard treatments for depression, anxiety, or trauma when stressful cultural encounters have contributed to the formation of symptoms. Barrera and Castro also described methods for testing the effectiveness of cultural adaptations once they have been developed. For example, instead of comparing an established treatment for anxiety to a purely multicultural treatment, these strategies could be combined. To test the relative effectiveness of different approaches to the treatment of stressful cultural encounters, researchers could assign subjects in a clinical trial to three experimental groups: (1) an established treatment for anxiety, (2) multicultural treatment, and (3) a combined treatment using strategies from both approaches. Hypotheses for such a study may predict that traditional treatment will reduce symptoms of anxiety but not have a significant impact on identity development. Multicultural counseling may have more impact on identity development but may not be as effective at reducing anxiety symptoms. Combined treatment may be predicted to have a positive impact on both symptom reduction and identity development. Both types of research may be helpful if multicultural counselors and psychotherapists would like to see their methods become recognized as empirically supported treatments.

Summary

This chapter started by reviewing different types of multicultural skills that are related to different phases of the multicultural counseling movement. To complement the established work on group-specific skills, two other categories of multicultural strategies were introduced. First, culture-centered skills were described as a way to develop an idiographic understanding of a client's identity within a unique constellation of cultural contexts. Second, multicultural adaptations were described that enable counselors and therapists to adapt established interventions to be more responsive to culture and to examine cultural interactions with other dimensions of human functioning. A catalog of the two new types of strategies was introduced. It was suggested that the current description of multicultural skills could be applied to the treatment of cultural adjustment disorders that result from stressful cultural encounters. This application of multicultural counseling may be used to develop a treatment manual that could be tested with empirical research, including clinical trials.

References

Altschul, D. (Chair). (2004a, July). *Multicultural skills training: Operationalizing a treatment, training, and research model.* Symposium conducted at the meeting of the American Psychological Association, Honolulu, HI.

Altschul, D. (2004b, July). Understanding the client's worldview. In D. Altschul (Chair), *Multicultural skills training: Operationalizing a treatment, training, and research model.* Symposium conducted at the meeting of the American Psychological Association, Honolulu, HI.

American Psychiatric Association. (2000). *Diagnostic and statistical manual of mental disorders* (4th ed., Text rev.). Washington, DC: Author.

American Psychological Association. (2003). Guidelines on multicultural education, training, research, practice and organizational change for psychologists. *American Psychologist, 58,* 377–404.

American Psychological Association. (2005). *Policy statement on evidence-based practice in psychology.* Retrieved May 16, 2011, from http://www.apa.org/practice/resources/evidence/evidence-based-statement.pdf

Atkinson, D. R., Morten, G., & Sue, D. W. (1979). *Counseling minorities.* New York: McGraw-Hill.

Barrera, M., & Castro, F. G. (2006). A heuristic framework for the cultural adaptation of interventions. *Clinical Psychology: Science and Practice, 13*(4), 311–316.

Beck, A. T. (1967). *Depression: Clinical, experimental, and theoretical aspects.* New York: Hoeber. (Republished as Beck, A. T. [1970]. *Depression: Causes and treatment.* Philadelphia: University of Pennsylvania)

Beck, A. T., Rush, A. J., Shaw, B. F., & Emory, G. (1979). *Cognitive therapy of depression.* New York: Guilford Press.

Brooks-Harris, J. E. (Chair). (2004a, July). *Culture-centered psychotherapy interventions: Adapting strategies from five theoretical approaches.* Symposium conducted at the meeting of the American Psychological Association, Honolulu, HI.

Brooks-Harris, J. E. (2004b, July). Facilitating cultural identity development. In D. Altschul (Chair), *Multicultural skills training: Operationalizing a treatment, training, and research model.* Symposium conducted at the meeting of the American Psychological Association, Honolulu, HI.

Brooks-Harris, J. E. (2008). *Integrative multitheoretical psychotherapy.* Boston: Houghton Mifflin.

Brooks-Harris, J. E., & Hamada, W. C. (2007). *Multitheoretical counseling and psychotherapy (Vol. V.): Multicultural counseling and psychotherapy* [Videotape]. Hanover, MA: Microtraining Associates.

Brooks-Harris, J. E., & Savage, S. (2008). Multicultural-feminist psychotherapy: Adapting to cultural contexts. In J. Brooks-Harris (Ed.), *Integrative multitheoretical psychotherapy* (pp. 370–412). Boston: Houghton Mifflin.

Buhin, L. (2004, July). Becoming aware of your own worldview. In D. Altschul (Chair), *Multicultural skills training: Operationalizing a treatment, training, and research model.* Symposium conducted at the meeting of the American Psychological Association, Honolulu, HI.

Cass, V. C. (1979). Homosexuality identity formation: A theoretical model. *Journal of Homosexuality, 4,* 219–235.

Castagnini, C. A. (2004, August). Culture-centered adaptation of systemic psychotherapy interventions. In J. E. Brooks-Harris (Chair), *Culture-centered psychotherapy interventions: Adapting strategies from five theoretical approaches.* Symposium conducted at the meeting of the American Psychological Association, Honolulu, HI.

Cross, W. E. (1971). The negro-to-black conversion experience. *Black World, 20,* 13–27.

Cross, W. E. (1995). The psychology of nigrescence: Revising the Cross model. In J. G. Ponterotto, J. M. Casas, L. A. Suzuki, & C. M. Alexander (Eds.), *Handbook of multicultural counseling* (pp. 93–122).Thousand Oaks, CA: Sage.

Hamada, W. (2004, July). Creating a culturally sensitive therapeutic relationship. In D. Altschul (Chair), *Multicultural skills training: Operationalizing a treatment, training, and research model.* Symposium conducted at the meeting of the American Psychological Association, Honolulu, HI.

Hanawahine, G. L. (2004, August). Culture-centered adaptation of interpersonal psychotherapy interventions. In J. E. Brooks-Harris (Chair), *Culture-centered psychotherapy interventions: Adapting strategies from five theoretical approaches.* Symposium conducted at the meeting of the American Psychological Association, Honolulu, HI.

Hayes, A., & Sahl, J. C. (2011). *Depression.* Retrieved May 16, 2011, from www.psychology.sunysb.edu/eklonsky-/division12/disorders/depression_main.php

Hays, P. (2008). *Addressing cultural complexities in practice: Assessment, diagnosis, and therapy* (2nd ed.). Washington, DC: American Psychological Association.

Helms, J. E. (1995). An update of Helms's white and people of color racial identity models. In J. G. Ponterotto, J. M. Casas, L. A. Suzuki, & C. M. Alexander (Eds.), *Handbook of multicultural counseling* (pp. 181–198). Thousand Oaks, CA: Sage.

Herring, R. (1999). *Counseling with Native American Indians and Alaskan natives.* Thousand Oaks, CA: Sage.

Hollon, S. D. (2006). Randomized clinical trials. In J. C. Norcross, L. E. Beutler, & R. F. Levant (Eds.), *Evidence-based practices in mental health: Debate and dialogue on the fundamental questions* (pp. 96–105). Washington, DC: American Psychological Association.

Hong, G. K., & Ham, M. D. (2000). *Psychotherapy and counseling with Asian American clients: A practical guide.* Thousand Oaks, CA: Sage.

Jennette, D. M. (2004, August). Culture-centered adaptation of cognitive psychotherapy interventions. In J. E. Brooks-Harris (Chair), *Culture-centered psychotherapy interventions: Adapting strategies from five theoretical approaches.* Symposium conducted at the meeting of the American Psychological Association, Honolulu, HI.

Lau, A. (2006). Making the case for selective and directed cultural adaptations of evidence-based treatments: Examples from parent training. *Clinical Psychology: Science and Practice, 13*(4), 295–310.

Nacapoy, A. (2004, July). Utilizing complementary roles beyond psychotherapy. In D. Altschul (Chair), *Multicultural skills training: Operationalizing a treatment, training, and research model.* Symposium conducted at the meeting of the American Psychological Association, Honolulu, HI.

Oliveira-Berry, J. (2004, August). Culture-centered adaptation of behavioral psychotherapy interventions. In J. E. Brooks-Harris (Chair), *Culture-centered psychotherapy interventions: Adapting strategies from five theoretical approaches.* Symposium conducted at the meeting of the American Psychological Association, Honolulu, HI.

Parham, T. A. (2002). *Counseling persons of African descent (multicultural aspects of counseling and psychotherapy).* Thousand Oaks, CA: Sage.

Pederson, P. (1990). The multicultural perspective as a fourth force in counseling. *Journal of Mental Health Counseling, 12,* 93–95.

Pederson, P. (1995). *The five stages of culture shock: Critical incidents around the world.* Westport, CT: Greenwood.

Polster, E., & Polster, M. (1973). *Gestalt therapy integrated.* New York: Brunner/Mazel.

Ridley, C. R. (2005). *Overcoming unintentional racism in counseling and therapy* (2nd ed.). Thousand Oaks, CA: Sage.

Rogers, C. R. (1957). The necessary and sufficient conditions of therapeutic personality change. *Journal of Consulting Psychology, 21,* 95–103.

Santiago-Rivera, A. L., Arrendondo, P., & Gallardo-Cooper, M. (2001). *Counseling Latinos and la familia.* Thousand Oaks, CA: Sage.

Savage, S. (2004, July). Responding to societal structures and values. In D. Altschul (Chair), *Multicultural skills training: Operationalizing a treatment, training, and research model.* Symposium conducted at the meeting of the American Psychological Association, Honolulu, HI.

Sue, D. W. (1981). *Counseling the culturally different: Theory and practice.* New York: John Wiley & Sons.

Sue, D. W., Ivey, A. E., & Pederson, P. B. (1996). *A theory of multicultural counseling and therapy.* Pacific Grove, CA: Brooks/Cole.

Sue, D. W., & Sue, D. (2007). *Counseling the culturally diverse: Theory and practice* (5th ed.). New York: John Wiley & Sons.

Task Force on Promotion and Dissemination of Psychological Procedures. (1995). Training and dissemination of empirically validated psychological treatments. *The Clinical Psychologist, 48*(1), 3–23.

U.S. Department of Health and Human Services. (2001). *Mental health: Culture, race, and ethnicity. A supplement to mental health: A report of the Surgeon General.* Retrieved May 16, 2011, from http://www.surgeongeneral.gov/library/mentalhealth/cre/sma-01-3613.pdf

Wagner, K. S. (2004, August). Culture-centered adaptation of experiential psychotherapy interventions. In J. E. Brooks-Harris (Chair), *Culture-centered psychotherapy interventions: Adapting strategies from five theoretical approaches.* Symposium conducted at the meeting of the American Psychological Association, Honolulu, HI.

Ward, C., Bochner, S., & Furnham, A. (2001). *The psychology of culture shock.* Philadelphia: Taylor & Francis.

Ecological and Culturally Responsive Directions for the Skills Identification Stage Model

19

Christine J. Yeh

Miguel E. Gallardo

Thomas A. Parham

Joseph E. Trimble

Given the increasing numbers of individuals from culturally diverse backgrounds in the United States (U.S. Census Bureau, 2008), therapists must reconceptualize their notions of what counseling/therapy looks like. We began this book with the story of the Maligned Wolf, which shared the Wolf's perspective in the classic story of Little Red Riding Hood (Fern, 1974). This story represents a much-needed paradigm shift that allows us to imagine culturally responsive methods of assessing, diagnosing, and interviewing clients (Ancis, 2004; Cardemil & Battle, 2003). Such a change also involves reexamining and relearning ideas about the self as situated in a larger social, political, and cultural context and exploring various ideas about how healing occurs. In this book, we presented five ethnocultural perspectives (African American, Latina/o, Asian American and Pacific Islander,

Native American and Alaska Native, and Middle Eastern) of the Skills Identification Stage Model (SISM; see Gallardo, 2004; Parham, 2002) as well as specific case studies demonstrating unique cultural issues, values, and concerns that may arise during counseling/therapy. We believe these chapters and case examples address the call for maintaining ethical standards in counseling/therapy (American Counseling Association [ACA], 2005; American Psychological Association [APA], 2002, 2003) and the "philosophical mandate" for a paradigmatic multicultural shift (APA, 2003) in therapy and counseling with culturally competent practices and interventions when working with ethnocultural communities (Chapters 2, 5, 8, 11, this volume).

In addition, our contributors presented and elaborated on the SISM skills and methods that counselors/therapists can use to provide culturally responsive and culturally competent services to clients (Aldarondo, 2007; Ancis, 2004; Gallardo, Johnson, Parham, & Carter, 2009; Toporek & Reza, 2001). These chapters highlight many important factors that influence the counseling process, such as generation level, language, socioeconomic status, family dynamics, cultural norms and stigmas, and many other critical considerations. This model requires a shift in traditional therapeutic interactions and settings and incorporates meaningful attention to issues such as community, family, political climate, history, and spirituality, while still attending to within-group heterogeneity. In Table 19.1, we present a summary of the six SISM skills across the five ethnocultural groups: connect with clients, conduct assessments, set goals, facilitate awareness, take action/instigate change, and assess for feedback and accountability. This summary enables us to see a snapshot of the main counseling/therapeutic values and priorities for each group. However, it does not include specific information about how the groups are directly different or the same. In this chapter, we explore future directions for training, practice, and research using these skills, in order to further understand their usefulness in terms of cultural specificity, adaptability, and generality.

We also present, compare, and contrast the five guiding domains of *ontology* (nature of reality), *axiology* (one's value orientation), *cosmology* (relationship to the divine force in the universe), *epistemology* (systems of knowledge and discovering truth), and *praxis* (one's system of human interaction). These domains undergird our philosophical stance that prioritizes culturally centered values, collectivism, relationships, oral history, and religious and spiritual guidance (see Table 1.1 in Chapter 1). In this chapter, we further incorporate contextual, ecological, and asset-based approaches to consider and discuss how best to apply the culturally adaptive SISM model to training, research, and therapeutic efforts.

Specifically, we further expand on ecological and multicultural approaches to therapy. Bronfenbrenner's (1994) development in context theory includes five contextual systems that exert reciprocal interactions across and between the systems (see Yeh & Kwan, 2009, for elaboration). The *microsystem* is composed of an individual's biology and immediate settings (e.g., school, friends, family, neighborhood). The *mesosystem* includes interrelationships

Table 19.1 Therapeutic Skills

Group / What	African American	Latina/o American	Asian American	American Indian/ Alaska Native	Middle Eastern American
Connecting With Clients	Create ambiance in the therapeutic space.	Allow the initial process to be informal and personal, using small talk, if needed. Implement *personalismo* and *platica* as priorities over any other task at hand.	Acknowledge importance of maintaining harmony, shame and stigma, shifting selves.	Review purpose, goals, and approaches of counseling.	Therapist's attire and office should project professionalism, cleanliness, and prosperity, with diplomas and credentials framed and available for client's scrutiny.
	Offer some food or drink.			Discuss counseling arrangements and negotiate conditions such as time, setting, etc.	Language, when English, should reflect the warmth, friendliness, and availability of the therapist, yet not imply informality.
	Use ritual (handshakes, music, poetry, libations).	Address members of the family with formal greetings depending on age, status, etc.	Explore stereotypes.		
	Exhibit congruent realness (self-disclosure).	Allow for nontraditional therapeutic hour/process, if needed.	Normalize the counseling process.	Accept long periods of silence.	Professional demeanor, using surnames of the client, particularly for older clients, is necessary.
	Shift context and setting.	Create culturally congruent therapeutic space (i.e., help develop a sense of "home" for clients).	Negotiate counseling environment.	Establish perceived levels of ethnic identity and acculturative status with client.	Allow for nontraditional therapy time.
	Be with the client (active listening).	Use self-disclosure as a therapeutic intervention and as a way to build a respectful relationship.	Demonstrate achieved and ascribed credibility.	Discuss trust and trustworthiness.	Educate client about the process; emphasize the confidential nature of the process.
			Use gift giving.	Acknowledge historical trauma conditions.	Offer positive self-disclosure to instill hope and foster trust.
		Assess cultural strengths and existing resources.	Save face.		Use of a close and trusted relative as an interpreter can be tolerated, but do not use children as
		Shift environmental context, if necessary (e.g., meet client		Value and use humor.	interpreters. If a member of the

(Continued)

Table 19.1 (Continued)

Group / What	African American	Latina/o American	Asian American	American Indian/ Alaska Native	Middle Eastern American
		outside office space, if necessary). Use ritual (*dichos*, music, poetry, prayer, bibliotherapy, *cuentos*). Educate client about counseling process. Identify what role your client wants you to take (e.g., limited, seek assistance only, gain deeper insight). Use gift giving (i.e., provide client with a sense of hope that therapeutic work might make a difference in their lives. It is not a guarantee, but a demonstration of faith in the healing process).			community is used for interpretation, he or she should be allowed some time to develop rapport with the client and to ensure client's confidentiality. Be open to discuss your education, training, and experience, and do not challenge their inquiry. The therapist's warm and personable demeanor fosters trust. Don't ask the client to educate you about the culture. More acculturated clients expect a universal treatment and may not appreciate the cultural emphasis by the therapist.
Assessment	Understand and identify cultural strengths. Understand client. Distress from a culturally centered frame of reference.	Assess generation status/ethnic identification/education history and acculturation history (information from these areas will help guide what the therapy process will look like). Trauma assessment: identify what, if any, traumas exist, either present or past.	Assess self as embedded in larger social and cultural context. Examine influence of political history, acculturation, SES, immigration.	Recognize that client may have different views of conventional psychological diagnostic categories. Provide opportunity for	Educating the client about the purpose of the assessment is indispensable. Assess the presenting problems first, then assess history of immigration, generation status, and ethnic identification. ICD-10 and *DSM-IV-TR* are readily utilized in technologically

Group / What	African American	Latina/o American	Asian American	American Indian/ Alaska Native	Middle Eastern American
	Use culturally normed assessment instruments. Help clients and therapist anticipate setbacks.	Ecosystemic understanding and influences (i.e., understand the context in which the client lives and the influences of any environmental factors). Language usage: provide treatment in language of preference and adapt language to meet clients' educational level and acculturation levels (avoid using psychobabble when not necessary and when incompatible with client's educational and linguistic competencies). Acknowledge spiritual/religious beliefs and the role they play in the client's life, if any. Family and community relationships: involve in therapy when appropriate. Use culturally appropriate clinical instruments/measures. Beliefs about healthcare: understand the client's cultural explanatory model.	Conduct family and community genogram. Explore holistic view of health, spirituality. Examine complexity of language and translation issues. Investigate preferred collectivistic coping styles.	client to discuss tribal and own history. Family and friend relationships may be a source of the problem; discuss and map relationships. Recognize that formal testing may be suspect. Use projective techniques such as "draw-a-person" procedure. Create a list of current stressful life situations, then create one for how client copes effectively with the situations. Identify and discuss unrealistic coping patterns.	advanced and modern societies within the region. Clients are open to share cultural experiences only in the context of being a unique window to their cultures. Somatic idioms often reflect mental anguish and distress and should not be misinterpreted as somatization. Natural and supernatural (will of God or evil eye) may comprise clients' view of their problems and should not be challenged. Externalizing is to ward off shame and not to be mistaken with shirking personal responsibility.

(Continued)

Table 19.1 (Continued)

Group \\ What	African American	Latina/o American	Asian American	American Indian/ Alaska Native	Middle Eastern American
		Understand client distress from a Latina/o-centered frame of reference (i.e., compare clients to a standard that matches their own developmental, cultural, and life histories).		Perform content analysis of client's spoken or written words.	
Facilitating Awareness	Rephrase as a way to help clients creatively synthesize opposites. Engage in reflection. Use metaphor. Analyze obstacles to growth (defenses). Summarize. Explore impact of social forces on client's life. Assign readings. Help clients understand their language and values.	Use cultural strengths and existing resources to help client gain awareness. Assess social and political forces: depathologize client and presenting concerns and separate what is connected to the individual from the environment. Increase insight into cultural coping methods. Use reflecting and reframing and validate, validate, validate before questioning, challenging, or confronting. Help clients understand their own language and values for explaining symptoms and where they come from. Help clients understand their struggle (social context).	Reduce shame associated with emotionality. Use creative approaches for deepening insight. Explore reciprocity in client's social systems.	Discuss values and beliefs and client's commitment to them. Recognize that clients may not be in harmony with their world. Identify presenting problem and client (or other) responsibilities. Promote the concept of mindfulness and deep openness to truth.	Provide a great deal of validation and normalization to ameliorate the shame associated with seeking help. Integrate a developmental and systemic exploration to enhance insight. Help client understand the influence of, or the process of, acculturation as a stressor toward a bicultural ethnic identity development. Explore the distance between the private and public senses of self and ways that the client can differentiate without damaging significant relationships. Explore the wants, needs, and the guilt associated with the individuation process.

318

Group / What	African American	Latina/o American	Asian American	American Indian/ Alaska Native	Middle Eastern American
		Use *dichos*, cultural and community-specific stories. Possibly connect clients to resources, people, or services in the community where further understanding can be developed. Analyze any obstacle that may be preventing growth. Assign readings, when necessary and when appropriate.			Help the client negotiate individual goals within the interpersonal network. For children and adolescents, educate parents regarding developmental challenges and ethnic identity development.
Setting Goals	Become a subjective companion. Reframe the environment while teaching improvisation, transcendence, and transformation. Help clients have a cultural corrective experience.	Understand and assess therapist's own process variables in therapy with Latinas/os (i.e., belief systems about Latinas/os, how one feels about empowering Latina/o clients, believes about the possibility of change for Latinas/os). Incorporate level of education, SES, etc. (feasibility of goal attainment). Active approach: use a collaborative approach with client/family/community, when necessary and appropriate.	Develop collaborative goals with client's social system. Understand who is involved in the decision-making process.	Recognize that gender makes a difference in client goals. Acknowledge the value of traditional healing ceremonies and accommodate client's interests. Relational counseling approaches should be considered.	Client expects that the therapist, as an expert, sets the goals. Educate the client regarding the collaborative nature of therapy and goal setting. For children and adolescents, parents should be involved closely in the process. Individual adult clients should be given a choice of the extent to which they want to involve their family system. Immediate concerns have priority: solving tangible problems, ameliorating symptoms'. First

(Continued)

Table 19.1 (Continued)

Group / What	African American	Latina/o American	Asian American	American Indian/ Alaska Native	Middle Eastern American
	Restore balance and harmony.	Address immediate and concrete concerns first. Design a clear, specific, focused treatment plan in collaboration with client/community. Expand role to community activist, consultant, advisor, case management, etc. when needed and appropriate. Include family and community in achieving goals, when appropriate.		Recognize that goal setting will involve a context and others, especially kin. Identify steps to achieving harmony, balance, and connectedness with the world.	set concrete and easily attainable goals, then focus on loftier goals of personal development. Account for gender, SES, faith practices, level of acculturation, and generational status in goal setting.
Instigating Change	Empower the client through self-knowledge. Teach clients to problem solve. Become a social advocate on behalf of the client.	Understand the research and culturally adapt any existing model or treatment intervention developed to address client's concerns, when needed and when appropriate. Get out and get connected; immerse and extend cultural learning experiences as a way to develop cultural empathy for your clients.	Facilitate counselor and client change. Negotiate changes at multiple systemic levels— ripple effect. Facilitate consciousness raising and giving voice.	Be open to use of family members, friends, and coworkers to promote change. Provide occasions for anger to be discussed and vented. Understand and implement the	Teach skills, advocate, or be a cultural liaison to facilitate adaptation. Educate the client regarding psychological factors and influence of culture in the process of change. Package insight from a developmental and social learning perspective to provide rationale for change.

Group / What	African American	Latina/o American	Asian American	American Indian/ Alaska Native	Middle Eastern American
		Role model for clients. Empower the client (self-knowledge) and help the client develop a stronger sense of connectedness to individuals in community and community context. Teach clients to problem solve. Become a social advocate on behalf of the client (culture broker). Use collaborative/active approaches in which you and client are participating in the process of change. Involve family and community, where appropriate.	Examine role of fatalism and external locus of control. Understand client's conceptualization of the healing process.	importance of gradual pacing of sessions.	Recognize holistic approaches and incorporating spirituality and alternative medicine, as well as the utility of pharmacotherapy, day programs, hospitalization, and rehabilitation. Cautiously explore fatalism and external locus of control, as well as negotiating the distance between the private and public selves.
Feedback/ Accountability	Review what is working in moving toward a goal. Examine congruence between goals and outcomes.	Assessing one's credibility: many Latina/o clients may see the therapist's overlapping roles in the community and as a therapist as a strength and someone they can trust. Understand and measure "success" in a Latina/o-specific	Use metaphors, storytelling, and written feedback. Reframe the notion of feedback, practice. Do not assume client will initiate	Use storytelling, legends, and inspirational writings. Use behavioral records of positive client changes.	Direct feedback is not culturally condoned even when solicited by the therapist. Educate the client about the process and discuss different roles that the therapist can play in providing the therapeutic service.

(Continued)

Table 19.1 (Continued)

Group / What	African American	Latina/o American	Asian American	American Indian/ Alaska Native	Middle Eastern American
	Examine spiritual energy and sense of harmony. Remind clients about the notion of being and becoming (concept of perfectibility).	context, not majority, universal standard of success. Examine congruence between goals and outcomes achieved. Assess therapist's role in creating change (i.e., understand what is helpful or not). Involve family and community if needed. Seek feedback from client, but know that feedback may not be direct, or may be limited, due to your professional role as a therapist/doctor/professional.	the feedback process. Structure feedback routine. Involve important others in client's social systems.	Have client summarize main points of each session in writing/ dictation on 3″ x 5″ card. Provide occasions to discuss letting go of control and options. Summarize each session and open sessions with summaries of previous sessions.	Assess for progress and utility of previous interventions on session-by-session basis to evoke accountability in the process. Use metaphors, stories, poems, and indirect communications to allow for more uncomfortable or undesirable feedback to be communicated more easily. Appropriate use of humor often softens the sharp edges of honest feedback.

between different immediate environments (e.g., student and school, family and community). The *exosystem* encompasses a developmental influence from a system in which the individual is not actively and immediately involved (e.g., availability of safe transportation, immigration resources). The *macrosystem* refers to the larger cultural environment (e.g., racist institution, political system), including the values and norms of society. The *chronosystem* includes sociohistorical conditions that intersect with and influence the individual's experiences (e.g., legalization of gay marriage). These ecological levels are interacting, reciprocal, and shifting (Borrero & Yeh, 2010). Moreover, they provide information about the client's life in a more comprehensive and holistic historical, political, social, familial, and cultural context. We now discuss the SISM in terms of training, research, and practical implications.

Training

Training in traditional counseling, clinical, and psychology programs has led us to the assumption that many specific counseling skills are universal and may be applied to various populations (Parham, 2002). In our introductory chapter, we described previous work that has identified four common factors in all healing approaches (Fischer, Jome, & Atkinson, 1998). Fischer et al. lay the framework for our SISM model and prioritize the therapeutic relationship as a basis for healing, a shared worldview of symptoms, clients' expectations for hope and faith, and the therapeutic ritual or intervention that entails active participation of client and therapist.

Further, Rebecca Toporek (Chapter 17, this volume) has discussed previous literature in multicultural training and future directions. In this review, she reveals the importance of balancing self-awareness, culturally specific information, and skill building (see also Pieterse, Evans, Risner-Butner, Collins, & Mason, 2009; Priester et al. 2008). As Toporek describes, it is important for educators to integrate skill building in the process of self-exploration through the use of interviews, case conceptualization, and so on. Moreover, it is also critical to continue skill development throughout the entire curriculum and to really unpack the counseling/therapy process so that each aspect of counseling/therapy is viewed in context. She offers many specific exercises to help better understand the client's context that are consonant with our ecological focus. These include the Career-in-Culture interview (Ponterotto, Rivera, & Sueyoshi, 2000) and the Person-in-Culture interview (Berg-Cross & Chinen, 1995).

Along with the proposed paradigm shift in the delivery of therapeutic services comes a necessary transition in how we train present and future psychologists. Training programs must also expand their expectations for competence and reconceptualize the healing process to include holistic beliefs about the interrelationship of mind, body, nature, and the spiritual world (Lakes, Lopez, & Garro, 2006; Yeh, Borrero, & Shea, 2011; Yeh, Hunter, Madan-Bahel, Chiang, & Kwong, 2004); empowerment of communities (Aldarondo, 2007); and appreciation of social, political, and cultural contexts in shaping clients' experiences (La Roche, 2005). Training needs to deconstruct notions of counseling/therapy in both theory and practice so graduate students learn the skills they need to be adaptive, responsive, and flexible (see Chapter 17, this volume). For example, training experiences may offer opportunities to counselors/ therapists in training to learn to work with community leaders, indigenous healers, religious organizations, and extended family systems (Hwang, 2009; Sue & Sue, 2003; Yeh et al., 2004). Training programs may also teach students to think about their role, not just as a therapist but as a cultural bridge (Amatea & West-Olatunji, 2007), cultural broker (Stone, 2005), social advocate (Parham, White, & Ajamu, 1999), social justice advocate (Goodman et al., 2004; Sue & Sue, 2003), healer (Parham, 2002; Yeh et al., 2004), mentor, teacher, role model, consultant, and advisor (see Chapter 1, this volume).

Research

As we move from clinical competence to cultural responsiveness and the need to integrate the two (Chapter 1, this volume), we need to consider research that will continue to raise our standards of cultural competence (Gallardo et al., 2009; Parham, 2004; Vera & Speight, 2003). The literature on culturally responsive counseling/therapy often focuses on culture-specific techniques and skills. Such approaches tend to conceptualize therapy in terms of specific values that are associated with a particular ethnic or racial group. Although these methods of counseling/therapy have the potential to provide validation and understanding of ethnocultural communities, we also need to consider our potential as therapists to incorporate common skills (as in our SISM) and approaches (as in the five domains) of counseling that may be adapted to many different groups. For example, Harris (Chapter 18, this volume) offers many important and relevant directions for improving multicultural counseling skills through research and practice using his specific multitheoretical psychotherapy model (Brooks-Harris, 2008). This includes a multidimensional model of human functioning that incorporates meaningful ecological, systemic, cultural, and personal variables (Brooks-Harris, 2008).

The culturally adaptive SISM does not intend to overgeneralize the experiences of individuals of African, Asian, Latina/o, Native, and Middle Eastern descent. Rather, we wanted to share some suggestions and examples for how we envision embarking on this necessary paradigmatic multicultural shift in counseling/therapy to interventions that are culturally congruent with clients' experiences (APA, 2003). We also acknowledge that there are many similarities as well as differences across the groups we discuss.

In order to further develop the SISM, it will be necessary to conduct future research on how best to connect with clients, conduct assessments, set goals, facilitate awareness, take action/instigate change, and assess for feedback and accountability (see Table 19.1). Research should account for within- and across-group differences as well as the many other demographic and cultural variables that shape one's experience. In Chapter 1 and throughout this book, we incorporate Evidence-Based Practices in Psychology (EBPP) by integrating research, clinical expertise, and cultural preferences and norms (see EBPP definition, APA Presidential Taskforce on Evidence-Based Practice, 2006). Research on culturally adaptive therapeutic techniques does not always incorporate a theoretical base such as the SISM. EBPPs also need to include client and community perspectives from the "bottom up" (Bernal, Jimenez-Chafey, & Domenech Rodriguez, 2009; Borrero, Yeh, Cruz, & Suda, 2010; Hwang, 2009; Yeh, Kim, Pituc, & Atkins, 2008; Yeh, Okubo, Cha, Lee, & Shin, 2008). Definitions of EBPP underscore that "culture is a multifaceted construct, and cultural factors cannot be understood in isolation from social, class, and personal characteristics that make each patient unique (APA Presidential Taskforce on Evidence-Based Practice, 2006, p. 278). This assertion connects well with our ecological and multicultural focus to researching and practicing the SISM.

Further, Jeff Harris (Chapter 18, this volume) provides an extensive overview of the development and publications associated with EBPP in clinical psychology (Division 12 of the APA); depression treatment (Hayes & Sahl, 2009); the relationship between research, clinical expertise, and client characteristics (APA, 2005); and the role of culture in clients' experience of therapy (APA, 2005). In addition, Harris describes the lack of EBPP research with ethnocultural communities and the importance of "contextualizing content" (see Lau, 2006).

Research exploring ethnocultural applications of the SISM need to move beyond the question, "Does this approach to counseling/therapy work?" Rather, while using the SISM as a conceptual guide, researchers could begin to investigate the specific mechanisms associated with each of the five skills listed above that may foster positive clinical change and growth. In addition, we need to consider how EBPPs contribute to this research agenda and investigate clients' perceptions of health and healing as a critical lens for developing EBPP (La Roche & Christopher, 2009; Yeh, 2000; Yeh et al., 2004).

Ideas for research questions and studies related to our six main SISM skills include the following:

1. Connecting with clients
   a. Interviewing clients about specific counseling strategies and skills in the SISM that fostered feelings of connection
   b. Measuring feelings of social connectedness in clients before and after implementing the SISM

2. Conducting assessments
   a. Using ecological and multicultural assessments (see Yeh & Kwan, 2009) in the SISM and examining how this method contributes to positive outcomes in counseling
   b. Having clients evaluate the helpfulness and meaningfulness of SISM assessments in their overall experience with counseling

3. Setting goals

a. Using pre- and posttest surveys to evaluate the integration of important relationships in the process of setting goals

b. Investigating community and individual client goals and how they change over the course of therapy

4. Facilitating awareness

a. Investigating counselors'/therapists' perceptions of factors that contribute to clients' awareness of how their past and present actions influence their future actions

b. Conducting narrative analysis of clients' awareness of important relational dynamics

5. Instigating change

a. Interviewing clients about ecological systems that are involved in the process of change

b. Observing how counselors/therapists are able to foster collaborative changes in clients

6. Assessing for feedback and accountability

a. Evaluating the reciprocity in client-counselor relationships and how this encourages clients' feedback

b. Using content analysis of therapy session transcripts to evaluate how counselors/therapists use creative methods to seek feedback about their clinical performance

Parham (2004) asserts that healers are persons who collaborate *with* the client in addressing the client's mental, physical, emotional, behavioral, and spiritual needs and strengths. Moreover, healers have access to and incorporate their healing wisdom into their own lives and facilitate clients' self-healing power. In order to continually raise the bar for what passes as competent, clinical and cultural competence must be conceptualized as inextricably linked (Parham, 2002).

Practice

In this book, we sought to demonstrate the cultural applicability of the SISM to various ethnocultural groups. Throughout the chapters, we described and discussed the structure and adaptability of the SISM in therapy and clinical practice. In this section, we further describe how to adapt the SISM in clinical practice using the strategies of connecting with clients, conducting assessments, setting goals, facilitating awareness, instigating change, and assessing for feedback and accountability.

Our culturally responsive skills model incorporates collectivistic and ecological approaches to understanding and assessing culturally diverse clients' needs (Yeh & Kwan, 2009). The therapeutic hour may involve the use of techniques that inquire about clients' meaningful relationships and contexts, such as families, peers, schools, and communities. For example, Borrero and Yeh (in press) describe several strategies that interface well with the culturally adaptive SISM: ecological asset mapping, examination of worldview, exploring family values and dynamics, and understanding community and cultural context.

Ecological Asset Mapping

Ecological asset mapping is a way of exploring and understanding clients' assets through an appreciation of their meaningful social settings (Borrero & Yeh, in press). Previous literature in community needs assessments (Beaulieu, 2002) defined asset mapping as the practice of identifying strengths and skills in a community or organizational setting. Borrero and Yeh (in press) expand this definition to ecological asset mapping, which is the identification, exploration, and integration of individual, family, institutional, community, and cultural assets for the empowerment of marginalized groups.

Counselors and therapists can use ecological asset mapping in their clinical work with diverse clients to support a systemic, strengths-based, collaborative, and contextual perspective. It may also help to identify how clients respond to societal structures and values, such as systems of privilege (see Brooks-Harris, 2008; Chapter 18, this volume). This approach may also provide validation for the communities in which clients interact. Guiding questions may include the following:

a. What are the most meaningful communities in your life (e.g., your family, neighborhood friends, members of a social organization)?

b. How would you describe some of the main assets in each of these settings?

c. What are some of the most relevant relationships that comprise this community?

d. What resources are available to you in each of these spaces?

e. What are some relationships that you could develop in these settings that could offer support to you?

Because ecological asset mapping emerges from the perspective of strengths and systems, this strategy and the above questions may encourage the use of the SISM in the areas of connecting with clients, conducting assessments, setting goals, facilitating awareness, and instigating change, in particular. For example, clients may feel more empowered and validated when their contextual background and assets are recognized (Aldarondo, 2007; Borrero et al., 2010). Similarly, therapists who are aware of the potential support networks and resources available may be able to better advocate for their client's relational, cultural, psychological, spiritual, and physical needs.

Examination of Worldview

In this book, we present numerous ideas and strategies that focus on culturally responsive counseling techniques, skills, and assessments. However, we also prioritize how our *own* cultural, personal, educational, and social class background and experiences influence our interpretations of the SISM and our interactions with clients (Yeh & Pituc, 2008) and are critical aspects of cultural competence (Arredondo, 1998). We also discuss how a shared worldview between client and therapist regarding the client's issues and attendant healing approaches can foster change (Chapter 1, this volume). Harris (Chapter 18, this volume) reviews and shares his multitheoretical psychotherapy work (Brooks-Harris, 2008), which prioritizes becoming aware of your own worldview and the client's worldview as critical culture-centered counseling skills.

Previous literature on *worldview* has defined the term as how a person interprets the world (Ivey, Ivey, & Simek-Morgan, 1997), one's subjective reality (Ibrahim, 1985), and a philosophy of life (Sue & Sue, 2003). Counselors' and psychologists' worldviews are created by their relationships, education, social class, racial/ethnic values and background, geographic location, religious/spiritual beliefs, life experiences, and family histories (Hays, 2008; Sodowsky & Johnson, 1994). We believe that all therapists and mental health practitioners must consistently question their assumptions, stereotypes, and biases that may exist or emerge during the counseling process (Yeh & Pituc, 2008).

A thorough examination of worldview can help therapists be advocates for their clients (Goodman et al., 2004; Ibrahim, Roysircar-Sodowsky, & Ohnishi, 2001; Parham et al., 1999; White & Parham, 1990). Ibrahim and Kahn (1987) have created the Scale to Assess Worldview (SAWV) to help counselors understand common beliefs, values, and assumptions that they may hold about others. Therapists may also collaborate with colleagues to challenge each other and examine daily beliefs, to deepen their self-awareness. Listed below are some questions to ask to begin examining one's worldview:

a. How have my relationships, education, social class, racial/ethnic values and background, geographic location, religious/spiritual beliefs, life experiences, and family history influenced my multiple identities?

b. How have my relationships, education, social class, racial/ethnic values and background, geographic location, religious/spiritual beliefs, life experiences, and family history shaped my interactions with clients?

c. What stereotypes and assumptions do I make about clients who are from a different cultural class than my own?

d. How do I participate in racism, sexism, classism, and so on?

Examining one's worldview coincides with the belief that counselors/ therapists must be active learners and engaged in the process of self-exploration. Hence, this technique not only fosters multicultural competence (Sue & Sue, 2003), but it also assists in the SISM in the areas of conducting assessments, facilitating awareness, and feedback and accountability. Specifically, counselors can more effectively encourage open feedback and discussion with clients when underlying or unspoken biases and assumptions are dealt with and addressed. Such examination of worldview and its impact on counseling processes will also foster greater counselor accountability.

Exploring Family Values and Dynamics

Often, therapy is an individualistic process that does not account for family values and dynamics (Yeh & Wang, 2000). When working with clients from collectivistic ethnocultural communities, the family is often the primary system for understanding client values, stigmas, and beliefs. For example, in Chapter 1, we explored the five guiding domains of ontology (nature of reality), axiology (one's value orientation), cosmology (relationship to the divine force in the universe), epistemology (systems of knowledge and discovering truth), and praxis (one's system of human interaction). These domains undergird our SISM model and prioritize many important family issues, such as lived family experiences and ancestral knowledge (ontology); one's collectivism to others, group identity, and cultural values (axiology); oral history, ancestral history, and storytelling (epistemology); and family guidance and shared wisdom (praxis).

Therapists have the opportunity and responsibility to serve as a *cultural bridge* between families and the members of the dominant culture (Amatea & West-Olatunji, 2007; Borrero & Yeh, in press). Therapy is often administered from the perspective of an autonomous being and does not always incorporate ancestral knowledge, family wisdom, or family oral history. Practitioners should explore avenues for learning about important family roles, relationships, and histories because families offer an entrée into role dynamics, cultural values and beliefs, gender expectations, lifestyle preferences, communication patterns, immigration histories, and socialization practices (Jones Thomas, 2005; Yeh & Kwan, 2009).

Therapists may begin by exploring how their clients define "family" in terms of membership (nuclear, immediate, extended, etc.) and associated roles (see McGoldrick, Giordano, & Pearce, 1996). In many ethnocultural communities, ancestor worship is a regular and important aspect of family relationships, decisions, and practices. Culturally relevant interview questions in therapy (Paniagua, 2005) and cultural genograms (Adachi Sueyoshi, Rivera, & Ponterotto, 2001) provide useful methods to examine family cultural beliefs and values. For example, cultural genograms create opportunities to better understand family patterns and psychopathology across generational levels. They may also highlight relational tensions that exist in family systems and partnerships.

Below we have listed some initial questions that explore family dynamics:

a. Who are the main people in your life that you consider to be family?

b. What are the roles and responsibilities of the different members of your family?

c. How does your family think about your ancestors and their contribution to your family life?

d. What are some expectations that you have of your family members and vice versa?

Exploring family dynamics prioritizes the view of the client as a collectivistic self embedded in ecological systems that include family and extended family (Yeh & Kwan, 2009). An understanding and appreciation of family dynamics helps to situate the client in a larger history of beliefs, norms, and values. This strategy is related to the SISM areas of conducting assessments, facilitating awareness, and instigating change/taking action. Helping clients understand their reciprocal interactions with family members will also further empower them in their family context. This process of exploration will also assist in identifying healthy and unhealthy modes of interaction that are informed and shaped by previous and current family dynamics.

Understanding Community and Cultural Context

Borrero and Yeh (in press) highlight the importance of community context when counseling clients from diverse ethnocultural backgrounds. Neighborhoods are often untapped resources that contain potential support networks (e.g., religious services, community agencies, programs for youth; Yeh, Inman, Kim, & Okubo, 2006). In order to be culturally competent, therapists must educate themselves about local community resources that offer instrumental support for basic living (e.g., legal issues, housing, employment, immigration services) as well as psychological, physical, and spiritual needs (e.g., traditional medicine healers, respected chiefs or elders; Yeh et al., 2004). A therapist's awareness of relevant community connections can offer support and validation for clients. These resources may also destigmatize the therapeutic process and underscore the critical role of community members in heal-ing, advocacy, and empowerment (Yeh & Kwan, 2009).

Therapists as social advocates (Goodman et al., 2004; Parham et al., 1999; White & Parham, 1990) should proactively investigate clients' cultural histo-ries, such as immigration context, political climate, language, and cultural values (Comas-Diaz, Lykes, & Alarcon, 1998). Such advocacy may involve learning current EBPPs, interviewing cultural liaisons, and searching Web sites that include U.S. Census data. Further, the therapist's potential role as a healer (Parham, 2002) must include active and collaborative engagement with local indigenous healers and learning about the physical, spiritual, and psychological interconnections of the holistic self that is present among many ethnocultural groups.

Questions to help explore community and cultural contexts include the following:

a. What are environmental barriers that may impede your ability to set and pursue culturally meaningful goals?

b. How do your social and community surroundings contribute to, or limit, your access to equitable conditions that foster positive develop-ment and success?

c. Which community settings do you interact with most frequently, and how do these exchanges promote or weaken your cultural assets?

An understanding and appreciation of clients' community context will help in connecting with clients, conducting assessment, facilitating aware-ness, setting goals, and instigating needed changes. Given our EBPP focus on "bottom up" community perspectives, this practice also intersects nicely with our research agenda.

Conclusion

Our culturally responsive SISM is grounded in the five domains of ontology, axiology, cosmology, epistemology, and praxis. Using the SISM, we incorpo-rate six ethnocultural approaches with diverse case studies that further expand our model. These perspectives highlight culturally centered (Parham, 2002), ecological (Bronfenbrenner, 1994), and multicultural (Yeh & Kwan, 2009) approaches to therapy, research, and training that encourage explora-tion of self, family dynamics, and community contexts that lead to empow-erment and liberation (Martín-Baró, 1994). Therapists need to remember their multiple roles that include mentor, social advocate, healer, advisor, and teacher. These multidimensional roles require adaptability, openness, and a commitment to collaboration and equity.

We hope that the contents of this book will assist researchers, thera-pists, educators, and students to explore, understand, and practice culturally responsive skills and relationships with their clients. We also hope that practitioners will challenge themselves to imagine therapy beyond the use of specific skills and incorporate indigenous methods and perspectives of health and healing. By using the SISM, clinicians and counselors will have a framework for engaging in therapy that incorporates common factors as well as culturally adapted and responsive techniques and methods. We also encourage our readers to continue to build the SISM for additional ethnocultural communities.

References

Adachi Sueyoshi, L., Rivera, L., & Ponterotto, J. G. (2001). The family genogram as a tool in multicultural career counseling. In J. G. Ponterotto, J. M. Casas, L. A. Suzuki, & C. M. Alexander (Eds.), *Handbook of multicultural counseling* (2nd ed., pp. 655–671). Thousand Oaks, CA: Sage.

Aldarondo, E. (2007). Rekindling the reformist spirit in the mental health professions. In E. Aldarondo (Ed.), *Advancing social justice through clinical practice* (pp. 3–17). Mahwah, NJ: Lawrence Erlbaum.

Amatea, E., & West-Olatunji, C. (2007). Joining the conversation about educating our poorest children: Emerging leadership roles for school counselors in high-poverty schools. *Professional School Counseling, 11*(2), 81–89.

American Counseling Association. (2005). *ACA code of ethics.* Retrieved November 19, 2010, from http://www.counseling.org/Resources/CodeOfEthics/TP/Home/CT2 .aspx

American Psychological Association. (2002). Ethical principles of psychologists and code of conduct. *American Psychologist, 57,* 1060–1073.

American Psychological Association. (2003). Guidelines on multicultural education, training, research, practice, and organizational change for psychologists. *American Psychologist, 58*(5), 377–402.

American Psychological Association. (2005). *Policy statement on evidence-based practice in psychology.* Retrieved May 16, 2011, from http://www.apa.org/ practice/resources/evidence/evidence-based-statement.pdf

American Psychological Association Presidential Taskforce on Evidence-Based Practice. (2006). Evidence-based practice in psychology. *American Psychologist, 61,* 271–285.

Ancis, J. R. (Ed.). (2004). *Culturally responsive interventions: Innovative approaches to working with diverse populations.* New York: Brunner-Routledge.

Arredondo, P. (1998). Integrating multicultural counseling competencies and universal helping conditions in culture specific contexts. *The Counseling Psychologist, 26,* 592–601.

Beaulieu, L. J. (2002). *Mapping the assets of your community: A key component for building local capacity.* Retrieved May 16, 2011, from http://srdc.msstate.edu/ publications/archive227pdf

Berg-Cross, L., & Chinen, R. T. (1995). Multicultural training models and the person-in-culture interview. In J. G. Ponterotto, J. M. Casas, L. A. Suzuki, & C. M. Alexander (Eds.), *Handbook for multicultural counseling* (pp. 333–356). Thousand Oaks, CA: Sage.

Bernal, G., Jimenez-Chafey, M., & Domenech Rodriguez, M. M. (2009). Cultural adaptations of treatments: A resource for considering culture in evidence-based practice. *Professional Psychology: Research and Practice, 40*(4), 361–368.

Borrero, N. E., & Yeh, C. J. (2010). Ecological language learning among ethnic minority youth. *Educational Researcher, 39*(8), 571–581.

Borrero, N. E. & Yeh, C. J. (2011). The multidimensionality of ethnic identity among urban high school youth. *Identity: An International Journal of Theory and Research, 11*(2), 114–135.

Borrero, N. E., Yeh, C. J., Cruz, I., & Suda, J. (2010). School as a context for "othering" youth and promoting cultural assets. *Teachers College Record, 114*(2), 2012.

Bronfenbrenner, U. (1994). Ecological models of human development. In T. Husen & T. N. Postlethwaite (Ed.), *The international encyclopedia of education* (2nd ed., pp. 1643–1647). New York: Elsevier Science.

Brooks-Harris, J. E. (2008). *Integrative multitheoretical psychotherapy.* Boston: Houghton Mifflin.

Cardemil, E. V., & Battle, C. L. (2003). Guess who's coming to therapy: Getting comfortable with conversations about race and ethnicity in psychotherapy. *Professional Psychology: Research and Practice, 34*(3), 278–286.

Comas-Diaz, L., Lykes, M. B., & Alarcon, R. (1998). Ethnic conflict and psychology of liberation in Guatemala, Peru, and Puerto Rico. *American Psychologist, 53*, 778–792.

Fern, L. (1974). The maligned wolf. In *Elementary assembly script 5–Topic 3A– Respecting diversity.* Retrieved May 16, 2011, from http://www.sacsc.ca/ Resources_School.htm#AssemblyScripts

Fischer, A. R., Jome, L. M., & Atkinson, D. R. (1998). Reconceptualizing multicultural counseling: Universal healing conditions in a culturally specific context. *Journal of Counseling Psychology, 26*, 525–588.

Gallardo, M. E. (2004, July). Working culturally and competently with Latinos: Shifting perspectives, facilitating change. In J. Resnick & J. Carter (Co-Chairs), *American Psychological Association pre-convention workshop: Implementation of the multicultural guidelines.* Workshop conducted at the meeting of the American Psychological Association, Honolulu, HI.

Gallardo, M. E., Johnson, J., Parham, T. A., & Carter, J. A. (2009). Ethics and multiculturalism: Advancing cultural and clinical responsiveness. *Professional Psychology: Research and Practice, 40*(5), 425–435.

Goodman, L. A., Liang, B., Helms, J. E., Latta, R. E., Sparks, E., & Weintraub, S. R. (2004). Training counseling psychologists as social justice agents: Feminist and multicultural principles in action. *The Counseling Psychologist, 32*(6), 793–836.

Hayes, A., & Sahl, J. C. (2009). *Depression.* Retrieved May 16, 2011 from http://www .psychology.sunysb.edu/eklonsky-/division12/disorders/depression_main.php

Hays, P. (2008). *Addressing cultural complexities in practice: Assessment, diagnosis, and therapy* (2nd ed.). Washington, DC: American Psychological Association.

Hwang, W. C. (2009). The formative method for adapting psychotherapy (FMAP): A community-based developmental approach to culturally adapting therapy. *Professional Psychology: Research and Practice, 40*(4), 369–377.

Ibrahim, F. A. (1985). Effective cross-cultural counseling and psychotherapy: A framework. *The Counseling Psychologist, 13*, 625–638.

Ibrahim, F. A., & Kahn, H. (1987). Assessment of worldviews. *Psychological Reports, 60,* 163–176.

Ibrahim, F. A., Roysircar-Sodowsky, G., & Ohnishi, H. (2001). Worldview: Developments and directions. In J. G. Ponterotto, J. M. Casas, L. A. Suzuki, & C. M. Alexander (Eds.), *Handbook of multicultural counseling* (2nd ed., pp. 425–456). Thousand Oaks, CA: Sage.

Ivey, A. E., Ivey, M. B., & Simek-Morgan, L. (1997). *Counseling and psychotherapy: Skills, theories, and practice.* Englewood Cliffs, NJ: Prentice Hall.

Jones Thomas, A. (2005). Family counseling and psychotherapy in racial-cultural psychology: Case applications. In R. T. Carter (Ed.), *Handbook of racial-cultural counseling: Training and practice* (Vol. 2, pp. 364–378). Hoboken, NJ: John Wiley & Sons.

La Roche, M. J. (2005). The cultural context and the psychotherapeutic process: Toward a culturally sensitive psychotherapy. *Journal of Psychotherapy Integration, 15*(2), 169–185.

La Roche, M. J., & Christopher, M. S. (2009). Changing paradigms from empirically supported treatments to evidence-based practice: A cultural perspective. *Professional Psychology: Research and Practice, 40*(4), 396–402.

Lakes, K., Lopez, S. R., & Garro, L. C. (2006). Cultural competence and psychotherapy: Applying anthropologically informed conceptions of culture. *Psychotherapy: Theory, Research, Practice, Training, 43*(4), 380–396.

Lau, A. (2006). Making the case for selective and directed cultural adaptations of evidence-based treatments: Examples from parent training. *Clinical Psychology: Science and Practice, 13*(4), 295–310.

Martín-Baró, I. (1994). *Writings for a liberation psychology.* Cambridge, MA: Harvard University Press.

McGoldrick, M., Giordano, J., & Pearce, J. K. (Eds.). (1996). *Ethnicity and family therapy* (2nd ed.). New York: Guilford Press.

Paniagua, F. A. (2005). *Assessing and treating culturally diverse clients: A practical guide* (3rd ed.). Thousand Oaks, CA: Sage.

Parham, T. A. (2002). Counseling models for African Americans: The what and how of counseling. In T. A. Parham (Ed.), *Counseling persons of African descent: Raising the bar of practitioner competence* (pp. 100–118). Thousand Oaks, CA: Sage.

Parham, T. A. (2004). Raising the bar on what passes for competence. *The California Psychologist, 37*(6), 20–21.

Parham, T. A., White, J. L., & Ajamu, A. (1999). *The psychology of blacks: An African-centered perspective* (3rd ed.). Englewood Cliffs, NJ: Prentice Hall.

Pieterse, A., Evans, S., Risner-Butner, A., Collins, N., & Mason, L. (2009). Multicultural competence and social justice training in counseling psychology and counselor education: A review and analysis of a sample of multicultural course syllabi. *The Counseling Psychologist, 37*(1), 93–115.

Ponterotto, J. G., Rivera, L., & Sueyoshi, L. A. (2000). The Career-in-Culture interview: A semi-structured protocol for the cross-cultural intake interview. *The Career Development Quarterly, 49*(1), 85–96.

Priester, P., Jones, J., Jackson-Bailey, C., Jana-Masri, A., Jordan, E., & Metz, A. (2008). An analysis of content and instructional strategies in multicultural counseling courses. *Journal of Multicultural Counseling and Development, 36*(1), 29–39.

Sodowsky, G. R., & Johnson, P. (1994). World views: Culturally learned assumptions and values. In P. B. Pedersen & J. C. Carey (Eds.), *Multicultural counseling in schools* (2nd ed., pp. 59–80). Boston: Allyn & Bacon.

Stone, J. H. (2005). *Culture and disability.* Thousand Oaks, CA: Sage.

Sue, D. W., & Sue, D. (2003). *Counseling the culturally diverse: Theory and practice* (4th ed.). New York: John Wiley & Sons.

Toporek, R. L., & Reza, J. V. (2001). Context as a critical dimension of multicultural counseling. *Journal of Multicultural Counseling and Development, 29,* 13–30.

U.S. Census Bureau. (2008). *U.S. population projections.* Retrieved May 16, 2011, from http://www.census.gov/population/www/projections/summarytables.html

Vera, E., & Speight, S. L. (2003). Multicultural competence, social justice, and counseling psychology: Expanding our roles. *The Counseling Psychologist, 31,* 253–272.

White, J. L., & Parham, T. A. (1990). *The psychology of blacks: An African American perspective* (2nd ed.). Englewood Cliffs, NJ: Prentice Hall.

Yeh, C. J. (2000). Depathologizing Asian-American perspectives of health and healing. *Asian American and Pacific Islander Journal of Health, 8,* 138–149.

Yeh, C. J., Borrero, N. E., & Shea, M. (2011). Spirituality as a cultural asset for urban youth in schools. *Counseling and Values, 5,* 185–198.

Yeh, C. J., Hunter, C. D., Madan-Bahel, A., Chiang, L., & Kwong, A. (2004). Indigenous and interdependent perspectives of healing: Implications for counseling and research. *Journal of Counseling and Development, 82,* 410–441.

Yeh, C. J., Inman, A., Kim, A. B., & Okubo, Y. (2006). Asian American collectivistic coping in response to 9/11. *Cultural Diversity and Ethnic Minority Psychology, 12,* 134–148.

Yeh, C. J., Kim, A. B., Pituc, S. T., & Atkins, M. (2008). Poverty, loss, and resilience: The story of Asian immigrant youth. *Journal of Counseling Psychology, 55,* 34–48.

Yeh, C. J., & Kwan, K.-L. K. (2009). Advances in multicultural assessment and counseling with adolescents: Community, ecological, and social justice approaches. In J. G. Ponterotto, J. M. Casas, L. A. Suzuki, & C. M. Alexander (Eds.), *Handbook of multicultural counseling* (3rd ed., pp. 637–647). Thousand Oaks, CA: Sage.

Yeh, C. J., Okubo, Y., Cha, N., Lee, S. J., & Shin, S-Y. (2008). Evaluation of an intervention program for Asian immigrant adolescents' cultural adjustment. *Journal of Immigrant and Refugee Studies, 6*(4), 567–590.

Yeh, C. J., & Pituc, S. T. (2008). Understanding yourself as a school counselor. In H. L. K. Coleman & C. J. Yeh (Eds.), *Handbook of school counseling* (pp. 63–78). New York: Taylor & Francis.

Yeh, C. J., & Wang, Y. W. (2000). Asian American coping attitudes, sources, and practices: Implications for indigenous counseling strategies. *Journal of College Student Development, 41,* 94–103.

Afterword _____

On Sending a Wolf of Color Out Into a Socially Unjust World

Janet E. Helms

If the reader has come this far in the journey to discover how Parham's (2002) Skills Identification Model may be adapted to fit the needs of clients other than, or in addition to, African Americans of otherwise unspecified ethnicity, then you will have discovered that absorbing the knowledge and skills that the authors offer will require many readings. I feel a bit like an ungrateful guest who, having just sated herself on a gourmet meal, expresses her gratitude by criticizing the chef. So, I begin by highlighting some aspects of the book that the reader has already recognized herself or himself. Time constraints do not permit me to address the merits of each of the chapters in the detail that they deserve. Perhaps the authors will forgive me for this inadequacy.

Nevertheless, I think there are some ingredients missing from this excellent presentation of applications of multicultural theory to the counseling and psychotherapy process, which, if added, might help to protect or buffer the well-intentioned culturally responsive therapist, researcher, and future therapists from the fate that befell the maligned wolf in the tale of the Wolf and Red Riding Hood with which Gallardo, Parham, Trimble, and Yeh began Chapter 1. These include (a) the invisibility of white culture, (b) racism and ethnoviolence as tapestries in the United States that are often mistaken for cultural psychopathology, (c) social interaction theory as a model for understanding the dynamics of the helping process at multiple levels, and (d) the nature of our ethical responsibilities to students trained to be culturally responsive therapists.

In this afterword, I briefly discuss each of these four themes and explain why I believe they deserve serious attention. I often refer to the fable in my examples because I think it was a charming way to introduce Chapter 1 and it is an easy way to make the invisible visible. However, in my culture, it is considered disrespectful to address a learned individual by a single name without a title. So, henceforth, the "maligned wolf" is Mr. Wolf in my examples.

Brief Highlights

Each chapter's authors want the reader to understand and incorporate into the reader's practice deep cultural knowledge of the specific ethnic group(s) whose cultural dynamics the authors discuss. Even therapists already engaged in the process of becoming culturally responsive therapists will learn something that they did not know about the culture or historical contexts of the specific ethnocultural groups that are represented, as well as how to be more responsive generally. Each chapter also presents one or more conceptual models and additions to the SISM to make it more responsive to clients' cultural needs. Interestingly, many of these embellishments seem to be focused on the assessment process. That is, how can we learn what we do not know about our clients? This assessment focus is important because it reminds us that not only do the theories we use require cultural refinement, so, too, do the standard assessment procedures that are routinely used for diagnostic purposes as if they are culture free. The chapter authors provide examples of the types of questions that should be asked to acquire information necessary to intervene appropriately. In the future, it would be useful to have available a model for integrating the various assessment recommendations across groups with respect to specific standard measures and procedures. Perhaps Yeh, Gallardo, Parham, and Trimble's integration of ecological models may serve as a framework for integrating cultural dynamics into the assessment process.

Another major contribution of the book is the inclusion of case materials along with descriptions of the relevant aspects of the clients' cultural origins that might have affected the presenting problem as well as the helpers' roles in resolving it. The case materials are excellent examples of the art of doing therapy as described by a person with in-depth knowledge of the focal ethnocultural group, even though some of the therapists and clients were from different cultural backgrounds. Sometimes the helper-client cultural mismatches were preferred by the client, which raises interesting questions about how best to manage culture-specific transference and countertransference issues in the helping process when the historical and cultural backgrounds of the client's and helper's communities may be additional parties in the helping relationship.

Nevertheless, the knowledge and skills demonstrated in the case materials may be quite intimidating if they are interpreted as meaning that such sophisticated knowledge and skills are required for providing beneficial mental health services to clients from every ethnic group in the United States, which, of course, is beyond the capacity of any person. Instead, I prefer to interpret the chapters as providing would-be culturally responsive therapists with a flexible frame for knowledge and skill development, regardless of the helpers' and clients' specific ethnocultural origins.

Missing Ingredients

Invisibility of White Culture

As I read each chapter, I wondered who the intended audience was. I figured that it must be people who do not have to routinely exist in cultural environments different from their own because the authors continually implicitly contrasted the cultural dimensions of their ethnocultural group with some other culture, although virtually none of them called it by name. Then, as I reached the end of the book, my wonderment was resolved. Virtually none of the authors or chapters discussed white American cultures, either at the level of specific ethnic groups (e.g., Irish, Italians, Greeks) or society (e.g., white cultural patterns). Consequently, the reader is left with the impression that culture is only manifested by people of color or recent immigrant groups and that, if cultural impasses occur, it is because of problems within the client's home culture or because the therapist misunderstands the client's culture.

However, every person, including therapists, is the recipient of some cultural socialization. Such socialization is what enables us to survive within our cultural units, whatever they may be; it is not necessarily pathological. Impasses occur when members of different cultures must interact and one cultural group has the power to define normality for the other(s). In the United States, white culture is synonymous with "American culture" (Torkelson & Hartmann, 2010). Yet white culture is invisible in the psychological literature, even though it is the norm for U.S. American society. In my quick search for empirical studies on white or American culture in the psychological literature, I located only five, and these were typically comparisons of some aspect of the culture of African Americans, Latina/o Americans, Asian American/Pacific Islander Americans, or Native Americans (ALANA) or related immigrant groups to a white sample. The implicit message is that either white people do not have describable culture, or it does not matter so long as others conform to it.

With the exception of the chapters on Indigenous people, most of the foregoing chapters dealt with immigrants to the United States who were transitioning in some manner from their cultures of origin to the dominant American culture, sometimes over many generations, while at the same time trying to hold onto those aspects of culture that defined their personhood and enabled their cultural units to survive. Many impasses occur because the rules of the culture into which the client and/or therapist have moved are unspoken and unacknowledged, but are enforceable through law, ethical codes, and U.S. American traditions nevertheless (Helms & Cook, 1999, pp. 316–318). Thus, what is needed is a cultural framework for allowing everyone to recognize white cultural values and/or patterns so that impasses can be anticipated, diagnosed, or recognized as they occur. The model should be taught to therapists in training as well as their clients. A conceptual model of white culture that I still find useful is Katz's (1985) sociopolitical description of its basic components. Although Katz's model should be studied empirically on white samples, Helms and Cook describe some of its possible applications to the counseling process. It might be comparably useful for helping people generally to understand how to engage in unfamiliar cultural contexts.

For example, Mr. Wolf entered a helping relationship without recognizing the alleged value of cultural dimensions such as "aesthetics" and "history" in U.S. American society. *Aesthetics* refers to the belief that the people (or entities) should exhibit European physical characteristics and cultural practices; *history* refers to the belief that the only worthwhile knowledge is derived from the experiences of European immigrants in the United States. Little Red Riding Hood, her grandmother, and the woodsman conformed to these values, but Mr. Wolf did not. Thus, he was immediately in the middle of a cultural impasse as soon as Little Red Riding Hood spoke to him, but so was she. Perhaps if Mr. Wolf had known what cultural patterns he was encountering in advance, he might have employed some of the intriguing compensatory strategies described in the previous chapters, including enhancing understanding of the two cultures by engaging the surrounding communities in difficult dialogues and the treatment process (Chapter 3, this volume). Mr. Wolf should not have had the complete responsibility for re-educating Little Red Riding Hood and her grandmother.

Racism and Ethnoviolence as Sources of Pathology

Insofar as I can tell, the authors did not actually define *ethnocultural*. I inferred that they intended their focus to be specific ethnic group cultures (i.e., ethnicity) rather than racial groups as socially defined (i.e., sociorace) or ethnic group classifications, which often are used as substitutes for racial groups. Some of the chapter authors subsumed "race" under "ethnocultural." Admittedly, there is considerable controversy (Helms & Talleyrand, 1997; Phinney, 1996) about whether "ethnicity" should subsume "race." One problem with conflating the two concepts is that doing so obscures the negative effects of ethnoviolence and racism on mental health and contributes to misperceptions of cultures rather than abusive social systems as problematic (Helms, Nicolas, & Green, 2011).

From my perspective, the interventions that follow from impasses attributable to race, or more accurately racial socialization, are quite different from the impasses attributable to cultural socialization. As the authors demonstrate throughout this book, culture has behavioral and psychological implications for individuals' levels of functioning, even when the rules of the culture are invisible. Race has no behavioral or psychological meaning (Helms, Jernigan, & Mascher, 2005). In the United States, individuals are treated or mistreated according to their perceived racial categories, whether or not such categories are consistent with how they conceptualize themselves. People also are mistreated because of their cultural practices or presumed practices, but this type of abuse may be difficult to recognize because race may be more salient in people's perceptions of others. Mistreating people because of their perceived race is racism and/or race-related emotional abuse; mistreating them because of presumed cultural practices is ethnoviolence or culture-related emotional abuse (Brubaker & Laitin, 1998). Racism and ethnoviolence are both types of inter-group relations that are imposed by members of more powerful out-groups. Helms et al. (2011) discuss a variety of issues associated with racism or ethnoviolence as catalysts for posttraumatic stress disorder (PTSD) with greater complexity than I can indulge in here. Also, Sue and associates (2007) provide a taxonomy of microaggressions (i.e., seemingly small, usually psychological assaults with potentially serious emotional consequences). Knowledge of their framework might be serviceable whether one is considering PTSD or less severe stress-related mental health issues associated with racism or ethnoviolence.

However, my main point is that we do clients, trainees, and ourselves a great disservice if we do not provide them with the skills to cope with threats to their self-integrity based on physical appearance (racism) or presumed common in-group cultural practices (ethnoviolence). Little Red Riding Hood engaged in microaggressions against Mr. Wolf not because of their cultural mismatches. She did not take time to know him well enough to understand his cultural values (e.g., *respeto*). Instead she reacted to him on the basis of his physical appearance and whatever stereotypes she had learned to associate with "big ears" and "big teeth."

Social Interaction Theory

In their introductory chapter, Gallardo, Parham, Trimble, and Yeh acknowledge disparities in power as a major contributing factor in the manifestation of cultural impasses and advocate empowerment as a goal for training programs and practitioners working with members of inappropriately served ethnocultural communities. Parham's (2002) Skills Identification Model, as outlined in Chapter 1, is a process model in that it pertains to four principles of facilitative helping relationships (positive relationships, shared worldviews, shared expectations, and participatory interventions or rituals) and five domains of cultures (nature of reality, value orientations, relationship to Divine force, systems of knowledge, and human interaction). The SISM provides six specific actions or themes (e.g., client connecting, culturally responsive assessment) by which these aspects may be integrated into culturally responsive therapeutic relationships. Each of the culturally responsive process dimensions are assumed to be universal or etic, in that they are expected to be appropriate for all groups, but emic or universal, in that it is noted that they must be adapted to the cultural dimensions of specific groups. Most of the chapters illustrate how such adaptations may occur.

However, the model and cultural adaptations of it do not appear to include a framework for diagnosing power dynamics in the therapy, training, or societal relationships. That is, helping clients, for example, develop "awareness of surrounding environmental circumstances that contribute to the establishment of behaviors and feelings of oppression" (Chapter 1) is a necessary condition for fostering empowerment. The capacity to diagnose the power dynamics in interactions at the person and system levels is a necessary skill because it allows the experiencing person to make wise decisions about how best to intervene and/or resist disempowering interactions.

The social interaction model (Helms & Cook, 1999) is useful for this purpose because it recognizes that any interaction, including therapy, involves expressions of power or lack thereof by each party or entity (e.g., pairs of individuals, groups, coalitions) involved in the interaction. Helms and colleagues have illustrated how the model may be used to understand the effects of power dynamics in therapy interactions (Helms & Cook, 1999), assessment (Helms et al., 2011), and therapy supervision (Jernigan, Green, Helms, Gualdron-Murhib, & Henze, 2010). Without going into great detail, interactions may be classified as parallel, regressive, and progressive. Each type has different implications for attitudes, values, behaviors, and emotions.

In *parallel interactions* or events, participants share power; no one's perspective is more valued than another's perspective. Maintaining harmony is a primary goal of such interactions. When culture is the underlying dynamic of the potential power differential, parallel therapy interactions are often supportive if both parties share a common manner of communicating from shared cultural perspectives, but they are not necessarily healing or empowering. *Regressive interactions* occur when the person or coalition with the most power in the interaction has the least understanding of or respect for the other person or group's cultural socialization. Such relationships are potentially harmful for all parties involved. For the least powerful, they contribute to psychological and perhaps physical withdrawal from the situation(s); for the most powerful, they contribute to entrenchment in culturally encapsulated worldviews. Although ostensibly in the more powerful role of counselor or educator, Mr. Wolf was actually in regressive interactions with Little Red Riding Hood, her grandmother, the woodsman, and seemingly the surrounding community. Although clients and trainees will probably not literally leap out a window when they experience regressive interactions, underutilization of services and premature termination may be an analogous form of withdrawing from potentially harmful experiences.

In *progressive interactions,* the person with greatest power (e.g., perhaps the therapist) has developed the skills and knowledge to help the persons understand and value the qualities of their own culture as well as the culture with which the persons are in conflict. The book *Culturally Adaptive Counseling Skills: Demonstrations of Evidence-Based Practices* is designed to promote progressive relationships with respect to culture and thereby empower helpers as well as those they seek to help.

Ethical Obligations for Changing Systems

The implications of teaching people to deliver culturally responsive interventions are contained throughout the chapters. Toporek (Chapter 17, this volume) proffers some specific training resources and strategies for engaging in progressive interactions with therapists-in-training during the training process. Nevertheless, every year around December through January, I am reminded of the resistance to change by an ethical dilemma that I think was not discussed in the foregoing chapters. Those of us who participate in the education of culturally responsive therapists perhaps recognize my timeframe as the period during which doctoral students in psychology participate in interviews to determine whether they will be selected for a predoctoral internship, a requirement that they must successfully complete in order to receive their doctoral degree.

Each year, candidates return with horror stories about their experiences at sites where the messages of the value and necessity of delivering culturally responsive services, such as those that permeate this book, apparently have not been received. Internship candidates are placed in multiple regressive interactions, where their potential benefactors barrage them with criticisms of who they are as people ("I'm afraid of you because you're so well dressed" or "Do you expect me to expose my clients to an Asian therapist?") as well as for their culturally responsive skills ("We don't do that 'cultural stuff' here; hopefully it's just a stage you're going through" or "Can you do real therapy?"). The parallels with Mr. Wolf's experiences are perhaps obvious. One might argue that candidates should not seek to match culturally unresponsive sites. But given that there are more potential interns than there are accredited sites, and even sites that advertise themselves as culturally responsive do not practice any SISM principles or guidelines or offer equivalent culturally responsive climates, such an argument is essentially nonsensical.

In effect, culturally responsive educators, supervisors, and mentors send our mentees off into systems in which they are often the only person who values what we have taught them. We expect them to change systems and advocate for client empowerment once they get into the system. However, often the only way to get into the required systems is to hide the skills and knowledge that we have taught them and they have taught us. Models exist for advocating for clients and teaching them to advocate for themselves in oppressive systems, but they do not exist for educators and supervisors. Ethical concerns for culturally responsive educators are (a) What do we do about ensuring the availability of internship placements for candidates who practice what we teach? (b) Should we be sending our mentees into potentially damaging environments? and (c) How might we best advocate for culturally responsive and socially just training environments once trainees enter the helping professions? Failure to attend to such systemic disempowerment issues means that the helpers we intend to train to be culturally responsive may eventually succumb to the pressures of the more powerful racially and culturally unjust systems, as did Mr. Wolf.

References

Brubaker, R., & Laitin, D. D. (1998). Ethnic and nationalist violence. *Annual Review of Sociology, 24*, 423–452.

Helms, J. E., & Cook, D. A. (1999). *Using race and culture in counseling and psychotherapy: Theory and process.* Boston: Allyn & Bacon.

Helms, J. E., Jernigan, M. M., & Mascher, J. (2005). The meaning of race in psychology and how to change it. *American Psychologist, 60*, 27–36.

Helms, J. E., Nicolas, N., & Green, C. E. (2011). Racism and ethnoviolence as trauma: Enhancing professional and research training. *Traumatology, 4*, 53-62.

Helms, J. E., & Talleyrand, R. (1997). Race is not ethnicity. *American Psychologist, 52*, 1246–1247.

Jernigan, M. M., Green, C. E., Helms, J. E., Gualdron-Murhib, L. G., & Henze, K. (2010). An examination of People of Color supervision dyads: Racial identity matters as much as race. *Training & Education in Professional Psychology, 4*, 62–73.

Katz, J. H. (1985). The sociopolitical nature of counseling. *The Counseling Psychologist, 13*, 615–624.

Parham, T. A. (2002). *Counseling persons of African descent: Raising the bar of practitioner competence.* Thousand Oaks, CA: Sage.

Phinney, J. S. (1996). When we talk about American ethnic groups, what do we mean? *American Psychologist, 51*, 918–927.

Sue, D. W., Capodilipo, C. M., Torino, G. C., Bucceri, J. M., Holder, A. M. B., Nadal, K. L., et al. (2007). Racial microaggressions in everyday life: Implications for clinical practice. *American Psychologist, 62*, 271–286.

Torkelson, J., & Hartmann, D. (2010). White ethnicity in twenty-first-century America: Findings from a new national survey. *Ethnic and Racial Studies, 33*, 1310–1331.

Index

Abdal-Ati, H., 225
Abe-Kim, J., 142
Abraido-Lanza, F. F., 87
Abreu, J. M., 13, 89, 118
Abudabbeh, N., 224, 225, 226
Abu-Laban, S. M., 225
ACA Advocacy Competencies,
    274, 276
Accountability. *See* Feedback and
    accountability
Acculturation of immigrants, 85–86
Acevedo-Polakovich, I. D.,
    114, 116
Achenbach, K., 280
Action and change, 15
    with African American clients,
        36–37, 57–59, 72–73
    with Asian Americans/Pacific
        Islanders, 149–150, 161
    helping students develop culturally
        adaptive skills with, 276–277
    with Latina/o clients, 103–104, 121
    with Middle Eastern Americans,
        230 (table), 238–240, 249–250,
        258–262
    with North American Indians and
        Alaska Natives, 193–194
Adachi Sueyoshi, L., 145, 330
Adaptations, multicultural, 288,
    300–303, 309
Ademuwagun, Z. A., 55
Adjustment disorders, 289, 305, 306,
    308–309
Advocacy, social, 36
Aesthetics, 340
African Americans
    aligning conscientiousness with
        destiny and, 35
    axiology and culture, 9–10 (table)

becoming a subjective companion
    to, 35
case study, 29–37
clinical application and intervention
    with AA-SISM for, 70–73
community and, 45–50
concept of mental health and,
    28–29
connecting with, 31–32, 45–54,
    67–69, 70–71
cosmology and culture, 10 (table)
cultural competence with, 65–66
cultural congruence, 28
culturally corrective experiences
    and, 35
culturally relevant assessment of,
    32–33, 54–55, 71
cultural strengths, 32–33
defenses, 34
empowerment of, 36
epistemology and culture,
    10–11 (table)
facilitating awareness with, 33–34,
    56–57, 71–72
family demographics, 26
feedback and accountability with,
    37, 59, 73
functional behaviors, 34
metaphors and, 34
need for distance, 36
ontology and culture, 9 (table)
praxis and culture, 11 (table)
problem solving by, 37
racial identity of, 25–26
reframing and, 35–36
remembering being and becoming
    with, 37
rephrasing and, 34
resilience, 47, 50

restoring balance and harmony for, 35, 37
ritual and, 50–51
self-healing power and, 28
self-knowledge, 28, 34
setting goals with, 35–36, 72
skill identification stage model (AA-SISM), 29–37, 70–73
social organizations, 47–48
spirituality and, 27–28, 33, 37, 52–54, 69–70
stereotypes of, 68, 72
taking action and instigating change with, 36–37, 57–59, 72–73
traditional healers, 53 (box)
transformative possibilities of the human spirit and, 27–28
understanding distress in, 33
understanding pain in, 33–34
using appropriate clinical instruments with, 33
Aguiar, L. J., 13, 100
Aguilar-Gaxiola, S., 85
Ajamu, A., 6, 8, 24, 27, 28, 324, 331
Ajei, C., 24
Akbar, N., 24, 27, 28, 50
Akutsu, P. D., 171
Alarcon, R., 14, 102, 331
Albert, R. D., 78, 79
Alberta, A. J., 280
Aldarondo, E., 3, 14, 314, 323, 328
Alderete, E., 85
Alegria, M., 82, 83, 91, 142
Alexander, C. M., 24
Ali, M. K., 160
Allen, J., 13, 188
Allison, K. W., 50
Almedia, R., 157, 160
Altarriba, J., 81, 88, 90, 115
Al-Timmi, N., 225, 226
Altschul, D., 296, 299
Alvarez, A. N., 157
Amatea, E., 324, 329
Ambience, 32
American Counseling Association, 3
American Indians/Alaska Natives
axiology and culture, 9–10 (table)
cosmology and culture, 10 (table)
epistemology and culture, 10–11 (table)
ontology and culture, 9 (table)
praxis and culture, 11 (table)
American Psychiatric Association, 305

American Psychological Association, 3, 4, 5, 25, 95, 114, 120, 122, 127, 156, 162, 288, 314, 325
evidence-based practice and, 292–293
Ancis, J. R., 3, 313, 314
Anderson, M., 185
Anderson, T. C., 89
Angold, A., 45
Ani, M., 8, 69, 70
Appleton, V., 195
Arciniega, G. M., 89
Arnold, M. S., 273, 274
Arntz, D. L., 4, 53
Aron, A., 273
Aronson, J., 72
Arora, A. K., 146, 149
Arredondo, P., 3, 24, 78, 94, 98, 129, 267, 274, 281, 290, 328
Arthur, N., 280
Asian Americans and Pacific Islanders
axiology and culture, 9 (table), 158
case study, 156–162
collectivism among, 140, 143–144
connecting with, 140–144, 158–159
cosmology and culture, 10 (table), 157
culturally relevant assessment of, 144–147, 159–160
demographics, 139–14
epistemology and culture, 10–11 (table)
facilitating awareness with, 147–148, 160
feedback and accountability with, 150–151, 162–163
gender roles and, 161
immigration and, 155
language and, 146–147
ontology and culture, 9 (table), 157
praxis and culture, 11 (table)
reasons for referral, 168–169
setting goals with, 148, 160–161
skills identification stage model (AA-SISM), 140, 141 (table)
stereotypes of, 142
taking action and instigating change with, 149–150, 161
Assessment, culturally relevant
of African Americans, 32–33, 54–55, 71
of Asian Americans/Pacific Islanders, 144–147, 159–160

About the Editors_____

Miguel E. Gallardo, Psy.D., is an associate professor of psychology at Pepperdine University's Graduate School of Education and Psychology, where he teaches courses on multicultural and social justice, intimate partner violence, and professional practice issues. He is a licensed psychologist and maintains an independent/consultation practice where he conducts therapy with adolescents and adults. Dr. Gallardo's areas of scholarship and research interests include understanding the psychotherapy process when working with ethnocultural communities, particularly the Latina/o community, and understanding the processes by which individuals develop cultural awareness and responsiveness. Dr. Gallardo has published refereed journal articles and book chapters in the areas of multicultural psychology, Latina/o psychology, ethics, and evidence-based practices. He is co-editor of the book *Intersections of Multiple Identities: A Casebook of Evidence-Based Practices with Diverse Populations,* published in 2009. Dr. Gallardo is a past president of the California Psychological Association. He is one of the founders and served as the first president of the California Latino Psychological Association and continues to be active in psychological organizations at the state and national levels. Dr. Gallardo is currently serving a two-year governor-appointed position on the California Board of Psychology. He is the recipient of several awards for his dedication and commitment to the field of psychology locally, statewide, and nationally. Dr. Gallardo is a Fellow of the American Psychological Association.

Christine J. Yeh, Ph.D. is professor and chair, Department of Counseling Psychology at the University of San Francisco. She was previously associate professor in counseling psychology at Teachers College, Columbia University. Her research has focused on ethnic identity, cultural adjustment, mental health, and coping of Asian Americans, Pacific Islanders, and Native Hawaiians. She is author of more than 70 articles, chapters, and other publications. Dr. Yeh has also received 22 grants from federal and local agencies, foundations, and universities, including a five-year National Institute of Mental Health grant for Asian immigrant mental health. She is the recipient of several awards, including Distinguished Fellow, Early Career, and the Okura Community Leadership Award from the Asian American Psychological Association; Outstanding

Research Award from the American Educational Research Association (Division E) and the American Counseling Association; the Community Service Award (Division 17, SERD, American Psychological Association); and five Outstanding Teaching Awards (Teachers College, Columbia University).

Joseph E. Trimble, Ph.D., is a distinguished professor in the Center for Cross-Cultural Research, Department of Psychology, at Western Washington University; also he is a President's Professor at the Center for Alaska Native Health Research at the University of Alaska, Fairbanks. Throughout his long career, he has focused his efforts on promoting psychological and sociocultural mental health research with indigenous populations, especially American Indians and Alaska Natives. He is the editor or author of 18 books and more than 100 journal articles and chapters and the recipient of 20 fellowships, awards, and honors, including the Excellence in Teaching Award and the Paul J. Olscamp Outstanding Faculty Research Award at Western Washington University; the Distinguished Psychologist Award from the Washington State Psychological Association; the Peace and Social Justice Award from the American Psychological Association's Division on Peace Psychology; the Distinguished Elder Award from the National Multicultural Conference and Summit; the Henry Tomes Award for Distinguished Contributions to the Advancement of Ethnic Minority Psychology by the Council of National Psychological Associations for the Advancement of Ethnic Minority Interests and APA's Society for the Psychological Study of Ethnic Minority Issues; and the International Lifetime Achievement Award for Multicultural and Diversity Counseling from the Ontario Institute for Studies in Education, University of Toronto.

Thomas A. Parham, Ph.D., is interim vice chancellor for student affairs and an adjunct faculty member at the University of California, Irvine. Dr. Parham is a past president of the National Association of Black Psychologists. For more than 30 years, Dr. Parham has focused his research efforts in the area of psychological nigrescence and has authored numerous articles in the area. Writing in the areas of African American psychology, identity development, and multicultural counseling remains his primary focus. Among the dozens of honors and awards he has received are election to Fellow status of Division 17 (Counseling Psychology) and 45 (Ethnic Minority Issues) of the American Psychological Association in 1994; the Samuel H. Johnson Award for Exemplary Service and Scholarship from the Association for Multicultural Counseling and Development in 1995; his election to the title of Distinguished Psychologist by the Association of Black Psychologists (ABPsi's highest honor) in 1998; the APA Dalmus Taylor Award for Leadership, Scholarship, and Advising in 1999; the Association of Black Psychologists Certification and Proficiency in African Centered/Black Psychology, Board Certified Fellow and Board Certified Diplomate, July 2007; the American Psychological Association Division 17 Society of Counseling Psychology Award for Lifetime Achievement in Mentoring, August 2007; and the Janet E. Helms Award for Mentoring and Scholarship in 2010.

About the Contributors _____

I. David Acevedo-Polakovich, Ph.D., is a faculty member at Central Michigan University, where he is assistant professor in the clinical psychology doctoral program and director of the Center for Community-Academic Initiatives for Development. His research and professional work focus on developing effective health and human services for historically underserved youth and families, with a particular emphasis on prevention and applied development programs targeted at adolescents. He is also actively involved in scholarship examining the development of successful community-academic initiatives and approaches to the development of practice-based evidence. More information on Dr. Acevedo-Polakovich and his work is available at www.cmich.edu/chsbs/x23916.xml.

Noha Alshugairi, M.S., MFTI, was born in Cairo, Egypt, and raised in Jeddah, Saudi Arabia. In 1984 she immigrated to the United States, where she has resided ever since. She received her B.A. in zoology from Rutgers University in 1986 and her M.S. in counseling from California State University, Fullerton in 2007. She is currently a licensed marriage and family therapist in private practice in Newport Beach, California. She co-hosts "Family Connection," an Internet Radio show, on www.onelegacyradio.com. As a Certified Positive Discipline Associate, she conducts parenting classes and frequently lectures on issues related to women and family. Her interests include divorce in the American Muslim community, parent and child relationships, and the intertwining of faith and culture in the American Muslim community.

Metra Azar-Salem, M.S., MFT Intern, was born in Kabul, Afghanistan, in 1978 after the country had just been invaded by the USSR and her family was on the verge of migration. After 9/11 she worked closely with new Afghan immigrant families, which inspired her to apply for her master's in marriage and family therapy (MFT). She completed her master's and is currently in the last phase of her dissertation.

She currently works at an Islamic school in Irvine, California, where she provides culturally sensitive therapeutic services to adults, children, and couples as well as parent education classes and groups. In 2008, she was awarded the Minority Fellowship by the American Association for Marriage and Family Therapy, which entailed a three-year training program under Dr. Kenneth Hardy as well as a full scholarship for her doctoral studies. She has been married for 13 years and has three boys of her own.

J. Manuel Casas, Ph.D., received his doctorate from Stanford University in counseling psychology. He is a Professor Emeritus in the Department of Counseling, Clinical, and School Psychology at the University of California, Santa Barbara. He has over 135 publications. He is the co-author of the *Handbook of Racial/Ethnic Minority Counseling Research* (Charles C Thomas, 1991) and is one of the editors of the three editions of the *Handbook of Multicultural Counseling* (Sage, 1995, 2001, 2010). His most recent endeavors have focused on Latina/o families, especially those who are immigrants, who are at risk for experiencing educational and psychosocial problems and trauma. His work in this area gives attention to resiliency factors that can help Latina/o families avoid or overcome such problems.

Angela M. Enno is a doctoral student in the Combined Clinical, Counseling and School Psychology Ph.D. Program at Utah State University. Ms. Enno has published in the areas of ethnic identity and community context, training for cultural competence, and interventions for treating anxiety spectrum disorders. Her future goals include working with American Indian communities in clinical settings and conducting community-based research and mentoring American Indian and other diverse students in psychology.

Anderson J. Franklin, Ph.D., is the Honorable David S. Nelson Professor of Psychology and Education in the Department of Counseling, Developmental and Educational Psychology at Boston College, Lynch School of Education, and Professor Emeritus of Psychology at The Graduate Center, The City University of New York. He directs the Nelson Chair Roundtable for Networking Community Based Programs and the Boston College Collaborative Extended Learning Project, strengthening ties between schools, families, and community partners. He was awarded an honorary doctorate of humane letters from Lewis and Clark College in Oregon and the 2010 Outstanding Alumnus Award from the University of Oregon College of Education, as well as the American Psychological Association's Presidential Citation for outstanding service as Distinguished Elder/Senior Psychologist at the 2009 National Multicultural Conference and Summit. He is the author of *From Brotherhood to Manhood: How Black Men Rescue Their Relationships and Dreams From the Invisibility Syndrome.*

Cheryl Gering, M.A., is currently a doctoral student in clinical psychology at Central Michigan University with interests in child clinical psychology and pediatric neuropsychology. Her professional experiences have focused on evidence-based assessment and treatment of children with disruptive behavior problems and/or a history of child maltreatment. Her research examines (1) cognitive and situational factors impacting parents' strategy use when interacting with their children and (2) predictors of social adjustment among typically developing children and children with neurodevelopmental conditions. Ms. Gering also has an active interest in the neuropsychological assessment and treatment of children and young adults with acquired or congenital brain dysfunction.

Cheryl Tawede Grills, Ph.D., is a clinical psychologist with an emphasis in community psychology. She is professor of psychology at Loyola Marymount University and associate dean in the College of Liberal Arts. Dr. Grills is also president-elect of the National Association of Black Psychologists and founder and director of Imoyase Community Support Services, a nonprofit program evaluation and consulting organization serving community-based organizations and foundations around the country. Among the honors and awards she has received is her election in 2004 to the title of Distinguished Psychologist by the Association of Black Psychologists. Her research interests and publications include African-centered models of treatment engagement with African Americans, substance abuse prevention and treatment, community psychology, community mental health, prevention, and the provision of action research and program evaluation services. She has also studied under traditional medical practitioners in Ghana, Nigeria, and Senegal and is a registered member of the Ghana National Association of Traditional Healers.

Jeff E. Harris, Ph.D., is an associate professor of psychology at Texas Woman's University. His Ph.D. in counseling psychology was awarded by The Ohio State University in 1990. Dr. Harris worked for several years at university counseling centers in Illinois and Hawaii. American Board of Professional Psychology certification as a specialist in counseling psychology was awarded in 2004. Dr. Harris is the author of *Integrative Multitheoretical Psychotherapy* (2008, Houghton-Mifflin) and coauthor of *Workshops: Designing and Facilitating Experiential Learning* (1999, Sage). As the originator of multitheoretical psychotherapy (MTP), Dr. Harris has trained psychotherapists at regional and national conferences and has been featured in five training videos. His current research focuses on applying MTP to depression and testing the effectiveness of key strategies training. Dr. Harris lives in Denton, Texas, with his wife and daughter. He enjoys biking, hiking, skiing, and reading about world religions.

Janet E. Helms, Ph.D., is the Augustus Long Professor in the Department of Counseling, Developmental, and Educational Psychology and director of the Institute for the Study and Promotion of Race and Culture at Boston College. Dr. Helms serves on the editorial boards of the *Journal of Psychological Assessment* and the *Journal of Counseling Psychology* and is on the Counsel of Research Elders of the *Journal of Cultural Diversity and Ethnic Minority Psychology.* She has written more than 60 empirical and theoretical articles and four books on the topics of racial identity and cultural influences on assessment and counseling practice. Her books include *A Race Is a Nice Thing to Have* (Microtraining Associates) and (with Donelda Cook) *Using Race and Culture in Counseling and Psychotherapy: Theory and Process* (Allyn & Bacon). Dr. Helms' work has been acknowledged with awards from national psychological associations and universities throughout the nation.

Arpana Inman, Ph.D., received her doctorate in counseling psychology from Temple University and is currently an associate professor in counseling psychology at Lehigh University. Her areas of research include Asian American coping and mental health, international counseling and psychology, multicultural competencies in supervision and training, and South Asian diasporic identity. She has presented nationally and internationally in these areas. She is also involved with the South Asian community at a national level and is a cofounder of the South Asian Psychological Networking Association, which runs a Web site and Listserv for South Asian concerns. She currently serves on the editorial boards of the *Asian American Journal of Psychology, Psychotherapy Research,* and *Psychotherapy: Theory, Research, Training, and Practice.*

Jeff King, Ph.D., is an associate professor and director of the Center for Cross-Cultural Research at Western Washington University's Department of Psychology, in Bellingham, Washington. He is a licensed clinical psychologist and has worked primarily with American Indian populations for the past 20 years. He is currently president of the First Nations Behavioral Health Association and active board member of the National Multi-Ethnic Behavioral Health Alliance. Both organizations work toward a reduction in the disparities in behavioral health for Native Americans and other ethnic minority populations. Dr. King is a tribally enrolled member of the Muscogee (Creek) Nation of Oklahoma.

Susana Ortiz Salgado, Ph.D., is the current president of the California Latino Psychological Association and is a licensed psychologist and coordinator for the Psychological Disabilities Program at Santa Ana College. Dr. Salgado has a strong passion for integrating multiculturalism and social justice into every aspect of her professional and personal life. She is a firm believer in integrating advocacy in her role as a psychologist and has a strong commitment to working toward social justice and serving disenfranchised communities. Her current focus is destigmatizing mental health concerns and access to mental health services within Latina/o communities. Dr. Salgado's clinical and research interests lie within an array of multicultural and gender-related areas. Her interests include gender socialization within Latina/o families, Latina/o mental health, and career development of Latina/o students.

Kao Chiu Saechao, M.S.W., is a registered associate social worker with the California Board of Behavioral Sciences. He is the program lead for the

Family and Children Division of the Mental Health Department at Asian Americans for Community Involvement in San Jose. Kao earned his master's in social work at San Jose State University and was recognized as the Outstanding MSW Field Student of 2008. He received his bachelor's in social welfare and double minors in education and ethnic studies from the University of California, Berkeley in 2005, played for the Cal Men's Volleyball team, and volunteered as a mentor and tutor to underrepresented youths in the community. Currently he is pursuing his clinical licensure and is involved with the Asian and Pacific Islander Social Work Council to promote social work as a profession. Kao's interests include community mental health, intergenerational conflicts in Southeast Asian family systems, and the transcultural practice of clinical social work.

Maryam Sayyedi, Ph.D., is the founder and clinical director of Omid Multicultural Institute for Development in Irvine, California. She is a licensed clinical child psychologist and an adjunct faculty member in the Department of Counseling at California State University, Fullerton. She obtained her Ph.D. in clinical psychology from Washington State University with concentrations in child development and neuropsychology. Dr. Sayyedi is bilingual and fluent in Farsi, and she has devoted her practice and research to addressing the mental health needs of Middle Eastern American adolescents, children, and their families.

Gayle Skawennio Morse, Ph.D., has conducted research for nearly a decade on examining the effects of polychlorinated biphenyls and other toxic chemicals on mental health. Currently she is looking at the neurological effects of toxic chemicals as well as cross-cultural studies of psychological measures and human health. In her role as the co-director of the American Indian Support Program, she is responsible for mentoring American Indian students and coordinating the Retreat and Convention of American Indian Psychologists. The unique design of the Retreat incorporates traditional views into the world of research and allows Native students to meet and interact with elders and leaders in the field of psychology. She is an enrolled member of the Mohawk Tribe and draws from the tribe the principles of respect, trust, and empowerment that have guided her both professionally and personally.

Nita Tewari, Ph.D., received her doctorate in counseling psychology from Southern Illinois University. She has served in positions of research psychologist at California State University, Long Beach; clinical researcher at the University of California, Irvine (UCI) Department of Psychiatry and Human Behavior; and most recently was a staff psychologist in the Counseling Center and adjunct faculty member in the School of Social Sciences and Asian American Studies at UCI. Dr. Tewari has provided clinical and consulting services to diverse populations since 1993 and has several publications in the areas of Indian American, South Asian, and

Asian American mental health. Her most recent book, *Asian American Psychology: Current Perspectives,* was published in 2009. She also cofounded the South Asian Psychological Networking Association in 2002 and served as vice president of the Asian American Psychological Association (2008–2009). She is currently a consultant in the area of multicultural and Asian American psychology.

Rebecca L. Toporek, Ph.D., is an associate professor in the Department of Counseling at San Francisco State University. She has written extensively on multicultural training, social justice advocacy, systemic interventions in discrimination, community engagement, and career and college counseling. She is committed to bringing others' work to the forefront, for example, as a coeditor of the *Handbook for Social Justice in Counseling Psychology, ACA Advocacy Competencies: A Social Justice Framework for Counselors, Handbook of Multicultural Competencies,* and, currently, the *Journal for Social Action in Counseling and Psychology.* She is involved in community partnerships in San Francisco and New Orleans focused on career and workplace issues integrating multicultural and social justice perspectives.

Jorge Wong, Ph.D., is the director of Behavioral Health Services at Asian Americans for Community Involvement in San Jose, California. He advocates for the advancement of cultural diversity in clinical practice, social justice, public service, and leadership development. He serves in local and statewide organizations, including the Mental Health, Alcohol and Drugs Contractors associations of Santa Clara County; San Jose's Independent Police Auditor; California Psychological Association; California Psychology Internship Council; Consumer and Family Leadership Committee of the Mental Health Services Oversight and Accountability Commission; Mental Health Loan Assumption Program; Office of Problem Gambling; and Kaiser Permanente's Research Project on Genes, Environment, and Health. He is clinical faculty at the Pacific Graduate School of Psychology at Palo Alto University, certified in healthcare compliance and ethics, and practices in community mental health and forensic settings. He enjoys volleyball, dragon boating, mud runs, and marathons with his interns and trainees.